# HISTORIAN

## Reconsiderations in Southern African History

Richard Elphick, Editor

# HISTORIAN

## *An Autobiography*

## HERMANN GILIOMEE

University of Virginia Press

Charlottesville and London

For Anette, as always

University of Virginia Press
© 2017 by Hermann Giliomee
Published by agreement with NB Publishers, a division of Media24 Boeke (Pty) Ltd
Originally published by Tafelberg, an imprint of NB Publishers, Cape Town, South Africa, in 2016
All rights reserved
Printed in the United States of America on acid-free paper

*First University of Virginia Press edition published 2017*
ISBN 978-0-8139-4091-5 (paper)

1 3 5 7 9 8 6 4 2

Library of Congress Cataloging-in-Publication Data is available for this title.

Translation from the Afrikaans, published simultaneously as *Historikus*: Linde Dietrich
Proofreading: Russell Martin
Index: George Claassen
Book design: Nazli Jacobs
All photos: Hermann Giliomee, except where otherwise indicated

The study of history is a training in humility. After more than twenty-five years of studying and writing I am impressed by the great difficulty of being an historian. Of all disciplines it is the most exacting and laborious. Few disciplines require a longer apprenticeship. The function of history is to put wisdom and experience at the disposal of each generation. A vigorous and independent historiography is more than an ornament of culture. It is the indispensable agent to wise and successful action in all human problems. In the world of scholarship the historian's craft comes the closest to statesmanship. Without historians a society cannot be mature or make its decisions wisely. Between democracy and a free inspired historiography there is a real equation. Amongst disciplines it is the greatest emancipator, releasing men from thraldom to the past, setting free their minds and their hearts for the tasks of each generation. The historian at his desk sheds hypocrisy in human relations, and is the declared enemy of what Norman Angell once called the unseen assassins – the words that defeat truth and accurate understanding by their prejudice or their falsity. In its fullness history is the meeting place of knowledge.

CW de Kiewiet, *The Anatomy of South African Misery* (1956)

# Contents

# Foreword

Historians who focus on South African history do not normally write autobiographies. Even CW de Kiewiet, the only South African historian who to my mind has come close to the elusive category of genius, never wrote about his own life. WM Macmillan, who together with De Kiewiet carried the liberal flag in the 1930s and 1940s, did write about his South African years, but he was neither born in this country nor died here. Phyllis Lewsen's autobiography, *Reverberations: A Memoir*, appeared in 1996. Arthur Keppel-Jones's *A Patriot in Search of a Country* was published posthumously in 2003. The only autobiography by an Afrikaans-speaking historian is AJ van Wyk's *The Birth of a New Afrikaner* (1991).

The two pillars of apartheid were theology and history. The theologian Jaap Durand recounts in his memoir *Protesstem: Oomblikke van herinnering* (2016) (Voice of protest: moments of memory) how he had made it clear in his doctoral dissertation that a racially divided church could not stand the test of the Christian gospel. This standpoint would radically influence his entire life and career.

History played an equally important role. The key myths were those of an "unoccupied land" in 1652 (except for small numbers of "Bushmen" and "Hottentots"), and of the "Bantu aggression and rapacity" which white farmers suffered from since the first contact in the 1770s, supposedly creating the need for boundary lines.

As a doctoral student I did extensive work on the frontier conflicts. I came to the conclusion that the conflict was about scarce resources, with arbitrary power rather than generally accepted rules being decisive. White farmers' first priority was not partition, but black labour.

From early on the white authorities proceeded under the delusion that they could enter into a treaty with a chief or a paramount chief that bound the whole "tribe". This was also the basic fallacy of the Bantustan policy of the second half of the twentieth century.

The main point on which I differed with other historians and social scientists was that of the root causes of social conflict. For me, it was not in the first place about the individual and his or her interests – as the liberals believe – or about class conflict – as the radicals would have it – but rather about the intrinsic competition between what can be called nations because they are based on different cultures.

In South Africa, up to about 1990, it was conflict between black nations that identified with Africa and a collection of ethnic minorities that had Europe rather than Africa as their reference point. In the 2016 election for the first time a strategically important segment in the electorate emerged that put a high premium on corruption-free and efficient government, not on "group identity".

While I had no illusions about the fact that the NP regime would do everything in their power to retain sole control for as long as possible, I did disagree with some of my English-speaking colleagues who were of the view that the regime would also do everything possible to oppress black people. I believe, for example, that Hendrik Verwoerd's policy of Bantu education was a rational attempt to provide mass education to a rapidly growing indigenous population within a political framework in which there was no enthusiasm from either Afrikaans- or English-speaking white voters for government expenditure on black education.

What has made my background somewhat different from that of most academics is that I spent the first half of my career at an Afrikaans university (Stellenbosch) and the second half on an English campus (University of Cape Town). I wrote books, academic articles and newspaper columns in both Afrikaans and English.

As a historian, I was fortunate in that I wrote about several "revolutions" and even experienced some at first hand. The first "revolution" was the first British occupation of the Cape (1795-1803), the subject of my first book. My study of this period enabled me to see how virtually the entire social order underwent a radical change, with paternalism, mercantilism and inequality supplanted by liberal principles, a market economy, and equality before the law. Not unlike today, leadership positions were occupied by the "Anglo men" who sought to replace Dutch-Afrikaans culture with English culture.

The second "revolution" I experienced as a child and a student: the rise of the Afrikaner nationalist movement. In 1938, the year of my birth, this movement reached one of its climaxes with the symbolic oxwagon trek in commemoration of the centenary of the Great Trek, which sparked mass Afrikaner enthusiasm. It was followed by a cultural blossoming over the next 20 to 25 years of Afrikaans as a literary and scientific language, and ultimately a republic outside the Commonwealth. Many Afrikaners expressed jubilation at the severing of this last link with Britain with a cry of "free at last".

The third "revolution" was apartheid, which still enjoyed a degree of respectability in my student years. Van Zyl Slabbert, my contemporary at Stellenbosch in the 1960s, would later describe "the excitement, even the thrill" experienced by academics and students in discussing this ideology. He added that apartheid had "a coherence and systematic quality which cannot be dismissed as racism pure and simple". It "made logical sense and addressed some very prickly issues".[1]

And then there was the fourth "revolution" with the ANC at its forefront, an increasingly intense battle against the apartheid state. In the mid-1960s, as a young cadet in the diplomatic services, it became abundantly clear to me that there was hardly any chance of apartheid winning support in the West. By the early 70s apartheid was already widely discredited outside of white, especially Afrikaner circles. For the next twenty years, the debate centred on how South Africa could become a more inclusive society without sacrificing steady economic growth and political stability.

It became ever clearer to me that the NP leadership regarded retaining their grip on power and salvaging party unity as their main priorities. I became increasingly critical in my newspaper columns, swiftly drawing the ire of NP-aligned academics who, against the evidence, kept clinging to the belief that they were influential within government circles.

By the late 1980s, with the struggle in South Africa at its most intense, I realised that newspaper columns and even books on politics and history have a short shelf life. I wanted to write a book which, in terms of its subject matter as well as accessibility to a general readership, might have a more lasting impact. There was only one big topic that interested me: the full story of the Afrikaner people from its beginnings in the 1650s to the present. I started working on the English version of *The Afrikaners: Biography of a People* in 1992 and completed the book ten years later, in 2002. My Afrikaans adaptation was published in 2004.

My next book, *Nog altyd hier gewees* (2007) (Always been here), dealt with the history of a coloured community that had been forcibly removed from the town centre of Stellenbosch. The research for this study gave me a perspective on my own people that was considerably less favourable than the one in *The Afrikaners*. In *The Last Afrikaner Leaders: A Supreme Test of Power* (2012) I attempted to understand the five Afrikaners who, politically speaking, dominated our lives between 1958 and 1994: Hendrik Verwoerd, John Vorster,

---

1    Ivor Wilkins, "This Man Who Guides the Ordinary People", *Sunday Times,* 19 April 1981.

PW Botha, Van Zyl Slabbert and FW de Klerk. I had conducted interviews with all of them except PW Botha. In the late 1980s he had reportedly warned members of the NP caucus against me and a co-author of mine, Lawrence Schlemmer, as snakes in the grass.

There was something special about the extraordinary times I lived through and that I researched and wrote about. In South Africa, unlike many other countries, history is central to our contemporary politics. The struggle around apartheid in the 1980s and 1990s was in many ways a propaganda struggle in which opposing interpretations of South African history played a crucial role. The convergence of my professional interests as a historian, my personal experience of dramatic social change, and my evolving understanding of South Africa have inspired me to write this book.

Hermann Giliomee
Stellenbosch
Winter 2016

*Chapter One*

# Origins

It was religious persecution that forced the Guillaumé family to flee France. Between 1670 and 1700 around 300 000 Huguenots bade their motherland farewell after long-standing discrimination and deadly attacks. The refugees settled in the Netherlands, the German states, England, Scotland, Ireland, Scandinavia, the American colonies and other predominantly Protestant countries. In 1688 some 200 Huguenots arrived at the Cape of the Good Hope from the Netherlands.

The flight of the Huguenots was one of the largest waves of migration Europe had seen up to that time. For France, it resulted in a massive loss of human capital. "*La grande catastrophe*" was President Charles de Gaulle's reaction when the South African ambassador in Paris told him about his own Huguenot forefather's flight.

The progenitor of the Guillaumé family in South Africa was François Guillaumé – in the primary sources the surname is also spelled Guilliaume and Guilliaumeth. He was born in 1680 in either Aimargues or the neighbouring village of Saint-Laurent-d'Aigouze, southwest of the city of Nîmes. The villages were part of Languedoc, a staunchly Protestant region between Nîmes and Montpellier, which was home to a flourishing silk industry.

François Guillaumé, who had left Languedoc as a child, married Claudine Cloy. By 1700 the couple were living in Berlin, where François most probably made silk clothing for a living. The Huguenot community, with their own church and congregation, numbered about 50 000 and constituted a quarter of the city's population. The Guillaumé couple's son Mathieu (later called Matthias) was born in 1711. Three other children were also born in Berlin.

In 1726 Guillaumé and his family travelled from Berlin to Amsterdam, and sailed from Texel to the Cape of Good Hope a few months later. François had two contracts in his pocket. One was a mandate that authorised him to negotiate on behalf of Jacob Labat, a Huguenot in London with a claim to the estate of a brother who had died at the Cape shortly before. It was likely, therefore, that Guillaumé was literate. [1]

The second contract was one he had entered into with the Dutch East India Company (the Vereenigde Oostindische Compagnie, or VOC) to start a silk industry at the Cape. He undertook to establish silkworm breeding and silk spinning as a business. The venture formed part of the VOC's efforts to set up an export industry that would make the Cape financially self-supporting. There had been unsuccessful attempts under two previous governors, Willem Adriaan van der Stel and Maurits Pasques de Chavonnes, to establish a silk industry.

## From silkworms to St Helena

In October 1726 Guillaumé and his family arrived in Table Bay aboard the *Berbices*. He had brought along some silkworms, but it appears that he might have spoken too highly of his own abilities. OF Mentzel, author of one of the best descriptions of the Cape in the first half of the eighteenth century, later wrote with a hint of schadenfreude that the so-called "expert" was not as competent as he had claimed to be.

Guillaumé soon discovered that he faced huge challenges. For one, his factory was situated at the top end of the Heerengracht in the small seaport town, while the mulberry trees were in Rondebosch. Slaves had to undertake daily trips to pick leaves for the silkworms. But there was a much graver problem: the worms Guillaumé had brought from Europe did not adapt well to the Cape climate.

The Political Council, the body that governed the Cape, was undeterred by these hurdles. The Council erected a three-storey building at the top end of Heerengracht and gave it the grand name of *De Oude Spinnerij* (the old spinning factory). The building was later demolished, but the name Spin Street has lived on as a reminder of the enterprise.

Though the outlook had been bleak from the outset, the Political Council was determined to persevere. In December 1727, just more than a year after his arrival, Guillaumé sent a gloomy report to the government. In the entire preceding year he had managed to harvest only six pounds of silk. Its value was far less than that of his salary of 20 florins per month plus living costs. Every year the enterprise's loss increased.

Towards the end of 1729, the members of the Political Council visited Guillaumé's spinning factory and expressed their disappointment at the poor

---

1    M Boucher, *French Speakers at the Cape: The European Background* (Pretoria: University of South Africa, 1981), pp. 145–46, 161–62.

progress. What he told them worsened their mood. He predicted poor results for the coming years as well, as few of the silkworm eggs had hatched.

In 1732 Guillaumé threw in the towel, overwhelmed by the problems with labour, worms and the mulberry trees. He saw no hope of a profit, and asked for permission to transfer the business to his son Matthias. In 1735 he informed the government of his intention to remain at the Cape as a free burgher. In that year, the name François Guillaumé appeared on the list of burghers of the district of Stellenbosch for the first time.

Matthias, too, decided that the silk industry was a blind alley, and became a blacksmith. Ten years later he abandoned this occupation as well, and in 1743 he started farming on the farm Vlottenburg (also called Vredenburg). He stayed there until 1756, when he sold the farm. In the last year he supplied the following information about his property for the *Opgaafrol* (the inventory of farming activities): 5 slaves, 13 horses, 10 head of cattle and 200 sheep. He also grew grain on a small scale.

A few years later Matthias moved to the farm Afdak which he had bought near present-day Onrus. His descendants would become pioneers of the Overberg, and specifically of the areas around Bredasdorp and Napier. [2] In the last years of the VOC's rule, the name Guillaumé was simplified to Giliomee in the Company's *Opgaafrol*.

My grandfather, Johannes Human Giliomee, born in 1867, was the son of an impoverished *bywoner* (tenant farmer) who worked on various farms in the Bredasdorp district. He married his cousin, Elizabeth Catharina Giliomee, and around 1890 the couple moved to the Republic of the Orange Free State. They settled in the town of Villiers on the southern bank of the Vaal River. Family tradition has it that they were as poor as church mice when they arrived in Villiers. There was a ray of light, though: my grandmother came from an affluent family in the Bredasdorp district.

With financial help from his in-laws, my grandfather soon found his feet. Villiers was on the main road to the Johannesburg goldfields, and my grandfather obtained the contract for the pontoon over the Vaal River. Later he was also awarded the contract for the mail coach between Villiers and Johannesburg.

When the war between Britain and the Boer Republics broke out in 1899, he joined the Free State forces and became a member of the Wilge River field cornetcy. British forces captured him and his brother Jurie at Groenplaats on 21 October 1900. They were sent as prisoners of war to the Deadwood Camp

2    Dirkie C Neethling, *Giliomee: 'n Pionierfamilie van die Overberg* (Private publication, 2010).

on the island of St Helena. Here he made a beautiful little wooden chest, which he brought back to Villiers.

My grandmother was determined that British troops would not capture her and her two children, both younger than ten, and send them to a concentration camp. They wandered around in the veld and lay low whenever a Britsh patrol was in the vicinity. The fact that she had hidden a sum of £60 in her belt assisted her greatly in the battle for survival.[3]

It has been estimated that by the end of the war, there were 2 000 Boer women and children in the Free State and 10 000 in the Transvaal who had been surviving in the open veld to escape internment in the concentration camps.

After the conclusion of peace, my grandfather was detained on St Helena for a further three months. On 19 August 1902, when he was about to depart, he wrote a simple yet moving letter to my grandmother that shows the extent to which the Dutch spoken in South Africa had already evolved into Afrikaans.

In the aftermath of the war, my grandparents managed to get back on their feet financially. Twelve years after the Peace of Vereeniging my grandfather took part in the Rebellion of 1914-15 along with many other farmers from the northern Free State, and was captured after a skirmish at Mushroom Valley. After the government had suppressed the uprising, the rebels were faced with huge claims for damages. In the northern Free State alone, the claims amounted to more than £200 000 (about R 240 million today). The Helpmekaar Vereniging (Mutual Aid Association), which had branches countrywide, was set up to raise funds for the purpose of assisting the rebels to pay their debt. The project was extremely successful, and by the end of 1917 all claims for damages had been settled from the fund.

The National Party, which had been founded by General JBM Hertzog in 1914, benefited greatly from this early form of nationalist mobilisation. Without the Helpmekaar movement, my grandfather and the other rebels would probably have been ruined financially. He and my grandmother were staunch Hertzog supporters for the rest of their lives. Their farming operations on their farms Wolwepoort and Prospect in the Villiers district prospered. They were able to send their eldest as well as their third-eldest son (my father) to Stellenbosch to further their education.

## A "Blommebuhr" from the Bokveld

I was named after my maternal grandfather, Hermann Henry Buhr (1876–1966), the son of Johann Jacob Buhr and Catharina Gesa Riege. His parental home in

---

3    *Seën- en groetewense aan die NG gemeente Villiers,* published on the occasion of the centenary of the Villiers congregation (Villiers, 2007), unpaginated.

Germany had been on a smallholding in the district of Ochsenwerder just out-side Hamburg. Here, several generations of Buhrs had grown vegetables for the Hamburg market and transported their produce to the city along the Elbe River.

Johann Buhr was an affluent banker and a member of the Senate which governed the city-state of Hamburg. According to family tradition, he was a "hard, unreasonable and unaffectionate man who was abnormally obsessed with the notion that one should not spend a single moment doing nothing".

Although Hermann had rebelled against his father in his youth, in his mature years he himself had little patience with children or grandchildren who sat around idly. He once asked a son-in-law who used to spend a long time on his morning devotions whether he could not pray under a fig tree instead and chase away the mousebirds at the same time.

After a few years at school, my grandfather ran away from home. His father discovered later that he had been working in a shoe shop in Berlin. He dis-appeared for a second time, intent on starting a new life in German South West Africa. According to research by my second cousin Riëtte Ruthven, his name does not appear on the passenger lists of any of the few ships that sailed to Africa in those days. The possibility that he was a stowaway cannot be discounted.

In 1895 my grandfather, aged nineteen, arrived in Table Bay. The ship's cap-tain refused to let him disembark, possibly because he lacked the necessary travel documents or financial means. Fortunately, the merchant William Spilhaus arrived and gave him an advance. The first that Hermann Buhr's family heard of his being in South Africa was when his sister Martha received a letter from him from Cape Town.[4]

He worked for a few months for Spilhaus to repay his debt. While his plan was still to seek his fortune in German South West Africa, he could not afford the trip to that territory. He applied successfully for the position of manager of the store on the farm Grasberg, fifteen kilometres outside the town of Nieu-woudtville on the Bokveld Plateau. This was how my German grandfather ended up on the farm where he would spend the rest of his life.

Grasberg belonged to Elias Albertus Nel, a well-off farmer who owned 40 000 morgen. He and his wife had two daughters, and at first they were dead set against the relationship that developed between their elder daughter, Hester Christina, and the young German. But my grandfather was resolute and enterprising.

When my grandmother left Grasberg in 1898 for a three-week visit to an unknown destination, he wrote her a poem that has been preserved. The fact

---

4    Communication from Riëtte Ruthven (born Buhr), 11 May 2015.

that he had it printed shows that his financial affairs had greatly improved. The poem gives the impression of a witty and literate suitor.

As poetry, it did not have much merit, but perhaps it cut the knot. Hermann Buhr's circumstances improved dramatically after Hester and her parents consented to the marriage. Their wedding took place in 1899. Hermann's brother Henri Buhr arrived from Germany for the occasion and brought along Hermann's inheritance from his father.

Farmers on the plateau of the Bokveld Mountains, with its erratic rainfall, poor soil and long distances from the market, struggled to make headway. My grandfather's inheritance enabled him to buy the store on Grasberg. A few years later he acquired a second store, on the farm Brandkop, on the road between Nieuwoudtville and Loeriesfontein.

My grandfather's stores attracted a considerable clientele from the surrounding farms. They would provide him and his family with a good income for the rest of his life. His brother Henri settled in South Africa in 1903, and bought a store in Loeriesfontein.

Despite not having completed his school career, my grandfather was an intelligent and well-read man. He later subscribed to both *Die Burger* and a Cape Town-based English newspaper, and to two influential American magazines, the *Saturday Evening Post* and *Life*. My cousin Constand Wahl, who had many conversations with him, wrote: "Oupa Buhr's contribution to the touch of difference that distinguished the Buhr family from the run-of-the-mill Northern Bokveld families was enormous . . . His policy was to give his children a good education, regardless of the cost. That was certainly a novelty for the Northern Bokveld."

My grandfather did not immediately become a South African citizen, which might have been cause enough to render him liable to internment during the First World War. Perhaps the real reason for his internment was the bitter animosity between him and his brother-in-law, who also lived on Graskop, and who had in all likelihood informed on him to the authorities. The fact that he had acquired South African citizenship as far back as 1909 did not protect him.

During the Second World War, the entire family was pro-German. Neighbours congregated at Grasberg to listen to the broadcasts of Zeesen, the pro-German short-wave radio station. One of my first political memories is of my disappointment at reading in the paper in 1945 that Germany had surrendered. I cannot recall, however, that the Nazi ideology or even Adolf Hitler was ever discussed. When the horrors of the Holocaust became known later, it was a great shock to the family.

My grandfather identified strongly with the Afrikaner community and was a member of the Dutch Reformed Church. Every Sunday he and my grand-mother would drive to Nieuwoudtville to attend the service. He was known for speaking his mind, and once took this habit to the extreme. Just as the service was about to start, he rose from his seat and walked up to the pulpit to inform the dominee that he disapproved of the church council's decision to build a new parsonage.

My grandfather retained a quality of "otherness" throughout his life. Johan Steyn, a frequent visitor to Grasberg in his childhood days, described him as follows: "He was a refined, cultured person, aloof from the then less cultured farmers of his district – in my view, the brains of Johann [his son] and his brother and sisters came from that side."

My grandmother, Hester, was renowned for her tact, empathy and talent for reconciling people with each other. But her almost endless patience with my grandfather had its limits. On one occasion she lashed out at him: "Now I can see why you're at odds with everyone." To which my grandfather's retorted: "Well, at least the two of us have got on for more than fifty years."

The couple had nine children. The eldest, Johann, was born in 1900 and my mother Rina, the third child, in 1903. Elias, the only other son, obtained a degree in agriculture and subsequently took over the farming operations on Brandkop and Grasberg.

Nowadays the tourism industry markets the Bokveld Plateau, with Nieu-woudtville as the commercial hub, as the "bulb capital of the world". My grandfather was the first person to see the potential of bulbs as a product for the Cape market. He was, after all, a child of Ochsenwerder where his family had produced vegetables for the market for generations.

My grandfather gained some prominence on account of the Dutch tulips he cultivated and his keen interest in the wild flowers of the area. One of the bulbous plants was named after him: *Hesperantha buhrii* (today better known as *Hesperantha cucullata*).

He also planted fields of *Sparaxis elegans* and marketed the bulbs. An article in the magazine *Sarie Marais* referred to him as the "Blommebuhr van die Bokveld" (flower farmer of the Bokveld). His son Elias inherited his interest in wild plants. He was the first collector of an aloe species that is named after him, *Aloe buhrii*.[5]

For me and all the other Buhr grandchildren, Grasberg was a wonderland we could never get enough of. Oupa had created a paradise of flower and vegetable

5    "Grasberg se Buhrs", memorandum compiled by Johann Hermann Buhr and his daughter Riëtte Ruthven.

gardens and orchards which he maintained in spite of periodic droughts. Once or twice every year my family would visit Grasberg, where we were always warmly received.

## A student prince

Johann Buhr, the eldest child in the Buhr family, was born in 1900.[6] I grew up with memories of "Oom Johann", as the Buhr grandchildren continued to refer to him. It was as if he were still alive, despite the fact that he had died as far back as 1940, two years after my birth. At Grasberg, nearly everyone had an anecdote to tell about him. As my cousin Hermann Spangenberg, later professor in psychology at the University of the Western Cape, put it: "His giftedness and modesty were so overwhelming that he was the favourite son of the area: he personified the innate intelligence and modesty of the people."

Johann was sent to Stellenbosch to complete his high-school education and in 1918 he enrolled as a student at the University of Stellenbosch, which had acquired university status in that year. He soon became known as someone with a keen intellect and unique sense of humour. In her autobiography *My beskeie deel*, MER (the writer ME Rothmann) recalled that everyone expected him to have a brilliant career, as he was already considered a leader in his student days.

His studies, however, got off to a slow start. He first took up agriculture, but dropped out of the course after a year or two and enrolled for a BA and later for a law degree. His class attendance was so poor that he was not permitted to write the final examinations for the BA degree. He informed his parents with a laconic three-word telegram: "Exams a fiasco".

To earn an income, Johann went to work for *Die Burger* for a few years. This was the beginning of what would become an association of almost twenty years with that newspaper and with the magazine *Die Huisgenoot*. Even after he had fallen ill with tuberculosis in 1930 and was no longer able to hold a full-time job, he still contributed newspaper reports, articles and short stories. In a preface to a collection of early Afrikaans short stories, Danie Hugo refers to "Johann Buhr's playfully mischievous style" with which he depicted his world more mercilessly than his predecessors had done.

In 1923 he returned to Stellenbosch and soon gained a reputation as an excellent debater. He was the opener of the university's team in a debate with the Oxford Union, the oldest debating society in the world. In 1925 he under-

---

6    Hermann Giliomee (comp.), *Buhr van die Bokveld: 'n sprankelende intelligensie' – 'n Bloemlesing uit die werk van Johann Buhr* (Cape Town: Africana Uitgewers, 2015).

took a debating tour through the country together with the 23-year-old Hendrik Verwoerd and LC Steyn, a future chief justice of South Africa.

They debated with each other in front of audiences in thirteen towns in all four provinces. With the exception of Middelburg, Cape, and Springs, the halls were packed. At Kroonstad, 700 people turned up to listen.

In 1924 Johann was elected chairman of the students' representative council (SRC). In that capacity, he was charged with the task of welcoming Edward, Prince of Wales, the heir to the British throne, on behalf of the students during the Prince's visit to Stellenbosch on 4 May 1925. Before the SRC approved the students' programme, there was heated debate about how the Prince should be received.

In the two weeks that preceded the visit, the university authorities, the municipality, and even the prime minister were anxious about the programme and what Johann might say in his speech. In a letter to his father, Johann wrote that the municipal and university authorities insisted on knowing to the last detail "what we are going to do and exactly how we are going to do it". Just before the visit, the prime minister finally approved the SRC's programme.

Great excitement prevailed on the day of the royal visit, but one person was absent when the reception started: Johann Buhr. His friends found him fast asleep in his room in Wilgenhof university residence, and rushed him to the venue of the reception. The following day, the *Cape Times* reported:

> The brilliant little speech in which the young student who had been elected to speak on their behalf addressed the Prince was such as to warrant the prediction that South Africa will hear a great deal in future years of Mr. J. Buhr, to whom the task was allotted.

The speech should be read against the backdrop of the near-hysterical way in which the press reported on the Prince's tour. One sensational event had involved a steeplechase in which the Prince, a keen horseman, took part. He had fallen from his horse and injured his collarbone. (On a press photo, he appears with a bandaged arm next to Oom Johann.) After the Prince's accident, the government had ordered him to stop participating in "such a dangerous sport".

In Ralph Deakin's book *Southward Ho!*, which was published officially after the tour, this account was given of the reception in Stellenbosch:

> A splendid rendering of Die Stem van Zuid Afrika, with words adapted to the occasion, led up to the jocular oration of Mr. Johan [sic] Buhr,

the president of the Students' Council, whose quips made the Prince, his entourage and the grand-stand full of students rock with mirth.

The Prince cabled the speech to his father, and it was included verbatim in the book. The speech, as it was delivered, read as follows:

> We have come here to-day because we like to see a man and we cheered because we know a man when we see one. Our presence here is intended as a tribute to your manliness, which the most persistent attempts of the whole world have not been able to spoil. This is, however, not the only reason for our enthusiasm over your visit. Next to a real man there is nothing we love better than a real sportsman, no matter for what side he happens to be playing, and it is a special pleasure to us to welcome here, to-day, one of the finest and most daring sportsmen of the British Isles.
>
> I am afraid your Highness will find that all our most popular heroes are people who have either been in gaol for political crimes or in hospital for fractured bones. I must admit that the fact that your Highness has never been in gaol is a serious disqualification, which I sincerely trust your Highness will manage to get remedied before leaving the country. On the other hand, your Highness has fortunately, on several occasions, managed to get yourself into hospital and I can assure you that on that count alone your visit would give us great pleasure.
>
> As regards our lady students, I would very much have liked to interpret their feelings also, but I am afraid their sentiments on this occasion are far too delicate for masculine interpretation, and for further information on the subject, I shall have to refer your Highness to the way they are looking at you. I trust that the mere fact that they have put me here will abundantly show just how enthusiastic they can be over good-looking young fellows with pleasant smiles.[7]

Markus Viljoen, famed editor of *Die Huisgenoot*, wrote about the speech: "After all the formal, lacklustre, rather cloying expressions of loyalty, the young student's speech was like a fresh spring breeze in a stuffy room, and it was a topic of discussion for weeks afterwards."

Oom Johann was not very impressed with the Prince, whom he described as follows:

---

7    See also the version of G Ward-Price, *Through South Africa with the Prince* (London: Gill Publishing Co, 1926), pp. 69-70.

The Prince, between you and me, is a rather hopeless specimen of humanity. He is extremely nervous, looks quite dissipated, and doesn't command respect in the least. He starts a sentence, and if you look him straight in the eye, he titters and starts a brand-new sentence.

So I soon dropped the etiquette and from that point on he seemed more at ease and we had quite a good chat, about the university and about sport. He has one good trait, which is that he makes an effort to be pleasant . . . He evidently does his best in very trying circumstances, and the strongest emotion he inspires in me is one of profound sympathy. He is a nice boy through and through, with no trace of haughtiness; but lacks all the qualities of someone in his position.

This assessment was not wide of the mark. Twelve years later, the Prince ascended the throne as Edward VIII. A few months later he abdicated after having committed the cardinal sin of refusing to give up his plan of marrying a divorced woman. Thereafter he took the title of Duke of Windsor. Winston Churchill dismissed him as "a little man, dressed up to the nines".

After obtaining a BA degree in 1925, Oom Johann worked in Pietermaritzburg for two years as editor of *The Times of Natal*. In 1928 he returned to Stellenbosch and completed his legal studies.

When the university Senate decided to ask a student to address the audience on graduation day, the choice fell on Oom Johann. After speeches by the rector, the vice-chancellor and one or two other office-bearers, it was finally his turn. "Ladies and gentlemen," he began, "you have listened to words of wisdom. Now you can listen to words of common sense." He continued:

I have been at Stellenbosch for ten years now. In the course of these ten years, there have been many changes. New university buildings have been erected . . . And whether it's true or not I can't say, but there are students who claim that during these ten years there have even been changes in some professors' notes.

The students cheered him, but the vice-chancellor, Professor Adriaan Moorrees, was not amused.

## "Brilliant writer"

Markus Viljoen considered Johann Buhr one of the most versatile and talented journalists he had ever encountered. "He was a born humorist who could be funny without even intending it." Because the editorial team of *Die Burger* was so small in those early days, Johann had scant opportunity to give his humoristic bent free rein. The paper even offered him the position of sports editor.

Among his best-known reports was his account of Malcolm Campbell's attempt to break the world land speed record at Verneukpan in 1929. He also accompanied the first Afrikaans theatre companies on their tours as a reporter, and wrote about pioneering actors such as Paul de Groot and Wena Naudé in his series of articles "Agter die sterre" (Behind the stars). The actor and director André Huguenet described Johann Buhr as a "brainy and brilliant writer" who did much to stimulate the public's interest in theatre.

In 1930, at the age of 30, he resigned for health reasons after having contracted turberculosis. In his entire life, he had spent less than six years in a full-time position. He returned to Grasberg, and for some while stayed in a mat hut at a remote cattle post in Bushmanland in the hope that the dry air would cure him of the disease.

Nevertheless, during the 1930s he still contributed several short stories and articles of exceptional quality to *Die Burger* and *Die Huisgenoot*.

A year or two before his death in 1940 at the age of 40, some of his student friends visited him at his lonely hut at the cattle post to say their goodbyes. ID du Plessis, who would later receive the Hertzog Prize for poetry, delivered this touching tribute:

> Judged by outward appearances, Johann Buhr was unimpressive. But it was only poor health that prevented him from achieving much, both as journalist and as literary writer with a light satirical touch; for behind that exterior lay a remarkable mind: a scintillating intelligence, a fine sense of humour, a quicksilver wit that could have given a new dimension to Afrikaans journalism.
>
> If he could have devoted his talents to column writing from the outset, no doubt we would have been enriched today by a contribution of lasting value in his particular field.
>
> In the last years of his illness he had to spend the winter months at an isolated cattle post. Through the agency of his friend Recht Malan, he received reading matter from Cape Town: a gesture for which he was poignantly grateful; because for this endearing person it always came as a surprise that others could be so good to him.
>
> My last impression of him was at Nieuwoudtville, when a few of us visited him in the final year of the eclipse. That day he told me: "What a wonderful privilege it must be to be able to fulfil oneself in poems."

What would have passed through his mind as he stood watching us
drive off: we who were headed for a life filled with all the possibilities
that he, with his shining talent, was not destined to enjoy?

On his death in 1940, *Die Burger* wrote: "As sincere and faithful as he always
was towards friends, so he was towards the Afrikaner cause, which he promoted
to the best of his ability." The *Cape Times* commented that his friends had
expected him to make a contribution to "the virile Afrikaans literature", but,
sadly, a very good brain had been housed in a weak body. In his memoirs
*Spykers met koppe* (1946), Johannes Steinmeyer referred to Johann Buhr as one
of his colleagues in journalism who were regarded as "men of great repute".

The tragedy of her brother's early death left a deep impression on my mother.
There must have been a strong bond between them, as he had nominated her
as executrix of his estate. Whenever I underachieved, I felt that my mother
was especially upset because she thought I was squandering my opportunities.

In 1980, forty years after Oom Johann's death, Anthony Heard, editor of the
*Cape Times*, and Gerald Shaw, the deputy editor, invited me to write a column
for the paper on the recommendation of the well-known journalist Anthony
Delius, whose acquaintance I had made during the 1977-78 academic year
at Yale University. I wondered what Oom Johann would have made of the
opportunity to write his own column – a role for which he had been eminently equipped.

## Chapter 2

# "The song of a nation's awakening"

My parents were Gerhardus Adriaan Giliomee (1905–1986), born in Villiers in the Free State, and Catharina Gesa Giliomee (1903-2001), whose birth-place was the farm Grasberg, near Nieuwoudtville on the Bokveld Plateau. My paternal grandfather's participation in both the Anglo-Boer War and the Rebellion of 1914-15 had shaped my father politically. Notable political influ-ences in my mother's case included her German father, Hermann Buhr, and the colonial patriotism that had developed among Cape Afrikaners in the nineteenth century.

At the time of my parents' birth in the early twentieth century, Afrikaners lagged far behind the English-speaking community. At the root of this dis-parity were the poor educational and cultural foundations that the Dutch East India Company had laid down in the first 150 years of the settlement. When the British first occupied the Cape in 1795, there were no locally produced newspapers, magazines or books. The Dutch-speaking burgher community was isolated, poorly educated, and far behind developments in Europe.

The British rulers decided to make English the only official language and the language of instruction in schools. The isolated life on farms and a huge shortage of schools in the country districts made it difficult for Afrikaners to establish a culturally conscious middle class.

By 1930, when my parents left university, a commission found that a quarter of the Afrikaners could be classified as poor whites – so impoverished that they lived far below the level that was considered then appropriate for white people. In the bigger towns and the cities, many lived in wretched conditions. Here, English was the dominant language. The English-speaking community set the tone in the spheres of fashion, architecture, language, good manners and polite conversation.[8]

---

8    Robert Ross, *Status and Respectability in the Cape Colony, 1750-1870: A Tragedy of Manners* (Cambridge: Cambridge University Press, 1999).

My parents studied at the University of Stellenbosch, where both of them trained for the teaching profession with the aim of devoting their lives to the building of the Afrikaner community. They married in 1933. In 1935 my father obtained his first permanent appointment, at a high school in the village of Ugie in Griqualand East.

Destitution was rife in Ugie. Those were the years of the Depression and prolonged drought. Many farmers had thrown in the towel and moved to town. In addition to all the poor farm children, the town had a large orphanage that could accommodate 400 youngsters. It had been established by the Dutch Reformed Church in the Cape Province in the wake of the flu epidemic of 1918, which left many orphans. Over the next forty years, the institution would send more than 4 000 children into the world equipped with a good school education.

Ugie influenced my parents' outlook on life in two ways in particular. They became aware of the vital importance of education in the upliftment of poor Afrikaners, and they reacted strongly against the tendency of some English speakers to look down on the orphans and other poor Afrikaners. My parents resolved to be unashamedly Afrikaans. Instead of calling our parents "Daddy" and "Mommy", we were taught to say "Vader" and "Moeder".

My parents moved from Ugie to Sterkstroom, where I was born in 1938. Six months after my birth, my father accepted the post of history teacher in the town of Porterville in the Western Cape. Porterville offered a much gentler and more pleasant environment than the Eastern Cape.

Porterville's history dates back to 1863, when the first plots were laid out on the farm Pomona. The town was named after William Porter, a popular attorney-general of the Cape Colony. The first school was opened in 1870. In 1876 the Dutch Reformed church was consecrated, and in 1880 the first minister was called. [9]

When the little school opened its doors in 1870, it had 82 registered pupils and one English-speaking teacher. But the average attendance figure was only 43. There was a fundamental problem: the teacher had lost control over the children. A replacement had to be found, and the school only re-opened a year later.

The Cape Colony only introduced compulsory education for white children in 1905. The school in Porterville, which was initially just a primary school,

---

9    A brief history of the town and its people appears in SW van der Merwe, *Porterville en die 24 riviere* (Stellenbosch: CF Albertyn, 1972), and in Francois du Bois's three self-published books *Land van die disa*, *Die mooiste disa* and *Gister se disas*. School yearbooks were also consulted.

became a secondary school as well in 1917, and it took another three years before a proper high school for white children was established in a separate building. This was fully two hundred years after the first burghers had settled here, and less than two generations before I went to high school in the early 1950s. Coloured children only gained access to a high school after 1994, when the white school was integrated.

The residents of Porterville had retained something of the independent spirit of their free burgher forebears. Many still kept their own cows so that they could be self-sufficient in terms of milk supply. In the mornings these cows would be taken to the pastures south of the town where they grazed, and in the evenings they were brought home to be milked. The municipality kept a bull in a kraal in the town to serve the cows. He was soon referred as "the Bull from Porterville", which is how Portervillers are known to this day.

Culturally, the town and district formed one of the most homogeneous communities in the country. Virtually all the inhabitants were either white or coloured, followed the Christian faith, and spoke Afrikaans. With a few exceptions, the coloured Afrikaans speakers were much poorer than their white counterparts. There were only two black African people in the town.

The number of Porterville residents who spoke English as their first language could literally be counted on the fingers of one hand. Most Afrikaans speakers' grasp of English was nonexistent or poor. English was, for all practical purposes, a foreign language.

## A Boland childhood

Porterville lies at the foot of the Olifants River Mountains, about 150 km north of Cape Town. It is a tranquil town, abounding in trees and water, with a moderate climate except for a quota of sweltering summer days. The Olifants River Mountains, which separate the coastal plain from the interior, stand sentinel over the town without dominating it.

For Jan Smuts, who had been born in nearby Riebeek West, the most beautiful spot in the world was the view from Riebeek Kasteel over the coastal plain to Cape Town. In my case, it was Porterville's town dam, from where you could look up at the Olifants River Mountains across the water to the east and down on the town to the west. On balmy summer evenings, my mother would often pack a picnic supper which we enjoyed at the dam. Porterville was a town where children felt safe and secure. You knew who you were, and who your family were. Porterville was my place.

We were three children in a happy family: Jan was born in 1936, I in 1938, and Hester in 1940. The three of us followed the same path through school and church in the town. As eldest child, Jan was the natural leader and he developed an interest in his environment, agriculture and the study of insects at an early age. He would later become a professor of entomology at the University of Stellenbosch, an eminent champion of environmental conversation, and an astute art collector.

I was named after my maternal grandfather, Hermann Buhr, an enterprising and innovative person, a great individualist and a strong family man, a German and an Afrikaner. I never really managed to connect with him. By the time I entered my teens he was already in his mid-seventies, and he had in any case never been disposed to small talk.

My sister Hester, a vivacious and energetic child, became a teacher. Many years later, when the television producer and director Herman Binge made the documentary programme *Stroom-op*, Hester revealed herself surprisingly as someone with a natural gift for appearing in front of the television cameras.

In our home in Porterville, I suffered from the typical "second-child syndrome" and routinely rebelled against Jan's authority and some parental decisions. "Against the government", my mother would remark about my protests.

My father was a well-informed, level-headed and positive person who dedicated his life to his family and to education. My mother was a strong woman, imbued with a great devotion to her family and a sense of duty towards the poor Afrikaners in the town.

My love for history came from my father. In his history classes at school, he tended to emphasise the "story" in history and the role of prominent figures such as Napoleon and the Boer Republic presidents Paul Kruger and MT Steyn. In his lesssons on the French Revolution, he would sometimes go as far as singing the rousing anthem "La Marseillaise".

After his retirement, my father wrote this message to the school: "Keep in mind that all knowledge and all experiences are of value to one and make one a richer and better person." He added that, despite temporary disappointments and setbacks, his teaching career had been "happy and fruitful years".

One of the disappointments had been an unsuccessful application for the principalship. He never applied for a principalship elsewhere. He could see no sense in it, as he identified with the local community and was able to find fulfilment in the town. Financially, there was no need for him to pursue a senior post. He did well with his investments on the stock exchange, especially in gold shares, and could send his three children to the University of Stellenbosch without taking out a loan.

He expressed himself exceptionally well in writing, and assisted me with the Afrikaans translation of *The Rise and Crisis of Afrikaner Power* (Yale University

Press, 1979), which I co-authored with Heribert Adam. Given the chance, he might have become an excellent historian.

## War and its aftermath

Both my parents supported the National Party (NP) except for a period in the 1930s, when my father lined up behind General JBM Hertzog, leader of the United Party (UP). The declaration of war in 1939, after General Jan Smuts had gained the upper hand in the UP, caused him to return to the NP. My parents remained loyal to the NP government through thick and thin. They would have voted for the proverbial broomstick if it had stood as the NP candidate in their constituency.

During the war years I was vaguely aware that my parents, like the majority of Afrikaners, were opposed to South Africa's participation as a member of the Allied Forces. The decision to join the war had been taken in Parliament in 1939 with a slim majority of thirteen votes, which mainly reflected the Afrikaans-English split in the country.

Afrikaner nationalists were not the only ones who felt that the country should not have entered the war on the basis of a split vote in Parliament. In her memoirs, the historian Phyllis Lewsen recounts that JS Marais, a respected liberal historian, told her: "No country should go to war except with multiparty support . . . The great majority of Afrikaners, and I include myself – though, as you know I am a liberal and hated the Nazis and the Nationalists – supported Hertzog's neutrality policy."[10]

The stories I heard from my parents about the victimisation of Afrikaners during the war would later prove to be true. The Smuts government suspended the policy of employing people on merit to a professional civil service during the war as, understandably, it did not want to run the risk of having anti-war Afrikaner nationalists in strategic positions. There were many stories of Afrikaners employed on the railways who were transferred against their will or forced to take early retirement. Another major grievance was that monolingual English officials were appointed in senior positions to replace officials who had joined the armed forces.

Rob Davies, in later years an ANC cabinet minister, wrote in his book *Capital, State and White Labour in South Africa, 1900 to 1960* (1979) that the dissatisfaction among railway officials was so widespread that Paul Sauer, who had become minister of transport after the election of 1948, appointed a Grievances Commission. A total of 2 875 complaints were received from Afrikaans-speaking employees who felt they had been disadvantaged.

---

10   Phyllis Lewsen, *Reverberations: A Memoir* (Cape Town: UCT Press, 1996). p. 110.

Following the 1948 election, in the case of two high-profile positions the NP government made appointment shifts that created a great stir: William Marshall Clark, who, during the war, had been appointed general manager of the SA Railways and Harbours over the heads of two Afrikaner civil servants, was ousted with a generous golden handshake, and Major-General Evered Poole, who had been first in line for promotion to chief of staff of the defence force, was sidelined. There are indications that the change of government disadvantaged another fifty officers who had been pro-war, including Afrikaans speakers, who were demoted or sidelined.

Leo Marquard, a respected liberal commentator, asserted in his book *The Peoples and Policies of South Africa* (1969) that the NP government reinstituted the policy of a professional civil service. The NP government did insist, however, on the strict application of the bilingualism requirement in the case of civil servants and on compensation for those who had been unfairly dismissed or denied promotion during the war. The predominance of English speakers in the higher ranks in the civil service still continued, and it was only by the early 1960s, more than fifty years after Unification, that people in those ranks reflected the white population composition.[11]

When I started writing about politics in the 1980s, I often had arguments with English-speaking commentators, notably Ken Owen, who claimed that the NP government had politicised the civil service by instituting a massive purge of English officials after the 1948 election. No evidence was supplied to substantiate these claims. It was more the case that, after the war, there was the perception among English speakers and pro-war Afrikaners that they would be discriminated against. The Civil Service Commission, however, would have acted against blatant injustice.

I have vague memories of how the war affected our household. White flour and rice were in short supply. Contrary to the government's orders, my father did not hand in his revolver at the police station but buried it in the garden instead. He probably obeyed the instruction that civil servants had to resign from the Broederbond. The fuel shortage meant that my parents sometimes had to cancel plans to visit Grasberg or other places.

In 1999 I asked the well-known South African business magnate and philanthropist Anton Rupert what had been the decisive factor in the NP's victory of 1948. He was unequivocal: "It was the war that clinched the election for the NP in 1948, not apartheid."

---

11    Leo Marquard, *The Peoples and Policies of South Africa* (London: Oxford University Press, 1969), p. 105.

I can still recall the great joy with which my parents greeted the news of the NP's victory. It was not apartheid in the first place that had motivated them, but their identification with the Afrikaner *volksbeweging* (national movement).

The NP fought the 1948 election with several planks in its platform. These included:

- a republican plank, which urged that the state should be as independent from Britain as possible;
- a cultural plank, which set great store by mother-tongue education and active involvement in the Afrikaans language and cultural movement;
- a nationalist plank, which maintained that the state as well as the white community should accept responsibility for the white poor;
- a populist plank, which was directed against the big English corporations, especially Anglo American, which towered over the economy. The aim was to establish an Afrikaner corporate sector (the first Afrikaner company had been listed on the Johannesburg Stock Exchange in 1945);
- a racist plank, which advocated white domination and comprehensive discrimination against coloured and black people.

The Afrikaners of my early years were very colour-conscious, and some were openly racist. Yet, on an interpersonal level, there often existed a paternalistic relationship between the "*baas*" and his "*volk*" (workforce) and between the "*miesies*" (mistress) and her "*bediende*" (domestic worker) that included responsibilities and obligations on both sides. A farmer was respected if he was someone who looked after "his people".

It was when the Afrikaners acted collectively as a group or party that they showed a much more inhumane face. The Immorality Act, the pass laws and Group Areas were harsh and merciless. Jan Smuts made a noteworthy observation late in his life: "I do not think people mean evil, but thoughtlessly do evil. In public life they do things of which they would be incapable in private life."[12]

The urbanised Afrikaner of today is already a generation or two removed from the traditional life on farms or in the small platteland towns. Nevertheless, there are many things Afrikaners still have in common: farm life, an interest

12   JC Smuts, *Selections from the Smuts Papers*, vol. 7, edited by Jean van der Poel (Cambridge: Cambridge University Press, 1973), p. 251.

in nature, and a love of *braaivleis* (barbequed meat). The custom of open-air braais took root among town and city dwellers during the 1938 celebrations of the centenary of the Great Trek.

## School and church

As schoolchildren, we soon heard that we had to prepare ourselves for a future that would not always be easy. Implicitly, the message was that uncontested white domination would not last for ever, and that a good education would become increasingly valuable.

As a state establishment, our school in Porterville encompassed the entire spectrum of the white community: from parents who were well off to those who struggled to get by, and from pupils who were gifted to those who found it difficult to keep up. The last-mentioned category included two of my class-mates, Org and Gys. Once I tried to justify my poor marks in an exam by saying: "Org and Gys fared even worse."

My mother made it abundantly clear that the poor performance of "Org and Gys" could not be my benchmark. She firmly believed that I was capable of greater things. "Org and Gys" became a saying in our home whenever one of us children offered a feeble excuse for a mediocre performance. On the other hand, we never got the idea that achievement was a precondition for parental love, which sometimes seems to be the case among the ambitious middle class of today.

The school in Porterville was relatively small, and in 1955, my matric year, we were only sixteen in the class. The teachers were generally committed to their work and to the welfare of the pupils. The one weakness was the quality of the English teaching. Combined with the monolingual nature of the town, this deficiency was certainly not a good preparation for university.

At university I would enrol for the subject English Special, the standard of which was considerably lower than that of English I. Even "Engels Spes" I had to abandon later on account of my low marks. I fell in the category of those whom our formidable lecturer Patricia McMagh used to call the "Kakamasians", or "Members of the Kakamas club" – students whose grasp of English was alarmingly poor. When she congratulated me in 2003 on the appearance of my book *The Afrikaners*, I reminded her kindly that I had once been one of her "Kakamasians".

Church and catechism were compulsory components of our education. Besides the great emphasis that was placed on the sermons and on the doctrine of predestination – which is still a mystery to me – I cannot remember much about my Christian instruction. Few churches had a task as daunting as that of the Dutch Reformed Church (DRC), which had to try to reconcile apartheid with Christianity's emphasis on the equality of all people.

Ben Marais, whose comprehensive study *Die kleur-krisis en die Weste* (the English version was titled *The Colour Crisis and the West*) appeared in 1952, was one of the ministers who rejected attempts to prove that apartheid had a Scriptural basis. When I worked in Pretoria from 1963 to 1965, I had the good fortune of getting to know him. In 1965 he perfomed our marriage ceremony when my fiancée Annette van Coller and I tied the knot.

"Oom Ben" was a respected and beloved minister who never complained about the opposition he encountered as a result of his views. He liked to tell the story of a session of the synod that took place in the election year of 1953, shortly after he had spoken out in his book against the efforts to justify apartheid on Christian grounds. An elder berated him: "Oh, dominee, you have now completely spoilt this year's wonderful election result for us."

## A sense of community

There was no neighbourhood in Porterville that was conspicuously rich or poor. In several streets, rich and poor lived side by side. While the homes of the more affluent were comfortable, there were no ostentatious houses. Plot size was the most noticeable difference. Some residents not only had a flower garden but also fruit trees, vegetable patches and even a vineyard. The big municipal dam was fed by water from a kloof in the mountain. The weekly turn to irrigate one's garden was a major event for the townspeople. Though my father was not a keen gardener, he did not easily miss his irrigation opportunity.

Wheat farming was the district's principal economic activity, but by the 1950s there was already considerable diversification. On the mountain farmers grew fruit, berries and disa plants, and on the farms below the mountain one found fruit, vineyards and mixed farming. Export grapes and wine grapes were produced in the Vier-en-Twintig-Riviere area, south of the town, while wheat farming predominated in the Rooi Karoo, northwest of the town.

Until about the year 2000 most of the farms were between 300 and 500 morgen in size, considerably smaller than those in the Swartland districts such as Malmesbury and Moorreesburg. This was the main reason why no significant class differences developed among the white community in the Porterville district. There was no question of poor Afrikaners belonging to a lower class. White people regarded each other as equals, irrespective of income differences.

Portervillers tended to look askance at anyone who paraded their wealth or education. People even hesitated to talk about an overseas trip for fear that they might be suspected of showing off. In the early 1960s, when my mother mentioned to an acquaintance, Oom Dais Toerien, that she and my father had just returned from a visit to London and Paris, he swiftly trumped her with an account of his recent trip to Oudtshoorn.

My recollection is that the Afrikaner community, whose lives revolved around the church and the school, were reasonably content with their lives, mainly on account of the lack of conspicuous class differences but also because there was no television that could broadcast images of the lifestyle of wealthy South Africans.

A scientific study carried out in the 1950s in more than a dozen countries around the world indicated that, on average, the citizens of poor countries were no less satisfied with their lives than those of rich countries. When a similar study was conducted in the mid-1980s, the results were dramatically different. According to their responses, citizens of richer countries were distinctly happier than those of poorer countries. The crucial difference was television. Almost everyone could see how the middle class lived in the world's advanced democracies, and almost everyone now hankered after that lifestyle and at the same time detested the rich.[13]

White people's strong sense of community had struck my parents from the outset. The church and the school occupied a central place in social life, and there was a spirit of mutual caring that went hand in hand with an engaging unpretentiousness. People showed respect towards the minister and the teachers, but did not shrink from criticism when they neglected their duties. The school achieved good academic results over the years.

In one of the school's yearbooks, three school inspectors highlighted the great value of "platteland schools for platteland children". My subjective impression at Stellenbosch, both as student and as lecturer, was that outstanding students who had matriculated at obscure platteland schools almost always performed better than good students who had attended the top schools.[14] Malcolm Gladwell recently proved this theory statistically in the context of American schools and universities in his *David and Goliath: Underdogs, Misfits and the Art of Battling Giants* (2013).

## A national movement

Participation in the *volksbeweging* was a formative influence in my life. It instilled in me a sense of involvement with Afrikaners as a community that was numerically small and still at an early stage of its cultural development. As

13   Benjamin M Friedman, "The Power of the Electronic Herd", *New York Review of Books*, 15 July 1999, pp. 40-44.
14   Malcolm Gladwell, *David and Goliath: Underdogs, Misfits and the Art of Battling Giants* (London: Allen Lane, 2013), pp. 63-96.

strange as it may sound today, the *volksbeweging* did not arise in reaction to any perceived threat from coloured or black people.

The *volksbeweging* was especially aimed at liberating Afrikaners from their sense of inferiority towards the wealthier and more confident English-speaking section of the white population. Besides the upliftment of the so-called poor whites, the national movement had other important objectives: the establishment of Afrikaner business enterprises which would, in turn, employ Afrikaners, and the development of the Afrikaans language and culture.

My mother played an active role in the upliftment of the town's poor. She was a member and, later, chair of the Porterville branch of the Afrikaanse Christelike Vrouevereniging (ACVV). This Christian women's organisation, which had branches across the Cape Province, had been founded in Cape Town in the wake of the Anglo-Boer War to relieve the distress of destitute Afrikaners.

My mother often visited the poor herself to distribute food, clothing or reading matter, and sometimes she would send Jan. Her greatest frustration was that the poor did not want to read. She wanted to help uplift them intellectually so that they could be full members of the Afrikaner community and not only candidates for charity. This was a message that went out particularly from Dr DF Malan, editor of *Die Burger* and the NP leader, and ministers of religion.

The Stellenbosch economist Professor Jan Sadie has pointed out that the project of middle-class Afrikaners to uplift their own poor was an unusual phenomenon. It had much to do with the fact that the English-speaking elite tended to look down on Afrikaners collectively as a lesser "race" or community. Some tried to substantiate this theory of inherent inferiority by noting that more than 80% of poor whites were Afrikaners.

As a young newspaper reporter, MER (ME Rothmann), the Afrikaans writer who worked full-time for the ACVV for much of her life, heard a speech by Sir Carruthers Beattie, vice-chancellor of the University of Cape Town, that upset her greatly. He stated that poor whites were generally "intellectually backward" and that there was something "inherent" in the Afrikaners that resulted in the phenomenon of poor whiteism assuming such alarming proportions in their case. MER wrote: "His audience raised no objections to this statement." As Sadie put it, Afrikaners of all classes resolved to form a united front against English speakers, who looked down on them, especially their poor.

Most of the coloured people were, of course, even poorer than the poor whites. I once asked my mother whether she should not try to help the coloured poor as well. Her reply was that one could undertake only one great social task in one's life, and the upliftment of the Afrikaner poor was her great task.

Economically, the Afrikaners still lagged far behind their English-speaking counterparts. In 1938, the year of my birth, the Afrikaner share of the private sector stood at less than 10% (excluding agriculture). Referring to the accepted correlation between Protestantism and capitalism, a respected analyst observed recently that "the failure of the Calvinist Afrikaners to develop a thriving capitalist system until the last quarter of the [twentieth] century" is an anomaly.[15]

In 1939 Sanlam and the Afrikaner Broederbond organised an economic *volkskongres* (people's congress) in Bloemfontein to promote the establishment of Afrikaner companies. From their side, Afrikaner companies had to undertake to employ Afrikaners and to place those who excelled in management positions. The central idea was to increase the Afrikaner share of the economy in a way that would command respect.

After the congress TE Dönges, who later became a cabinet minister, defended the economic mobilisation of Afrikaners in a way that was also wholeheartedly endorsed by my parents. The Afrikaners, he said, were determined to act as a group to increase their share of the economy fairly and peacefully. They felt that they had no right to expect others to help them, and were too proud to ask for help from others to work out their economic salvation. Dönges emphasised that the Afrikaners had no intention of boycotting English firms. All that they asked was for the English-speaking community to maintain at least a "benign neutrality" to allow Afrikaners to find their "economic feet".

This was the idealistic side, but there was certainly also the dark side. After the NP came to power in 1948, Indians were forced to move from business centres to the outskirts of towns. My parents ordered us not to buy from Hassim, an Indian who had a shop in the main street. Few enterprises were owned by coloured people, and up to the last decade or two of NP rule the government or local authorities made virtually no attempt to help coloured entrepreneurs grow their own businesses.

By the time I reached the age of ten in 1948, there was still only a smattering of Afrikaner-owned businesses that were bigger than the town café or the town shop. It was only in 1945 that the first Afrikaner company listed on the Johannesburg Stock Exchange (JSE): Anton Rupert's Distillers Corporation. Bonuskor (in the Sanlam stable) followed a few years later.

Fortunately, there was no question of English companies having to lend the

---

15    Francis Fukuyama, *Trust: The Social Virtues of Prosperity* (New York: The Free Press, 1995), p. 44.

Afrikaners a hand in establishing themselves economically. The Afrikaners had to earn their respect by creating their own successful enterprises. I asked Anton Rupert in 1999 if he could think of any Afrikaans company that had been "empowered" by an English company. He reflected for a moment before answering: "Not one, and I'm very grateful for that."

My father had joined the Afrikaner Broederbond (AB) shortly after his arrival in Porterville. After the congress of 1939, the AB encouraged its members to invest in Afrikaner companies. My father had started buying shares on the JSE at an early stage. He bought gold shares in particular, but also invested in Rembrandt, Federale Volksbeleggings and Federale Mynbou.

Something that irked my father was the poor quality of *Die Burger*'s business page. In 1959 he asked in a letter to *Die Burger*'s managing director, Phil Weber, that the newspaper "should become just as authoritative in the economic field as it already is in other fields". He described *Die Burger*'s financial reporting, justifiably, as "formal, technical, stiff and dull". English-language papers, on the other hand, were chock-a-block with analyses of the value of particular shares.

To illustrate his point, my father referred to the shares of Federale Mynbou (later known as Fedmyn), a Sanlam subsidiary that was established in 1953 and that soon achieved success. In 1958 it went public with Bonuskor and Federale Volksbeleggings as the major shareholders.

My father was keen to buy shares in Fedmyn but could not find the necessary information in *Die Burger*. He complained to Weber about the difficulty investors had in trying to evaluate the transactions of the emerging Fedmyn. To do that, he wrote, "information and yet more information" was required. As matters stood, "we have to hunt around for it everywhere in the English magazines".

Weber forwarded the letter to the paper's editor Piet Cillié for answering, with the comment: "Apparently the man means well." It would still take almost ten years before *Die Burger*'s business page improved.

## The Broederbond "gang"

My father's Broederbond membership gave him a sense of participation in the Afrikaner nationalists' debates on policy issues. Along with other branches of the organisation across the country, the Porterville branch studied the working documents that the Johannesburg head office circulated among members for comment. I sometimes chanced upon some of these documents, for instance an analysis of the Tomlinson Commission's report. As children, we enjoyed playing along to maintain secrecy when the local branch of the AB met at our home. Naturally, I never talked to my friends about the AB. Now and then I would tease my father light-heartedly about his "secret gang", but I soon saw that I was on dangerous ground.

In the mid-1950s the Porterville branch lodged a complaint because a member from another branch had rejected a teacher they had recommended for membership. At that stage the rector of the University of Stellenbosch, Prof. HB Thom, was chair of the AB's Executive Council, and the AB management referred the complaint to him. Thom and my father had been classmates at Stellenbosch.

It later transpired that the objection had come from someone who suspected the nominee of having cheated as a referee in a school rugby match. The person in question never became a member. Maybe the AB did not want to take a chance with someone who had a reputation as a crooked referee.

My father never derived any personal benefit from his AB membership. He was shocked when it was alleged in later years that the AB pulled strings to advantage its members, and that some people joined the organisation for their own advantage. "That was never what the Bond was intended for," he often said.

However, my father did not have any first-hand experience of the modus operandi of the AB outside the confines of Porterville. The dissident Afrikaner theologian Nico Smith relates in his book *Die Afrikaner-Broederbond: Belewinge van die binnekant* (The Afrikaner Broederbond: Experiences from the inside) (2009) how he was appointed as Broederbonder at the Theological Faculty of Stellenbosch over the heads of two other candidates who were much better qualified. The historian Ernst Stals, who conducted an in-depth study of the AB, writes that from early on it had been the AB's aim "not only to promote the interests of the Afrikaners in general, but also to help its members advance in their careers". I would later have reason to wonder whether the AB had something to do with the apparent dead end my career at Stellenbosch reached towards the end of the 1970s.

## "The man who refuses to participate"

"Be proud of your own" were words that I and other children of my generation heard repeatedly when language and culture came up for discussion. We took part in *volkspele* (Afrikaner folk dances) in the church hall and enjoyed them. Rev. Theron, who was our minister during my school years, was vehemently opposed to dancing. It was at university that I first discovered dancing was a harmless social activity and regretted the fact that I had not learnt to dance at school.

The *volksbeweging* placed great emphasis on the notion that every individual's contribution counted. This applied in particular to the promotion of Afrikaans as a public language which, constitutionally, enjoyed equal status with English. At school I was struck by ID du Plessis's poem "Soet is die stryd" (Sweet is the struggle) from his collection *Land van die vaders* (Land of the Fathers) (1945), which stressed that, despite the pessimism of those who considered the obstacles too daunting, what mattered was the effort one put into the collective struggle, regardless of the eventual outcome. The last two lines underlined the personal responsibility of the individual: *Maar die man wat sy deelname weier, / Is die MAN wat sy Nasie VERMOOR!!!* (But the man who refuses to participate / is the MAN who KILLS his nation!!!).

When I became involved in the language struggle at the University of Stellenbosch many years later, these words still inspired me.

The message of the *volksbeweging* in the 1950s was that one should never regard one's people and one's language as inferior. Our household at Porterville was well aware that Afrikaans literature, especially in the field of prose, still ranked far below the literatures of the major European languages. A momentous event for us was the appearance of *Die Afrikaanse kinderensiklopedie*, a children's encyclopedia, the first volume of which was published in 1948. The editor noted in the introduction that the work had been written by "friends of children". One of the writers was the poet and intellectual NP van Wyk Louw, whose notions of "*lojale verset*" (loyal resistance, or rebellious loyalty) and "*liberale nasionalisme*" (liberal nationalism) would later exert a great influence on me.

We were avid readers of the youth magazine *Die Jongspan*, which, like the encyclopedia, was edited by Dr CF Albertyn. On his retirement from the publishing company Nasionale Pers, he came to live on his farm in the Porterville district. Following his own retirement from teaching, my father assisted Albertyn on an almost full-time basis with his ambitious project of publishing an adapted version of the Dutch *Winkler Prins ensiklopedie* through his own company. It involved the translation of articles from Dutch into Afrikaans and the incorporation of additional entries on South African topics written by local experts. Sadly, the project was not a financial success.

During the first half of the 1950s, when I was a high-school pupil, it seemed as if the great ideal of a republic was close to being realised. It was a time of surging optimism. For me, the spirit of the times is represented by the first lines of "Die lied van jong Suid-Afrika" (The song of young South Africa), which we sometimes sang in classes at school:

*En hoor jy die magtige dreuning*
*Oor die veld kom dit wyd gesweef*
*Die lied van 'n volk se ontwaking*
*Wat harte laat sidder en beef. . .*

With its stirring description of the "mighty roar" of "the song of a nation's awakening", the verse still says something to me about the optimism with which the Afrikaners of my generation faced the future. A "nation's awakening" had little or nothing to do with apartheid. As children, we felt we were part of a movement that would place us on an equal footing with the English community, that would proclaim a republic, that would expand Afrikaans, and that would conquer economic and cultural worlds. Viewing the *volksbeweging* and apartheid as one and the same is simply false.

After the NP's election victory in 1948, Afrikaans was for the first time treated on an equal basis with English in practice as an official language. Over the next forty years Afrikaans grew rapidly as a public language, especially because it was so firmly embedded in schools and universities. Afrikaans enabled me to master universal knowledge in my mother tongue and made it possible for me to express myself optimally. It has become an inextricable part of my social identity. After the appearance of my book *The Afrikaners: Biography of a People* in 2003, I was often asked what had been decisive factors in the Afrikaners' rise in the twentieth century. My reply was always: mother-tongue education and committed teachers.

Jean Laponce, a French-Canadian expert on the survival of smaller languages, later informed me that Afrikaans is one of only four languages in the world – the others are Hebrew, Hindi and Indonesian-Malay – that in the course of the twentieth century were standardised and developed from a low-status, informal language to one used in all branches of life and learning, including postgraduate teaching, science and technology. Hebrew and Afrikaans were the only two languages spoken by a very small speech community that had achieved this feat.

How did Afrikaans manage to achieve the near unthinkable? An e-mail message I received after the appearance of *The Afrikaners* demonstrated the misconceptions about this issue that exist in some quarters. My correspondent posed the question: "How did Afrikaans reach such a level?" He provided his own reply: "It was forced on schools' curricula and imposed on the civil service as a so-called official language."

The facts, however, are quite different. The Constitution of the Union of South Africa (the South Africa Act), passed in 1909, established Dutch and

English as the official languages of South Africa, with equal status under the law. Neither language was "imposed" or "privileged"; the bilingual character of the state was the primary symbol of reconciliation between the country's two white groups.

In a contemporaneous article in *The State*, the writer and historian Gustav Preller described the Union's promise to place the two official languages on a footing of "most perfect equality" as essential to Afrikaner support for the Union.[16] Without recognition of the equal status of English and Dutch (which would be replaced by Afrikaans in 1925), it is most likely that a debilitating conflict would have developed between the two white communities, with grave consequences for the economy.

But misunderstandings about what had been decided at the National Convention, the body that drafted the Constitution of the Union, would bedevil relations between the two white communities for a long time. FV Engelenburg, Louis Botha's biographer and a staunch supporter of the South African Party's ideal of English–Afrikaner cooperation, later wrote that whereas the fathers of the Constitution had accepted the absolute equality of both languages in good faith, English-speaking South Africans never took the matter seriously. Bilingualism was regarded as nothing more than a polite gesture towards the other section. According to Engelenburg, the average English-speaking South African was inclined to regard every form of political recognition of the Dutch language as a threat to the interests of "his own race".

From 1910 to 1948 the government of the day postponed consistent enforcement of Section 137 of the Union Constitution several times. The lack of suitable candidates in the civil service who were proficient in both languages was one of the reasons that were advanced for the lack of progress. By 1948, however, this was no longer a valid excuse. After its election victory in that year, the NP decided to systematically enforce the use of both Afrikaans and English as official languages in the civil service.

Economic mobilisation and the development of Afrikaans as a public language went hand in hand with acknowledgement of the Afrikaners' history and their contribution to the establishment of the South African state. In 1952 I attended the Van Riebeeck Festival in Cape Town, which celebrated three centuries of white settlement, as an adolescent member of the Voortrekker youth movement. There was one memory that lingered in my mind. As part of a torchlight procession of thousands of Voortrekkers who marched from Signal Hill to the stadium in the Foreshore area, I met with disaster. My torch died

16    Gustav Preller, "The Union and the Boer", *The State*, 1, 6, 1909, p. 638.

while we were still on the mountain, and I was mortified at having to complete the march with an unlit torch. In subsequent years, I would often wonder whether my extinguished torch had any symbolic meaning.

It would be wrong to equate the *volksbeweging* with the National Party, or to regard the NP as an institution that dictated to the *volksbeweging*. In the first decade of NP rule there were still between 10% to 20% of Afrikaners who supported the United Party (UP), which had been formed out of a merger between General JBM Hertzog's then National Party and General JC Smuts's South African Party (SAP) in 1934. UP supporters were still commonly known as "Sappe" because of the link with the erstwhile SAP. Many Afrikaner "Sappe" felt equally strongly about the Afrikaans language and the upliftment of the white poor. The big difference between them and fellow Afrikaners who were NP supporters ("Natte") lay in their support for South Africa's participation in the Second World War and their veneration for the towering figure of Jan Smuts. I once asked Christo Wiese, who grew up in a "Sap" family in Upington and later became an outstanding entrepreneur, what had been the distinguishing factor between the "Natte" and the "Sappe" in our youth. His answer was simple but spot-on: Jan Smuts.

## Coloured Portervillers

Porterville's coloured residents spoke Afrikaans, but they were not regarded as part of the *volksbeweging*. The law determined the fate of white and coloured from the cradle to the grave. Everyone adhered to the same faith, but white and coloured worshipped separately; everyone spoke the same language, but white and coloured did not attend school, church or concerts together. Everyone played the same sports, but white and coloured never participated together in organised sports. There were undoubtedly secret relationships across the colour line. The many light-skinned children with reddish hair in the coloured neighbourhoods of Pella Park and Monte Bertha attested to that.

The coloured community of Porterville consisted of people who were no longer able to live on the farms, or had chosen to leave of their own accord. While a few managed to make a living as artisans such as builders or carpenters, the majority worked as "servants" or gardeners for white people. In my childhood days, every white home seemed to have its servant.

For a while our household also employed Japie, a coloured boy of my own age, who did odd jobs in the garden. He was exceptionally well built and self-confident. Japie used to play cricket and rugby with me and my white friends in the backyard or in the street in front of the house. We were unable to get the better of him either physically or figuratively, which boosted his confidence even more.

One day there was a confrontation between the two of us, and I spat in his face. As the enraged Japie made a rush for me, I fled into the house. It was only indoctrination that prevented him from pursuing me into the house and getting even. I was bitterly ashamed of the incident, and spoke to no one about it until Athol Fugard told me years later that he had been involved in a similar incident in his youth. It provided the inspiration for his play *Master Harold and the Boys* (1982).

Farmworkers were worse off than most of the coloured people in town. In my schooldays, I sometimes stayed over with friends who lived on farms. The tot system of providing workers with wine throughout the working day was still in common use, and there was no pressure on farmers to abandon the practice. Still, there were also farmers who realised that it was wrong and who promoted abstinence from alcohol. They were also very critical of the heartless practice of some farmers to let their workers go after the harvesting season.

On Saturday mornings, many farmers would bring their "volk" to town, and by twelve o'clock intoxicated farmworkers were a common sight on the pavements in the vicinity of the two bottlestores in the main street.

Although coloured men who met the requirements of the Cape's qualified franchise could vote up to the 1950s, I never heard of a single one in the town who was eligible to vote. *Die Burger* did not write about the fierce competition for the coloured vote during the 1920s in which the National Party had also participated. The paper frequently alleged that coloured voters were "open to bribery" and, by implication, did not really deserve the vote.

My parents supported the policy of apartheid. Their standpoint was that the policy was not only intended to bring about separation between white and coloured, but also helped to develop and uplift the coloured people by providing them with better mass education and social services. No doubt they endorsed the statement PW Botha made to his biographers: "The coloureds must first be uplifted and the consequences of that accepted."[17]

The government's spending on coloured education in the Cape Province had started increasing rapidly from 1935. In 1953 it was almost ten times what it had been in 1935. Between 1948 and 1951 it increased by 41%, and it did not slow down thereafter. In 1953 a study asked whether the "financial burdens" in this regard were not perhaps "disproportionate to the province's carrying capacity".[18] Of course, the spending on white children was much higher, but

---

17    Dirk and Johanna de Villiers, *PW* (Cape Town: Tafelberg, 1984), p. 90.
18    NJ Marais, "Die voorsiening en administrasie van Kleurlingonderwys in Kaapstad, veral sedert 1910", MEd thesis, University of Stellenbosch, 1953, p. 129.

no one asked whether this was disproportionate to the country's "carrying capacity".

But there was also another problem, which NP supporters only realised later. Improving a community's education levels without giving them meaningful rights is a recipe for political alienation and revolt.

The Group Areas Act was the central aspect of the political debate in the early 1950s, at the time I started becoming politically aware. By law, coloured people had to be moved from the "white town" to separate coloured "towns" on the outskirts of, or a short distance from, the main town. It was said that the resettled people would get their own houses and shops there.

In Porterville, a relatively small proportion of the coloured community was moved during the period of NP rule to Monte Bertha, a coloured suburb that had been established as far back as 1937. But there were several towns in the Boland, notably Stellenbosch, Paarl and Wellington, which had large coloured or racially mixed neighbourhoods that were situated in the central business district. In the first two decades of NP rule, these neighbourhoods were all proclaimed white areas and the coloured residents were forced to move. The most prominent mixed area in the Cape was District Six in Cape Town, which had about 65 000 residents. While the majority was coloured, there were also black, Indian and white residents, including Afrikaners. NP propaganda portrayed District Six as "a den of iniquity".

As an avid newspaper reader from an early age, I was certainly exposed to this propaganda that was peddled in *Die Burger*. This is apparent from my first article that ever appeared in print. It was written in 1951, when I was in standard 6 (now grade 8), and appeared in the school's yearbook three years later.

In the article I gave an account of my first visit to Cape Town, and related how I had lost my way in the city centre and later found myself in a slum quarter where I saw only hovels around me. I wrote that I had no idea of how to find my way back, but fortunately ran into a policeman. He informed me that they had been looking for me everywhere, and that I had wandered into the heart of District Six. I wrote the story as if my straying into District Six had put my life in danger.

For coloured people, the forced removals and the break-up of established communities were a source of immense grief and heartache. I would only grasp this fully many years later, when I wrote about the forced removal of the coloured community from the centre of Stellenbosch in the late 1960s. This same story repeated itself in numerous towns without any protest from Afrikaners.

The only serious conversation I had with a well-educated coloured person

at the time took place in 1966 aboard a ship on the way to Europe. He was a
teacher headed for Canada to start a new life there, and I was travelling to the
Netherlands to study at the University of Amsterdam. The sadness in his voice
as he spoke of his humiliation made a lasting impression on me.

As I have mentioned, there were virtually no black people in Porterville.
When the homeland policy was discussed, it was as if one were talking about
some exotic experiment in a far-off land. In our student days at Stellenbosch,
the only black people we interacted with were the waiters in the residence.
Black residents of the town were subject to a curfew; every night at ten o'clock
a siren would go off, which meant that no black person was permitted to be
outside the township of Kayamandi. We did not think of the flagrant denial
of a person's citizenship it represented.

## "The open conversation"

Our household subscribed to *Die Huisgenoot* in which the column "Die oop
gesprek" (the open conversation) of NP van Wyk Louw, one of the leading
Afrikaner intellectuals, appeared. On 8 August 1952 Louw's column took the
form of a letter adressed to "My dear young friend". Van Wyk Louw's article
was prompted by the NP government's efforts to remove coloured voters from
the voters' roll.

Louw was at that stage a professor in Amsterdam, and he wrote in general
terms instead of criticising the decision to put coloured voters on a separate roll.
In a letter to a friend at the University of Cape Town, he wrote that legislation
"was not necessary for our preservation as a people". It would be better to
make the coloured people "nationalists again than to put them on separate rolls".

Louw was referring to the 1920s when coloured voters constituted about a
quarter of the electorate in constituencies such as Stellenbosch and Paarl.
Along with the other parties, the NP competed fiercely for their vote. In 1929
Bruckner de Villiers, the victorious NP candidate in Stellenbosch, was carried
shoulder-high into Parliament by coloured voters. After the 1938 election,
in which De Villiers lost the Stellenbosch seat to the UP's Henry Fagan by
30 votes, he commented scathingly on the "bright young men" in Parliament
whose "clever plans" had cost the party several Cape seats, while they managed
to win only one seat in the Transvaal.

In the battle to remove the coloured voters from the voters' roll in the 1950s,
the NP leaders and *Die Burger* kept silent about this history, or, when it did crop
up, shrugged it off with the comment that coloured voters were bribable.

In his article of 1952 Van Wyk Louw wrote that a people could be faced
with various crises of national survival: one was military conquest, and

another would be if a critical mass of its members no longer considered it important to continue existing as a separate people. And then there was the third case: when a people, after it had done all in its power to survive, was faced with the last temptation: "*to believe that mere survival is preferable to survival in justice*" (Louw's emphasis).

Louw realised that people would ask why an ethical crisis like this could threaten the survival of an entire people. He replied with a counter-question: "How can a small people continue to survive if it is something hateful and evil for the best within – or without – it?" He added: "I believe that in a strange way this is the crisis from which a people emerge reborn, young, creative, this 'dark night of the soul' in which it says: I would rather perish than survive through injustice."

I have no memory of having read the article at the time, and Jaap Steyn writes in his biography of Louw that *Die Huisgenoot* received no letters from readers in response to the particular column. The article was republished in 1958 in Louw's collection of essays *Liberale nasionalisme* when I was in my third year at university as a student of Afrikaans-Nederlands. There was no mention of this work in our classes.

But Piet Cillié, editor of *Die Burger*, wrote in an exceptionally positive review that Louw excercised his influence as an intellectual midwife. "He was more skilful and subtle than many other thinkers, but without the pretensions of absolute certainty." During my student years, such thinkers were extremely rare at the Afrikaans universities.

## Chapter 3

# A university with attitude

In 1956 I enrolled as a student at the University of Stellenbosch (US) with no expectations of becoming an academic. As my aptitude for maths was nothing to write home about, I did not do particularly well in the final matric examination. My brother Jan and my sister Hester would later enjoy reminding me that both of them had obtained a better symbol than I did in their matric exams. In his history classes my father told the story of the past well, and was respected by his friends for his political judgement. I decided to choose history as one of my major subjects.

My student years were largely carefree. I thoroughly enjoyed life in Simonsberg residence, especially the inter-residence sport. In 1958 I was a member of the team that won the Sauer Cup for the first league of residence rugby. I was on the editorial team of the student newspaper *Die Matie*, but preferred writing about sport rather than student politics. The ardent nationalists on the campus put me off.

To my surprise, I was elected to serve on the SRC in 1960 despite not having published my policy in *Die Matie* as all the other candidates had done voluntarily. When I was questioned about this at the pre-election mass meeting known as "the Circus", I had a pat answer. I argued that experience had taught us that candidates' promises were seldom carried out, and that all I would promise, therefore, was to do my best according to my lights. It sounded principled, but the real reason was that I decided to stand at such a late stage that the opportunity to publish my policy had passed by.

In 1960 I was also elected *primarius* (head student) of Simonsberg, a residence that accommodated 280 male students. This was at a time when students had started questioning the official ban on alcohol and female visitors in the rooms. To the annoyance of Prof. Chris Gunter, the residential head, I maintained that it was not the responsibility of the house committee to be moral guardians, but only to act against students who openly flouted the rules.

Towards the end of my term as *primarius*, I received my first lesson in how power operates. Late one evening, about twenty Simonsbergers invaded a female residence and overturned the beds of the sleeping residents. The university authorities considered this a serious offence, and immediately requested the names of the culprits from the house committee. Without the committee's cooperation, however, they were powerless.

I contended that the house committee had no say with regard to offences committed by Simonsberg residents outside the residence, and that we were only prepared to comply with the request if the authorities undertook not to punish the culprits. The undertaking was given verbally. Accordingly, the house committee persuaded the culprits to provide their names, with the assurance that they would not be punished.

A few days later I heard to my dismay that the university authorities had written to the parents of the offenders, informing them that their sons were guilty of a serious offence in a female residence and that any further mis-demeanours would be punished severely. Evidently the authorities felt that because no one had been punished, they had kept to their undertaking. I felt that the university's action flew in the face of the promises that had been made, but it was too late to do anything about it.

On the other hand, there were also times when the university decided not to act. One day "Vloog" Theron, an obstreperous second-year student, asked me for permission to bring two elephants to graze on the lawn in front of the residence. I thought he was joking, and did nothing to stop him. Lo and behold, a day or two later he turned up at Simonsberg with two circus elephants in tow. The following day *Die Burger* published a photo in which I and a few other residents looked on laughingly as Vloog and the two giant animals made themselves at home on the lawn. There was no reaction from the administration. Clearly, elephants on the loose on Simonsberg's lawn was much less dangerous than male students on the loose at 11 pm in the bedrooms of a female residence.

## A symbiotic relationship

By the time I started my studies, the university had entered the "era of Thom". Prof. HB Thom, who was rector from 1954 to 1969, was also the only person from the south of the country who ever served as chairman of the Afrikaner Broederbond's Executive Council. He occupied this position from 1952 to 1960. This undoubtedly boosted the AB's membership figures on the Matie campus.

The US was a university with attitude: all students and lecturers were supposed to be extremely grateful for the privilege of being part of the US's proud legacy. Between 1919 and 1978, all the prime ministers were US alumni.

There was a symbiotic relationship between the university and Afrikaans as an official language. It was the first institution with full university status in the country that used Afrikaans predominantly as the medium of instruction. The offices of the *Woordeboek van die Afrikaanse taal*, a comprehensive descriptive dictionary aimed at reflecting Afrikaans in its entirety, were situated on the campus. And, of course, Stellenbosch had Danie Craven, who was practically synonymous with South African rugby.

The US as an institution that was unmistakably Afrikaans was founded on the winged words "Stellenbosch stands for an idea", expressed by Dr DF Malan in 1913. By that he meant that Stellenbosch was the place from which the Afrikaner nation could best realise its ideals. The US was established a few years later through a generous bequest of the philanthropist Jannie Marais, a Stellenbosch businessman and politician, which stipulated that Dutch or Afrikaans had to occupy no lesser place than English at the institution. Almost a hundred years later, no one seems to know any more what the famous Stellenbosch "idea" was. Without much compunction, the university has allowed English to elbow out Afrikaans relentlessly as medium of instruction.

At the time of my enrolment at Stellenbosch, there were certain departments and lecturers that were justifiably rated highly. The Law Faculty was universally recognised as excellent, and the students had the greatest admiration for the dean, Prof. JC de Wet. Prof. PJ van der Merwe of the History Department was the most influential Afrikaans historian.

## Encountering Verwoerd

I was a student at a time when it seemed as if white rule would remain inviolate for decades to come. Except for three or four months after the Sharpeville tragedy in 1960 – when the police shot dead 69 black people as a large crowd protested against the pass laws at the Sharpeville police station – we did not really have any fears about security. My generation was the last one which was not subject to military conscription, and we were also the generation that experienced the excitement of the final push towards a republic. I voted "yes" for the republic in the referendum of 1960. In the general election of 1961, I voted for the NP for the first and last time during the era of that party's rule.

In 1958, when I was in my third year, Dr Hendrik Verwoerd became NP leader and prime minister. I have two personal memories of Verwoerd that are unrelated to his political ideas. At the age of about 12 or 13, I collected signatures of celebrities as a hobby. Most of the cabinet ministers replied to my written request with a brief note from their private secretaries to which the signature had been added.

Verwoerd was the only one who responded to my request with a personal handwritten note. He wrote that he had a child who was left-handed like me, and another who was the same age as me. I read later that a little girl once asked him for permission to call her pet rabbit Hendrik Verwoerd. He replied that he did not think it was a suitable name for a rabbit, but he was prepared to give his permission nonetheless. It says something about the man that he took this kind of trouble with children's requests.

My other instance of contact with him was in June 1960, when a few students and I spent the winter holidays with our fellow Simonsberg resident Siebert Wiid at his father's farm Welgevonden, near Groblersdal. Verwoerd and his wife arrived at Welgevonden shortly after us. He was due to address a huge crowd at Groblersdal the following day, one of his first public appearances after the failed attempt on his life three months earlier. (David Pratt, a farmer from the Magaliesburg district, had shot Verwoerd in the face while he delivered a speech at the Rand Easter Show.) We students had our meals together with the VIP guests in the main house. I sat next to Verwoerd, and I remember how calmly and convincingly he formulated his standpoint in a way that made complete sense.

On the Sunday morning of the Verwoerds' weekend at Welgevonden, the local NP branch presented Verwoerd with a painting of him as a gift. He received it graciously, but remarked that it had a minor flaw: something was missing. There was a moment of consternation. "My beauty spots," he explained smilingly, pointing to the bullet scars on his face. In my layperson's view, it was clear that the assault on his life had caused no psychological damage. Thereafter I took scant notice of claims that Verwoerd regarded his survival as tangible proof of divine intervention and of the special blessing that supposedly now rested on him.

Years later, in my book *The Last Afrikaner Leaders* (2012), I gave a more favourable assessment of Verwoerd than is the norm. I believe this had much to do with my first-hand exposure to the force of his personality and his powers of persuasion during that weekend in 1960.

The publisher Koos Human had a similar experience. He and José Burman, the author of a book on mountain passes in the Boland, asked Verwoerd to write a foreword, as it was known that Verwoerd and his wife were keen mountaineers. Verwoerd invited Human and Burman to his office where, after informing them that he had read the entire manuscript and had written the foreword himself, he elaborated expertly on the subject in a ten-minute monologue. Human made an observation that I can endorse wholeheartedly after the weekend at Welgevonden: "Never before (or since) have I been in the presence of such an almost unbelievably dominant personality. After this brief encounter, there was no doubt in my mind that he had his cabinet, caucus and party under his absolute control."[19]

## The struggle against the English

The political struggle of the 1950s had two facets: one was the overt competition for power between the National Party and the United Party (UP); the other was the veiled competition for status between the Afrikaans- and English-speaking white communities. By 1955 English South Africans had started realising that the UP would in all likelihood never regain political power. Like the Afrikaners after their loss of power in 1994, they were resentful of their diminished status and political marginalisation.

The political activist and writer Patrick Duncan expressed their sense of disgruntlement as follows: "English South Africans are today in the power of their adversaries . . . They are beginning to know what the great majority of South Africans have always known – what it is to be second-class citizens in the land of one's birth."[20]

After 1948, it was English commentators who "interpreted" the Afrikaners to foreign journalists and diplomats and, through them, to the entire world. Some commentators and historians declared that the Afrikaners were simply and solely driven by apartheid and other racial obsessions.

English South Africans' opposition to apartheid and their dissatisfaction about the fact that the Afrikaners were in power were often indistinguishable. David Yudelman, an esteemed historian, criticised English-speaking opinion-makers for disseminating a distorted picture of Afrikaners to the world. South African anglophones, he wrote, were not significantly more liberal than the Afrikaners on race questions, yet they tended to present the Afrikaner as "the villain, the fanatic, who created or at least perfected institutionalised racial discrimination". Whites of British extraction, on the other hand, supposedly accepted segregation and apartheid only passively.

The anglophones, Yudelman added, were quite prepared to "use apartheid as a pretext for indirectly expressing their culturally chauvinistic distaste for the Afrikaners while continuing to enjoy the benefits of white supremacy".[21]

---

19  Koos Human, *'n Lewe met boeke* (Cape Town: Human & Rousseau, 2006), p. 157.

20  Patrick Duncan, *The Road Through the Wilderness* (Johannesburg: Hygrade Printers, 1953).

21  David Yudelman, *The Emergence of South Africa* (Westport: Greenwood Press, 1983), pp. 13-14.

The person who had the greatest political influence on me up to the mid-1960s was Piet Cillié, who became editor of *Die Burger* in 1954. Long before Yudelman, he expressed a similar view. He was a razor-sharp political commentator and, along with NP van Wyk Louw, the best political essayist in Afrikaans. Cillié headed a brilliant team that included three outstanding journalists: Schalk Pienaar, JJJ Scholtz and Rykie van Reenen.

From my high-school days I read the daily editorial in *Die Burger* as well as the political column under the pseudonym "Dawie" that appeared on Wednesdays and Saturdays. The collection of articles from this column, *Dawie, 1946 tot 1964* (Tafelberg, 1966), provides a better perspective on the surging Afrikaner nationalism of the 1950s than any other book. This was before the dogma of apartheid began to stifle Afrikaners' cultural nationalism.

Cillié often drew attention to the far-reaching way in which the "first-past-the-post" electoral system influenced politics and racial policy in particular. In the first place, the system made it possible for a party that had won a minority of votes to form a government. This was indeed what happened in South Africa between 1948 and 1958. Secondly, in countries that used this electoral system, there was a strong tendency that power ended up in the hands of the biggest ethnic group among the electorate and that the leaders tightened their grip on the group through a form of ethnic mobilisation that radicalised the political system. Between 1948 and 1994, Afrikaners at all times constituted more than 50% of the voters.

There was also a third trend associated with the system. Vulnerable racial or ethnic groups that held the balance of power between two big parties were often shut out. An example of this is what happened in the southern states of the United States in the 1890s when the Democratic Party spearheaded the large-scale disenfranchisement of black people. During the 1960s, it would take all of President Lyndon Johnson's legendary ingenuity to get black people back on the voters' roll. He did this even though he knew his party would pay a high price in the South for a generation or two.

In the general elections of 1948 and 1953 the English voters voted solidly against the NP, while the UP captured about 20% of the Afrikaner votes. In the 1948 election there were only 130 000 more potential Afrikaner votes than potential English votes. Up to the mid-1950s, NP fears that the UP could win an election with the help of coloured votes were not unrealistic. These fears are sometimes dismissed with the statement that there were only eight constituencies in which coloured votes could tip the scales. This argument misses the point that in 1948 the NP had an effective majority of only five seats.

Piet Cillié was pre-eminently the person who took up the cudgels against the view that the English-speaking community was supposedly above racial discrimination and racism. During election campaigns he seldom defended apartheid on its own terms, but described the English–Afrikaner contest and the contest between white and non-white as struggles that were inextricably intertwined. He rejected the liberals' insistence that they had no ulterior motives in promoting equal rights for all. To Afrikaner nationalists, he wrote, the English liberals had always seemed to be more English than liberal, and more interested in power for the white English speakers than in power for black or coloured people.

A recent biography by Jaap Steyn clarified for me why I felt such an affinity with Cillié. In 1952 Cillié wrote to the Rev. Ben Marais, whose aforementioned book *Die kleur-krisis en die Weste* had just been published: "I agree wholeheartedly with you that the efforts to find Scriptural supports for apartheid, in the naive form that this quest mostly assumes, are doomed to failure . . . I know only one old man who believes that coloured people are descendants of Ham and eternally cursed, and no coherent pseudoscientific myths about race are being propagated deliberately in South Africa."

He expressed his doubts as to whether the statistics Marais had quoted to prove that, inherently, races and ethnic groups differed very little from each other, were of any practical value for the problem in South Africa – how would it help Jews and Arabs in Palestine, for instance, to know that there were more similarities than differences between people?[22]

According to Cillié, colour was only salient in South African politics to the extent that it represented the boundary between "peoples" or "nations". He referred to the Afrikaners' reaction to the superior number of black people as "national instincts". He criticised Ben Marais for not addressing the issue of "political power that lies at the root of race relations". For Cillié, apartheid had to ensure that the Afrikaners and the broader white community retained power over themselves while they were building the state and the economy in the ultimate interest of all.

Cillié had an element in him of Niccolò Machiavelli, whose thinking had interested me from an early age. The Florentine is often erroneously described as a thinker who was prepared to argue that power be gained through the most immoral methods. Machiavelli did believe that the state's task was not in the first place to be fair to all, but to ensure its citizens' safety. But that was not an end in itself. The ultimate goal was a strong, effective state from which all its citizens benefited. I believe that this is also what Cillié strove for.[23]

22   JC Steyn, *Penvegter: Piet Cillié van Die Burger* (Cape Town: Tafelberg, 2002).
23   Maurizio Viroli, *Machiavelli* (London: Granta, 2008).

## Arnold Toynbee's warning

An important element in Afrikaner nationalists' thinking was the notion that the NP government would only succeed in building an effective state and a well-ordered society on the basis of a united Afrikaner nation. Growing Afrikaner unity was a new phenomenon. Oral tradition has it that in the 1938 election in the seat of Stellenbosch, university lecturers were split right down the middle.

The Afrikaner unity that developed in the 1950s was based on the possession of state power and the ideal of a republic. Many historians have gone looking in the Afrikaners' past for a unity that never existed. A question we often discussed as students was whether Afrikaner unity was necessarily a good thing, for the survival of the Afrikaners as well. Would an Afrikaner unity that attempted to incorporate all factions not lead to a political paralysis that could stymie urgently needed reforms?

My interest was piqued by an essay by Arnold Toynbee, a British historian who had studied the rise and decline of two dozen civilisations since the earliest times. Entitled "History's warning to Africa", it appeared in 1959 in the opinion magazine *Optima* which the Anglo American Corporation distributed to its shareholders, of whom my father was one.

I tore the essay from the magazine and kept it in a file in which I preserved the most stimulating articles I came across. By that time Toynbee was no longer the international star he had once been when he graced the cover of *Time* magazine in 1949, but in this essay he anticipated the Afrikaners' failure to adapt timeously to South Africa's political challenge.

In his essay, Toynbee considered the different roads open to dominant minorities in empires. He first looked at the Spanish colonies in Latin America. The Spanish also exploited the native peoples, but here the division between first-class and second-class citizens did not follow racial lines and was therefore not impassable. The barriers to upward mobility were predominantly based on class, not race, and the colonial rulers allowed the elite from among the oppressed into the ranks of the dominant group. The result was continued Spanish predominance, even after their colonies became independent. The same applied to people of European (or mainly European) descent in the former Portuguese colony of Brazil, where they constituted just more than half of the population. After independence, they continued to call the tune at almost all levels of society.

The colonies the Dutch and the British founded in Africa provided a stark contrast. Upward mobility for coloured or black people was difficult, and intermarriage with white people was virtually ruled out. Toynbee noted that there was "no easy way of entry into the . . . dominant caste for an able and adaptable Bantu [*sic*]", and continued: "The Graeco-Roman precedent shows that, even after a thousand years, the roots of domination may still be as shallow as they were in the first generation."[24]

He stressed the aspect of demography. If the dominant minority was ahead in technology and culture, as was the case in South Africa, the struggle would be more drawn out and morally more complex than in a clear-cut military struggle. But, he emphasised, "the dénouement may be more tragic".

Toynbee warned that it would be fatal for a dominant minority to hold on to its supremacy by sheer force against a rising tide of revolt. "Even if its belief in its own cultural superiority was justified, numbers would tell in the long run, considering that culture is contagious, and that an ascendancy based on cultural superiority is therefore a wasting asset." He expressed some sympathy for the dilemma of minorities: "Voluntary abdication in favour of a majority whom one feels to be one's inferior is a very hard alternative for human pride to accept."[25] As a prophet of what would happen in South Africa thirty years later when the Afrikaners relinquished power without having been defeated, Toynbee is without equal.

## Afrikaner warnings

GD Scholtz, editor of the newspaper *Die Transvaler*, came to a similar conclusion in his book *Het die Afrikaanse volk 'n toekoms?* (Does the Afrikaner nation have a future?) I bought this book in my fourth year and, judging by all the underlined sentences, read it attentively. If the white people failed to impose what Scholtz called "total segregation" in good time, he warned, black people's numerical superiority and the knowledge that they could revolt successfully would be decisive. Unfortunately, the book failed to explain what form "total segregation" should take.

By the end of the 1950s it was already evident that great tension existed in Afrikaner ranks between those who wished to cling to white power and those who were in favour of making radical adjustments in good time in order to avoid the fate Toynbee predicted. Among the Stellenbosch students of my time, a split between the ideologues and the pragmatists started to manifest itself.

For the ideologues, apartheid was an end in itself and racial segregation the answer to virtually any form of social interaction. Theological students, or *tokkelokke* as they were popularly known, abounded in this camp. Manie van der

---

24   Arnold Toynbee, "History's Warning to Africa", *Optima*, 9, 2, 1959, p. 56.
25   Toynbee, "History's Warning to Africa", pp. 55-56.

Spuy, a contemporary of mine who studied psychology, has rightly observed recently that there were two gospels of salvation in our time at Stellenbosch: "Christianity as personal salvation", and "apartheid as the Afrikaner gospel of salvation". In both cases, one only had to believe and was not judged by one's deeds but by one's faith. Those who deviated in any way from the prescribed dogma ran the risk of being stigmatised as "heretics".

I sided with the pragmatists, who came from "Nat" as well as "Sap" homes. We believed that especially between white and coloured there should be no sharp division, and that rigid apartheid had to change rapidly to a system where leaders of the various communities exchanged views and cooperated on projects. Universities were the very places where people should make contact across the colour line. The Extension of University Education Act of 1959, which provided for racially separate tertiary education, destroyed the possibility that future leaders could get to know each other and hone their views in debates. In my residence there was considerable sympathy for Bertie van der Merwe and a fellow Simonsberger on the SRC, who were forced to resign in 1959 because they opposed the Act.

Stellenbosch had a tradition of tolerating dissidents. In his student days my father was a supporter of Prof. Johannes du Plessis, a professor at the Theological Seminary, who had played a leading role in the 1920s in bringing leaders from white and black churches together and in mitigating segregation. He was expelled from his post for doctrinal reasons. My father used to refer jokingly to Du Plessis's opponents by their nickname *"oupajane"*. (One of the leaders had written a book with the title *Op die ou paaie* (On the old roads).)

In my time, the only reminder of this church struggle was a statue of Du Plessis that had been erected by his admirers. Owing to the pink hue of the marble, the statue was commonly known as Pink Piet. It was frequently vandalised in late-night pranks by intoxicated students who used to daub it with various colours, especially pink. Our lecturers did not think of informing us of the ground-breaking role of Du Plessis in the fields of theology and race relations.

Another prominent dissident was Bennie Keet, also a professor of theology. In my third year I bought and read his book *Suid-Afrika waarheen? 'n Bydrae tot die bespreking van die rasseprobleem* (Whither South Africa? A contribution to the debate on the racial question) (Stellenbosch: Universiteitsuitgewers, 1956). He was unequivocal in his rejection of any biblical justification of apartheid. In his view, increased segregation was "a flight from reality". The challenge for every Christian was: What does Scripture say?

The following year I purchased and read Henry Fagan's booklet *Ons verant-woordelikheid* (Our responsibility) (1959), which shaped my thinking to a significant extent. A graduate of Stellenbosch, Judge Fagan was a former journalist of *Die Burger* and a former UP cabinet minister. As chair of a commission that had investigated the issue of black urbanisation in 1947 and concluded that it was irreversible, he had a much greater understanding than almost anyone else of the political implications of this process.

I could see that Fagan's argument was very similar to Toynbee's: as the economy became more sophisticated, the need for communication between the groups would become more and more urgent. Fagan warned that whites, as the dominant group, had far more to lose than blacks from a lack of contact between their respective groups. The homelands offered only a limited solution, as they could accommodate only a small proportion of black people.

In 1956 a commission chaired by Prof. FR Tomlinson recommended that the state should spend £104 million (about R45 billion today) over the next ten years to develop the homelands. As Minister of Native Affairs, Dr Verwoerd rejected some of the key recommendations and budgeted for a much smaller amount. He also torpedoed a recommendation that white private capital be allowed to facilitate industrial development in these territories. This gave rise to the question that would haunt me later: Was the government really serious about its policy of viable homelands?

## Verwoerd's clever plans

And then, in 1958, Verwoerd became prime minister. Within the first year or two he transformed apartheid from unvarnished white supremacy into a coherent ideology of a "commonwealth" that would ultimately consist of a white state or two and a number of prosperous black states. NP followers started believing in this model with growing conviction.

Frederik van Zyl Slabbert, who arrived at Stellenbosch in 1960 to study theology, would later describe "the excitement, even the thrill" of academics and students in discussing this ideology. The policy, Slabbert added, had "a coherence and systematic quality which cannot be dismissed as racism pure and simple". It "made logical sense and addressed some very prickly issues".[26] The homelands were still just an abstraction at the time, and, like many of my contemporaries, I initially saw the policy as one that, under a dynamic leader, could open up new possibilities.

Verwoerd's policy with regard to coloured people was a huge disappointment. In 1960 he sharply rejected Piet Cillié's call in *Die Burger* that coloured MPs

---

26   Quoted in Ivor Wilkins, "This man who guides the ordinary people", *Sunday Times*, 19 April 1981.

be permitted to represent the coloured community in Parliament. Cillié also wrote approvingly of the resolutions of church leaders at the Cottesloe conference which declared that certain aspects of apartheid were incompatible with the demands of the Gospel. Verwoerd reacted critically, however, and at his urging the synods of the various Reformed Churches quickly condemned the Cottesloe resolutions. Cillié later told me: "When Verwoerd cracked the whip, you just saw coat-tails flapping as the ministers took to their heels and disappeared round the corner."

My sympathy lay with Cillié, but the majority of the students at Stellenbosch regarded Verwoerd as an infallible political giant. Verwoerd not only impressed NP supporters. Allister Sparks once told me how he had been riveted by Verwoerd when, as a young reporter at the *Rand Daily Mail*, he sat listening to him explaining his policy in a hotel room.

In 1964 CW de Kiewiet, the liberal historian whom I would later come to admire above all, wrote in the influential American journal *Foreign Affairs* that Verwoerd was confronting the country's grave problems with "boldness, shrewdness and even imagination", and that it was by no means absurd to suggest a comparison between him and Charles de Gaulle, "the stern, headstrong but deeply imaginative leader of France". In August 1966 *Time* magazine featured an article that was highly critical of apartheid yet described Verwoerd as "one of the ablest white leaders Africa has ever produced".[27]

## Job hunting

My studies as a full-time student progressed reasonably successfully. In 1958 I obtained a BA degree with history and Afrikaans as majors. At the end of 1960 I was awarded the honours degree in history with distinction, and the following year I embarked on my master's thesis. I was very conscious of my limitations, however, which included a poor mastery of English. Having remained a "Kakamasian" through all my years of study, I decided that only drastic measures could resolve the problem. When I heard that Graeme College, an English-medium state school in Grahamstown, was looking for a social studies teacher, I notified the principal of my availability.

In 1962 I spent a productive year in the major stronghold of the British settlers. My spoken English improved with the help of my colleagues, and that of a music teacher in particular. Socialising with colleagues and with teammates in the Albany rugby team helped me gain a much better understanding of the English community.

27 *Time*, 26 August 1966, pp. 20-23.

On completion of my MA thesis in mid-1963, I accepted a position as cadet in the Department of Foreign Affairs in Pretoria. At the time, apartheid was not yet as discredited as it would be a few years later. De Kiewiet's article in *Foreign Affairs* offered the hope that at least in some countries there could be a meaningful debate on South Africa. It was in any case not expected of diplomats to defend apartheid in all its facets but rather the standpoint that peaceful change in the country was possible.

On 1 July 1964 I started my employment at Foreign Affairs at the Union Buildings in Pretoria. I had the good fortune to work directly under Donald Sole, with whom I had had my job interview in Cape Town. He was one of the most respected persons in the department.

Eric Louw was still the responsible minister till the end of 1963, and GP Jooste the secretary of the department. Pik Botha, however, roamed the corridors with a furrowed brow in a way that could suggest to the uninformed that all of South Africa's diplomatic burdens rested on his shoulders, which in due course would indeed be the case. At that stage he was chief law adviser charged with the coordination of South Africa's defence at the International Court of Justice against the claim that the country had violated its mandate over South West Africa (now Namibia).

After just over a year in the Department of Foreign Affairs, I abandoned the idea of a career in the diplomatic service and became a history lecturer at the University of South Africa (Unisa). There were certainly people such as Neil van Heerden, a colleague in the department, who would continue to serve the country and the cause of reform with great distinction, but my heart was not in a career of that nature.

Instead of trying to influence international opinion-makers, I wanted to lecture and to participate in the debate in Afrikaner ranks about apartheid and an alternative form of survival. I was itching to delve much deeper into issues than I had been able to do in the short pieces I wrote as part of my responsibilities as a cadet. I also resolved to embark on a doctorate in history as soon as possible.

The Pretoria of the mid-1960s was an ideal city for young graduates, who lived in large numbers in Arcadia and Sunnyside and worked for the state, for parastatals or for professional firms. I threw myself wholeheartedly into the rugby world and played for a season for the Pretoria Rugby Club's first team in the formidable Carlton league.

In Pretoria I met Annette van Coller. She would qualify as an architect at the University of the Free State shortly after our marriage, and had started working at an architectural firm in Pretoria in 1963. Our family backgrounds were very similar: our paternal grandfathers had both fought in the Anglo-Boer War, our parents were all teachers at Afrikaans schools, and she and I both identified with the Afrikaner *volksbeweging*. For me, she was the ideal partner from the outset. Today, fifty years later, she is still my greatest source of inspiration, strength and encouragement.

We were married on 3 April 1965 in the Pretoria East Dutch Reformed church, which is adjacent to the Loftus Versfeld Stadium. The date coincided with the start of the rugby season. I knew that if I failed to take the field for the Pretoria Club team at Loftus at 15h00 on that day, I would lose my place in the first team. The marriage service was due to start at 17h30, and I contemplated combining a rugby match and a marriage ceremony in one afternoon. My mother considered it highly irresponsible, and I had to drop the plan. This was also the end of my rugby career, which would in any case not have reached great heights.

In 1966 I took a year's leave from Unisa to pursue postgraduate studies in history in the Netherlands. Annette and I spent an unforgettable year in Amsterdam. At the University of Amsterdam I completed a course that focused on Hitler's assumption of power, but the other courses dealt with themes such as "The Medieval Diary", which held no appeal for me. There was a lively group of South African students in Amsterdam who met once a month for a sociable "*koffietafel*".

One day, out of the blue, I received a letter from Prof. Dirk Kotzé, professor in general history at the University of Stellenbosch, asking me to apply for a vacant post in the department. My application was successful, and I started at the beginning of the 1967 academic year. I was back at the "university with attitude" and in the town of Stellenbosch. Francine, our elder daughter, was born in that year, and Adrienne about three years later. They have continued to give us great joy in our lives.

In the general election of 1970 Annette and I decided to support the Progressive Party with its policy of a qualified franchise. Though my parents were dyed-in-the-wool Nationalists, I was not worried that our decision would result in a family squabble. Nonetheless, I decided to inform my parents of our decision by way of an ambiguous letter that read more or less like this:

> For the sake of the children we have decided that our ways should part, and that we should sever a relationship that was once beautiful and precious, regardless of how hard it may be. We know that you will be shocked, but it is better that we part ways now instead of later.

I elaborated further in the same vein, and wrote right at the end: "What we would actually like to tell you is that we have decided to vote Progressive." My mother told my father: "They're not getting divorced, they're going to vote Prog," and then added in relief: "The bloomin' fools."

*Chapter 4*

# Apprentice

Prof. HB Thom had been rector of the US when I enrolled as a first-year student in 1956. In 1967, his shadow still hung over the History Department which he had headed from 1937 to 1954. His writings were not the *"volks-geskiedenis"* Gustav Preller had produced at the beginning of the century, but a form of academic historiography with a clear nationalist agenda. Among the documents preserved in Thom's private papers is a letter from a student who thanked him because his classes had transformed him from a *"louwarm"* (luke-warm) to a *"vuurwarm"* (red-hot) Afrikaner.[28]

Thom was the "history man" par excellence of the Afrikaner nationalists of the 1940s and 1950s. In speeches and articles during this era, he called on historians to be faithful to the demands of their discipline. They had to research the facts thoroughly and at the same time approach Afrikaner history in a way that would serve the spiritual welfare of the *volk*.

For Thom, the light that Afrikaner historians cast on the past had to help the Afrikaners understand their political challenges. The key feature was the momentous struggle the Afrikaners had waged for a large part of their history to maintain their belief that they could develop within their own community, in spite of unsympathetic governments and great isolation. In so doing, they had developed a sense of self-worth.

Another aspect was racial policy. According to Thom, a study of the past would show how deeply the principle of racial segregation was rooted in the Afrikaner past, and how persistently the Voortrekkers had advocated an "auth-entically Afrikaans" policy of "differentiation". In his biography of the Voor-trekker leader Gert Maritz he wrote of "the brave generation of unforgettable Afrikaners who . . . with their primitive muzzle-loading rifles freed the greater part of South Africa from barbarism and conquered it for white civilisation".[29]

---

28  Albert Grundlingh, "Politics, Principles and Problems of a Profession: Afrikaner Historians and Their Discipline", *Perspectives in Education*, 12, 1, 1990, pp. 1-3.
29  HB Thom, *Die lewe van Gert Maritz* (Cape Town: Nasionale Pers, 1947), p. ix.

From the late 1940s Thom had been involved in the planning of the first complete academic history of the country, viewed through the lens of Afrikaner nationalism. The two-volume work of more than 1 400 pages appeared in 1955 under the title *Geskiedenis van Suid-Afrika* (History of South Africa). Two of the three editors and several of the 23 contributors had a connection with Stellenbosch, and specifically with the History Department. At the start of my first year of study, students were told that those who intended to major in history had to buy the two volumes.

While the work was presented as the first scientific history in Afrikaans, the past was still seen as a battle between "civilisation" and "barbarism". Some of the writers still used derogatory terms for indigenous people. The first volume of *Geskiedenis van Suid-Afrika* provides a chronological overview of the European settlement. It starts with a chapter titled "The discovery of South Africa", as if no one had lived at the southernmost tip of Africa before 1652. The first third of the book contains virtually no mention of the San ("Bushmen") or the Khoikhoi ("Hottentots"), except for passing remarks about the "rapacity" of the Hottentots and the "obstacle" represented by the Bushmen to white advance.

The first mention of the Xhosa people on the colony's eastern frontier comes on page 178, where the text refers to "the terrible depredations" perpetrated by the Xhosa, who had moved across the Great Fish River boundary in "great hordes". There is no reference to the "depredations" committed by the frontier farmers' commandos.

The second volume of *Geskiedenis van Suid-Afrika* contains a chapter entitled "The native people of South Africa". It states that the "Bushmen" soon "ceased to play any role", and that the "Hottentots" "bartered away" their cattle wealth. As to where the black people had lived prior to 1652, it was merely said that existing knowledge in this regard was very limited.

The best chapter in the two-volume work was PJ van der Merwe's interpretation of the Dutch East India Company's native policy. He explained well how the Company, with its gaze focused on the sea and maritime trade, devoted little attention and limited funds to the frontier conflicts. In the absence of troops or a police force, the frontier farmers had to fend for themselves in defence of their families' lives and property. But Van der Merwe, too, erred in arguing that the Fish River, which Governor Joachim van Plettenberg had proclaimed as a boundary after consultations with a few minor Xhosa chiefs, was supposed to apply as a boundary to all other Xhosa groups in the territory as well.

The two volumes assumed without any argument that white people had the right to exercise political control over the greater part of South Africa.

This view of history underwent a radical revision during the 1960s. Radio-carbon dating of artefacts showed that Bantu-speaking communities had occupied the region between the Limpopo and the Vaal as far back as the eleventh century. Subsequent archaeological finds have placed the first black occupation south of the Limpopo several centuries earlier. By the 1750s some of the western Xhosa had already settled west of the Fish River. This was twenty-five to thirty years before Van Plettenberg proclaimed his boundary and the first trekboers (white migrant farmers) arrived in the area.

The first volume of the *Oxford History of South Africa* (1969), edited by Monica Wilson and Leonard Thompson, provided a good summary of the new research. At the time when the Voortrekkers crossed the Orange River, vast parts of the interior were indeed depopulated in the wake of the *Mfecane*, a period of devastating conflicts among black communities that had resulted in a great loss of life. On the other hand, it was indisputable that black and coloured people had occupied vast parts of southern Africa long before white people first landed in Table Bay. The NP government and many of the Afrikaner historians preferred to avert their eyes and pretended that this information could be wished away.

There was a reason for this: for the NP of the 1960s, the historical right to the land had become the cornerstone of the ideology of apartheid. Apartheid was no longer based on white superiority but on white people's supposed right to more than 80% of South Africa's land, which was considered "rightfully theirs" on historical grounds.

Missiologists, anthropologists and sociologists were in the forefront of the academics who helped construct the ideology of apartheid. There were few historians in their ranks.

They had no problem, however, with the vision of South Africa as a pre-dominantly white country. This view was also reflected in the Afrikaans press. Schalk Pienaar, one of the most respected Afrikaans journalists, wrote:

> South Africa is by no means Bantu territory wrested from its rightful owners by the white man. There were no established Bantu home-lands in South Africa when Van Riebeeck landed at the Cape in 1652. The Whites moving northwards and the Bantu moving southwards did not meet until more than a century later. If newcomers is the word one wants, then the Bantu are as much newcomers to South Africa as the Whites.[30]

---

30   Schalk Pienaar and Anthony Sampson, *South Africa: Two Views of Separate Development* (New York: Oxford University Press, 1960), p. 5.

In 1968 Prime Minister John Vorster declared: "We have our land and we alone shall have authority over it."[31] The "land" Vorster had in mind was the entire territory of South Africa except for the 13% that was classified as black areas.

By the time I embarked on my postgraduate studies in 1960, NP politicians had stopped using crude and hurtful terms in public when referring to people who were not white. The main reason for this change was Britain's policy of granting independence to its colonies in Africa, which had started with the "liberation" of Ghana in 1957. The NP government was quick to embrace the new terminology. All nations were now equal, but this did not mean that all individuals in South Africa were equal.

As a result of the high economic growth in the 1960s, the black labour force and consumer market kept expanding. In spite of influx control, black people were urbanising rapidly, and fewer and fewer believed that this stream to the cities could be reversed. A need arose for an interpretation of history that was inclusive rather than exclusive.

When I joined the staff of the History Department at Stellenbosch in 1967, *Geskiedenis van Suid-Afrika* was no longer the frame of reference. A year later history lecturers from the University of South Africa published a new collective work, *Vyfhonderd jaar Suid-Afrikaanse geskiedenis* (Five hundred years of South African history). The history of the black ethnic groups before 1652 was covered in an addendum at the back of the volume. In this book, it was mainly white people that had taken the initiative in building the country.

For a period of about forty years, between 1930 and 1970, the battle between liberal and nationalist historians dominated historiography in South Africa. Numerous dissertations in Afrikaans were published in the annual *Archives Year Book for South African History*, which first appeared in 1938. After the NP assumed power in 1948, more and more Afrikaner historians received university training. The ideal was scientific historiography, but the question was: from what vantage point?

Members of my generation knew that we neither were nor wished to be liberal historians; at the same time, we did not want to write nationalist "*volksgeskiedenis*" as many of the previous generation had. As late as 1966 Prof. HB Thom still characterised the University of Stellenbosch as a "*volksuniversiteit*". By implication, the history taught here would be *volksgeskiedenis*. It proceeded from the assumption that the Afrikaners were in the first instance the people who had historically taken responsibility for what Thom called "Christianity and civilisation, and specifically law and order and progress in history".

---

31   BJ Vorster, *Geredigeerde toesprake* (Bloemfontein: INEG, 1976), pp. 102–03.

However, there had increasingly been a shift from *"volksgeskiedenis"* to what was referred to at Stellenbosch as "scientific-objective" historiography. Piet van der Merwe was the personification of this new approach. By 1944, when he was still only 32 years old, he already had three excellent scientific studies to his name. (There was a fourth work, *Die Kafferoorlog van 1793* (The Kaffir War of 1793), which, apart from the title, had other serious flaws.)

His focus was the trekboers, those pastoral farmers who had trekked away for non-political reasons from the southwestern part of the country that is now South Africa. But his major works had been written at a time when white domination still seemed unassailable.

Van der Merwe refused to practise any self-censorship. He told me once that he had stumbled upon something terrible in his research on the Voortrekkers and the Ndebele people, but would not elaborate on the matter. I wondered sometimes whether it was this incident that had kept him from sending the manuscript on the subject to the printers. A comprehensive work that dealt with the Voortrekkers and the Ndebele was published after his death in an *Archives Year Book*. It contained a detailed account of a massacre of the inhabitants of a black village that had been perpetrated by a Voortrekker commando under Hendrik Potgieter.[32]

What I as a historian was searching for in particular was a way in which to describe and analyse white-black interaction on the colonial frontiers at a time before the whites had consolidated their control over black people. My contemporaries as postgraduate students at Stellenbosch included Henning van Aswegen and Ernst Stals, who worked on white-black relations in the nineteenth century in the area between the Vaal and Orange rivers and in Ovamboland respectively, and Pieter Kapp, who critically analysed the liberal views of the missionary Dr John Philip on the Cape Colony's eastern frontier.

Van Aswegen noted the major problem that confronted all of us: "The few available 'non-white' sources and the masses of available white sources constantly had to be interpreted and re-interpreted in order to arrive at a better understanding of the attitude of the non-whites."[33] In my work on inter-ethnic relations on the eastern Cape frontier, I became more and more convinced that the conflicts on colonial frontiers should be analysed as a struggle

---

32    PJ van der Merwe,"Die Voortrekkers en die Ndebeles", *Argiefjaarboek van die Suid-Afrikaanse geskiedenis,* 1986, pp. 312-20.

33    Henning van Aswegen, "Die verhouding tussen Blank en Nie-Blank in die Oranje-Vrystaat, 1854-1902", unpublished doctoral dissertation, University of the Orange Free State, 1968, p. ii.

characterised by conflicting claims to a disputed territory where no generally accepted authority existed because of the inability of any one ethnic community to impose its will on the others and gain the upper hand.

## Ranke, the founder

Piet van der Merwe was largely responsible for the esteem in which the History Department was held in both Afrikaans and English circles. He had stamped the approach of "scientific-objective" historiography on the department. The German historian Leopold von Ranke (1795-1886) is generally regarded in the West as the founder of modern source-based or scientific historiography. His standpoint was that the historian had to record the past as it had actually happened: "*wie es eigentlich gewesen*", as he put it. He was not under the illusion that the historian could ever be completely neutral or objective, but insisted that the historian had to determine as precisely as possible what had really happened and be impartial in his treatment of conflicts and disputes.

The chief principles of "scientific-objective history", as I was introduced to the concept, were derived from this approach. The first duty was that of verification, for which primary or documentary sources were usually the best. Second, every epoch had its own unique particularity, with people who had their own time-bound moral convictions, values and mindsets. The views of the present should not be imposed on the past. At the same time, however, every era posed its own questions about the past. The historian who did not want to be considered antiquarian had to present history as realistic and relevant to his or her readers.

Van der Merwe was a formidable instructor who went through all theses and dissertations with a fine-toothed comb. One could not fail to admire his thoroughness and devotion to the discipline. On the other hand, he was a poor lecturer and could bore his students stiff in class when he endeavoured to thrash out the history of his specialist field, the trekboer movement, in minute detail. We used to joke that history was actually about whether the Voortrekkers had trekked to the left or to the right of a particular koppie.

Van der Merwe put the stress on what had occurred and how it had happened, and less and less on why things had happened as they did and not in any other way. Though the critcism he levelled at theses, including my own, was sometimes excellent, it could also be so destructive that the entire process of getting a thesis accepted would leave a bitter taste and a wry smile.

Flagrantly absent in the department was any focus on the theory or philosophy of history as a discipline. While it is true that Prof. Dirk Kotzé lectured enthusiastically on nationalism and communism as historical phenomena in Europe, in terms of his remit he could not present courses on theory or on

South African history. In the case of Van der Merwe's offering, there was scant reflection on theory or philosophy. I think he realised that his lectures were poor but was loath to admit it. Once when I mentioned to him that a lecturer from another university had asked me to send him my notes on his lectures, Van der Merwe said he definitely did not consider this a good idea.

We received virtually no guidance on where we could go for further reading on our subject and especially what books or journals we as prospective historians needed to acquaint ourselves with. There was a course in early historiography, but it was never explained how this could broaden our perspective.

Van der Merwe also made no effort to introduce his students to the world of thought of the leading historical figures. There was no scope for students to come up with imaginative insights, to speculate creatively, and to bring historical characters and their worldview to life. As a redoubtable examiner he made a huge contribution to the training of future historians, but it was also due to him that the department stagnated.[34]

Worst of all, the poor offering we were given went hand in hand with what Van Aswegen has rightly referred to as "the self-satisfied Stellenbosch tradition".[35] St Elmo Pretorius was the only lecturer who encouraged us to read books and journal articles, and to do so critically. It was certainly no coincidence that he was the only lecturer who had not been trained at Stellenbosch.

## "A particular way of thinking"

I am grateful that I received the technical side of my apprenticeship as historian in the Ranke methodology. Few qualities are more important to a historian than a reverent respect for facts coupled with constant vigilance against an anachronistic treatment of the past. A historian wants to engage with the past as something that actually happened, not with the past as fiction.

Our inadequate theoretical training forced us to start doing our own thinking and reading about the value of history as a discipline. Aphorisms about the study of history abound, but the one that struck me most was a statement by GJ Renier, a Dutch historian who was influential between the two world wars: "The study of history is not just another field of study; it is a particular way of thinking."

---

34   PH Kapp, *Verantwoorde verlede: Die verhaal van die studie van geskiedenis aan die Universiteit van Stellenbosch, 1866-2000* (Somerset West: Mediator Drukkers, 2004), p. 143.

35   Henning van Aswegen and Pieter Kapp, *Verandering en vernuwing in geskiedbeskouing: 'n Gesprek oor die ervaringe van twee tydgenote* (Vanderbijlpark: Kleio, 2006), p. 23.

The essence of historical understanding lies in being attuned to complexity, context and causality, and to change over time. Historical reflection implies the obligation to take all sides of a matter into acount, but also assumes the adoption of a particular position. Like the novelist, the historian has to imagine that the characters in the "story" cannot foresee the future and the outcome of their actions. The Dutch historian Johan Huizinga advises historians to constantly put themselves at a point in the past where the known factors will seem to permit different outcomes.[36]

Historians should ask themselves why there was ultimately a specific outcome instead of a different one, and what the decisive factors had been. In so doing, they will soon learn that the best-laid plans go awry, that the unexpected tends to be the norm, and that few things are as important as the character of leaders. There *is* something like thinking historically, which also helps one to understand the present better. History offers a particular perspective that is absent from other disciplines.

In the second half of my career, when I lectured in political studies at the University of Cape Town, I experienced a strong sense of the difference between political science and history as disciplines. In political science, one looks from the present at the past; in history, it is precisely the opposite – and there is a massive difference between these ways of looking.

The difference goes further. There is a tendency on the part of political scientists and sociologists to argue that what had occurred was inevitable, and that history could not have happened in any other way. Historians, on the other hand, endeavour to put themselves in a different era and place. They attempt to imagine that various possibilities are still open and that they are unaware of how the historical narrative would actually unfold. Their observations are inductive and tentative.

The major lesson I learnt at Stellenbosch is that the writing of history is only of value when one tries one's utmost to establish the truth and does not attempt to put this truth at the service of a particular political ideal. I felt, however, that at Stellenbosch the "scientific-objective" method had become a fetish that created the illusion on the part of some that they were recording history impartially. According to the British historian AJP Taylor, the historian who believes in his own impartiality runs a greater risk of being biased than others do.[37]

---

36   Niall Ferguson, *Virtual History: Alternatives and Counterfactuals* (London: Picador, 1997), p. 1.
37   See AJP Taylor's essay on Ranke in his *Europe: Grandeur and Decline* (Harmondsworth: Penguin, 1957), p. 115.

While guarding against one's own biases and ensuring that one's facts are correct are both crucial, it is impossible to ever arrive at the full truth or to say the final word. Pieter Geyl, an eminent Dutch historian, referred to historiography as "a debate without end". It is inevitable that one will write history from a particular ideological perspective. Verification of facts to ensure accuracy is the duty of any historian, regardless of which "school" he or she belongs to, and not an exceptional virtue.

I started asking myself more and more who I wanted to write for and how I should approach my target group. In 1943 HB Thom argued that the historian should search for the historical truth from within "the bosom of the *volk*" with the aim of serving "the spiritual welfare of the *volk*". The problem with this approach is that the attempt to give a sympathetic interpretation of Afrikaner history became conflated with defending white supremacy, segregation and apartheid. My contemporaries included a number of historians such as Ernst Stals, Henning van Aswegen, Pieter Kapp and Johann Bergh who did not want to use their history writing in the service of the existing order, but instead wished to show how white, coloured and black had shaped one another. Like them, I was not a liberal historian but rather a pluralist who interpreted the country's history as one of contesting communities in which group interests rather than individual attitudes were decisive.

Up to the early 1970s, everything I wrote was in Afrikaans and I addressed myself to an Afrikaner audience in the first instance. But I started believing less and less that separate development offered a solution to South Africa's problems. From 1970 onwards I voted for the Progressive Party and its successors, despite having strong doubts about whether the classical liberal solutions were appropriate for South Africa.

I decided to write as someone who stood on the margins of the Afrikaner community. Though I would attempt to understand the Afrikaners in particular and explain them to others, I would be unsparing in my criticism where necessary.

I identified with NP van Wyk Louw's dictum that one loves a nation because of its "misery," and also with the words of William Faulkner, the great writer of the American South, who said that one does not love "because" but "despite"; "not for the virtues, but despite the faults".

## A liberal outlook

During the 1960s Afrikaner historians and their English-speaking counterparts, who had long worked in separate silos, started making closer contact, especially in the South African Historical Society and on the editorial board of the *South*

*African Historical Journal/Suid-Afrikaanse Historiese Joernaal.* At Stellenbosch, how-ever, the department still largely ignored the publications of liberal historians, all of whom wrote in English.

It was almost as if Van der Merwe thought that the Ranke school, to which he subscribed, was in opposition to the liberal school. Unlike the Ranke approach, the liberal historians advocated values such as individual freedom and equality. There was a tendency to interpret the past in terms of these values.

In our research, however, it was impossible to be indifferent to three eminent liberal historians who produced important work on South African history, namely CW de Kiewiet, Leonard Thompson and Rodney Davenport. Their studies challenged certain key views of Afrikaner historians.

Whereas Afrikaner historians had long regarded segregation as the only solution, De Kiewiet wrote that history showed segregation offered no solution to South Africa's racial problem, and that any renewed efforts to intensify it were bound to fail.[38] Thompson made the most significant contribution to the history of the constitutional development of South Africa. While the NP government contended in the 1950s that the sovereignty of Parliament was the only Afrikaner tradition, he pointed out that in the Republic of the Orange Free State the constitution had been sovereign, as in the case of the United States. Hence constitutionalism was not a foreign concept but part of the Afrikaner tradition.[39]

Davenport showed that between 1880 and 1910 the Afrikanerbond, the first political party in the country, did not stand on a platform of segregation but defined the term "Afrikaner" inclusively and eagerly sought allies, also across the colour line.[40]

On the other hand, anglophone historians tended to be blind to English chauvinism and the strong conservative element in the English-speaking com-munity. A section of the anglophone elite accused the Afrikaners of various forms of racism, including their insistence on equality for Afrikaans within the context of the official policy of bilingualism. In the first two decades of the Union of South Africa this attitude was so pronounced that the writer,

---

38   CW de Kiewiet, *A History of South Africa: Social and Economic* (Oxford: Oxford University Press, 1941) pp. 242-45.
39   Leonard Thompson, "Constitutionalism in the South African Republics", *Butter-worths South African Law Review*, 1, 1954, pp. 50-71.
40   TRH Davenport, *The Afrikanerbond: The History of a South African Political Party 1880-1911* (Cape Town: Oxford University Press, 1966).

journalist and politician CJ Langenhoven asked in exasperation in a speech in front of an English audience: "Why do you always call our politics racialism, but your racialism you call politics?"[41]

Against this backdrop, a debate between history students from Stellenbosch and Cape Town would have been stimulating. On one occasion Davenport, then a lecturer at the University of Cape Town, proposed that one be held on the topic of General JBM Hertzog's political thinking. The Stellenbosch professors were dismissive; "Davenport just wants to politicise history," was their reaction. As if Stellenbosch did not politicise history.

## "Insurmountable objections"

The department I joined at Stellenbosch had two professors and four lecturers. There was little collegiality in our departmental relations. The model was evidently that of the hierarchical university in the Netherlands and Germany between the two world wars. As lecturers, our status was not much higher than that of senior students. There were no departmental meetings or social gatherings such as shared tea-time where we could discuss history as a discipline. The professors did all the senior departmental work. We were later instructed to mark the third-year students' assignments, but the professors themselves wanted to decide on the topics.

I expressed the desire to lecture on South African history as well, but my request was rejected. I had to continue with courses on American and European history. In 1976 I suggested that the department admit Henry (Jatti) Bredekamp, a coloured lecturer at the University of the Western Cape with whom I had become acquainted, as a doctoral student. Van der Merwe's reply was that we should not "dirty our hands" with this matter.

I ran into a brick wall when I wanted to tackle a fairly recent topic for my doctoral dissertation. Van der Merwe, in particular, was unwavering. It was impossible, he declared, to be "scientific-objective" when writing about the recent past. I tried to persuade him, but he was adamant and did not give me much chance to argue my case.

His standpoint was completely in line with the official stance of the time. In the archival depots, the government records for the preceding fifty years were closed. In 1965 the Joint Matriculation Board's history curriculum excluded political events in South Africa between 1910 and 1965. As Van der Merwe put it to me, there were "insurmountable objections to contemporary history".

Frustrated, I sat down and wrote an academic article on Van der Merwe's

41    Quoted by CR Swart, *House of Assembly Debates*, 22 February 1944, col. 1705.

"insurmountable objections". It appeared in the February 1969 issue of *Stand-punte*, a journal that covered both the arts and the humanities. I had sufficient ammunition at my disposal. In 1966 I had obtained a credit in a subject called contemporary history at the University of Amsterdam. The major part of the course consisted of a case study of Adolf Hitler's assumption of power in Germany during 1933-34, just more than thirty years earlier.

I wrote that a great urge had arisen among the leading historians in Europe to write the history of their own times as a result of the horror evoked by the mass slaughter in the two world wars, and especially the extermination of the Jews and other minority groups. It was no longer advisable to wait until the time was supposedly ripe before taking up the pen to deal with particular historical events. The great disillusionment on the part of Westerners in particular and the moral confusion of the time demanded that historians provide answers to the question of why European civilisation had lost its way to such a degree.

Regarding the Afrikaners, I wrote: "Has there ever been, with the exception of Germany, a greater impulse or a stronger motivation for a nation to account for its history, and especially its recent history, to itself and to the world?" I also asked: "Does the Afrikaner, in the light of all the allegations about the nature and essence of his character, not also have a duty and calling to search for the answers in the past century?"[42]

The writing of contemporary history did not require any new skills, I argued; it did, however, bring the huge challenges of historiography into sharp focus. No one in the department reacted to my article. In all likelihood my modest revolt never came to the attention of the professors. I wonder if Van der Merwe would have deigned to discuss the article with me if he had read it.

## In turbulent times

With no possibility of writing on a contemporary topic, I accepted the professors' suggestions. My master's thesis dealt with the first years after the second British occupation of the Cape in 1806. For my doctoral dissertation, the professors proposed that I write on the period 1795-1803 when the Cape was occupied by Britain for the first time, after having been governed by the Dutch East India Company for 143 years.

In the end, it turned out to be a very good exercise for me to write about an entire society in a time of crisis. In fact, the British seizure of power in 1795 was not a mere change of government but a regime change that was accom-

---

42   Hermann Giliomee, "'Onoorkoomlike besware' teen kontemporêre geskiedenis", *Standpunte*, February 1969, p. 43.

panied by radical changes in the form of government, the economic system and social values. I was surprised and thrilled to discover how challenging the history of turbulent times could be.

After 1795, as in the case of South African society after 1994, the population within the colonial borders – officials, burghers, slaves, Khoikhoi, San and Xhosa – had to adjust to sweeping changes and new ideas. To them it seemed as if the world had been turned upside down. Whereas, prior to 1795, there had been a hierarchy of legally defined groups consisting of officials, burghers and slaves, each with its respective status and different rights, there were now only "British subjects", who had to be put on an equal footing before the law in due course.

In many respects, the state of mind in the colony in the early 1790s resembled that in South Africa in the early 1990s. In the early 1790s, the burgher JF Kirsten encapsulated the spirit of the times as follows: "The government has lost the respect of the people; everyone wants to command and no one wants to obey."[43]

In 1972 I obtained my doctoral degree, and thereby formally completed my apprenticeship in history. But this was not the time to sit back complacently. Stellenbosch was decidedly not at the cutting edge of developments in Western historiography.

## A momentous meeting

While doing research for my doctoral dissertation at the Cape Archives in 1968, I happened to meet Rick Elphick, who was working on his doctoral study on the Khoikhoi. He was a Canadian citizen and a student of Leonard Thompson at the University of California at Los Angeles. In 1969 Thompson became professor in African Studies at Yale University and had Elphick's enrolment transferred to that institution.

My chance meeting with Elphick would prove to be of crucial significance to my career. Elphick is one of the most subtle and innovative historians who write on South African history. My friendship with him and our professional collaboration have been among the most formative influences on my career.

In the course of his archival research Elphick also visited Stellenbosch, where I introduced him to several local academics. He recalls that I was optimistic about radical reform. The Afrikaners were not monolithic, I told him, and a younger generation was starting to shake the pillars of Afrikaner power.

---

43    Quoted in my *Die Kaap tydens die eerste Britse bewind, 1795-1803* (Pretoria: HAUM, 1975), p. 31.

He writes that I assured him I had no intention of becoming an anglicised Afrikaner or *volksvreemd* (alienated from my community).[44]

On completion of his research in Cape Town Elphick travelled to Maseru, where he joined Thompson, who was working on a biography of Moshoeshoe. Thompson reacted negatively when Elphick told him about the fruitful conversations he had had with me and other Afrikaners in Stellenbosch. He hinted that Elphick might have been infected with racism, which was absurd. Nevertheless, Elphick's relations with Thompson improved to the extent that he could persuade him to invite me to Yale as a postgraduate fellow.

Thompson, too, would play a huge role in my career. Born in England in 1916, he was first educated there and then in South Africa, to which his parents had emigrated. He fought in the Second World War and was a Rhodes Scholar at Oxford University. After his studies he lectured in history at the University of Cape Town (UCT) for just more than ten years. As a member of the Liberal Party, he was actively involved in the fight against the removal of coloured people from the voters' roll.

Thompson and Monica Wilson, an anthrolopogist attached to UCT, were the co-editors of the *Oxford History of South Africa*, the first volume of which appeared in 1969 and the second in 1971. The book could well be described as revolutionary. For the first time, eminent scholars from various disciplines collaborated on a work that depicted South African history as African history, with black people as the principal actors instead of bit players in a white-centric history. Whereas earlier historians, like Eric Walker, had seen the Great Trek as the central event in this history, this work portrayed the trek as an invasion to which the Zulu in Natal and the black polities on the Highveld had to react.

The second volume of the *Oxford History of South Africa* was less controversial. Notably the chapters on agriculture and urbanisation, by Francis Wilson and David Welsh respectively, approached the history in a fresh way. Chapters on Afrikaner nationalism by René de Villiers, a journalist, and on African nationalism by Leo Kuper, an anthropologist, were less successful. They confirmed the old rule that liberals find it hard to write about nationalism with insight and understanding.

The expectation was that the two-volume work, which ran to a thousand pages, would be accepted as the new orthodoxy. Instead, it became the target of a fiery assault by radical scholars, who were mostly people of my generation. They

---

44    In this section I rely mainly on Rick Elphick's account of our meeting and collaboration. See Richard Elphick, "Hermann Giliomee and *The Shaping of South African Society*: Memories of a Collaboration", *South African Historical Journal*, 60, 4, 2008, pp. 553-62.

contended that the liberal approach, as displayed in the *Oxford History*, was out-dated, despite the fact that it was sharply critical of white domination. According to them the emphasis had to be placed on structural analysis, and especially on capitalist exploitation, which, in their view, was the real driving force in history.

I agreed with neither the radicals nor the liberals. What I did not know, however, was that certain Afrikaner historians, particularly Floors van Jaarsveld, would react with disgruntlement to my decision to pursue postgraduate studies at Yale under Thompson. To Van Jaarsveld, this was confirmation of the suspicion that I had crossed over to the liberal side.

## A special year

The year that I spent with Annette and our two young daughters, Francine and Adrienne, in New Haven, Connecticut, in 1973 was an enriching experience. For me as a historian, it was a great stimulus. Of all the top American universities, Yale was the one where the largest proportion of undergraduate students majored in history.

I had a spacious office in the department and also spent long hours in the magnificent library. For Annette and the children, though, it was hard at times. We stayed in a minuscule apartment in the Divinity School. Our funds were limited and there was little opportunity for sightseeing trips and tours. At best, we were part of the "Greyhound set".

At Yale I soon discovered that Thompson harboured suspicion towards me as an Afrikaner. I think he had expected me to be far more openly critical of the NP government and NP supporters. But I had no intention of passing myself off as a "detribalised Afrikaner". It was clear that Thompson, who identified with the cause of black liberation under a liberal order, was upset by the criticism levelled at the *Oxford History* and was in search of allies.

Thompson thought highly of Van der Merwe as a historian, but his assessment of the Afrikaners was negative. He wrote that from the time of the first free burghers to the Voortrekkers only one social order had obtained, namely one in which the Afrikaners and their ancestors regarded people of African, Asian or mixed origin as a subspecies of humanity, as "creatures" rather than "people". This view was, according to him, engraved in the minds of the Voortrekkers, who cemented it in legislation. Hence Thompson concluded: "That was what custom prescribed, self-interest demanded, and God ordained. That was how it always has been and always must be in South Africa."[45]

---

45   Leonard Thompson, "The Zulu Kingdom and Natal", in Monica Wilson and Leonard Thompson (eds), *Oxford History of South Africa,* vol. 1 (Oxford: Clarendon Press, 1969), p. 367.

I found it surprising that a historian as sophisticated as Thompson could make such an unhistorical statement, almost as if he simply had to give vent to a sense of resentment against the Afrikaners. It was completely at variance with the positive comments he had expressed in a scholarly article fifteen years earlier about the Republic of the Orange Free State whose constitution was based on that of the United States.[46] He ignored the history of the Afrikaner-bond in the Cape Colony and that of the early National Party, between 1915 and 1929, which had been in favour of the political and economic integration of the coloured people and had competed zealously for their vote.

Once Thompson asked me directly what I thought of the two volumes. I replied that the *Oxford History*'s stress on the interaction between people of different races and cultures provided an important corrective to the orthodoxy that white people had always just insisted on segregation, but that I had problems with the book's view that the Afrikaners and their forebears were inveterate racists. He listened to my explanation in silence.

Thompson was someone with a huge ego and a thin skin. But I would always be grateful to him for the doors he opened for me. In the end we did establish a relationship based on mutual respect. In 1975 he was one of my referees in my application for the vacant King George V Chair in History at UCT. (He had previously occupied the chair.) When Colin Webb, an English-speaking historian, was appointed, he expressed doubt in a letter as to whether Webb's long residence in Natal would help him to understand the Afrikaners.

## Influential people

In 1973, and again in the academic year of 1977/78, I got to know several of the other professors in the History Department at Yale. I always made a point of asking historians which book outside their particular field of research had influenced them the most. A name that cropped up frequently was that of Reinhold Niebuhr. His influential work *Moral Man and Immoral Society* had appeared in 1932 when the system of segregation in the southern states of the United States was at its worst.[47]

Niebuhr believed that an oppressive system such as segregation in the American South was not primarily the result of ignorance, erroneous doctrines

---

46   Leonard Thompson, "Constitutionalism in the South African Republics", *Butterworths South African Law Review*, 1, 1954, pp. 50-71.

47   Reinhold Niebuhr, *Moral Man in Immoral Society* (New York: Charles Scribner's Sons, 1932) and *The Children of Light and the Children of Darkness* (New York: Charles Scribner's Sons, 1944).

or irrationality. People organised themselves in communities in order to protect their particular political identity, interests and social values. Contrary to what the liberal creed maintained, such groups did not dissolve easily. As members of a community, they tended to be much more unmerciful towards other groups than in their personal relationships with individuals from other communities. This struck me as an apt description of the Afrikaners.

Niebuhr did not believe that solutions lay in finding "reasonable leaders" who were prepared to talk to the leaders of competing parties or communities and come up with a clever solution. A nation, an ethnic community or a class believed in the justness of its cause. Appeals to people's conscience and to "reasonableness" and "fairness" would fall on stony ground until the balance of power had shifted sufficiently to make a community change its course. A democracy only became possible once people's fears about security and their sense of self-worth in a new dispensation were allayed.

Naturally, I also asked Thompson which historians I should study. He singled out De Kiewiet and WM Macmillan, and added that I did not have to take much notice of Lewis Gann's recently published article on liberal interpretations of South African history. Needless to say, I immediately made a point of reading the relevant article in the *Rhodes-Livingstone Journal* of 1959.

Gann, a historian of German-Jewish descent, had received his university training in England and worked in the British colonial service before accepting a university position in Rhodesia (today Zimbabwe). He had written books on the history of Rhodesia and about the African continent.

Gann's argument was that liberals sought to impose an inappropriate model on South Africa. The model was that of British society, which had first granted the franchise to its middle class before extending it to its working class. Unlike South Africa, British was a homogeneous society in terms of race and culture, and a rich and prosperous country to boot.

Gann rightly pointed out that if historians were looking for a model, they should rather study the history of ethnic conflicts in eastern Europe. In these societies ethnic and class differences coincided, as in South Africa; and in eastern Europe, too, ethnic groups had long been engaged in a fierce power struggle.

The dominant group made sure that it kept all the others subordinate. Gann emphasised that while the refusal of the NP government to give black people any representation in Parliament after 1948 could be described as selfish, from a short- to medium-term perspective it was not irrational.

Gann asserted that the fate of political minorities with no power was seldom pleasant, and that the loss of political power by the NP might well also mean the end of the Afrikaners as an ethnic minority.[48]

During the year at Yale I attended a memorable public lecture by the writer Alan Paton. In many respects a "Christian realist", like Niebuhr, Paton was also one of the leading voices in South Africa in favour of a liberal alternative to apartheid. He firmly believed that if the international world were to force the Afrikaners to accept majority rule in a unitary state, they would rather "be destroyed than yield".

But he did not exclude the possibility of a voluntary transfer of power. Paton posed the key question: "When total apartheid is seen to be impossible, what will the Afrikaner intellectuals and religious leaders do? Will they choose white domination or the common society?" In this speech and in various articles, he answered the question himself: "Surely, with their intellectual qualifications and moral views, they must choose the common society." In Paton's view, the Afrikaners would not be forced from power. The initiative, he believed, would remain with them until they chose to give it up.[49]

## Historian of the South

I was particularly fortunate in getting to know C Vann Woodward, the most eminent historian of the American South. His influential study *The Strange Career of Jim Crow* (1955), which dealt with the evolution of American race relations, was at one stage considered the best-known historical work in the United States. Martin Luther King Jr called it "the historical Bible of the civil rights movement".

Though Woodward, like the later president Bill Clinton, hailed from the southern state of Arkansas, he was nonetheless unflinching in his insistence on liberal values. Woodward's studies of the emergence and mutation of segregation in the southern states of the United States after the abolition of slavery were of great help to me in understanding race relations in South Africa. In both cases one had to do with a dominant white community that refused point-blank to incorporate black people in their political and social system.

I had several conversations with Woodward over lunch at Mory's, the popular faculty club. He could become extremely annoyed with the northeast elite (particularly that of the New England region) who were, in his view, hypocritical about the race question and labelled the South as backward, dumb and myopic without being conscious of their own racism.

Woodward told me of the formative influence Niebuhr's books had had on

---

48    LH Gann, "Liberal Interpetations of South African History", *Rhodes-Livingstone Journal*, 1959, pp. 40–62.

49    Peter Alexander, *Alan Paton* (Oxford: Oxford University Press, 1994), p. 300.

him. As a Southerner himself, Woodward highlighted the contrast between the New Englanders and the Southerners in a way that immediately reminded me of the differences between Afrikaners and the English-speaking whites in South Africa. Like the "New Englanders" in the US northeast, the English-speaking community in South Africa had a shared experience of economic prosperity. This went in hand in hand with their protestations of innocence on any charge of black exploitation and oppression.

The history of the Afrikaners, on the other hand, corresponded largely to that of white people in the American South. In both cases there was an era of slavery and later a devastating defeat in war (the American Civil War and the Anglo–Boer War), followed by another century of segregation. (South Africa took the term "poor white" as well as "segregation" from the South.) Like those of the Southerners, Afrikaners' hands were stained in respect of both slavery and apartheid – the two great moral issues about which the West had developed an obsession. But Woodward did not feel that whites had the duty to pay off their debt in perpetuity.

In 1976 Thompson and Woodward travelled together to South Africa to attend a conference on apartheid in South African universities held on the UCT campus. This was just after the first wave of uprisings in Soweto and other black areas. Along with many others, I wondered whether we were heading for a full-blown civil war over the race question. I hosted Woodward at Stellenbosch, where I showed him separate entrances, separate residential areas and schools, and the other manifestations of apartheid.

We subsequently exchanged letters on a number of occasions. In 1998 he referred to the "black carpetbaggers" in the United States of that time, black people who sought to benefit personally from affirmative action even though they had not suffered under segregation themselves. To him, this was proof that advocates of white supremacy were correct in their assumption that skin colour was the overriding factor in the white–black conflict. On 15 June 1998 he wrote that it seemed to him as if racial rhetoric in America had been much worse than in South Africa:

> The racial rhetoric here [in America] was framed in terms of hatred, bitterness, contempt, and personal violence. It appeared in these forms among the courts, the police, the militia, prisons and mobs. Was there anything in South Africa comparable with the Ku Klux Klan, the lynching mobs, the mass brutality in the South?

Once I asked Woodward a question that had long preyed on my mind. Would the white people in the American South have been able to abolish segregation if those states had been independent? He pondered it for quite a while and then replied: "No, we wouldn't have been able to do it."

## Unintended consequences

In the course of 1973 Rick Elphick and I decided to compile a book of essays on the early shaping of Cape society, about which so many conflicting theories existed. We wanted to obtain contributions from young historians who had focused on the early colonial history of the Cape in their doctoral dissertations. Rick himself had written on the Khoikhoi at the beginning of the VOC era, while I had written on the last decades of the eighteenth century, of which the first white-black conflicts on the eastern Cape frontier were such an important facet.

Our pool of authors and their doctoral research topics included Leonard Guelke on the burghers, Gerrit Schutte on the Cape Patriots, Robert Shell and James Armstrong on the slaves and free blacks, Martin Legassick on the Griquas and Southern Sotho on the northern frontier, and William Freund on the transitional governments from 1795 to 1806. All of them accepted the invitation to contribute to the volume. I ended up being the only contributor who was still based in South Africa. It was a striking illustration of the migration overseas of the historians who were engaged in a radical reinterpretation of our early history.

We started our work on the book in a time before electronic communication. During the planning and editing stages of the manuscript, streams of letters made their way across the ocean. Rick still has a 30cm-high pile of correspondence between the two of us and between us as co-editors and the various authors.

Gradually we realised that our book had the potential to challenge the views of historians on the early colonial era fundamentally. With a friend, Mike Peacock, at the helm of Maskew Miller Longman, we were assured of a sympathetic publisher and an effective marketer. The book was published in 1979 as *The Shaping of South African Society, 1652-1820*. An Afrikaans version in collaboration with Karel Schoeman, who had translated a large section, appeared in 1982 under the title *'n Samelewing in wording: Suid-Afrika, 1652 tot 1820*.

The reviews were generally positive, but Anna Böeseken, the historian who had introduced me to Elphick in the Cape Archives in 1968, called it a "presumptuous book" in *Die Burger*. She stated that it reflected the modern obsession with racial differences which resulted in scant attention being paid to interpersonal differences, and added: "Thus theories are constructed and conclusions drawn on the basis of insufficient data."

Böeseken, an authority on the seventeenth and eighteenth centuries, evidently felt that we as young scholars were still too wet behind the ears to mount the radical reinterpretation to which the book laid claim. Nevertheless, the book sold very well. The University of South Africa prescribed it for their students, and within a few years several other universities followed suit. By the end of the 1980s the total sales exceeded 50 000.

We then embarked on a substantially revised and extended second edition which took the analysis up to 1840. The new edition, which appeared in 1989, comprised more than 600 pages and included essays by new contributors such as Candy Malherbe, Nigel Worden, Robert Ross and Jeffrey Peires. This work, too, sold well, but it went out of print when Pearson took over our publisher ten years later. In 2015 the Wesleyan University Press made it available as an electronic book.

Rick and I consider our most significant contribution the synoptic final chapter in which we posed the question: How did white control and black exclusion become entrenched while at the same time there were large-scale interracial sexual relations outside wedlock?

Up to about 1775, the government and the burghers virtually never used the terms "race" or "white people". Laws did not differentiate or discriminate on the basis of race or colour. A racist ideology did not exist. The word "black" was used very rarely except in the formal term "free blacks", which referred to former slaves who had been freed by their owners. The police force consisted of black men who were called "kaffirs". They were colour-blind in the execution of their duties and arrested people without making any distinction based on colour.

How did it come about that the Afrikaners developed the system of apartheid from such a pioneer history? It was a question one could indeed ask oneself. Liberal historians and social scientists enthusiastically offered explanations. According to some, the blame for white racism had to be laid at the door of the burghers' "primitive" Calvinism with its doctrine of predestination. The problem with this interpretation was that, up to the end of the eighteenth century, the burghers had not been particularly devout.

Other historians again traced the origins of racism back to the conflict on the eastern frontier where the burghers and the Xhosa clashed in six frontier wars between 1780 and 1836. What was never explained was how the poorly educated frontier farmers managed to influence the much more cultivated inhabitants of Cape Town and its surrounding areas.

After numerous conversations on the stoep of the Lanzerac Hotel in Stellenbosch and many letters, Rick and I formulated an argument with five legs. The first leg was the administrative framework that the VOC initially imposed on the Cape, which distinguished between three legal status groups: Company officials, free burghers and slaves. The government imported slaves (who were exclusively black or Asian) from Africa and the East Indies as labourers. The free burghers were almost exclusively people who hailed from Europe.

Over the first 150 years of the settlement, the legal status group and race/colour started to correlate more and more closely. The burghers were white people and the slaves black people; those who owned land were white, and the landless people were black or coloured. There were many white people who did not own land, but they had the status of burghers. Among other things, they helped defend the landowners' farms and livestock.

Burgher status went hand in hand with certain rights, obligations (such as commando service) and social status. For example, the VOC appointed only burghers as *heemraden* and field cornets. Until well into the nineteenth century members of the burgher community did not regard themselves as a race, but referred to themselves as burghers or "*ingesetenes*" (inhabitants).

The second element was demography. By 1725 the initial imbalance between men and women in the European community, which had given rise to several mixed marriages, had largely disappeared. The European men who managed to find a European wife got married, and a large majority of the others took a black or coloured concubine. As a general rule, children born from such extra-marital interracial liaisons were not absorbed into the European community.

Thirdly, there was the role of the church in the promotion of a racially exclusive white community. The Dutch Reformed ministers were officials of a trading company, the VOC, which saw no profit in christianising black or coloured people. With regard to baptism, some ministers distinguished between born Christians (infants whose parents were Christians and who were baptised immediately) and baptised Christians (whose parents were not Christians). Those in the latter category often had to first prove that they understood the basic teachings of Christianity before they could receive baptism.

After *Shaping* had already been published, I came across the words of the Stellenbosch minister PB Borcherds. He had to explain to the British governor why, in a district as large as that of Stellenbosch, so few slaves had been baptised. Borcherds replied that he could not baptise slaves before they answered his questions about Christian doctrine to his satisfaction. He expected them to know the answers by heart. According to him, while they did have the "fear of God" in their hearts, they were too "*stomp*" (obtuse) to answer the questions.[50]

A fourth element was the system of Roman-Dutch law, which gave women in the Netherlands and in Dutch colonies more rights than those enjoyed by women in any other European legal system. In the event of adultery, a woman could divorce her husband and she then received half of the estate. During the eighteenth century, a pattern was established where women took the lead in becoming confirmed members of the church, and where they insisted that men who courted their daughters first had to be confirmed.[51]

Finally, the economy was so basic that no need arose to free a limited number of slaves to fill positions (such as those of merchants and soldiers) for which there were not enough Europeans and for which slaves were unsuitable. By contrast, in certain parts of Brazil an intermediate category of mulattoes emerged because of this need. An order without sharp racial distinctions developed in that country, which was completely different from that of the Cape.

During the time Rick and I were working on our final chapter, Cillié de Bruyn carried out genealogical research in the Archives which we would cite. He found that in a sample from the year 1807, only 5% of more than a thousand children had a grandparent that genealogists designated as non-European. Our conclusion was that by 1800 a community had emerged which intermarried and which had developed a high rate of endogamy. Thus a white "nation" emerged in South Africa without there initially having been any plan to "found" one. The VOC was succeeded by a British regime which, in a different way but equally purposefully, entrenched white power and white status.

My collaboration with Elphick provided me with the best possible exposure to the complexity of history and the unintended consequences of historical processes. It was a lesson that stayed with me and that I would find very useful in the last quarter of the twentieth century when the political order again changed fundamentally.

## A sometimes venomous debate

In the last three decades of the twentieth century a heated debate raged at academic level between so-called radicals and liberals. It had been sparked in large part by the publication of the two volumes of the *Oxford History of South*

---

50    PS de Jongh, "Sendingwerk in die landdrosdistrikte Stellenbosch en Tulbagh, 1799-1830", unpublished MA thesis, University of Stellenbosch, 1968, pp. 78-79.

51    I only became aware of the important role of women and that of the legal system later, thanks to the work of Andreas van Wyk, but include these aspects here for the sake of completeness.

*Africa* in 1969 and 1971.

The debate was about the question whether race (white versus black) or class (the "haves" who owned land and other fixed assets versus the "have-nots") had been the key factor in the evolution of human relations in South Africa. Liberal historians tended to argue that certain myths and superstitions about descent or race (such as the idea of "Ham's descendants", the Calvinist notion of predestination, and beliefs about white "genetic" superiority) were responsible for white people's subjugation and exploitation of black people. Radical historians (also called Marxists), on the other hand, proceeded from the assumption that the dominant class exploited other people, for example through slavery in the eighteenth century or through cheap labour in the twentieth century. The capitalist exploiters tried to justify this by means of a racist ideology.

A variant of this question was the following: Were the Afrikaners, with particular ideas that had been shaped by Calvinism, slavery, frontier conflicts and apartheid, the real culprits in the political crisis that started mounting in the country in the 1970s? Or were the real culprits the capitalists, with their exploitation particularly of the black working class?

From the outset I had reservations about the manner in which the race-class debate was conducted. There was a tendency among some liberal historians to serenely blame the Afrikaners for racial conflict in the country's history while appropriating all the credit for economic growth for the English community and ignoring the massive disruption and exploitation of the capitalist system. Radical historians such as Martin Legassick saw through this and forced the liberal historians to engage in introspection. The Marxists, in turn, regarded nationalist movements as the work of a "petty bourgeoisie" who mobilised people through culture-mongering in order to derive the most benefit from the movement for themselves.

What surprised me was the arrogance and venom with which some radicals in particular fought against the liberals. The reason, of course, was that this was not merely an academic debate but a civil war in the ranks of the English-speaking intelligentsia. If someone considered class the determining factor, it followed almost automatically that he or she also believed that capitalism was the root cause of the South African problem, and that the solution lay in sanctions, boycotts and, for some, revolution. Those who adhered to race (or ideas) as the key element believed instead that capitalism was the solution. If capitalism were to be given free rein, apartheid would be swept away by economic growth, like a sandcastle by the incoming tide. Hence sanctions had to be opposed with might and main.

What the radicals did successfully was to draw attention to the illusions of sections of the English-speaking community and to the ideology of liberalism in South Africa. It was hard to believe that this community, which dominated the economy, had played only a minor role in the development of racism as dominant ideology. The much lower wages that English employers paid their black workers were most likely backed up by a view of black people that hardly differed from racism. By the beginning of the 1970s the white-black ratio for earnings in the private sector was a shocking 21:1 in the mining sector and 6:1 in the manufacturing sector. The vast majority of these employers were English speakers who, until 1987, had voted faithfully for the opposition parties.

In general, neither the liberals nor the radicals showed much interest in the interpretations of the Afrikaans-speaking historians. In his book on the debate, *The Making of the South African Past: Major Historians on Race and Class* (1988), Christopher Saunders states categorically that Afrikaner historians made no contribution to the liberal-radical debate. He writes that this "may be explained at least in part" by their "more unquestioning acceptance of white supremacy".[52]

Saunders's view is wide of the mark. It is a myth that English speakers as a community were significantly more liberal than the Afrikaners. In 1988, when the Progressive Federal Party for the first time resolutely propagated a non-racial form of majority government, their policy was supported by nearly all the English newspapers. There was, however, a huge gulf between the editors and their readers. In an opinion poll conducted in the same year, only 10% of English speakers supported majority government, compared with 3% of Afrikaners.[53]

Afrikaner historians were generally not interested in participating in a debate whose basic terms had been formulated by academics outside the group. Pieter Kapp makes the valid point that the Afrikaner historians attempted to answer the questions put to them by their Afrikaans readers.[54] Until about 1960 the most important questions on the part of Afrikaans readers related to the establishment of white control and to what was called the "struggle between Boer and Briton", which only started to fade away after the advent of a republic in 1960.

## The aftermath of humiliation

---

52   Christopher Saunders, *The Making of the South African Past: Major Historians on Race and Class* (Cape Town: David Philip, 1988), p. 3.

53   Hermann Giliomee and Lawrence Schlemmer, *From Apartheid to Nation-Building* (Cape Town: Oxford University Press, 1989), p. 156.

54   For a good overview, see Kapp, *Verantwoorde verlede*, pp. 143-45.

Instead of the old nationalist historiography, what I identified with was the approach known as pluralism. It seeks to understand deeply divided societies, where a common social will and shared values are lacking, in a particular way. It emphasises the cultural as well as material influences that have shaped the Afrikaners. In this approach, culture represents a force in its own right and is not merely a component of the ideological superstructure that serves to legitimate particular interests, as the radical historians would have it.

Pluralists also grasp the great extent to which politics are driven by national or cultural humiliation.[55] My study of Cape society during the first decades of British rule made it clear to me that what had united the burghers as a community was their culture and the disdain with which they were often treated by British officialdom, rather than their material interests.

After the British conquest of the Cape, a small group of burghers, the so-called "Cape Dutch", offered their services to the new government, adopted English customs, swore unconditional allegiance to the new government – and soon became anglicised. But they were an unrepresentative elite. The majority of the burghers continued to identify with the culture and institutions to which they were accustomed, namely the system of landdrost and *heemraden*, and their church and congregation. They were well aware of the contempt with which leading figures in the English community regarded "the Dutch" and their culture.

In British eyes, most of the burghers remained nothing more than Hollanders – with the implication that this was an inferior status. Thirty years after the second British conquest of the Cape, Christoffel Brand, a leading Afrikaner in Cape Town, wrote that "their conquerors had continually worked to remind them that they were Hollanders".[56]

History studies written in English tend to assess the Great Trek largely in terms of material interests, such as the emancipation of slaves and the hankering after land beyond the colonial borders. What they overlook, however, is the scornfulness on the part of many government officials and the grave lack of representative institutions through which burghers could air their views.

The writer Olive Schreiner, who had worked as the governess of Afrikaner children in Cradock and other eastern Cape districts a few decades after the

---

55    Gideon Rachman, "Politics of humiliation drives international relations", *Financial Times*, 12 March 2015.

56    Quoted in my *The Afrikaners: Biography of a People* (Cape Town: Tafelberg, 2003), p. 199.

Great Trek, commented on the trek as follows:

> [What] most embittered the hearts of the colonists was the cold indif-
> ference with which they were treated, and the consciousness that they
> were regarded as a subject and inferior race by their rulers ... [The] feeling
> of bitterness became so intense that about the year 1836 large numbers
> of individuals determined for ever to leave the colony and the homes
> they created and raise an independent state.[57]

After 1994, two hundred years after the regime change of 1795, it was again the
humiliation that had been imposed on black people during the previous
two centuries that determined the new government's politics.

## The central question

The big question I asked myself at the start of my career was the following:
From what perspective would I tell my story? Tony Judt, one of the most
respected historians of our time, was born of Jewish parents in London and
grew up there. He never felt himself to be specifically Jewish or English, but
identified with both identities at different times. He was neither a radical nor
a conventional liberal.

Judt has pointed out that in everyday life, the person we tend to trust the most
is the one who is upfront about the perspective from which he comes and from
which he tells his story, rather than the one who tries to pass himself off as
totally objective.[58] Of course, one does not reject the need to avoid partisanship,
but in the final analysis one gives one's personal interpretation.

I also learnt that one can derive great benefit from seeking information from
a historian with an ideological perspective that differs from one's own. My
collaboration with Rick Elphick on the analysis we did of early Cape society
in the final chapter of *The Shaping of South African Society* taught me more
about historiography than all the classes at Stellenbosch had done.

A focus on both the overall picture and the detail is important. Without the
detailed study I had done of Cape society between 1780 and 1812, I would
never have grasped the bigger picture of the shaping of a particular society.
The same holds true for the transition from white to black control in the years
between 1960 and 1994. Perhaps Piet van der Merwe was right in insisting that
every aspiring historian first has to undergo an apprenticeship by writing a

57   Olive Schreiner, *Thoughts on South Africa* (Johannesburg: Ad Donker, 1992), p. 205.
58   Tony Judt, *The Memory Chalet*, (London: Vintage Books, 2011), pp. 200-16.

conventional dissertation on a demarcated period from the past before tackling a topic from contemporary history.

During the year at Yale, I often asked myself the following question: How can the study of history serve to make people, and notably the Afrikaners, aware of the way in which they were liberated from English political, economic and cultural domination, and, on the other hand, inspire them to fight for freedom for all in South Africa?

# Chapter 5

# "A snake in our midst"

My move away from apartheid and, along with it, from the National Party came about in an unusual way. As I have mentioned before, in mid-1964 I started working at the Department of Foreign Affairs as third secretary and cadet in the diplomatic service. My task was to summarise the reports of the heads of mission in a weekly bulletin and distribute it among senior members of the department.

These reports dealt particularly with South Africa's international image. I could see virtually week by week how the West's initial wait-and-see attitude with regard to the homeland policy was changing to one of disapproval and ever-mounting condemnation.

The main reason for this was the Cold War and the accompanying rivalry for the support of African countries between the West and the Communist bloc. Unlike in the case of the Israelis, support for Afrikaners was absent among voters in Western countries. Their governments increasingly found it an embarrassment to be denounced as protectors of apartheid by the Communist bloc.

I realised that it would hold serious implications for stability if both Western countries and our country's black majority categorically rejected apartheid. In Afrikaner ranks, this was an unpopular standpoint. Few Afrikaners had travelled internationally, and South Africa still lacked a television service. Only a thin layer of the white elite read foreign newspapers and journals. People believed local political leaders and newspaper editors as if they were prophets.

A poll conducted in 1966-67 showed how conservative even the opinion-forming elite in South Africa was. When asked what they perceived to be the biggest political threat, a random sample of parliamentarians indicated that "a lack of understanding by the West" (80%) and "international communism" (65%) were more serious threats than "black nationalism in South Africa" (12%). The responses of top officials and business leaders were largely similar to those of the parliamentarians. [59]

---

59   Heribert Adam, "The South African Power-Elite", in Heribert Adam (ed.), *South Africa: Sociological Perspectives* (London: Oxford University Press, 1971), pp. 91-96.

There was a tendency among Afrikaner nationalists to view "liberalists" as more dangerous enemies of the "Afrikaner cause" than communists. It was hard to put across the view that Western countries increasingly disapproved of apartheid, without being suspected of communist or liberalist sympathies.

Pretoria was a hotbed of political disagreements that quickly resulted in animosities. Critics were regarded with mistrust. Without the benefit of my fifteen-month stint at the Department of Foreign Affairs, I would probably have been much less outspoken at that stage.

However, I was not convinced that a classic liberal solution would work. In the course of the 1960s, democracy failed in most of the independent states in Africa. Liberal analysts invariably put the blame on ethnicity or nationalism, but my impression was that it was rather the liberal model of democracy that had failed because it was so unsympathetic towards minorities and their respective cultures.

## My Unisa year

After little more than a year at Foreign Affairs, I resigned and became a history lecturer at the University of South Africa (Unisa). I was impressed by what the department did. The offering at undergraduate and honours level was much better than that of Stellenbosch. So, too, were the relations between junior and senior staff members, compared with what I would experience later as a lecturer at Stellenbosch.

One of the senior lecturers in the department at Unisa was Floors van Jaarsveld, who typecast me fairly soon as someone who opposed his brand of historiography. Van Jaarsveld was a highly gifted as well as a highly complex individual. His brother-in-law Manie van der Spuy, who later became a professor of psychiatry in Canada, has described him as follows:

> He was a complex personality, who was simply referred to as "*bedui-weld*" (cantankerous) in the family. He suffered from the unfortunate combination of a brilliant intellect and totally immature emotional development. High intelligence and emotional immaturity are always a difficult combination. He was unable to deal with criticism, and took any criticism intensely personally. He was also incapable of admitting to mistakes, and never apologised – both characteristic of emotional immaturity. If you did not admire everything about him, you were a threat to him.[60]

---

60   E-mail communication from Manie van der Spuy, 25 September 2014.

Van Jaarsveld was the author of *Die ontwaking van Afrikanernasionalisme* (1957) (The awakening of Afrikaner nationalism) and a collection of essays titled *Lewende verlede* (1961) (Living past), which I rate highly. His criticism of Afrikaans historiography brought him into disfavour with historians attached to his alma mater, the University of Pretoria, in particular. They made the ridiculous allegation that he had been so heavily influenced by the Marxist Jan Romein, an esteemed Dutch historian under whom he had studied, that he became a Marxist himself.[61] As a result of his controversiality, Van Jaarsveld never became a member of the Broederbond.

Van Jaarsveld read more widely and in more languages about his field of study than anyone else. Yet it was only in 1958, at the age of 36, that he obtained a lectureship, at Unisa. He would only become a professor ten years later, in 1967, at the Rand Afrikaans University (RAU, now the University of Johannesburg).

In the early 1960s Van Jaarsveld's views changed radically. One of the reasons was the scathing attacks in the English press on a series of history textbooks for schools that he had written. Some of the criticism was unfair, in my view. A second reason was his conflict with Leonard Thompson. In 1964 Van Jaarsveld went on a three-month study visit to the United States. In Los Angeles he stayed at Thompson's home. There is no consensus about what occurred between the two of them, but a lifelong enmity was born there.

Van Jaarsveld wrote later that the relationship between the two of us at Unisa went wrong because of a disagreement about the marking of students' assignments.[62] I cannot recall anything of that nature, and am fairly sure that politics was the root of the problem. In 1965 Van Jaarsveld told Gerrit Schutte, a Dutch postgraduate student in history who spent that year at Unisa: "Giliomee is not of the Afrikaner historiography school . . . Giliomee is a liberalist!" As Schutte rightly observes: "In those years 'liberalist' was a damning label – something much worse than a communist."[63]

And yet Van Jaarsveld extended a hand of friendship to me after I became a lecturer at Stellenbosch in 1967. On 26 February 1969 he wrote in reply to a letter of mine that he had read my article "Onoorkomelike besware teen kontemporêre geskiedenis" (Insurmountable objections to contemporary history) in the journal *Standpunte* with "great satisfaction". He added that it was "well

---

61 FA Mouton, "FA van Jaarsveld (1922-1995): A Flawed Genius?"*Kleio*, 27, 1995, pp. 6-7.
62 Mouton, "Van Jaarsveld: A Flawed Genius?", p. 9.
63 E-mail communication from Gerrit Schutte, 23 November 2014.

motivated", and that it was in keeping with an essay he had published on the topic in 1966. He also wished me success with my doctoral dissertation and asked me to send him a copy.

On 27 July 1972, after having received a copy of my dissertation, he congratulated me on "the superb piece of work" and added that I had "truly left no stone unturned in acquiring information". He trusted that this would be the start of "a fruitful life of research". "We Afrikaners", he wrote, "have a deficit in historiography, but if everyone does his duty, it will gradually be eliminated."

As for my plan to spend 1973 at Yale University as a postdoctoral student of Leonard Thompson, he wished me a successful period of study, but added: "Resist the temptation to adopt the ideology of American liberalism there, also as far as your vision of history is concerned. They are looking for disciples; but we have to remain who we are."[64] Van Jaarsveld had mounted a campaign against the *Oxford History of South Africa*, and Leonard Thompson and those Van Jaarsveld referred to as his "disciples" were in his crosshairs. Both Afrikaner nationalism and apartheid were based to a crucial extent on a particular interpretation of history. Consequently, the battle among historians about divergent interpretations of South Africa's history was of vital importance, and anyone who deviated from the orthodoxy could expect strong and sometimes venomous criticism.

## Typical Stellenbosch "liberalists"

When I accepted a lectureship at Stellenbosch in 1967, the US was no longer the university of the early 1960s when Prime Minister Hendrik Verwoerd and Rector HB Thom had wielded the sceptre. While still an Afrikaner university, it was no longer an avowed *volksuniversiteit* built on the idea of an exclusive Afrikaner identity. There was space for debate and dissenting views, naturally within limits.

Few lecturers made better use of that space than Johannes Degenaar, an exceptional individual and an extraordinary philosophy lecturer. Unfortunately I had not been taught by him, but friends told me how he used to challenge them by means of the Socratic method to critically re-examine long-cherished truths. He was a Socratic "gadfly" who was intent on making the establishment as intellectually and morally uncomfortable as possible. He was at no stage an outsider, but rather operated in the tradition of loyal resistance, to use NP van Wyk Louw's term. He identified with Afrikaners and delivered his criticism from a position on the margins of the community.[65]

---

64   US Manuscripts Collection, letters from FA van Jaarsveld to the author.
65   André du Toit, Tribute at a memorial service for Johan Degenaar, 1 August 2015.

Because Degenaar had raised doubts in the minds of so many theological students about their calling, the university parked him in a separate department called political philosophy in 1963. This was to enable the *tokkelokke* to study philososphy without the risk of being confused by Degenaar. In 1969 André du Toit joined him in his department.

In 1958 Degenaar established a discussion group that consisted mainly of Stellenbosch lecturers, and followed this up with a second one a few years later. In the year of my arrival at Stellenbosch he formed a third group, known as the Junior Discussion Group. All three groups met monthly on a Friday night to thrash out an issue of topical interest after an introductory talk by a member or an informed outsider.

Among the members of my "junior group" were outstanding lecturers such as Frederik van Zyl Slabbert from sociology, André du Toit from political philosophy and Wolfgang Thomas from economics. The Junior Discussion Group became the forum for heated arguments in which Slabbert with his impressive analytical abilities and debating skills excelled in particular. He debunked one NP dogma after another.

Du Toit, who, like me, would later move across the Cape Flats to the University of Cape (UCT), observed in 2015: "I only really grasped the exceptional nature of Degenaar's Stellenbosch discussion group when I moved to Cape Town and UCT where no equivalent of this forum existed (and where we also failed, despite several attempts, to keep a similar discussion group going)."[66]

By the end of the 1960s John Vorster as prime minister and Dr Gerrit Viljoen as leading figure in the Broederbond made it clear that apartheid was not an end in itself but merely an instrument to promote Afrikaner power. It became more and more acceptable for lecturers to criticise aspects of apartheid. Whether an anti-apartheid lecturer would be promoted or not depended to a great extent on his or her departmental head. In the Sociology Department, for instance, where SP Cilliers was the head and Van Zyl Slabbert a lecturer, there were no problems, but I soon realised that the chances of "dissenters" in my department to be promoted were slim.

Van Jaarsveld had an ambivalent attitude towards Stellenbosch. Though he had a high regard for the History Department, and especially for the work of Piet van der Merwe, he had an aversion to those whom the English press referred to as the "Cape liberals". The term originated in the years 1960-61 when Piet Cillié, editor of *Die Burger*, led a short-lived revolt against Verwoerd's rigid apartheid policy and also pleaded for coloured MPs to represent coloured people in Parliament.

---

66   Du Toit, Tribute, 1 August 2015.

Besides SP Cilliers, Nic Olivier (Bantu law) and Jan Sadie (economics) were known for their support of radical adjustments to apartheid policy. After a speech that Cilliers had delivered by invitation at RAU, Van Jaarsveld stood up and declared: "Ladies and gentlemen, you have now had the opportunity to listen to a typical Stellenbosch liberalist." In reality, the extent of "Stellenbosch liberalism" was quite limited. Apart from Bennie Keet at the Theological Seminary, few strong voices of protest were raised from Stellenbosch in the 1950s when apartheid policy was finalised. In the late 1960s, when 3 500 coloured people were forced to move from Die Vlakte, a neighbourhood in the centre of Stellenbosch, *Die Burger* supported the evictions and Stellenbosch lecturers, with a few exceptions, kept silent.

Slabbert and I often attended an informal discussion group together with Nic Olivier, Jan Sadie, SP Cilliers and the United Party politician Japie Basson on the farm Joostenberg, which belonged to the father of a friend from my student days, Philip Myburgh. Sadie was incisive as well as cynical about Afrikaner politics, but Nic Olivier, an academic with a keen intellect, still spoke with resentment about Verwoerd.

Olivier was once part of a delegation from the South African Bureau for Racial Affairs (Sabra), an NP-aligned think tank, that went to see Verwoerd about the need for accelerated development of the homelands. He started reading out the memorandum he had prepared on the issue, only to be interrupted by Verwoerd, who declared: "I have read the document. Let me state what you wanted to tell me, and then say what you actually should have told me and then I shall give you my reply." Olivier considered this an enormous insult.

In 1967 the growing rift between conservative and more progressive elements in the NP over the issue of apartheid was given a name when Wimpie de Klerk, a newspaper editor, described the two factions as *verligtes* and *verkramptes*. While *verkramptes* were in favour of a return to rigid apartheid, *verligtes* remained loyal to the NP but advocated reforms and attempted to exert an influence from within the structures of the *volksbeweging*, notably the Broederbond.

People like Slabbert, Du Toit and I never regarded ourselves as *verligtes*, as we were not part of either the NP or the Broederbond. We did, however, propagate our point of view in the Afrikaans press or on platforms at the US. The distinction between our strategy of exerting influence and that of the *verligtes* can be likened to the one made by the economist and social scientist Albert Hirschman between "voice" and "exit" in his book *Exit, Voice, and Loyalty: Responses to Decline in Firms, Organizations, and States* (1970).

The "establishment *verligtes*" – a term coined by the *Rand Daily Mail* journalist Helen Zille – used the strategy of "voice" to advocate within the NP and Broederbond system for comprehensive reform. Olivier, Sadie and a few of us

younger academics had undergone an "exit" and criticised from outside the
system. Our argument against the *verligtes* was increasingly that their "voice"
did not amount to much if they kept silent in public, while not achieving a great
deal within the secret circle of the Broederbond either.

## Coloured citizenship

During the first ten to fifteen years of NP rule there was little criticism of apartheid from the Afrikaans university campuses. For a handful of law professors,
the moment of truth in the mid-1950s was the government's circumvention
of the entrenched clause in the Constitution that guaranteed coloured voting
rights, in its bid to remove coloured people from the voters' roll. After a number of court defeats the government enlarged the Senate and packed it with
NP-aligned senators, which enabled it to get the required two-thirds majority
to change the Constitution. In 1955 thirteen academics (two from Unisa and
eleven from the University of Pretoria) issued a statement in which they
rejected this measure. Not a peep was heard out of either Stellenbosch or the
University of the Orange Free State.

In the late 1960s the government introduced a Coloured Persons' Representative Council which would be responsible for affairs that affected only so-called
coloured people (as if a white-coloured division were possible at local government level). This body would liaise in an unspecified manner with Parliament,
which would remain white. Coloured local authorities would also be established. It would later prove that not a single coloured town had a sufficient tax
base to make the local authority self-sustaining. "Dormitory towns" was a term
that soon gained currency. What was very clear was that the coloured representatives would have limited funds and even more limited powers at their disposal.

And then, on 30 July 1971, a handful of Afrikaner academics cautiously
stirred the waters. A total of 29 academics from three universities issued a
public declaration in Pretoria in which they rejected the government's segregation of the coloured community and advocated full citizenship for them. A
few weeks later, a petition was issued by 109 Afrikaners in the Western
Cape, most of whom were Stellenbosch academics, which declared their support in principle for the Pretoria declaration and called for "equal and full
citizenship" for coloured people.[67]

My name was among those who had signed the petition. I also participated
in a conference that was subsequently held over a weekend in Grabouw to
work out comprehensive proposals, where I met coloured peers for the first

---

67   For a discussion, see Pierre Hugo, "The Politics of 'Untruth': Afrikaner Academics
     for Apartheid", *Politikon*, 25, 1, 1998, pp. 31-55.

time. Franklin Sonn, with his unique blend of self-mockery and satire, could convey harsh truths about apartheid in a way that made people blush.

My support of coloured rights was rooted in the realisation that the political exclusion of the coloured community was having the effect of completely alienating people with the same language and culture as the Afrikaners. The NP was in any case no longer in the precarious situation in which it had been when it embarked on its efforts to remove coloured voters from the voters' roll. As I noted before, in the early 1950s the NP had an effective majority of only five seats, and 100 000 fewer votes had been cast for the party than for the United Party (UP).

In 1970, however, the NP had 70 seats more than the UP in a 165-member House of Assembly, and almost 300 000 more votes had been cast for the NP than for the UP. It was inconceivable to me that the UP could mobilise 300 000 coloured votes for the explicit purpose of trumping the NP without running the risk of losing a large portion of its white support.

Moreover, the whites' sense of "being a nation" was no longer as fragile as it had been in the aftermath of the Second World War, when it was feared that competition for the coloured vote would exacerbate Afrikaner-English divisions in the white community. Military conscription for all white males, which had been in force since 1968, had given a considerable boost to a sense of white nationhood.

And yet the NP-aligned press and certain Afrikaner academics slated the two declarations in favour of coloured civil rights as an act of profound political ignorance and gross irresponsibility. Some claimed, with no substantiating proof, that the Progressive Party had inspired the petition, despite the fact that Helen Suzman, the sole Prog MP, had seldom if ever set foot in Stellenbosch.

The biggest disappointment for me was the stance taken by the *Burger* editor Piet Cillié, who had had a huge influence on my political thinking in my high-school and university days, and by Schalk Pienaar, whose Sunday paper *Die Beeld* had been at the forefront of innovative Afrikaner thinking in the late 1960s. (In 1970 *Die Beeld* merged with *Dagbreek en Landstem* and became the Sunday paper *Rapport*.)

Although the circumstances were now materially different, in an editorial in *Die Burger* Cillié persisted with his narrative of the early 1950s that an increasing coloured vote "holds the possibility of a calamitous disruption of our entire political system and a splitting apart of the white population". The editorial called for "ironclad guarantees" that coloured voters would not become a decisive factor in the white power struggle, "otherwise we only open the way to national schism and civil war".[68]

---

68   *Die Burger*, 3 September 1971.

Schalk Pienaar argued in his column in *Rapport* that white-coloured integration in Parliament was just as "nonsensical" as a coloured homeland. He foresaw that a parallel structure of white and coloured institutions could be developed. There was "an infinite amount" that could be done to make such a structure possible.[69] The column appeared under the heading "Stop scratching where it doesn't itch"– and that more than fifteen years after the NP had removed the coloured people from the voters' roll.

Some pro-NP Stellenbosch academics also immediately piled into us in letters to *Die Burger*.[70] Seven years later, Ivor Wilkins and Hans Strydom's book *The Super-Afrikaners: Inside the Afrikaner Broederbond* appeared, with 155 pages of membership lists. The lists revealed that six of the nine male lecturers from Stellenbosch who had written letters denouncing us were between 35 and 45 years old and had joined the AB fairly recently. (Two of the remaining three were probably members too, but they were close to retirement.)

The arguments of the critics varied. Dr Julius Jeppe maintained that the "declaration moles" were subtly propagating "the revolutionary democratic" (*sic*) standpoint of the Progressive Party; Prof. Sampie Terreblanche objected to the circulation of the petition as an anonymous document; Prof. Mike de Vries slammed the demand for full citizenship as premature; and Prof. Christoff Hanekom contended that the academics were prejudicing their profession "by compromising themselves with unknown groups". No evidence was provided for the claims.

The Rev. Nico Smith, who would later become a prominent opponent of apartheid, deplored the petition as something that would only serve to make the government's task more difficult. Prof. DJ Kotzé of the History Department, who had asked me five years earlier to apply for a post, declared that the government had created "gateways to development" for the coloured people during the preceding parliamentary session.

The negative attitude of the letter-writers came as a severe disappointment to me. In the discussion groups in Stellenbosch there was a great measure of consensus that the white-coloured relationship had to be resolved as speedily as possible so that the white-black "problem" could be tackled. A frustrated Slabbert gave *Die Burger* a message for the letter-writers: "Don't stroke my lapel in my lounge and make '*verligte* noises' which you are not prepared to avow in public."[71]

---

69   *Rapport*, 8 August 1971.
70   For the letters, see Hugo, "Politics of 'Untruth'".
71   Letter from F Van Zyl Slabbert, *Die Burger*, 12 August 1971.

The Labour Party, which had attracted the majority of votes in the election for the first Coloured Persons' Representative Council, endorsed our call for full civil rights. It was an illusion that relatively well-educated coloured people would support the government's plan, and this was precisely the stratum that the government sought to engage.

## Loyal resistance

Fifteen months after the petition, in October 1972, *Rapport* published a full-page article of mine under the heading "Loyal resistance: We must become real free burghers again". I cited NP van Wyk Louw's well-known essay of 1939 on the topic of loyal resistance, in which he wrote that the loyal critic should see it as his task to identify fossilised ideas that were inimical to the life of a *volk* and dispose of them through analysis.

I also drew attention to his warning that the danger for intellectuals did not lie in their being too remote from the *volk*. As Louw put it, it was rather the case that they were too deeply embedded in and part of the *volk*, "that they are imbued with its prejudices, its values, and are geared to winning its favour".

I added that we as academics had become semi-politicians – too mindful of what was practically possible "instead of positioning ourselves on the moral basis of: What is ethically permissible? What is right? What is fair?"

My assessment was that there would be little opposition from academics above the age of 35 if the government refused point-blank to redistribute power and income. I made a distinction between political nationalists, who put Afrikaners' political-power interests at the centre, and the cultural nationalists, who insisted on the pursuit of fairness, truth and justice. The latter group also demanded that the intellect and creativity of people with an Afrikaans background be harnessed for the refinement of the Afrikaners' national spirit and national character and the advancement of "common human values", as Van Wyk Louw called them. I added:

> It implies that we as Afrikaners, out of concern for our people, refuse to tolerate irrational arguments, half-truths and injustices from Afrikaners who act in the name of Afrikaners. It implies the refusal to slavishly accept the diktat of a party, a church or an establishment – Nat, Sap or Progressive.
>
> It implies the refusal to keep silent merely for the sake of party-political interests, and the renunciation of petty party-political loyalties – even if you lose your support in that party.

When I received an invitation from a student society to address them, I decided to talk about the way in which academics could promote reform. I started with Winston Churchill's words "We must be better British and worse nationalists", and added that if Afrikaners were to do the same, they had to become "better Afrikaners and worse nationalists".

It implied that as an Afrikaner you should not shrink from stating your view in public, and that if your view proved to be unpopular, "you do not relinquish it or go looking for support from another ethnic group". It boiled down to "retaining your freedom of speech and action in every matter". In so doing, the Afrikaners could become real free burghers again.[72]

## "Stellenbosch: Is anything happening there?"

The absence of any student support for the petition convinced me that fundamental political change among Stellenbosch lecturers and students would not happen soon. As a form of provocation, I wrote an article titled "Stellenbosch: Gaan daar iets aan?" (Stellenbosch: Is anything happening there?), which was published in *Deurbraak*, the Progressive Party's Afrikaans monthly. I used the pseudonym "Willem Adriaan", as I anticipated that NP-aligned academics would seize on an article under my own name as conclusive proof that I had always been motivated by "Prog" sympathies rather than my own convictions.

In the article I referred to the Stellenbosch tendency to assert: "What happens at Stellenbosch today is an indication of what will happen in South Africa in twenty years' time. What happens at Stellenbosch matters." It seemed to me as if students were unable or unwilling to adopt their own political course. I argued that, in reality, not much was happening at Stellenbosch.

Now and then an address by an NP speaker was poorly attended or the SRC sounded a timidly critical note, but almost all Afrikaans-speaking students still voted NP and about the same percentage was still firmly committed to the Dutch Reformed Church, which was in solidarity with the government on apartheid. In SRC elections, candidates who were aligned to the NP fared much better than those who were liberal. The *Matieland* magazine assured alumni that the conduct of the activist minority was unrepresentative.

To prove my point, I referred in my article to a conference held in Cape Town in 1971 where, for the first time, white student leaders conferred together with their black counterparts, including Steve Biko. The various conference papers were published in the volume *Student Perspectives on South Africa* (1972), edited by HW van der Merwe and David Welsh and published by David Philip.

---

72  *Rapport*, 18 October 1972.

Michiel le Roux, a member of the Stellenbosch SRC, candidly outlined the position of the Afrikaner students at the Cape Town conference. The political situation, he wrote, was too complex to be solved by means of a single scheme. *Verligte* students knew that even if they found a partial solution, it would be rejected by the political leaders and students themselves would not make the sacrifices it would require. Hence they had decided that they could best exert influence by remaining "acceptable to their community".

My article concluded: "Nothing is happening at Stellenbosch. In any event, nothing that matters to South Africa . . . There is a realisation of the deficiencies of separate development without alternatives being considered. *Verligtheid* is in the final instance the shallow political expression of a permissive society that still fills the church on Sundays."

On my return from the United States at the end of 1973, what disappointed me most was the cynical political commentary of Piet Cillié of *Die Burger*. For him, party politics was no longer about extending the more positive elements of NP policy, but about delivering a knock-out blow to the UP, which was in any case on its last legs. To this end, he resorted to obsolete forms of ethnic mobilisation. In the campaign for a by-election held in Oudtshoorn in 1972, he had written that the UP was driven by "*Boerehaat*" (hatred of Afrikaners). I said in an address to the student society SAAK at Stellenbosch that "*Boerehaat*" was an insult to voters' intelligence, and nothing more than "*Boerebedrog*" (duping of Afrikaners).[73]

## "Broeders" and "Ruiters"

I often wondered what lay behind the apparently spontaneous identification of Stellenbosch students with Afrikaner nationalism and apartheid, which was conspicuous on the campus up to the first year or two of the 1970s. Students of my generation had drawn inspiration from the proclamation of a republic and the rise of Afrikaans-oriented companies such as Rembrandt and Federale Mynbou/General Mining. In those days, the hope still existed that the home-land policy would offer a viable solution.

By the early 1970s, the picture was very different. Apartheid had become more and more controversial, and a new generation of black students, organised in the Black Consciousness Movement, rejected white domination unequivocally.

I only realised many years later that the student body's solid support for NP-aligned student leaders owed much to the behind-the-scenes machinations of the Afrikaner Broederbond (AB) and its youth wing, the Ruiterwag (RW).

---

73   *Cape Argus*, 24 April 1974.

The AB was not, as some studies would have it, the "power behind the throne", which devised policy on behalf of the cabinet. The Stellenbosch *verligtes* in the AB did encourage John Vorster's reform politics. But the major political influence resided in the church, in universities and in senior position at schools, where AB candidates had an inside track. It goes without saying that all the rectors of the Afrikaans universities were members of the AB in the 1970s.

Broeders went to great lengths to combat anyone who was perceived as a threat to the power and influence of the government, the AB or the RW. In 1965 Nico Smith, an AB member, was by his own admission appointed as professor in missiology at Stellenbosch over the heads of much better qualified candidates such as Jaap Durand and David Bosch. The latter two theologians were both critical of the dogma of apartheid.

In *Die Afrikaner Broederbond*, his insider's account of his experiences as an AB member, Smith told of his own involvement in forms of manipulation to promote NP and AB interests among the students.

The main organisation for this purpose was the RW, which had been established in the late 1950s to involve young Afrikaner men in a secret body that would serve as a source of potential members for the AB. According to Ernst Stals's authoritative study of the AB, Prof. HB Thom, the US rector, did not like the name that was initially used by the organisation, but he evidently supported the idea of such a body.

In August 1958 the organisation adopted the name Ruiterwag, while branches were called "*wagposte*" (guard posts). A senior AB member with the title of "*hoofwag*" (chief guard) was appointed to supervise the activities of the guard post in his town or city suburb.[74] Shortly after his arrival in Stellenbosch, Nico Smith became the "*hoofwag*" in the town. In that capacity he had to report regularly to the local Broeders on the activities of the Ruiterwag branch.

By the early 1970s the AB executive in Johannesburg noted with dismay that a "liberal spirit" was spreading among students. The executive dispatched two representatives to Stellenbosch to explore ways in which it could be curbed, and possible causes for this tendency were discussed. Smith wrote: "The conclusion was that certain lecturers were responsible for engendering the critical spirit towards Afrikaners and the government." When it was suggested that RW members be asked to act as informants in the classes of

74 ELP Stals, "Die geskiedenis van die Afrikaner-Broederbond, 1918-1994", manuscript commissioned by the AB Executive Council, submission date September 1998.

certain lecturers, the proposal was vehemently opposed by Jannie de Villiers, the US rector and himself a RW member, and the plan was dropped.

The RW was obviously active on the US campus, but its influence varied from year to year. One of its main functions was to ensure that the right people were elected or appointed to key positions in the student community. They had to attend meetings and sound early warnings if an individual or a student society was unsympathetic towards the "Afrikaner cause".

The RW put in much effort to get the right people elected to the SRC. In 1972 all the RW-backed candidates were elected, and they formed the majority of members on the council. At a post-election meeting held at Smith's home, an RW member who had been an election officer recounted gleefully how he had entered the names of RW candidates into the machine by utilising unused punch cards. Smith wrote that he had been appalled by this election fraud, but the RW members downplayed the matter as part of student politics and nothing more than "healthy student fun".

The US academics who were AB members performed a special function by serving as as a think tank for the NP and the government. The working papers they prepared carried weight with the AB executive and were distributed countrywide among AB divisions. Ministers and even prime ministers often came to address the AB divisions in Stellenbosch. For the Stellenbosch Broeders, it was important that the university in the town be seen as an institution that was in the vanguard of Afrikaner nationalist thinking.

In May 1973 Smith resigned from the AB. His action was prompted by a request from the AB's executive council in Johannesburg that all AB members confirm their undivided loyalty to the NP with their signatures. Getting the AB members to declare their loyalty to the NP leadership was part of Prime Minister John Vorster's battle against the ultra-rightists under the leadership of Jaap Marais and Albert Hertzog.

Throughout the years the AB's official policy had been that the organisation promoted the Afrikaners' cultural interests, not those of any political party, and that it refrained from interference in party-political differences in Afrikaner ranks. The party-political demand from the head office finally shattered that illusion. Smith was not prepared to sign his name as a confirmation of his loyalty to the NP, and withdrew from the AB.

After his resignation, Smith attended my second-year course on European history as a registered student. In this course I put the emphasis on revolutions and uprisings in European history. I wondered why a theology professor would attend my classes. Perhaps my lectures had drawn the attention of the AB at an earlier stage, and he wanted to find out for himself what they were all about.

## A question of relationships

One of the first things that struck me on my return from the United States at the end of 1973 was the alarm among political observers about the political stagnation that had set in in the Vorster government. Among the first expressions of this concern was the establishment of the movement known as Verligte Aksie. Advocate Johann Kriegler from Johannesburg, who would serve as chair of the Independent Electoral Commission twenty years later, was appointed national president.

In 1974 Kriegler visited Stellenbosch to found a branch in the south. To this end, one of the very first racially mixed public meetings was held since the advent of a republic. What soon became clear was how deeply rooted the coloured people's grievances were. Not only had more than 3 000 residents been forced to move from Die Vlakte, an established neighbourhood in the centre of town, five or six year earlier, but in the new "coloured township" of Cloetesville, on the outskirts of town, there was intially an acute lack of public amenities.

In "white" Stellenbosch there were virtually no cafés where people other than whites could enjoy a cold drink. Except for the square behind the town hall, there were hardly any public toilet facilities. Cafés where coloured people could sit down at a table were nonexistent. Restaurants and hotels admitted only white customers. The university was reserved for white students.

After Kriegler had addressed the audience, it was decided to set up a committee that would work towards improved facilities for coloured people, and I was appointed to take the matter further. The community leaders I approached to serve on the committee all agreed to participate.

The founding meeting of what was called the Stellenbosch Public Liaison Committee took place on 6 August 1975. Piet Lombard, a former mayor, was elected as chairman and I became secretary. There were eighteen other members who represented various organisations. Meetings were held five times a year.

The greatest revelation for me was, on the one hand, the large-scale neglect of the needs of coloured and black people, and, on the other, the cautious approach of the committee to avoid offending white people. For example, the Stellenbosch committee requested developers to "consider" rest and recreation facilities for coloured workers in the town's central business district.

Sometimes matters were raised that only coloured members felt strongly about, such as not being able to conduct burials on Sundays because of municipal regulations. After representations by the liaison committee, the request for permission was granted. I could scarcely imagine anything less radical than serving on a committee of this nature, but for those who suffered the effects of the "sticking points" the alleviation of these burdens was a priority.

The government subsequently jumped on the liaison committee bandwagon, as nearly all the white members were pro-NP and all of the coloured members were moderate, and established similar committees across the province. After the introduction of the Tricameral Parliament, these committees disappeared.

## An anonymous defamatory letter

On 24 September 1972 Professor Kotzé, at that stage the chair of the History Department, received a letter that put me in a very bad light. The letter was anonymous, but purportedly came from students and ex-students. There was little doubt in my mind that the sender was one of the lecturers in the department.

The sixteen-point "charge sheet" lodged both academic and political complaints. According to the former, I frequently came to class unprepared and had a "casual attitude" towards my work. In addition, there was no structure in my work, I was never on time for my lectures, my marking of tests and practical assignments was sloppy, and the marks I awarded were "unjustified". I left most of my work to students in the form of self-study, and prescribed English textbooks because I was "too lazy" to adapt the material in my notes.

The political charges included the following: that I subtly sought to put the government in an unfavourable light during my lectures; that I had alienated numerous ex-students from the university through my political views and engagement in anti-government correspondence in the press; that I approached history subjectively and slanted it to fit my personal "progressive political views". The letter demanded that these problems be rectified, or that I be removed. Such measures would supposedly be to the "advantage" of the department and of history as a subject.

Professors Van der Merwe and Kotzé summoned me and asked for my response to the charges in the letter. I replied that no reputable institution paid attention to anonymous letters, and that I expected the university, and the department in particular, to do the same. The professors indicated that because of the anonymity of the letter, they would give it no further consideration.

I was going the leave the matter there, but a week or so later I heard that an identical letter had been sent to the chairman of the University Council. On 10 October 1972 I requested the registrar to destroy the anonymous letter and to ask the professors in the department to do the same. If this was not acceptable, I wrote, the university should appoint a committee with the power to summon students to testify and to read all my notes in order to establish whether any of the allegations were true. It should then make a finding as to whether I had broken any rule. I sent copies of my letter to the registrar to the two professors in my department.

No record exists of a reply from the university. Perhaps the matter was settled verbally, but it is also possible that the university did not reply to my request. My experience with the anonymous letter made me realise that there was an invisible enemy somewhere who had no scruples about using dirty tricks to undermine me.

## A first book

Early in 1974 I began revising my dissertation, which had been accepted for publication by HAUM Publishers. In the last year or two of my work on the dissertation I had had several disagreements with Prof. Kotzé, the supervisor, and Prof. Van der Merwe, the internal examiner. Kotzé insisted on stylistic changes with which I disagreed, while Van der Merwe made me keep strictly to what the documents said about a particular matter. The external examiner, Prof. JJ (Os) Oberholzer of the University of the Orange Free State, observed afterwards: "My overriding impression was: Here is a student who was reined in too tightly."

I was eager to revise the manuscript for publication as I saw fit. Apparently this sparked anxiety on the part of my professors, and they gave permission for publication on the express condition that I declared in the preface that the supervisor and the internal examiner accepted no responsibility for the amendments. The dissertation of Diko van Zyl, a fellow lecturer, was published a year later, without a similar declaration in his preface.

I wrote a new preface for my book, *Die Kaap tydens die eerste Britse bewind, 1795-1803* (HAUM, 1975). I thanked both my professors for their comments which had improved the dissertation, and also expressed my gratitude to Leonard Thompson, who, as I put it, "stimulated me to try and view South African history also as a process of interaction between the different population groups".

I noted that many of the previous studies of the late eighteenth century overestimated the whites' military power and displayed a strong aversion to social equality between the races. On the other hand, there were historians who had no appreciation of the fears of the whites, espcially those who farmed in the unsafe frontier zone. I added that I had attempted to offer a "non-ideological" interpretation that met the demands of our time. Actually, I was a bit naïve, as no one can ever be free of an ideology of some kind.

After the year at Yale I found myself on the horns of a dilemma. On the one hand there was Thompson, who certainly expected initially that I would subscribe to the liberal approach in due course, while Floors van Jaarsveld, on the other hand, regarded me as a protégé of Thompson. In the Afrikaans world, Van Jaarsveld was the most prominent historian on the South African scene between 1970 and 1990. He was a prolific author of textbooks and works on the theory of history.

## Rebellion or anarchy?

In 1971 Van Jaarsveld delivered a series of seventy radio talks on Afrikaner history, which were subsequently published as *Afrikaner, quo vadis?* (Voortrekkerpers, 1971). The work was reminiscent of that of HB Thom in the 1940s and 1950s. Both saw the Afrikaners as exposed to the fierce assaults of the time and endeavoured to use nationalist historiography to fortify them against the attacks.

In *Afrikaner, quo vadis?* Van Jaarsveld projected the origins of the Afrikaner nation back into the distant past. Jan van Riebeeck was portrayed as the founder of the white nation, and Simon van der Stel as the "father" of the Afrikaner *volk*. According to Van Jaarsveld, "a new person" had been born from Dutch, German and French ancestors: the Afrikaner. Van Jaarsveld's view amounted to an anachronistic projection of his present-day nationalist sentiments onto the past. It was the "*volksgeskiedenis*" from which professional historians, including Van Jaarsveld himself in his pre-1960 publications, had broken away.

In one of the talks Van Jaarsveld attacked the *Oxford History* for its interpretation of the burgher rebellions of 1795 in Graaff-Reinet and Swellendam, when disgruntled burghers rose up against the authorities. In the *Oxford History*, the uprising was portrayed as a protest against the attempt of the government in Cape Town to use the courts to curb farmers' abuse of their workers. For Van Jaarsveld, however, it was a revolt, aimed at self-determination, against an oppressive government. He saw it as comparable to the American War of Independence.[75]

In my research for my doctoral dissertation, I had read all the primary sources regarding the rebellions in the Cape Archives. During my year at Yale University I worked on an academic article in which I argued that the rebellions should not be seen purely and simply as an expression of democracy. A small group of burghers from one or two divisions had seized power and tried

---

75   FA van Jaarsveld, *Afrikaner, quo vadis?* (Johannesburg: Voortrekkerpers, 1971), p. 50.

to impose their will on the burghers in the other divisions. The rebellions could even be regarded as a case of lawlessness.

The leaders of the rebels from the southeastern divisions of the Graaff-Reinet district were known for being stormy petrels. They insisted that commandos be called out to drive the Xhosa in the Zuurveld back across the Fish River and to recapture the cattle they had seized from the burghers in the 1793 frontier war. The burghers from the northern divisions, on the other hand, maintained that they were fully occupied in fighting the Bushmen, and that the Graaff-Reinet district lacked the resources to open a new front against the Xhosa. Landdrost Honoratus Maynier supported them.

Some burghers from the southeast then deposed the landdrost and chose self-styled *"representanten des volks"* (representatives of the people) who attended the meetings of the Board of Heemraden. There is no evidence that they were democratically elected. In both Graaff-Reinet and Swellendam the rebels expressed a desire for their districts to fall directly under the rule of the new republic in the Netherlands, but there was no indication that they had the support of the burghers in the other divisions. I argued that the rebellions were not democratic as such. They were at the same time expressions of individualism, which is a prerequisite for democracy, and of anarchy, which is a denial thereof.

When I submitted the paper to the *South African Historical Journal*, it was sent to Van Jaarsveld for review. He rejected it. Rodney Davenport, the editor, was upset about this, and advised me to amend the article slightly by including a similar rebellion on the American colonial frontier and comparing it with the rebellions on the Cape eastern frontier. This article appeared in the *Journal* in 1974, probably to Van Jaarsveld's consternation. Not only was my article in English, but it had been published as a result of the intervention of an English-speaking editor.

## A controversial review

Unbeknown to me, I made a sworn enemy of Van Jaarsveld because of reviews I wrote of his work. The first one, written while I was in the United States, appeared in *Die Burger* on 20 September 1973. Here I referred to the question Van Jaarsveld had posed with regard to the *Oxford History*: "Can a foreigner with a hostile mindset construct a historical image of the Afrikaner that is acceptable to the Afrikaner?"

In the review, I made a distinction between *volksgeskiedenis* and scientific history, and explained that in the case of *volksgeskiedenis* one was dealing with collective memories of past events, heroes and glorious deeds. It could be viewed as a community's memory, which is often a mixture of facts and fiction. To me, Van Jaarsveld's notion of a national history that is "owned" by a people was irreconcilable with scientific historiography. It should rather be termed *volksgeskiedenis*, or nationalist history. An approach like this, I wrote, would turn history into "a hermetically sealed system". Afrikaans historiography would "only have a future if it strives to free the past from mythical and ideological interpretations".[76]

In contrast to *volksgeskiedenis*, I wrote, scientific historiography sought to create a truthful representation of history, based on sound source-based research and the rejection of prejudices. I added that if Afrikaans historians were to disregard new insights in the field of scientific historiography, it would be a great loss. "The Afrikaner historian who prioritises the demands of *volksgeskiedenis* runs the risk of allotting the Afrikaner a position that is un-African (not from Africa), while at the same time cutting himself off from ties that connect him as a scholar to European historiography."

For Van Jaarsveld, the last straw was my review of his collection of essays titled *Geskiedkundige verkenninge* (Historical explorations) that appeared in *Die Burger* of 8 August 1974. This work included his sharp criticisms of the *Oxford History* in an essay that dated back to 1969, in which he argued that the book presented an unacceptable image of the Afrikaners. Van Jaarsveld wrote: "Every cultural group will construct its *own* historical image, as it is part of its national myth, part of itself." He noted that he objected violently if this image came under attack. He concluded with the observation: "A historical image is [part of] the spiritual heritage, the cultural heritage, of every ethnic or cultural group." In his eyes, the *Oxford History* was aimed at impairing the Afrikaner's "spirit", at degrading his or her "cultural heritage".[77]

On 21 August, two weeks after the publication of this review, Van Jaarsveld wrote to my departmental chairman, Prof. Dirk Kotzé. He objected strongly to my review, as well as the one that had appeared on 20 September 1973. His main grievance was that I had labelled his views as propagating *volksgeskiedenis*, and had presented scientific history as the kind of historiography that professional historians should practise.

Van Jaarsveld asked why I was so intent on protecting the *Oxford History*. In his opinion, the only explanation was that I subscribed to liberalism and was a

---

76   *Die Burger*, 8 August 1974.
77   Van Jaarsveld's article originally appeared in *Standpunte* in 1969. It was republished in FA van Jaarsveld, *Geskiedkundige verkenninge* (Pretoria: Van Schaik, 1974), pp. 166-186.

member of the Progressive Party. He warned that I was harming the image of the department and informed Kotzé that he had heard from various quarters that they had a "liberalist" on their staff. The letter concluded as follows: "Needless to say, I have always held your department in high regard. It would be a pity if Giliomee were to continue publicly (and possibly in front of students) with his practice of discrediting and suspicion-mongering."[78]

Kotzé replied:

> We are aware of Giliomee's views and actions, and we in the Department are keeping a vigilant eye on him. Up to now, however, in his work in the Department he has not given us any reason to act. He makes sure that when it comes to his academic work in the Department, he keeps to the laid-down rules, regulations and code . . . But I can assure you that within the Department, we have no intention of putting up with nonsense; outside it, however, it is more difficult.
>
> As far as Giliomee's academic future is concerned, it would not surprise me if he saw it as outside the Afrikaans universities. He is in close contact with lecturers in his age group at several English universities, including UCT and Wits.

On 23 August Van Jaarsveld wrote to Diko van Zyl, one of my colleagues in the department. He offered him a lecturership in the History Department of the Rand Afrikaans University, which he headed. After stating that a great task of writing the country's history awaited Afrikaner historians, he continued:

> More needs to be done, precisely from the side of Afrikaans speakers, who have originated here and who love the country. The country has to be "fallen in love with" historically. We must reveal the past to ourselves – also to others. We may not follow foreign gods. This can lead to scientific alienation and barrenness, yes, to disloyalty.

Van Jaarsveld also noted the high regard he had for the department at Stellenbosch, and considered it regrettable that there was "a negative voice emanating from the History Department that is causing great and, yes, near irreparable damage to the university's public image". He continued:

---

78   This letter and other letters quoted in this section are part of the FA van Jaarsveld Collection in the library of the University of Pretoria. The collection has been opened for research.

[It is] the voice of a liberalist, who discredits and sows suspicion where it is unwarranted. This has set tongues wagging here in the North, believe me. The little grey fox sometimes feeds off the prey caught by the lion – with ingratitude.

On 4 September Van Zyl replied in a letter to Van Jaarsveld:

Unfortunately, we indeed have a snake in our midst. This just re-emphasises the fact that in appointing someone in a department like this, one should not take only academic grounds into account. Now we are stuck with a person (who is a very poor lecturer to boot) who arrogates to himself the right to criticise competent, honest and sincere historians and other academics and put them in a negative light.

I can assure you that he is a huge embarrassment to me and other colleagues in our History Department, and to our university. But one should take it from whom it comes: a little grey fox who himself has not yet achieved anything to speak of, and who is bent on fraternising with liberalist English-speaking historians in South Africa and America.

Van Jaarsveld wrote back on 25 September. He stated that he was glad the department now realised it had "a snake in their midst", and that it was fortunate this tendency was limited to a single individual.

## A lawyer's letter

In 1977 Piet van der Merwe reached the compulsory retirement age of 65. There was a tragic air about him during the last decades of his academic career. The fact that he had not published any book of stature since 1944 was a source of intense frustration to him. He told me once that he had done enough research to produce eight books, but that he could not bring himself to finalise the manuscripts for publication. In my first years as lecturer I occasionally played a round of golf with him at the Stellenbosch golf course, and got to know him as a man with wide interests and an original outlook.

Gradually our relationship deteriorated. I objected to the department's refusal to allow lecturers to do any important teaching work and wrote him a long memorandum on the issue, but received no reply. On one occasion he told me: "You are the only one who has raised your horns in the department, and you shouldn't complain now if you run into problems." When I asked Prof. H van der Merwe Scholtz, professor in Afrikaans at UCT, why Van der Merwe's interpersonal relations were so poor, his response was: "The problem with Piet van der Merwe is that he doesn't like himself."

Both Diko van Zyl and I applied for Van der Merwe's post. C Vann Woodward agreed to be one of my referees. After Woodward's death in 1999, David Brion Davies, a colleague of his at Yale and one of the foremost authorities on the history of slavery in America, described Woodward in the *New York Review of Books* as "the most respected, honored, and influential American historian of the post-World War II era".

During Woodward's visit to South Africa the year before he had hosted one of my honours seminars. Though he was unable to read Afrikaans, he had read my English publications as well as the first drafts of my chapters on the Afrikaners that were subsequently published in *Ethnic Power Mobilized*. In his letter in support of my application he commented positively on my work. I realised later that Woodward's letter would not have been of much help. The history of race relations in the United States was not taught in our department, and few people at Stellenbosch had any knowledge of Woodward.

To fill the vacant chair of South African history, the university appointed a three-person subcommittee consisting of two geographers and Prof. Kotzé of the History Department. The panel recommended to the Senate that Van Zyl be appointed. When the recommendations came up for discussion at a Senate meeting, several members enquired from the floor why I had not been recommended. One was Prof. Sampie Terreblanche from the Economics Department, who described me as the better candidate, and another was Prof. John Thompson from the English Department. He told me afterwards that he had initially intended to refrain from comment, as he saw the matter as an intra-Afrikaner issue, but then he imagined the likely reaction of his wife if he kept quiet: "John, you sat there and said nothing!"

Kotzé became upset during the Senate meeting and made certain allegations about my work that were untrue. Among other things, he said that large parts of my study *Die Kaap tydens die eerste Britse bewind*, which people were now enthusing about, had in fact been written "by yours truly" (in other words, by himself), and that I had done virtually no archival research.

I was strongly advised to insist that Kotzé withdraw his allegations, otherwise they would leave a black mark on my reputation as an academic. I requested Deon Malherbe, a lawyer friend, to take the necessary steps. On 18 August 1977 he informed the rector in a letter that both senior and junior advocates had told him Kotzé's allegations could be cause for "a viable defamation lawsuit". He added: "It is, however, Dr Giliomee's explicit request that the dispute be resolved in a collegial manner."

Malherbe then had a meeting with the rector, the registrar and the dean of the Law Faculty, where it was decided that the following declaration would be included in the agenda of the next Senate meeting:

1   That in so far as the impression may have been created during the Senate meeting of 5 August that Dr HB Giliomee's work as a researcher is not of a meritorious nature, such an impression is erroneous;
2   That Dr Giliomee, for the purposes of his doctoral dissertation as well as his publications, and particularly the publication *Die Kaap tydens die eerste Britse bewind*, spent long periods doing personal research, in respect of archival sources in particular;
3   That the above-mentioned publication, namely *Die Kaap tydens die eerste Britse bewind*, is Dr Giliomee's own work.

As promised, the declaration was included in the agenda of the next Senate meeting.

Van Zyl was appointed professor in South African history at the end of 1977. According to the book *The Super-Afrikaners*, he became a member of the Broederbond in the same year.

Early in 1978 Kotzé informed me that I could henceforth lecture on South African history. As I have mentioned, I had been keen to do so since my arrival at Stellenbosch, but Prof. Van der Merwe kept turning down my requests.

As head of the department after Van der Merwe's retirement, Kotzé was in a position to reconsider the decision. While knowing full well that I would not teach the kind of South African history he would have preferred, he granted my request nevertheless. It was an attempt from his side to put relations between us on a slightly better footing.

## Tarring and feathering

Meanwhile, the Soweto uprising of 1976 and escalating international pressure had brought about a new reversal of Van Jaarsveld's views. Now he contended that nationalist historiography had become obsolete and hidebound. In 1979, in a conference paper, he placed the vow the Voortrekkers had taken before the Battle of Blood River in December 1838 within a secular context. He stated, inter alia, that the Afrikaner people were not the only nation to have believed that God was on their side.

Just before he was due to speak at the conference, a group of forty men from the right-wing paramilitary group the Afrikaner Weerstandsbeweging (AWB) stormed the stage, grabbed Van Jaarsveld and tarred and feathered him. Among the ten people who were later charged was Eugène Terre'Blanche, who had founded the movement ten years earlier. Their advocate declared that they had adopted Van Jaarsveld's book *Afrikaner, quo vadis?* as their own philosophy of life. They were appalled that Van Jaarsveld, who had signalled the way ahead for them, had now gone off the rails and even slighted the Day of the Vow.[79] Evidently they regarded Van Jaarsveld as a snake in the grass.

---

79   *Hoofstad*, 29 June 1979.

*Chapter 6*

# Civil war in "The John"

Before I left for Yale University in January 1973, my intention had been to remain in the History Department of the University of Stellenbosch until my retirement. Moreover, I had been especially keen to become involved in the Afrikaner debate on apartheid and nationalism. Ten years later I was in the employ of the University of Cape Town as professor of political studies, a subject I had never studied, and virtually all my popular and academic writing was now conducted in English.

By the mid-1970s history started to catch up with white South Africa. In 1974-75 Portugal's control over its colonies in southern Africa collapsed and the tide turned against the Smith government in Rhodesia. Towards the end of 1975 South African troops invaded Angola to help impose a government of national unity. In spite of the fact that conscripts were also involved, the public was kept completely in the dark for several months.

In June 1976 the report of the Theron commission of inquiry into the position of the coloured people was tabled. Erika Theron, the chairperson, and two other members, Sampie Terreblanche and Ben Vosloo, signed the majority report. It, too, stressed the large-scale neglect of coloured interests and needs and called for coloured representation at all levels of government.

On 16 June 1976 the Soweto uprising erupted. Three months later, while the riots were still raging, I drew a parallel in *Die Burger* of 18 September 1976 with the riots that had broken out in the summer of 1965 in the black neighbourhood of Watts in Los Angeles. For four "long, hot summers" (from 1965 to 1968) there had been riots in black neighbourhoods in major cities across the United States.

In my article I pointed to the report of the Kerner Commission which had been appointed in 1967 to investigate the causes of the United States riots and recommend solutions. Its basic conclusion was that their nation was "moving toward two societies, one black, one white – separate and unqual". The commission found that black people's destruction of buildings and public facilities was not "senseless", as many in the United States (and also in South Africa) claimed. On the contrary, the destruction had succeeded in casting a sharp light on the alienation of black people, a large proportion of whom lived in wretched circumstances.

I wrote that the alleviation of extensive poverty and unemployment was one of the preconditions for stability. Even more critical, however, was the need for a political dispensation that would ensure black people could identify with the government, the police and the social order. The message for South Africa from the four long, hot summers in the United States was clear.

## A programme on southern Africa

I was invited to spend the 1977/78 academic year at Yale University as one of four research fellows in their newly established Southern African Research Program, commonly known as SARP. Leonard Thompson was the director. Until 1994 the programme awarded year-long fellowships to three or four reseachers annually. Fellows had no lecturing duties, but it was expected that they would make full use of the opportunity to publish their research on southern Africa in books or articles.

Richard Elphick and I were now able to meet regularly as co-editors to finalise the editing of our book on early South African society, the project we had started in 1973 and to which nine historians eventually contributed. *The Shaping of South African Society, 1652-1820* (Wesleyan University Press and Maskew Miller) was published in 1979.

I also started working with the political philosopher André du Toit on a source publication of relevant primary documents that would show how Afrikaners had reacted to various major challenges in the past. We pointed out how difficult it was to define "the Afrikaner", and highlighted the great diversity that existed within Afrikaner thinking. In 1983 the first volume, *Afrikaner Political Thought, 1780-1850*, was published by the University of California Press and David Philip Publishers in Cape Town.

Most of my time, however, was spent on a project in which I collaborated with Heribert Adam, one of the other SARP fellows, in analysing the political, economic and social position of the Afrikaner community. We also asked whether the Afrikaner power elite would be able to introduce necessary reforms before the country became caught up in a civil war. In 1979 Yale University Press published our book under the title *Ethnic Power Mobilized: Can South Africa Change?* in which Adam and I published our chapters under our own names.

Adam and I struck up not only an academic relationship but also a close friendship. Our backgrounds differed radically. Whereas I had grown up in a peaceful country town, he had narrowly survived the Allies' bombing attacks on his home town near Frankfurt in Germany as a young boy. While I had completed my studies at the *"volksuniversiteit"* of Stellenbosch, he had received his doctoral degree from the Frankfurt Institute for Social Research, which was held in high esteem in radical leftist circles in particular at the time.

Adam read widely and reflected deeply, which enabled him to come up with fresh and challenging ideas. In his first book, *Modernizing Racial Domination: South Africa's Political Dynamics* (1971), he argued that South Africa was not a police state but rather a pragmatic racial oligarchy. The NP government would in the short to medium term retain the ability to adjust its strategies in order to preserve Afrikaner power. He added, however, that apartheid would require ever greater sacrifices.

In his chapters for *Ethnic Power Mobilized*, Adam made many points with which I identified completely. He attacked the notion that black exclusion should be explained as a manifestation of racism based on the supposed biological inferiority of black people. For him, it made more sense to see it as a case of whites clinging to power because they feared blacks' numerical superiority and their ability to compete at certain job levels. Adam also contended that a group that found itself under pressure would not necessarily become more unified; it was also likely that they might split under pressure. This was indeed what happened three years later with the Afrikaners.

In my own chapters I focused on Afrikaner identity, Afrikaners' economic interests, and the political system that was dominated by the NP government. In an earlier book, Dirk Kotzé of the US History Department had defined an Afrikaner as a member of an exclusive, white community who belonged to "typically Afrikaans institutions", such as one of the Reformed Churches and the National Party.

I disagreed strongly with this definition and demonstrated how over more than three centuries the construct of Afrikaner identity had undergone frequent changes depending on political circumstances. During the nineteenth and early twentieth centuries, leaders often used the term "Afrikaner" for those in the white community, regardless of language, who were loyal to South Africa. During election campaigns in the 1920s, some NP leaders referred to coloured people as fellow Afrikaners when attempting to capture their vote. In the 1970s, half of the Afrikaners indicated in a survey that they were prepared to accept a coloured person as an Afrikaner.

In my chapter on the Afrikaners' economic rise, I could rely on research by Jan Sadie and Sampie Terreblanche that showed how rapidly the Afrikaners had advanced between the early 1930s and the mid-1970s – from a community in which blue-collar workers and struggling farmers predominated to one where a middle class took the lead. The income gap between Afrikaners and English-speaking whites had shrunk considerably.

I described the changing economic scene. Appeals that Afrikaners still needed to stand together to narrow the gap between them and the English community were fading. Instead, the government and business people now strove to persuade black people to use the free market to make blacks as a community more prosperous, as the Afrikaners had done between 1910 and 1975. I was sceptical of the likely success of these efforts, noting that there was a clear tendency on the part of blacks to regard political power and control of the state rather than the capitalist system as the key to the economic rise of the black population.[80]

I emphasised that influx control was skewing the labour market completely. Black workers with urban residential rights earned five to six times more on average than rural blacks. The urban areas were sucking in desperate people from farms and homelands who were in search of a job and a better life. The demolition of the squatter settlements that had sprung up around the cities would not stem the tide of black urbanisation.

In a third chapter I described how the Afrikaner *volksbeweging* operated under John Vorster. The church, the universities, the FAK (Federation of Afrikaans Cultural Assocations) and the Broederbond were still closely connected under the overarching leadership of the NP government. As prime minister, Vorster ran the cabinet like a ramshackle family firm in a country town. Proper minutes were not kept of cabinet meetings, and state departments were allowed great freedom of action as long as they kept within broad policy. This lack of firm direction and control made it possible for some officials to undermine the government's dismantling of apartheid.

## A glimpse into the future

By the time 1980 arrived I sensed that South Africa's fate would be decided in the coming decade. As I never managed to interview Vorster's successor, PW Botha, I was unable to form an impression of the kind of leader he was. Botha was aware of my existence, however, and in 1988 he would warn the NP caucus against me and my co-author Lawrie Schlemmer as "snakes in the grass".

---

80   Hermann Giliomee and Heribert Adam, *Afrikanermag: Opkoms en toekoms* (Stellenbosch: Universiteitsuitgewers, 1981), p. 143.

I increasingly commented critically in the English press on the reforms that were introduced under the Botha administration. The *Cape Times* and the *Rand Daily Mail* published a lunch-time lecture I had given at the University of the Witwatersrand (Wits), titled "Botha's First Year as Prime Minister", as a centre-page article. In this lecture I argued that serious conflict was brewing in a situation where blacks enjoyed the same rights as other workers under labour legislation yet were still excluded from any meaningful political rights.[81]

As a result of the attendant publicity I was invited to join the discussion group Synthesis/Sintese, which had 25 to 30 members, most of whom lived in Johannesburg. It was made up of business leaders, black and white newspaper editors, black community leaders, progressive politicians and a few academics. The group met once a month in Johannesburg, usually at the home of Clive Menell, one of the senior executives of the Anglovaal mining conglomerate. The business leaders set up a fund from which the travel and accommodation costs of black members and "poor" academics (in whose ranks I fell) were paid. The regular contact with these opinion-formers assisted me greatly in looking further politically than the top of Stellenbosch's Papegaaiberg.

An important influence on my thinking was the work I did in my spare time as political coordinator of the Unit for Futures Research, which was housed in the Economics Faculty at Stellenbosch. The unit was sponsored by Rembrandt and several other top companies, and analyses were sent to the sponsors on a regular basis. Philip Spies, the head of the unit, and I had been residence friends during our student days. He believed that the way in which historians studied change over time could also be used to examine the political future that was unfolding in the country.

In one of my first political analyses I quoted from the American economist Robert Heilbroner's well-known book *The Future as History: The Historic Currents of Our Time and the Direction in Which They Are Taking America* (1960). Despite being a life-long socialist, Heilbroner was one of the few who declared, prior to the collapse of the Soviet Union, that the capitalist system had defeated socialism decisively. He did not see the future as an endless series of surprises, but as the past playing itself out in a predictable manner.

In my first newsletter, "The Message from Zimbabwe", which the unit issued in March 1980, I noted that Robert Mugabe's movement, with which the Smith government had not wanted to negotiate, had received almost two-thirds of the votes in an election – the first democratic election in independent

---

81    Hermann Giliomee, *The Parting of the Ways: South African Politics* (Cape Town: David Philip, 1981), pp. 14-23.

Zimbabwe – that was considered legitimate by the international community. The lesson for South Africa was that moderate black leaders who were acceptable to whites were soon rejected by their traditional followers when a revolutionary movement was allowed to enter the country and participate in politics.

My major blind spot was that I did not foresee the resurgence of the African National Congress (ANC) between 1980, when it was still largely an ineffective organisation in exile, and September 1992, when it effectively assumed power.

Another development I failed to foresee was that the ANC would replace its futile strategy of guerrilla warfare with a much more effective "people's war" in the early 1980s. Nor did I anticipate that ethnic differences in the black community, with the exception of the rural Zulu people, would fade away when Nelson Mandela emerged as a unifying figure even while he and his comrades were still in prison. By making Mandela into a martyr and by alienating Mangosuthu Buthelezi, the NP government ensured its own demise.

## The political pulse

In early 1980 I travelled through the country in an effort to gauge the political pulse. In Ulundi I had a long interview with Mangosuthu Buthelezi. He was one of the most complex politicians I ever met. He could be charming, frank and sociable, but became cold and unapproachable the moment he suspected a lack of respect. I got the impression he was surprised that white leaders and white academics had such a poor grasp of black politics. In 2010 he told me during a conversation that the NP leaders had evidently not studied the way the ANC operated in the 1980s.[82]

In Pretoria I talked to Fanie Botha, then minister of labour, who told me enthusiastically how he intended to transform trade unionism. His plan was to give urban blacks the right to receive training and to form trade unions, but to withhold these rights from "nations" such as the Xhosa and the Tswana whose homeland governments had become "independent". These workers would have to join trade unions in their own homelands. Nothing came of this idea.

I had a fruitful discussion with Dr Nthato Motlana, chairperson of the Committee of Ten, which had been established in Soweto. The committee was at that stage the only black organisation without any ties to homeland leaders which enjoyed great support among urban blacks.

In April 1980 I had an interview with John Vorster. He was still chancellor of the University of Stellenbosch but had already been forced to retire from

---

82   Interview with MG Buthelezi, 15 September 2010.

politics. The interview was conducted at his son's home near the University of Cape Town. Vorster reminded me of an old lion that had been pushed out of the troop.

When I introduced myself, he remarked in his usual gruff way: "I don't know you; all I know about you is that you're far left, which I find a pity." I asked him why he had not reformed apartheid more rapidly and comprehensively. NP policy attracted only the poorer and less educated coloured people, but left the middle class cold.

His response was: "Oh, you're like the English earlier in our history. They wanted the rich Afrikaners like the Van der Byls and Cloetes, but not the Vorsters and Giliomees." I recalled something Piet Cillié had written about him: "His priority is not people as an abstract mass but YOU."

I argued that the Soweto uprising of 1976 showed that the Afrikaners could not continue to suppress blacks indefinitely. No, he said, it had merely been a case of "poor intelligence": the police had failed to recognise that school-children could be a security threat. "Suppose I get a bunch of children together, arm them with nice big stones, line them up along De Waal Drive and tell them to let fly at the passing cars. No doubt they will cause great damage and chaos. But the next time the police will be ready for them."

I asked him why he had not fired his justice minister, Jimmy Kruger, when Kruger remarked that Steve Biko's death in detention left him cold. "No, you don't drop a colleague at a moment like that," he replied. "And besides, Biko would have had no mercy at all for the Afrikaners if he had come to power."

What did he think of Ian Smith, whose worst fear was realised when Robert Mugabe was sworn in as president? Vorster replied that Smith had had many options to get a better settlement, but had squandered them all. Each time Smith had the opportunity to make a deal, he wanted to postpone the inevitability of majority rule. Though the lesson for South Africa was obvious, it was evident to me that there was one thing Vorster did not want to discuss: the future.[83]

The conversation made me understand why Henry Kissinger described Vorster as very intelligent after they held talks in West Germany. Helen Suzman once told me: "PW Botha was a bully, so you won't listen to him. But Vorster had a mind: I liked listening to him."

Shortly after Vorster's death I wrote about our meeting in an article in the November 1983 issue of *Frontline* magazine: "What struck me most about

---

83    I elaborate on this conversation in *Die Afrikaners: 'n Biografie* (Cape Town: Tafelberg, 2004), p. 538.

Vorster was that he was at the same time a very charming and a very chilling man." The charm worked on Afrikaners in particular, but even some liberal English speakers had felt drawn to him.

In the article I referred to the newspaper editor Donald Woods, who fled the country in the wake of Steve Biko's horrifying death. I was present at a public meeting on the Yale University campus where Woods launched an excoriating attack on the Vorster government. But halfway through the speech he started telling jokes about Vorster and imitated Vorster's thick English accent. I could see the puzzled expression on the student faces. This was not how a refugee from the Soviet Union or Iran would have spoken about Leonid Brezhnev or Ayatollah Khomeini.

One could sense Vorster's "chilling" side when he spoke about radical black leaders and the white-black power struggle. I wrote: "If there was any compassion for his black opponents or any sense that they were fellow South Africans, I failed to detect it."

## A Soweto conversation

My meeting with Motlana had planted the idea in my mind of flying a group of Stellenbosch student leaders and lecturers to Johannesburg for a weekend-long discussion on our common future. It would be left to Motlana to invite a number of black students as participants. I discussed the idea of a "Stellenbosch-Soweto conversation" with Dick Goss, the managing director of South African Breweries (SAB). Though sceptical of the possibility of success, he agreed to sponsor such a meeting.

Motlana, a Wits-trained medical doctor, had studied at Fort Hare together with Robert Sobukwe, Robert Mugabe and Mangosuthu Buthelezi. He had been a co-founder of one of the first branches of the ANC Youth League and had taken part in the Defiance Campaign. In 1980 he was widely regarded as the black leader inside South Africa who enjoyed the greatest support among urban blacks after Nelson Mandela.

Motlana was razor-sharp, humorous and charismatic. He was the kind of leader with whom the government had to come to terms if they wished to avoid the prospect of black revolutionaries determining the future. Tragically, the government did its best to undermine him and his Committee of Ten. Motlana responded enthusiastically to my suggestion that a group of Stellenbosch students and lecturers undertake an expedition to Soweto for talks about the future with himself and a group he would assemble.

I had discovered in the meantime that a new group of student leaders had emerged at Stellenbosch. The turning point had been the Soweto uprising in

1976 and the advent of television, which had exposed the public to images of young stone-throwers braving live ammunition. It had brought about a significant mental shift on the part of many students.

Few students or lecturers were still openly conservative. Most of them were aware that the future was being determined by the "dictatorship of numbers" and had accepted the compelling need for change. The real dividing line was between those students who identified openly with the National Party, the Afrikaner Broederbond and the Ruiterwag, and those who distanced themselves from these organisations and were independent thinkers.

As Hilgard Bell, who was the SRC chairperson in 1979–80, later described the stance of the latter group, they were opposed to the government's inexplicable foot-dragging in respect of Nelson Mandela's release and its proposal for a Tricameral Parliament that would exclude blacks. They expressed their views on burning political issues without having been influenced by any institution or organisation.

On the Stellenbosch campus and that of the university's medical school at Tygerberg, the independents started devising plans to outwit the Ruiterwag and take control of the SRC. They had their work cut out for them, given that the university management overtly supported the NP-aligned students.

Besides Bell, the leading figures in the independent faction included Chris Heymans, Freddie Human, John van Breda and Johan Naudé. People from this group formed the majority on the SRC that was elected in 1979.[84]

Nobody in this group belonged to any political party, according to Bell. As in the case of the so-called "Civil War in 'The John'" two years later (see p. 126), the NP-aligned faction did not attack their opponents for advocating liberal principles, but instead tried to discredit them politically as individuals who were leftist, radical and possibly even Marxist.

Bell puts it well: "It was puzzling, as the normal liberal concepts of personal liberties, a free market and equality before the law were part of the everyday mindset of the majority of the students – they just could not bring themselves to accept that these concepts should also apply to people who were not white." [85]

In February 1980 the SRC under Bell's chairmanship adopted a motion in which the council pronounced itself against racial discimination. It also described the NP's proposal for a Tricameral Parliament as unworkable.

In the same month, I told Bell about my idea of a "Stellenbosch-Soweto

---

84    E-mail communication from Anton Naudé to Johan Naudé, 14 September 2015,
       and from Hilgard Bell to Anton Naudé, 28 September 2015.
85    E-mail communication from Hilgard Bell to Anton Naudé, 28 September 2015.

conversation". He reacted enthusiastically, and I asked him to invite a small group of student leaders to join us. I stressed that we had to take along a balanced group with diverse views. Since we anticipated that there would be considerable opposition to this venture, Bell and I drove to Cape Town to discuss the matter with Piet Koornhof, then minister of cooperation and development. He encouraged us to go ahead, though politicians close to PW Botha probably took a different view.

The SRC members whom Bell approached were initially all keen to participate, but as things tended to go in Stellenbosch in those days, some soon withdrew, probably as a result of AB and RW intervention. Fortunately, there were several SRC members who did not succumb to the pressure. In mid-March 1980, about twenty of us flew to Johannesburg.

We first went to Motlana's home in Soweto and held discussions there. Motlana spelled out in stark terms how apartheid affected his life. He was classified as a Tswana; when Bophuthatswana became independent two years earlier he had automatically lost his South African citizenship, despite never having lived in his so-called "homeland". When we asked whether influx control did not also help protect the established black urban areas against being swamped, he wordlessly produced his own passbook and showed it to us. Like the poorest migrant labourer, Motlana, too, had to carry one.

The absurdity of apartheid had never hit me as hard as it did at that moment. Francis Fukuyama, an American writer and political theorist who would later cause a great stir with books such as *The End of History and the Last Man* (1992) and *Political Order and Political Decay* (2014), wrote after a visit to South Africa that the government wanted to build a modern industrial economy, which was largely dependent on black labour, while at the same time it sought not only to prevent black urbanisation but to actively reverse it. He remarked: "No communist apparatchik ever devised a policy so contrary to the fundamental laws of economics."[86] The policy depended on pass laws that rigorously controlled black people's movements.

After the meeting at Motlana's house, the Soweto contingent and the Stellenbosch group travelled together to the Hunter's Rest holiday resort near Rustenburg. We were accompanied by several newspaper editors, including Ton Vosloo, Harald Pakendorf, Tertius Myburgh and Ken Owen.

The original plan had been that the discussions should take place mainly between the white and black student groups. To our disappointment, apart from the adults the Soweto group consisted almost exclusively of high-school

---

86   Francis Fukuyama, "The Next South Africa", *SA International*, 22, 2, 1991, p. 72.

children. It was the first time we became aware that in the black community the term "student" also referred to high-school pupils. They were not really equipped for the conversation, with the result that Motlana and the other adults did most of the talking. Motlana's wife Sally observed that there was an imbalance in the conversation, and that "next time" they had to make sure there were also real students in their group. Hilgard Bell recently recalled the tour as follows:

> I got the impression that on the black side of the conversation there was surprise that there was not a very strong sentiment in favour of the continuation of apartheid on our side, and that we agreed so easily on the ideals of equality and a non-racial state for the country. The first time that a difference of opinion really manifested itself was when it came to the redistribution of land. The issue drew a clear dividing line between the groups.

After our return to Stellenbosch, Chris Heymans stated at a meeting that the government was not talking to the real representatives of black people. The blacks rejected the community councils and the homelands. It was a mistake to think that the transfer of power lay far in the future, he warned. Whites had to obtain certain guarantees for their survival in the country as soon as possible.[87]

The conversation led to a subsequent visit to Stellenbosch by Motlana and Fanyana Mazibuko, an impressive young man from Soweto who had participated in the discussions. When Mazibuko was placed under house arrest shortly afterwards, there was a flood of letters of protest from Stellenbosch that reportedly surprised the responsible minister. Ton Vosloo criticised the decision in an editorial in *Beeld*.

I could sense this new spirit at a meeting PW Botha held during this time at the university's DF Malan Centre. The SRC members, who sat in the front row, did not stand up as he entered the venue. At question time, one asked why Mandela was not being released. More questions followed. Botha lost his temper and started wagging his famous index finger. The meeting became more and more raucous. The following day the reporter from the *Cape Times* quoted my remark that the evening had "offered the most amazing political theatre".

In a move in which the RW probably played a prominent role, NP-aligned

---

87    *Die Matie*, 26 March 1980.

student leaders succeeded with the adoption of a motion of no confidence in the SRC under Bell's chairmanship. This put paid to the chance of a continuation of the Stellenbosch-Soweto conversation.

In 1985 I published my impressions of several conversations with Motlana in the magazine *Die Suid-Afrikaan* under the headline "The conversation begins". Just below his photo were his recent words: "We shall win the liberation struggle." During our discussions back in 1980 he had not spoken in these terms. The sands of time were running out.

## More intractable than elsewhere

In 1980 the World Peace Foundation, a think tank in Washington, invited fifteen South Africans – white and black, English- and Afrikaans-speaking – on a tour to New York, Washington, Atlanta and Boston to meet some of the foremost American opinion-formers. We had fruitful discussions with Walter Cronkite, one of the biggest names in television at the time, as well as with the editor of the *Washington Post*, the president of Harvard University and black community leaders in Atlanta.

Our group included several leading role-players in South Africa, such as the Inkatha politician Oscar Dhlomo, the Toyota boss Albert Wessels, the *Beeld* editor Ton Vosloo, and the sugar magnate Chris Saunders.

In the 25 years since the US visit I have never had reason to change my first impression of Ton Vosloo: calm and collected, yet capable of attacking and counter-attacking with a vengeance. He was an analyst with acute political insight; a man of integrity, but, thankfully, unlike most members of that rare species, blessed with a good sense of humour.

At the end of a memorable tour we were hosted at a formal dinner in Washington. The main speaker was one of the leading black figures in President Jimmy Carter's administration, Donald McHenry, the US ambassador and permanent representative to the United Nations. His closing remarks were:

> To us Americans, this looks like a magic moment for South Africa to extend civil rights to all her peoples. Is there anything we Americans can say to persuade you of the need to seize this chance and by so doing save yourselves from sure destruction?

Our visit gave rise to the book *The American People and South Africa: Publics, Elites and Policymaking Processes* (1981) in which various dimensions of non-governmental US relations with South Africa were examined. Alfred Hero, the co-editor along with John Barratt, asked me to respond to McHenry's speech.

In my chapter I warned that the problem of fundamental political reform in South Africa was far more intractable than in any other multiracial country. In the United States black people were granted civil rights and affirmative action after a great struggle in the 1950s and 1960s, but blacks there represented just over 10% of the national population.

In Brazil, an intermediate category of mulattoes between the dominant whites and dirt-poor blacks had developed over the previous two centuries as a result of economic needs and the role of the Catholic Church. They constituted about 40% of the population, which made rigid segregation impossible.

In South Africa, the proportion of "urban insiders" who, like the mulattoes, wanted to be assimilated into the dominant group, was still very small. The key question was whether these people would see their interests as different from those of rural blacks and migrant labourers. There was a good chance that these black "insiders" had become so alienated that they would further radicalise the black "outsiders".

The book also included a contribution by Dr Chester Crocker, who, as assistant secretary of state for African affairs, would play a major role in the Reagan administration's policy towards South Africa from 1980 to 1988. Crocker stressed that reforms should not appear to be minimal concessions made under pressure. He pointed to the pattern that dramatic events, such as the outbreak of violence in a country, elicited dramatic American reactions. This was indeed what would happen to US policy towards South Africa five years later.

## In the wrong order

With PW Botha at the helm, the government's policy was no longer apartheid but "sensible reform" of apartheid. What did this mean? In the introduction to my book *The Parting of the Ways: South African Politics, 1976-1982*, I referred to David Low's famous cartoon in which the Colonel Blimp character said: "Gad, Sir, reforms are all right as long as they don't change anything." The problem was that the Botha government was opposed to doing anything that would affect its political power monopoly in a significant way.

The government's first major step was the reform of the labour market in 1979-80 after the commission chaired by Prof. Nic Wiehahn had issued its report. Black workers could now be trained as artisans and join a trade union that could engage in collective bargaining over wages and better working conditions. The next significant reform measure was the Tricameral Parliament in which whites, coloureds and Indians would be represented in separate chambers according to a ratio that corresponded to population size, but from which the African population would be excluded.

At a Synthesis meeting in Johannesburg, an English business leader told me of an Afrikaans business leader who had tried to elicit his support for the Tricameral Parliament by explaining that it was an attempt at "sharing power without losing control". [88] This naïve remark was an apt description of what the government aimed to achieve with the new parliament. Instead of genuinely attempting to negotiate, the government sought to impose its own model, which was based on the statutory groups of apartheid. The scheme was rejected by the greater part of the middle class in the coloured and Indian communities.

Even worse, it alienated the entire black population. Blacks wanted to be South African citizens and to be represented in Parliament. Now they found themselves excluded from the Tricameral Parliament while Indians and coloureds had been given representation.

To crown it all, the government's reforms were introduced in the wrong order. In most countries, political citizenship (representation in the legislative body) was granted first, and industrial citizenship thereafter (trade unions that participate in collective bargaining in the labour market).

In South Africa, the order was reversed. On 21 November 1979 an article of mine appeared in *Die Vaderland* under the headline "Wiehahn and Riekert: Now open residential areas and the vote must follow". (Appointed at the same time as the Wiehahn Commission, the commission headed by Dr Piet Riekert, chairman of the prime minister's Economic Advisory Council, was asked to make proposals for the training, employment, housing and governance of black workers in industry.) I started off by stating that it would be foolish to think the "economic citizenship" granted to blacks after the adoption of the Wiehahn report did not also have implications for political citizenship. I warned: "To prevent escalating conflict and irreparable damage to white interests, economic rights have to be extended to include participation in the political decision-making process . . ."

The homelands could form part of a new political system, I wrote, but everything would depend on whether "the national foundation is firmly established in the 1980s". This could only be achieved by expanding economic citizenship to embrace political and social citizenship.

It was only when the minutes of the National Party caucus were opened thirty years later that it became clear that Prime Minister PW Botha and Labour Minister Fanie Botha had painted a very different picture. In my book *The Last Afrikaner Leaders* (2012), I relate that PW Botha told the party

---

88   Hermann Giliomee, "The Botha Quest: Sharing Power Without Losing Control", *Leadership SA*, 2, 2, 1983, pp. 26-35.

caucus that labour reforms were important to help the government withstand
foreign pressure, while Fanie Botha pointed out that it was no longer possible
to refuse to let black workers talk to their bosses. One of his main aims as
labour minister was to win proper control over the black unions by forcing
them to register. This would enable government to obtain reports on their
finances and prohibit them from participating in politics.

The NP caucus was highly satisfied with this picture, and Andries Treurnicht and Ferdie Hartzenberg, future leaders of the breakaway Conservative
Party, even congratulated Nic Wiehahn in the lobby. Up to the end of the
1980s there was still a strong faction in the cabinet under the leadership of
FW de Klerk that saw a partial solution in linking urban blacks to their various
homelands.

In less than ten years the black unions would develop into the government's
most formidable internal political opponent. They refused to register as trade
unions and flouted the prohibition on political participation. They became
the ANC's strongest battering ram. The black urban elite remained alienated
because they had not been granted any effective political representation. Instead,
the government had excluded them from its Tricameral Parliament and alienated
them once and for all.

In the campaign that preceded the referendum of 1983 on the draft constitution for the Tricameral Parliament, there was much talk that a "yes" vote
would indicate approval of the new system as "a step in the right direction"
and that the issue of black rights would be tackled immediately after the referendum. I had no qualms about voting "no".

In 1984 I wrote an article in *Leadership SA* on the internal contradictions of
the government's policy, titled "Changing Everything (Except the Way We
Think?)" (This was a reference to Albert Einstein's comment in 1945 that the
release of atomic power had changed everything except our way of thinking.)

I wrote: "The historian would be at a loss to explain how South Africa could
allow an acute contradiction between 'excorporating' blacks as political citizens by denationalising them, but incorporating them as industrial citizens
by granting them the right to form trade unions and engage in collective
bargaining."[89] By the mid-1980s the so-called black trade unions had already
largely freed themselves of the government's control measures. There could
be no question of migrant labourers being excluded from the system.

89   Hermann Giliomee, "Changing Everything (Except the Way We Think)", *Leadership SA*, 3, 3, 1984, p. 125.

## From academic to columnist

One of the most interesting people I met at Yale was Anthony Delius, who participated in the seminars of the Southern African Research Program in 1977. Endowed with a sharp analytical mind, a delightful sense of humour and an innate rebelliousness towards authority, he was also an exceptionally gifted essayist. During the 1950s and early 1960s he gained renown as a parliamentary writer in South Africa with his *Cape Times* column "Notes in the House". In 1962 he was suspended from Parliament and subsequently, in 1964, banned from its press gallery.

By the time we met in 1977 Delius had long been residing in London, but he had kept his finger on the pulse of South African politics. In the light of my interest in politics, he suggested that I write a political column in the English dailies, an idea that had not occurred to me before. Delius advised Anthony Heard, editor of the *Cape Times,* and Gerald Shaw to ask me to write a regular column. As they were both great admirers of his, they approached me at once.

The first of my columns appeared in the *Cape Time*s on 7 March 1981. They were published simultaneously in the *Rand Daily Mail*, under the editorship of Allister Sparks, and, after the *RDM*'s demise, occasionally in *Business Day* as well. I continued with the *Cape Times* column until the end of the century, initially on a monthly basis and later twice a month. Throughout, I received nothing but encouragement from Heard, Shaw and Sparks, despite our political differences.

I soon discovered that column writing is an art in itself, and studied the techniques of the masters. My models were Schalk Pienaar in *Die Beeld*, Stanley Uys, then London correspondent for the English dailies in South Africa, Simon Jenkins in the *Sunday Times* (London) and William Pfaff, an American who wrote for the *International Herald Tribune* from Paris.

There is a fundamental difference between the approach of a columnist and that of an academic writing a paper for a scholarly journal. The academic tends to think his fellow subject specialists are more or less obliged to read the new insights he has arrived at through exhausting research; the columnist, on the other hand, knows he is competing in a tough market. He has to capture his readers' attention in the first paragraph, and thereafter a clear "flow" has to ensure that the column is read to the end. A good columnist presents not only an opinion but an assessment. Few readers are interested in mere opinion that is not buttressed by facts and especially by a sound assessment.

In a preface to my book *The Parting of the Ways,* a collection of essays in political journalism, the veteran journalist Stanley Uys drew a distinction between the journalistic opinion pieces of English-speaking academics and those of their Afrikaner counterparts. According to Uys, the former wrote about apartheid with great indignation; they analysed all the facets of an issue but were completely uninvolved. They remained outsiders – observers that peeped into the arena of power.

Uys contrasted them with the Afrikaner academics, who, in his view, placed themselves within the political arena and were emotionally involved with the country and the Afrikaner community. Such commentators had a better grasp of which reforms were politically negotiable and which were non-negotiable. That was precisely what enabled them to make an important contribution. Uys's words were a great encouragement to me.

Helen Zille, who was the political reporter of the *Rand Daily Mail* at the time, reviewed *The Parting of the Ways* in the magazine *Frontline*. "With a historian's penchant for order and analysis," she wrote, I had set out "to satisfy a basic South African craving – the need to make some sense out of the confusion of events, issues and trends that make up South African politics". She continued: "But Giliomee doesn't only describe. He prescribes. He takes a position. And the price of taking a position, in South African politics, is opposition."

Zille also highlighted what I was for and what I was against. "He believes in the kind of reform that would destroy or radically alter the political and social structures of apartheid – 'homelands', the Group Areas, separate schools, the pass laws. Especially the pass laws. His top priority is the need to scrap influx control. 'It is not everything, it is the only thing,' he says, quoting what an American football coach once said about winning."

"On the other hand," she added, "Giliomee does not believe in majority rule in a unitary state. Instead he backs the idea of a negotiated regional federation, something like that proposed by the Buthelezi Commission of which he was a member."

She noted, too, that PW Botha, after his promising start, did not seem to me like the kind of leader who could carry through radical reforms.[90]

## Someone who refused to be intimidated

An informal perk of being a columnist is that one comes into contact with much more interesting figures than if one remained in one's own little circle. One of the most remarkable South Africans I came to know was Lawrence Schlemmer, director of the Centre for Applied Social Sciences at the University of Natal.

Schlemmer's father was of German descent and his mother was Afrikaans.

---

90    Helen Zille, "Making Sense of South Africa", *Frontline*, September 1982, pp. 17-18.

Despite having only an honours degree to his name, his academic standing as an all-round social scientist continued to rise as a result of his incisive analyses, which were often linked to opinion polls that he had either conducted himself or helped to coordinate. In 1999, when he was already in his early sixties, he obtained a doctoral degree at UCT under my supervision. His research topic was the changes in Afrikaners' political attitudes during the last quarter of the twentieth century.

We collaborated on six books as co-editors or co-authors. Our topics ranged from influx control and an alternative to apartheid to the future of Afrikaans as a public language.

Even more important than our academic collaboration was the firm friendship we formed. What struck one most was his intensity and passion. He made a huge impression on everyone who met him. Schlemmer wanted to help huild a political dispensation in South Africa in which the demands of the majority and the fears of minorities would be reconciled in a democratic system. Though he had misgivings about the influence of the South African Communist Party on the ANC from the outset, he wanted to exclude neither the ANC nor Inkatha from a future system.

Schlemmer soon had formidable enemies in the ranks of the ANC. He was prepared to establish the Inkatha Institute and serve as its director. On the same day, a white ANC supporter set fire to his home and another to his office. Schlemmer refused to let himself be intimidated. He told Monica Bot, his girlfriend and later his wife: "Living in South Africa is a good test of character."

The last time we had one of our extended lunches, I invited the Stellenbosch philosopher Johan Degenaar to join us at a restaurant in the Strand that overlooked Melkbaai. Degenaar remembered three things about Schlemmer: his broad-mindedness, his intense interest in life, and his sociological approach to things in general. The following day, when I asked Schlemmer's opinion about our lunch, he replied that the company had been delightful but the food rather disappointing. Typically, he made a sociological observation: "Always avoid a restaurant with a beautiful ocean view if you want to have a quality meal."

Schlemmer had qualities that were both indispensable and rare: insight, good judgement and an exceptional zeal for work. He set himself the task of finding out what was really happening in politics. In this regard he was the exact opposite of Vladimir Lenin, of whom a biographer wrote: "Lenin didn't know that he believed; he believed that he knew."

In Schlemmer's view, the government, the opposition and ivory-tower academics did not actually know what was going on in politics. He insisted on the need for ongoing fresh research in order to keep abreast of what people thought and wanted. Hence he was keen on conducting opinion polls, which he would always conceptualise and interpret with a great sense of responsibility. But he also read widely, and was well acquainted with the theoretical literature on deeply divided societies.

He always questioned the idea – which was prevalent among *verligte* academics at the time – that the political solution lay in extending the homelands and making them more economically viable, even if this required huge financial sacrifices from the taxpayers. His polls showed that more Afrikaners would oppose such a policy than those who would accept it, and that more English speakers than Afrikaners supported it. Schlemmer analysed the results of this poll along with those of similar polls, and came to the conclusion that Afrikaners preferred a well-controlled degree of integration at the higher levels to making sacrifices for separate development in the homelands.

Like Schlemmer, I increasingly came to the conclusion that the real purpose of the homelands was to justify the pass laws and the withholding of voting rights from blacks. This policy was stoking black resistance more and more.

In their book on black urbanisation titled *Swart verstedeliking: Proses, patroon en strategie* (1981) (Black urbanisation: process, pattern and strategy), Flip Smit, a former classmate of mine at Stellenbosch, and his co-author Jan Booysen showed that the process of black influx to the cities was irreversible. They noted the inescapable facts. The big metropolitan areas would have to absorb most of the additional black urbanites before the end of the century. Blacks who urbanised could improve their economic position so dramatically that they were prepared to risk prosecution in the cities.[91]

At the launch of the book, Piet Cillié said that the Afrikaner's dream of "a piece of the earth that is irrevocably his own or ought to be his own" belonged to the past. In his opinion, Afrikaners were now being forced to make a "reassessment so painful that one could pray that this cup would rather pass us by, yet there was no alternative". One would have liked to hope that the NP-aligned academics at Stellenbosch would take the message of Smit and Booysen's book and Piet Cillié's words to heart and throw their weight behind a plea for the abolition of the pass laws. But this hope would be disappointed.

## Squandered opportunities

By 1980 it was clear that the KwaZulu government under the leadership of Mangosuthu Buthelezi had no intention of accepting independence. This was

---

91    P Smit and JJ Booysen, *Swart verstedeliking: Proses, patroon en strategie* (Cape Town: Tafelberg, 1981), pp. 105–06.

the deathblow to the South African government's plan of establishing a confederation of independent white and black states. There was now an urgent need for an alternative plan, but the government did not seem to have anything on hand.

Schlemmer played a leading role in setting up a commission to work out a proposal for integrating the homeland of KwaZulu and the province of Natal in a second-tier government based on power-sharing.

Five other academics and I were asked to research various aspects as commission members. The group included Arend Lijphart, an authority on power-sharing in deeply divided societies; Marinus Wiechers, a constitutional expert; Jill Nattrass, an economist; Heribert Adam, a sociologist; and Jan Sadie, a demographer. I was tasked with trying to establish how the NP leadership would respond to the idea of an integrated KwaZulu-Natal.

It was an impossible task. The Botha government had been opposed to the commission from the outset and declined the invitation to send a representative. I was unable to find a leading figure in the government who was prepared to talk seriously about possible support in the party for a second-tier government based on power-sharing. The one minister I did speak to was Dr Piet Koornhof, but I knew from experience that his opinion did not carry much weight in the cabinet.

In October 1981 the Buthelezi Commission completed its report in which it recommended an integrated regional authority based on power-sharing, with strong guarantees for minorities. Botha's response to the commission's proposals was in the classic apartheid mode. He said Buthelezi was welcome to investigate matters that concerned "his own country", but had no right to deal with matters under the central government's control.

With that, the Botha government squandered its great opportunity to take the initiative in respect of constitutional reform. If it had backed regional integration in KwaZulu-Natal (without trying to control it), it could have sparked similar initiatives in other regions of the country. As a next step, the central government could have appointed duly elected leaders from the various regions to the national cabinet. Powerful, legitimate black leaders in the regions would have lessened the pressure on the central government considerably.

## Up against the fences

Schlemmer and I decided to expand the research on influx control for the Buthelezi Commission, with the help of Jan Steyn of the Urban Foundation. We asked various experts to prepare papers for a conference that was held early in 1982 under the umbrella of the Unit for Futures Research. Our co-edited volume *Up Against the Fences: Poverty, Passes and Privilege in South Africa* issued from this.

Describing it as an "impressive collection", a review in the American journal *Foreign Affairs* noted that the book demonstrated in minute detail that the homelands were not viable economic entities and that influx control measures failed to stem the flow to the cities. Despite the huge income gap and hence growing class differences between urban and rural blacks, there was virtually no black support for maintaining insider-outsider distinctions through influx control.

In the book, Schlemmer wrote strikingly how the system of influx control represented a fence around the cities. Desperate people fleeing rural poverty were piling up against the fences in ever-increasing numbers. Although their living conditions in these peri-urban areas were poor, the job prospects were nevertheless much better than in their homeland villages.

The scope of the system was mind-boggling. Over a twelve-month period in 1968-69, close to 700 000 blacks were arrested for pass law offences. In the first half of the 1980s, an average number of 300 000 pass offenders were arrested annually. A poll among migrant labourers showed that influx control was an even bigger grievance to them than their working conditions.

In February 1982 I undertook a trip to the Ciskei at the request of Jan Steyn in order to provide him with a report on the "resettlement camps" in the homelands. A few months earlier he and I had paid a visit to the black squatter camp at Onverwacht, an hour's drive outside Bloemfontein. We were astounded at the shack settlement with its more than 40 000 residents that had mushroomed here within a few years. In terms of official policy, people in these "black spots" had to be resettled in camps in the homelands.

My visit to the Ciskei's resettlement camps was an unnerving experience. The conversations I had with some of the women and old people revealed their sense of rejection and hopelessness. It made all the talk in Parliament of "development" and "self-realisation" in the "homelands" sound surreal.

Driving back after this experience, I was reminded of the words from NP van Wyk Louw's historical verse drama, *Germanicus*. Like Rome, South Africa had become a "rancid old empire" in which "a hotchpotch, a cold, drab, smooth blend of peoples" had been "whisked together". Yet, I thought to myself, the NP would still rule this old empire for many years, provided that it remained united.

Just as I was driving past Grahamstown on my way to the airport, a news flash interrupted the radio broadcast: the NP had split, with Andries Treurnicht and 21 followers having walked out of the NP caucus. "This is the end of the

NP and of white domination," I told myself. I read later that this had also been the first thought of Pen Kotzé, an MP who was well acquainted with the inner workings of the party.

## Afrikaner ethnic power

In 1980 my father and I translated *Ethnic Power Mobilized*, which I had co-authored with Heribert Adam, into Afrikaans. As PW Botha had replaced John Vorster as leader in the meantime, I updated the new book considerably to cover Botha's totally different leadership style. The South African edition of the English text appeared under the title *The Rise and Crisis of Afrikaner Power*.

I also wrote a new final chapter, titled "Oorlewing in die toekoms" (Future survival), in which I examined demographic and other trends which would determine the politics of the next twenty years. For this I was able to draw on the projections of the Unit for Futures Research, with which I cooperated closely. *Afrikanermag: Opkoms en toekoms* was published in the second half of 1981.

The final chapter highlighted the rapid black population growth and the sharp decline of the white proportion of the population. Jan Sadie's projections indicated that the proportion of whites in the age group 5-25 would decrease from 12.8% of the total in 1980 to 7.7% in the year 2000. In the case of blacks, it would rise from 74.4% to 83%.

Between 1980 and 2000 the number of black pupils who successfully completed the highest school standard would increase from 22 920 to a projected 185 807, while the number of white pupils would remain virtually static at around 50 000. Studies showed that relatively well-educated blacks were much more militant than those who left school at an early age.

While the South African state would be able to maintain itself well against guerrilla fighters, no police force or army could guarantee industrial peace. "An alienated skilled working class, occupying strategic positions in the economy, would increasingly develop the capacity to disrupt politics and the economy through strikes, industrial sabotage, arson, consumer boycotts and protest marches." An unwillingness to embrace radical reform could lead to endemic industrial unrest and an ever-growing lack of stability. The only solution was to scrap all racially discriminatory laws and abandon the illusion that South Africa was a white country.

The chapter warned: "Without creative reforms, the spiritual content of Afrikaner survival will become so attenuated that growing numbers of Afrikaner intellectuals will refuse to identify themselves with the political order. The new generation of English-speaking whites and potential allies in the coloured and black middle class will become totally alienated. The West will start with-drawing its considerable military and moral support unless South Africa moves towards a fundamental reform of political policy in the 1980s." I concluded with the words: "Seldom has the saying been more true that they who seek to pre-serve all will lose all."

The most incisive discussion of the book was a long article by Helen Zille in the *Rand Daily Mail* of 7 November 1981. With reference to the final chapter, she observed that the government's policy was failing on numerous fronts. The facts were catching up with apartheid. "Nowhere is this spelt out more clearly and concisely than in the new book ... *Afrikanermag: Opkoms en toekoms*."

In his review of *Afrikanermag* in the Johannesburg daily *Beeld*, Ebbe Dommisse, who would become editor of *Die Burger* ten years later, wrote: "It forces the reader to think more deeply than possibly ever before." Stanley Uys, the London correspondent for the English-speaking dailies, recommended it as "one of the most important books ever written on South Africa".

By contrast, Louis Louw, deputy editor of *Die Burger*, condemned it in his review. The book was dominated by my "negativism and scepticism", he wrote, and I was evidently not well enough informed about the Afrikaner and his institutions. If I had to be believed, "it was curtains for the Afrikaner and all his institutions – his church, his party, the Broederbond, even his newspapers".

Louw concluded: "[Giliomee's] approach indicates that he has not really come close to the glow of the fire in the Afrikaner's inner court; that his impressions are therefore unsound and his eye and heart cold. Maybe he is right about the future, but I hope that is not the case."

## Civil war in "The John"

Over the years *Die Burger*'s opinion columns had acquired a reputation for fiery debates. I had a hand in instigating two big fights: the first was in 1982 about the NP government's inability to abolish influx control, and the second, in 2005, about language as medium of instruction at the University of Stellenbosch.

Helen Zille gave an excellent account of the first-mentioned "war" in an article in the November 1982 issue of Denis Beckett's magazine *Frontline*. There were two factions, she explained. The one side consisted of the "*oorbeligtes*" (literally, the "overexposed" ones), those who, in the opinion of the *verligtes*, received too much exposure in the English press. This little group comprised André du Toit and Johan Degenaar, the two lecturers in the department of political philosophy, and myself. On the opposing side were those Zille called the "establishment *verligtes*": Sampie Terreblanche (economics), Willie Esterhuyse (philosophy) and Julius Jeppe (development administration). With the exception of myself, the members of the two teams all had offices in the John Vorster Building, also known as "The John".

*Die Burger*'s cartoonist Fred Mouton drew a cartoon of the "Civil war in 'The John'" that depicted two teams running onto a field in rugby togs under a banner that read "Academics' Intervarsity". My fellow *oorbeligtes* and I looked skinny and sheepish compared to the three robust and resolute *verligtes*, all of whom were Broederbond members.

"The Civil War in 'The John'" eventually turned into a national debate, with academics from five other universities joining the fray. Zille summed the debate up well as a fight about the limits of NP reforms. In the view of the *oorbeligtes*, these reforms were insufficient and the *verligtes*' praise for them constituted an obstacle to fundamental reform.

According to Zille, the first salvo of "round one" of the "war" was a review of Esterhuyse's book *Die pad van hervorming* (The path of reform) that I wrote for *Die Burger*. She described my criticism as "simple and straightforward, a hammer blow on a raw *verligte* nerve".

In my review, I argued that Esterhuyse's book attempted to be academically grounded and loyal to the claims of Afrikaner nationalism at the same time. In an earlier work titled *Afskeid van apartheid* (1979), published in English as *Apartheid Must Die*, Esterhuyse had endorsed the homeland policy by proposing that concrete content be given to the "freedom ideal of the black nations of South Africa". There was no need to suspend the goal of independent black states.

In *Die pad van hervorming*, Esterhuyse sought to achieve a balance between reform and the "legitimate claims of Afrikaner nationalism". While advocating greater freedom of association across ethnic lines in respect of various relevant matters on the one hand, he insisted on "drastic curbs" on political competition across colour lines on the other. Such competition would give rise to "a group race for political power and group domination", something which, according to Esterhuyse, did not make allowance for "minority groups and their rights and claims" and for the "requirement of justice". My question to him was: Why can the coloured people only participate in politics as a group and not simply, like Afrikaans- and English-speaking whites, as individual citizens in a common system?

I expressed my doubt as to whether Esterhuyse's proposal for a new constitution stretched further than the government's proposed constitution which was based on the statutory groups of apartheid (whites, coloureds, blacks and Indians) and a prohibition on coalitions across the colour line. The book should rather have had a different title, I concluded, such as *Die pad van magsbehoud deur sosiaal-politieke aanpassings* (The path of retaining power through sociopolitical adjustments).

Anton van Niekerk, a junior colleague of Esterhuyse, replied to my review with the question whether I regarded reform as structural only if it destroyed all institutions on which Afrikaner power was based and replaced them with institutions in which Afrikaners, or whites in general, had no power.[92]

This outrageous question was a good indication of the tone in which the subsequent debate would be conducted. There was, however, one good thing about Van Niekerk's response: at least he had responded in the same newspaper in which my article originally appeared. In a later letter I expressed my dislike for Terreblanche's practice of giving in *Die Burger* his own representation of what I had written in the English press, and then passing sentence on this version.

In Zille's reconstruction of events, round two kicked off with an article I wrote for the *Sunday Times* of 27 June 1982. I referred to rumours that the NP government had requested a donation of R6 million from a group of business leaders, both English and Afrikaans, in order to nip Andries Treurnicht's newly founded Conservative Party in the bud. As a quid pro quo, I suggested, the business leaders should demand real reforms from the government, and specifically the scrapping of the pass laws.

This time it was Terreblanche, "the veteran war horse", in Zille's words, who stormed in. As she put it, understatement was certainly not an element of his style. On 29 June, in *Die Burger*, he lashed out against my *Sunday Times* article and my other essays in the English press in hyperbolic fashion.

In describing my article, he used terms such as a "growing element of maliciousness and suspicion-mongering", "poison-tipped arrows" and the fomenting of "raw ethnic hatred and ethnic suspicion" as well as "hatred" and "spite". Terreblanche warned English businesspeople not to waste money on the "Prog horse" despite the support of some Stellenbosch academics for the party.

In my reply, I remarked that his letter reminded me of a question that might be asked in a word-choice game: "*Party mense se geleerdheid dryf hulle tot rasery/raserny.*" (Some people's learning drives them to inanity/insanity.) On a more serious note, I stated that my *Sunday Times* article had resulted from my growing concern about the subsistence crisis in the homelands and the pass laws. Scrapping influx control was the best way to prevent an escalating crisis in the homelands and create a freer, more just and more prosperous system. For me it was not about whether the Nats or the Progressives were gaining ground, I wrote in conclusion, but whether urgently needed reforms would be implemented in time.

---

92   Letter from Anton van Niekerk, *Die Burger*, 24 June 1982.

Terreblanche replied that he, too, was concerned about the policy of influx control, but I was being simplistic in thinking that the abolition of influx control would in itself create job opportunities, prosperity and justice "out of thin air".

It seemed as if the debate would end there: Terreblanche declared himself the winner, while I left for Cambridge University on study leave. But then Johan Degenaar made a speech at a student meeting where he used the term "morally critical Afrikaner" for people who were prepared to fight against apartheid outside the NP framework. He warned the *verligtes* that *verligtheid* was "an obstacle on the path to peaceful fundamental change" if they did not make a clear choice in favour of power-sharing, free association and the abolition of racial discrimination.

Meanwhile, Floors van Jaarsveld was still burning to get at me. On 3 August he wrote to Diko van Zyl, my colleague at Stellenbosch: "To me, ultra-left radicalism is as objectionable as the ultra-right kind. Giliomee has long been a worry to me, namely as an exponent of the vengefulness of [Leonard] Thompson."

A few days later he wrote to Pieter Kapp at the History Department of the Rand Afrikaans University. He portrayed my work as "ideologically coloured" and posed the question: "Will we still be able to practise '*volksgeskiedenis*' as advocated by Prof. Thom in the past?" He continued:

> I believe history finds itself in a contentious position today. We are experiencing a total onslaught, also on the history front. What is being published in English about the past sends cold shivers down my spine. I wouldn't have participated in the Stellenbosch academic civil war, as Giliomee calls it, were it not that I had been asked telephonically to do so.

The telephone call evidently bore fruit, as Van Jaarsveld entered the debate a few days later. The aim was to unmask me as a "neo-Marxist". Among the "evidence" he produced for my being under Marxist influence was the fact that, as co-editor of *The Shaping of South African Society, 1652-1840*, I had allowed a Marxist historian, Martin Legassick, to write one of the chapters. The chapter in question dealt with the Griqua and Sotho-Tswana on the northern frontier of the Cape Colony, which hardly offered much scope for class analysis.

Van Jaarsveld described my chapters in this book as having been conceptualised from "a historical-materialist perspective" in which "class is central, as is the case with the neo-Marxists". As "proof" he noted, inter alia, that I distinguished between members of the community of farmers in the Bruintjieshoogte region northeast of Cradock where the Slagtersnek Rebellion of

1815 had taken place. My contention had been that the more affluent farmers had too much to lose to take part in an armed rebellion against British authority, unlike the predominantly poor rebels.

Van Jaarsveld's portrayal of me as a neo-Marxist was the only time I have been labelled as such. I have always maintained that people are motivated by their ideology and culture as well as by their material interests.

In the course of the 1980s Van Jaarsveld once invited me to write a chapter for a book he was editing on the interface between the disciplines of history and political studies. For a moment I thought it was an attempt on his side to bury the hatchet and considered agreeing to the request. On reflection, however, I declined.

In 1992 Van Jaarsveld stated in an interview with the editor of a Dutch history journal that he had promoted apartheid because he believed it could succeed. If he could have rewritten his books, he added, he would have slated apartheid right from the start "as a mistake, a historical mistake". [93]

In the 1982 epistolary war, Terreblanche and Julius Jeppe had meanwhile informed *Die Burger*'s readers of two articles André du Toit had written a few months earlier in *Frontline* and the *Sunday Times*. In one, Du Toit had called on Afrikaner intellectuals to distance themselves from the government and take a stand against apartheid together with non-Afrikaners, even if it would entail support for black movements on their terms. For Jeppe, this was "revolutionary language and unacceptable propaganda".

Terreblanche went a step further in his eagerness to settle scores with us. He wrote: "In our delicate situation, surely we cannot allow destabilising and neo-Marxist propaganda to be spread unpunished under the guise of intellectualism."

Jakes Gerwel, a lecturer in Afrikaans at the University of the Western Cape (UWC) with a strong interest in Marxism, was rightly appalled. He wrote in reply: "Whether Messrs Degenaar, Du Toit and Giliomee are influenced by neo-Marxism or not – and anyone who knows something about Marxism, among whom I rank the economist Terreblanche, will know that none of the three (and Giliomee least of all!) comes close to being neo-Marxist – is not principally at issue in my argument with my colleague Terreblanche."

What was at issue for Gerwel, however, was Terreblanche's statement that our views should not be allowed to go "unpunished". I, too, considered it a reckless choice of words. As Gerwel put it, the manner in which Terreblanche participated in the debate was "not part of our rules of engagement" as "academics and intellectuals".

---

93   See Leonard Blussé *et al., Pilgrims to the Past* (Leiden: CNWS, 1996), p. 269.

Christopher Saunders from UCT and Jeffrey Butler from Wesleyan University added their voices to the debate, warning against the vilification of dissident historians. In my last contribution, I proposed a truce to give combatants an opportunity to read the books they had referred to, so that they could at least acquaint themselves with the subject on which they wrote letters to the press.

This extraordinary episode made me wonder if all that was now left of the old Afrikaner "*volksbeweging*" was a dogged defence of the policy of the NP and of its dominant position in white politics.

## Civil war: a post-mortem

What did all of this mean? Fundamentally, the fight between the *verligtes* and the *oorbeligtes* was not about influx control, which was the major policy question I had raised. It was hard for any academic to defend the pass laws and the exclusion of blacks from the Tricameral system. The fight was rather about whether the NP still served the Afrikaners' long-term interests the best, and whether the NP government was the most appropriate vehicle for reform. The *verligtes* called on the public to keep trusting the government.

They maintained that the *oorbeligtes* were not "academically objective" and "politically uninvolved", but instead inspired by our "neo-Marxism" and our sympathy with the Progressive Federal Party (PFP). At the same time, the *verligtes* tried to create the impression that their own position had nothing to do with their association with the NP and the Broederbond.

In a by-election held in Stellenbosch later that year, the NP candidate scored a resounding victory over the PFP candidate. Two young Stellenbosch lecturers, Elrena van der Spuy and Hans van der Riet, pointed out in *Die Burger* of 27 November 1982 that the three *verligtes* had publicly declared their support for the NP prior to the election. As they put it, there had been no sign of the *oorbeligtes* – the so-called "Proggish professors" – during the election campaign.

After the NP victory, *Die Burger* described the Stellenbosch "civil war" between *verligtes* and *oorbeligtes* in the controversy earlier in the year as having been a good preparation for the "massacre" in the by-election. Van der Spuy and Van der Riet asked in their letter whether the three *verligte* professors were going to distance themselves from the reflection this cast on what had motivated them to launch their attacks. They wrote in closing: "Let there be no misunderstanding about who puts party-political involvement first, and who puts academic objectivity first." The *verligte* professors failed to respond to their letter.

It would transpire later that the NP was split right down the middle on the abolition of the pass laws and that the cabinet did not want to take a decision, not even after Flip Smit, the co-author of *Swart verstedeliking* and the cabinet's adviser on the issue, had proposed that the laws be scrapped. The black majority were left out in the cold and alienated even further. The pass laws were only abolished in 1986, after nearly two years of widespread rioting. The government earned no credit for this belated reform. Instead the United States instituted comprehensive sanctions.

In the main, the leadership at Afrikaans universities was not very sympathetic towards those who criticised the NP's reforms. Several outstanding academics felt compelled to pursue their careers at other campuses either inside or outside South Africa. Among them were the theologians Murray Jansön, Wentzel van Huyssteen and Vincent Brümmer, the jurist Johan van der Vyver, the psychologist Manie van der Spuy and the sociologist Jan Loubser.

## Respite at Cambridge

In 1953 Cambridge University established both a Smuts Professorship of Commonwealth History and a Smuts Visiting Research Fellowship in memory of their renowned alumnus and chancellor JC Smuts. The university awarded one fellowship annually to an academic from a discipline in the humanities or the social sciences who was attached to a university in the British Commonwealth. Despite our country having left the Commonwealth twenty years earlier, South Africans were eligible for the fellowship. I applied, and was awarded the fellowship for the academic year 1982/83.

During the second half of 1982, comfortably housed in Clare Hall, my family and I were able to enjoy the wonderland of Cambridge. We would often play tennis in summer till eight or nine o'clock at night on the grass courts of Clare College.

Cambridge was a welcome respite after the acrimonious controversy in *Die Burger*. Annette and I had the opportunity of attending John Lonsdale's brilliant lectures on Africa's colonial history and recent political developments. I focused on getting abreast of the latest literature on the development of ethnicity and nationalism, and completed a lengthy study of the beginnings of Afrikaner ethnic consciousness and nationalism in the nineteenth and early twentieth centuries. It was published in 1989 in Leroy Vail's collection of essays, *The Creation of Tribalism in Southern Africa*.

In November 1982 I returned to Cape Town for a week to attend a conference on South Africa's future. One evening Prof. Francis Wilson from the Economics Department at UCT visisted me at the Holiday Inn next to the

Eastern Boulevard where I was staying. He asked me to apply for the vacant professorship in political studies at the university. I was surprised, as I had no formal qualifications in the subject.

Because I was due to return to England the following day, I wrote a formal letter of application on the hotel's stationery and handed it to Wilson. Shortly after my return to Cambridge, the UCT vice-chancellor Stuart Saunders phoned me with the news that the selection committee had recommended my appointment. When I informed my family, with Saunders still holding on, Adrienne expressed her disgust with a single word: "Sis!" She had no intention of leaving her friends at Bloemhof Girls' High School in Stellenbosch.

As a family, we arrived at a compromise. We would stay on in our beloved house in Stellenbosch that had been designed by Annette, and I would commute between Cape Town and Stellenbosch.

Leaving the US was not an easy decision, and one evening at Cambridge I went as far as writing a letter to the registrar at Stellenbosch in which I declared my willingness to stay if they offered me an associate professorship – a position between that of a senior lecturer and a professor. I remembered, however, that between 1978 and 1982 I had applied for such a position on three occasions, without success. The next morning I tore up the letter.

On 27 January 1983 in Cambridge, just after the news of my resignation had become public, I received a letter from Prof. Erika Theron, whom I held in high regard, not only because of her commission's report but also for the way in which she had defended herself against NP politicians' attacks. She wrote:

> Just a short note to say that I am so sorry you are leaving Stellenbosch. Your departure is a great loss to our university – our academic life will certainly be the poorer for it. Now you will just have to stay on the right course among the bunch in Cape Town. Here in South Africa, the pace is accelerating more and more towards – I don't know where. And who are worried? Not the whites.

I deeply appreciated her letter.

My last day as a US lecturer was 31 March 1983. That evening I cleared out my office, unscrewed my name board from the door, and consigned it to the wastepaper basket.

# Chapter 7

# Among the English

Up to the 1970s the debate within the Afrikaner nationalist movement had centred on how the Afrikaners could assert themselves and raise their status vis-à-vis the English community. It encompassed various spheres of Afrikaner life: businesspeople wanted to prove that they, like the English, could build successful enterprises without state support; universities and schools wanted to prove they could become the equal of English institutions; the leading Afrikaans writers, poets and dramatists wanted to prove Afrikaans could be a vehicle for literature of high quality. Between the 1930s and the 1970s the income gap between the two white communities had narrowed considerably. This had not resulted from a forced redistribution of wealth but from the expansion of opportunities for the Afrikaner.

After the Soweto uprising in 1976 the political discourse changed radically. The Afrikaner-English rivalry over which white community was dominant was a thing of the past, and the top priority was an economic growth rate that would be conducive to jobs and food for all. The African National Congress (ANC) had emerged as a competitor for state power. The debate was now about whether a negotiated settlement could be reached before the country became mired in a low-intensity civil war.

On 1 April 1983 I took up my position as professor in political studies at UCT. A few years later, in my inaugural lecture, I commented on my surprise at finding myself in a department as well as a university for which I had not been programmed.[94] For me as a schoolchild, this university on the slopes of Table Mountain had been "the other place". For the History Department at Stellenbosch, their UCT counterpart was the seat of the opposition – liberal historiography – against which they positioned themselves.

In the Political Studies Department I had colleagues such as Robert Schrire,

---

94   Hermann Giliomee, *The History in our Politics* (Cape Town: University of Cape Town, 1986).

David Welsh, André du Toit and Annette Seegers, who all did important work on contemporary South African politics. Unlike at my previous workplace, there was no divide between professors and ordinary lecturers but rather a culture of collegiality born out of respect for each other's work. During the 1980s and the early 1990s, UCT was a far more stimulating and dynamic environment than the University of Stellenbosch. I soon realised that my departure from the US had been a blessing in disguise.

I delivered my professorial inaugural lecture on the evening of 11 June 1986. Driving to Cape Town, we saw some Casspirs (armoured police vehicles) next to the N2 highway. Palls of smoke hung over the black township of Crossroads. A national state of emergency would be declared the following day. As I took my place at the rostrum, I was amazed to notice my mother in the front row of the lecture hall. Aged 83, she had insisted on attending the event.

Academics generally use inaugural lectures to spell out a particular approach to a discipline. I used mine to distinguish between two different approaches one could take in the study of politics. In *politics as an arena*, I explained, the focus of study was the nature of political power, the dynamics of political institutions, the role and functions of the bureaucracy, and interstate relations.

What attracted me was *politics as a process*, an approach where one studied the process by which political and economic power had become concentrated in the hands of a particular party or group. This direction also included investigating how conflicts about power, status and economic opportunities had built up over time, and why they were resolved in some cases while in others they led to rebellions and revolutions. It was common cause that South Africa was on the brink of make-or-break changes.

I argued that a large part of the national debate was about whether the current ethnic and racial groups were a transient or a permanent phenomenon. Could minorities be disregarded by a new constitution, or should they be accommodated?

My standpoint was that historical identities were not immutable, but any future settlement would need to take into account that social identities changed slowly. It was unlikely that a community such as the Afrikaners would suddenly decide to relinquish all control over matters that affected them directly, such as schools and universities. I cited NP van Wyk Louw, who had declared in the 1950s that if the Afrikaners lost power and became a political minority, "they would be as helpless as the Jews were in Germany". He was referring to the intensified discrimination in areas such as employment and university admission that Jews were subjected to in the 1930s.

I said that the ANC had a case in questioning *white* minority rights. But the movement was too rigid in its insistence that it only recognised individual rights. My position was that in a future constitution there had to be a sound balance between the majority and minorities, and rules for dispute resolution should be written into the constitution.

Moreover, the university should do everything possible to serve as a venue where all the parties could conduct a rational debate on these and other issues. I wanted to invite speakers from all political parties to address students in my courses on South African politics.

It was a vain hope. Two years earlier a lecture by Mangosuthu Buthelezi had been disrupted, and there was no chance that some of the students would allow representatives of Inkatha or the Labour Party (which participated in the Tricameral Parliament) to speak on the campus. The final phase of the struggle for control of the South African state had already begun, and students would play a role in the mass protests.

## Worlds apart

I commuted between Stellenbosch and Cape Town three or four days a week by car, leaving early in the morning and returning in the late afternoon. I soon became aware of the vast differences between the two campuses. The driving distance was less than 50 km but they seemed to be worlds apart. For one, there was very little communication between the two universities. In 1961 the Stellenbosch SRC of which I was a member had turned down an invitation from the UCT SRC to hold a debate on politics, as we believed the political divide was too great. Some of us, myself included, had doubted privately whether our English was good enough for a debate that would probably have been conducted in that language.

We suspected that there was a potent anti-Afrikaner prejudice among some UCT lecturers and students. Like the Afrikaners today, English speakers were understandably resentful over their apparent permanent exclusion from power despite being, as a community, considerably better educated and more affluent than the Afrikaners.

WH Hutt, an eminent economist, was a former UCT lecturer who had displayed a marked anti-Afrikaner bias. In his book *The Economics of the Colour Bar* (1964) he advocated the free-market system because it supposedly freed people from their racial and ethnic prejudices. He singled out Afrikaners as the stumbling block since, in his view, they still clung to myths about racial differences that had long been discarded by most others.

According to Hutt, Afrikaners associated white with goodness and purity, and black with sin, evil, dirt and death. This was the reason, he claimed, why urban Afrikaners preferred white fish and chicken, "especially the white meat", for "invalids and children". The sole source he cited for these startling revelations was research done by a student. Hutt's views were certainly bizarre and, to my knowledge, not shared by others.

By the time I joined UCT in 1983 there was no longer any question of such blatant stereotyping, but it was hard to avoid the impression that some academics and members of the executive looked down their noses at Afrikaners. JM Coetzee, a lecturer in English at UCT who started distinguishing himself as a novelist in the 1970s, recently commented as follows on the historical relationship between the two white communities:

> I understand very well that the eye of the Afrikaner was on the English and that English superciliousness was galling. The English have never (to my knowledge) been called to account sufficiently for the way they looked down on the Boers/Afrikaners from 1795 onward, and pretty consistently saw the worst in them rather than the best . . . The English intellectuals like Olive Schreiner believed that the great future question about South Africa was the black-white, African-European question. Afrikaner nationalism, locked into its project of self-assertion against the English, never gave enough weight to this question until it was too late.[95]

My colleague David Welsh maintained in his publications that English speakers had historically been equally complicit in the entrenchment of racial discrimination. They were generally more liberal than the Afrikaners, but the difference between the two language communities on the racial problem constituted a difference of degree, not of principle.[96] To my mind, this encapsulated the issue very well.

On the campus and in seminars, negative remarks about the Afrikaner community were made in my presence. There were the inevitable Van der Merwe jokes, often a veiled form of expressing English ethnic superiority, and people referred to "the damn Nats" in a way that made one wonder whether the attitude conveyed did not actually pertain to the Afrikaner community as a whole.

What struck me was the lack of understanding for the position in which

---

95   E-mail communication from JM Coetzee, 17 March 2015.
96   David Welsh, "English-speaking Whites and the Racial Problem", in André de Villiers (ed.), *English-speaking South Africa Today* (Cape Town: Oxford University Press, 1976), p. 236.

the NP found itself in respect of the Afrikaners as its primary support group among the white electorate. The party had to reckon with the fear of a large section of its voters that their material position could weaken significantly under a black government. As recently as 1960, 40% of Afrikaners had still been factory workers or manual labourers, who feared competition on a level playing field with black and coloured workers.

The NP also had to take account of the Afrikaners' fears for their cultural survival. These concerns were mostly incomprehensible to English speakers. Charles Simkins, an economist at UCT whose work I respected, wrote that the South African English, "like English elsewhere, have never organised themselves politically in any major way around their Englishness. They are culturally incapable of it; they take their Englishness for granted and mobilise around another issue – that of social class."[97]

Against this, there was deep anxiety on the part of many Afrikaners over whether Afrikaans as a language and the Afrikaner community would survive without political power. I have always been struck by NP van Wyk Louw's articulation of the struggle in South Africa as one between a white and a black nationalism, each insisting on its right to self-determination. As he put it: "It was the typical tragic situation of history: two 'rights' which confronted each other implacably." A victory for either of the two rights would in itself become unjust. In Louw's view, liberals condemned themselves to sterility by demanding "full democracy" in a country where uniform equality could be realised only "over the dead body of an entire people [the Afrikaners]".

What stood out for me as someone who worked at the US for nearly fifteen years and at UCT for fifteen years was how little the universities knew about each other and how limited the interaction was between the staff and students of the two institutions. My impression was that, with a few exceptions, the US lecturers did not read English newspapers. On the other hand, as a UCT lecturer, I rarely heard a colleague mention something he or she had read in *Die Burger*.

From the early 1970s Van Wyk Louw's ideas were frequently quoted in political discussions on the Stellenbosch campus, but I seldom heard a reference to him on the UCT campus or saw his name in any publication. Likewise, the thinking of Alfred Hoernlé, the great English-speaking philosopher of the 1930s and 1940s, was virtually unknown among US academics.

---

97   Charles Simkins, *Reconstructing South African Liberalism* (Johannesburg: SAIRR, 1986), p. 43.

## The US under the spotlight

At the time of my move to UCT in 1983, the English universities were far ahead of their Afrikaans counterparts when it came to scholarly publications. There was consternation at Afrikaans universities when the state decided that the allocation of research grants in the natural sciences and engineering would in future be evaluated on the basis of international norms. Academics who were rated as top researchers on the strength of their published work (categories A and B) could count on generous state funding from the Council for Scientific and Industrial Research (CSIR). Those who were unable to prove their worth would have to look elsewhere for research funding.

In 1985 I conducted an interview with Prof. Jack de Wet from UCT, one of the architects of the new peer evaluation and rating system, which we published in the magazine *Die Suid-Afrikaan*. He did not mince his words in outlining the inferior position of some Afrikaans universities. At UCT the number of researchers in categories A and B came to 13 and 38 respectively, and at the University of the Witwatersrand (Wits) the corresponding numbers were 12 and 41. At the US, however, the numbers were only 1 and 8, and at the University of Pretoria 2 and 7.

De Wet stressed the difference that good management could make to a university's research output. He referred to the example of Prof. Wynand Mouton, rector at the University of the Orange Free State, who had vigorously expanded the research component and budgeted generously for this purpose. "Free State, with a 'weight' of 5, lies halfway up the ladder along with the University of Port Elizabeth while the English universities are at the top, virtually in a class of their own, with Stellenbosch and Potchefstroom right at the bottom."[98] When the news of the poor research record of the lecturers in the natural sciences and engineering became known, John Thompson, a professor in English at the US, quipped: "And they keep giving each other prizes."

We published the interview with De Wet alongside a cartoon by Cora van Eeden. The CSIR was portrayed as a fat woman with a bag of money. A little boy labelled "Wits" was cosily ensconced on the woman's lap; another boy, with "US" on his chest, was seen slinking away shamefacedly after apparently having received a hiding. I was told that the US executive had been offended by our article. When I once bumped accidentally into the US rector, Prof. Mike de Vries, he made no pretence of hiding his dissatisfaction.

While one does not know how Stellenbosch academics in the arts faculty

---

98   "Ons universiteite en hul navorsingsgehalte", *Die Suid-Afrikaan,* Winter 1985, pp. 8-11.

would have fared in a similar evaluation, it was conspicuous how seldom members of the faculty published anything with university presses or in respected international journals. Many lecturers' sole focus was on teaching and the examination of ideas they had expressed in their classes. In some cases, knowledge of prescribed literature was tested as well. When they did publish research, it tended to be in local scholarly journals.

The harsh truth was that the lawns of too many Stellenbosch lecturers were too neatly manicured. It was only after the turn of the century that the US started catching up significantly with UCT and Wits in the area of published research.

## A fiery debate

At Stellenbosch, we had seldom argued about the great history debate between liberals and radicals. At the core of this debate was the question whether ideas such as predestination or racial prejudice were the root cause of white racism and white supremacy, or whether these ideas were merely rationalisations that served to justify the occupation of the original inhabitants' land and the exploitation of coloured and black workers.

At UCT, it was a different story. The *Oxford History of South Africa* (1969 and 1971) had spawned a fierce and often acrimonious debate between liberals and radicals. In the case of volume one, both editors and all three of the contributors had been attached to UCT at some point. In the case of the second volume, both editors and two of the six contributors had links with UCT. Three of the *Oxford History*'s four most prominent radical critics (Shula Marks, Stanley Trapido and Martin Legassick) had either studied at UCT or taught there at some stage.

The race-versus-class debate was central in seminars and lectures in more than one faculty at UCT. I could not isolate myself from the debate. Students argued about it among themselves and waited for lecturers to show their colours. The issue cropped up regularly in the weekly African Studies seminars, which were attended by lecturers.

It was not purely an academic debate without political implications. For some radicals, it was about exposing the capitalists' historical complicity in the exploitation and humiliation of coloured and black workers. They advocated stringent economic sanctions to bring the state to its knees and argued for the radical redistribution of land and capital.

The liberals, with whose viewpoint I identified in the sanctions debate, contended that the biggest burden of sanctions would fall on those who were already suffering great hardship. The risk was that politics could become so polarised that the possibility of a democratic settlement would be ruled out.

The aspect on which I differed fundamentally from both the radical and the liberal historians was their assumption that materialist considerations were always the overriding factor, whether for individuals (in the case of the liberal view) or for a class, as the Marxists would have it. Non-materialist considerations had been decisive in three of the critical decisions the Afrikaners had faced in their history: the Great Trek, the Anglo-Boer War, and the choice of Afrikaans above Dutch as official language. It was on account of these three great gambles they took that NP van Wyk Louw described the Afrikaners as one of the most daring peoples in history.

But academic debates remain academic unless they have tangible results in practical politics. While radical academics succeeded in giving great impetus to the anti-apartheid movement in Britain in particular, their influence on the white electorate in South Africa was limited. Many academics at UCT enthusiastically supported the ANC's internal ally, the United Democratic Front (UDF). The UDF tended to support the ANC on the necessity of sanctions.

I observed a material difference in the way in which academics at the US and those at UCT liaised with the primary community from which they and their students hailed. At the US there was a tradition that academics participated in political controversies in the Afrikaans press. They generally wrote as Afrikaners, and tried to convince readers that they were not only propagating their individual views but also had the Afrikaners' interests at heart.

The situation at UCT was radically different. English speakers on the campus had never organised themselves around an English identity or acted as champions for a party or a community. The majority of academics and students felt politically marginalised, a position which found expression in sentiments of cynicism or apathy with regard to white politics.

UCT academics expressed strong criticism of apartheid in their scholarly publications, but seldom wrote letters or articles for newspapers or made sensational statements in the press. They regarded the government and the security forces as "the other" which was tolerated only because people tended to fear anarchy more than a revolution. While most US academics talked about the orderly reform of apartheid, UCT academics were inclined to insist on the total abolition of apartheid, although there was no support for this stance among the vast majority of white voters, including English speakers.

## Black presence

In contrast to the situation at the US, black students had started influencing the classes and campus life at UCT from the early 1980s. For them, the lines in politics were sharply drawn between liberators and collaborators of the "regime". When I once mentioned unsuspectingly in a lecture that I had been a member of the Buthelezi Commission on the future of Natal and KwaZulu, many black students burst out laughing.

Black students adopted an implacable position on apartheid. As lecturer, I often asked if there was any concrete evidence I could cite to persuade them of the opposite of their argument on a particular issue. "No" was usually the answer, whereupon I would suggest that they study theology instead, seeing that they chose to believe rather than to know.

I especially enjoyed my first-year course on South African politics. Between 1983 and 1998, the year I retired, the proportion of black students in the class had grown from a small minority to a substantial majority. For many of these students politics was not merely of academic interest, but a burning issue that would directly determine their life chances. On many occasions, about eight to ten black students would stay behind after a lecture to ask questions or to express alternative opinions. I never experienced any open hostility.

At third-year and honours level I lectured on the topic of democratisation, which was one of the most exciting themes in the field of political studies at the time. The overthrow of the dictatorship in Portugal in 1974 had signalled the beginning of the so-called "Third Wave" of global democratisation. (The previous two "waves" or major surges of democracy had started in the early 1820s and the early 1960s.) Outside South Africa the question was no longer whether the days of white domination were numbered, but what system would replace it.

## What should our democracy look like?

At the time of my departure from the US, the debate on that campus had still been about whether the government's plans for political reform would attract any significant coloured or black support. Majority government did not come up as a topic of discussion.

By the 1990s more than thirty democracies had already come into being in the Third Wave. In 1991 the political scientist Samuel Huntington from Harvard University published his influential work *The Third Wave: Democratization in the Late Twentieth Century*, which I could draw on to good effect in my classes and newspaper columns. Internationally, the expectation was that South Africa would soon get a democracy, whether through violence or through negotiations.

On the nature of a future democracy in South Africa, I related in particular to the work of David Welsh and of Charles Simkins from the Economics Department. *South Africa's Options: Strategies for Sharing Power* by Welsh and

Van Zyl Slabbert had appeared in 1979. Welsh, who had been a member of the Liberal Party in the 1950s and subsequently supported the Progressives, was one of the few academics who were well acquainted with the literature on deeply divided societies. He pointed out that transitions to a democratic system of government in deeply divided societies only succeeded where power-sharing between the groups was institutionalised.

*South Africa's Options* stressed that while safeguarding individual rights in a bill of a rights was important, it was even more vital that a form of power-sharing be built into the political system. The authors proposed a minority veto of 10% to 15% to force parties to negotiate and seek compromises in respect of contentious matters. It was the kind of plan the NP would look for desperately ten to twelve years later. But at the time of the book's publication in the late 1970s, the immediate instinct of pro-NP opinion formers had been to slate such a scheme as a form of "selling out". Welsh told me recently that he could not recall a single substantial review in an Afrikaans newspaper or journal.

The NP was also urgently in search of a new ideology. During this time Simkins delivered an absorbing series of lectures on the theme "Reconstructing South African Liberalism", which was published shortly afterwards by the South African Institute of Race Relations (SAIRR). He argued that a liberal system of power-sharing could be designed as long as the state did not define the groups, as the apartheid regime had done. The right to mother-tongue education was a legitimate group right. Simkins's preferred electoral system was based on a single transferable vote, a system where voters rank candidates in order of preference on a ballot paper. A stipulated minimum of support would give a party the right to a seat in the cabinet and to veto certain laws.

The NP leaders, however, ignored this contribution as well. There was a belief that the NP was in a position to dictate the post-apartheid constitution. But even in the circles of the Progressive Federal Party (PFP) or of English-speaking academics, the book evoked little discussion. In the mid-1980s the PFP under Slabbert adopted a new policy which advocated a bill of individual rights but for the rest did not differ significantly from simple majority rule. This crucial issue was never put under the spotlight and debated.

## A controversial Irishman

By September 1986 widespread unrest had been continuing unabated for two years. The state detained thousands of people without trial, with no immediate prospect of normality. There was a pent-up rage among urban blacks in particular. After a visit to South Africa in 1985, Conor Cruise O'Brien, a razor-sharp Irish writer and academic, wrote that he had put the following propositions to South Africans he met: "The maintenance of the status quo is impossible. Reforms acceptable both to the white electorate and to politicised blacks are impossible. Revolution is impossible."

Welsh, who was at that stage head of the Department of Political Studies, invited O'Brien to present an undergraduate course on "siege societies", with special reference to the conflicts in South Africa, Israel and Northern Ireland, in the fourth quarter of 1986. The other members of the department and I welcomed the idea of a visit by O'Brien, a commentator held in high regard in Britain and the United States. We did not anticipate any problems. He was, after all, an outspoken opponent of apartheid and a supporter of economic sanctions.

But trouble lurked just around the corner. In 1986 the leadership of the ANC in exile called for an academic boycott of South Africa. Just before his departure for South Africa, O'Brien wrote in *The Times* of London that he rejected such a boycott. He indicated that he was on his way to deliver a series of lectures at UCT. In the fourth week of his stay in Cape Town, a storm erupted.

Groups of students, at the instigation of the ANC and O'Brien's enemies in London and Belfast, held protest meetings and disrupted a lecture and a public meeting that O'Brien had been scheduled to address. As a member of the audience at the latter event, I witnessed how a small group of students kept raising the temperature by harassing and taunting him. At one point an exasperated O'Brien called the academic boycott "Mickey Mouse stuff". The fat was in the fire, and it was clear that further disruptions would follow.

During this time a group of about forty students turned up at my office one afternoon. Their leader, a well-known activist called Comrade Ziko, addressed me: "Comrade Professor, you must tell us where that fellow O'Brien's office is." Fearing that the group planned to throw O'Brien out of his office, I refused to give the information. "The Comrade Professor is reactionary," Comrade Ziko told his followers contemptuously before leading the retreat.

After deliberations between O'Brien and the university management, it was agreed to terminate the lecture series. The subsequent commission of inquiry, headed by a former vice-chancellor of the University of the Witwatersrand, unfairly put part of the blame for the debacle on O'Brien. The truth was that the university authorities were unwilling to take the strong disciplinary measures against black students that they would have employed in the case of white students. Over the next thirty years, the same pattern would unfold on other campuses.

In *Ideas Matter: Essays in Honour of Conor Cruise O'Brien*, Welsh wrote that there was little indication that the ANC was willing to respect the autonomy or neutrality of the universities. He predicted that this attitude was likely to prevail even after the organisation's unbanning. O'Brien warned at the time of his visit to South Africa that the academic boycott and the intransigence of some of the students threatened the South African universities with the same forces that destroyed the Chinese universities during the Cultural Revolution at the instigation of Mao Zedong.

Directly after these events, I wrote in the Spring 1986 issue of *Die Suid-Afrikaan*: "It is very difficult to enforce academic freedom when black students, who represent an ever growing proportion of the student numbers, put no premium on it, and are incited by the ANC to do so."

In my *Cape Times* column I made the point that the manner in which South Africa conducted the struggle for freedom for all would be decisive for the political system that replaced apartheid. If the nature of the struggle was such that it expanded freedoms peacefully, the result would be a freer South Africa. Likewise, if freedom of speech was restricted in this struggle, we would get an intolerant South Africa.

Hence the nature of the future democracy would be determined by the kind of struggle waged to achieve it. As Dr Danie Craven used to say to the rugby teams he coached: "The way in which you practise during the week is the way you will play your match on Saturday."

In the O'Brien case, sympathy on the UCT campus was on the side of the students. A total of 81 academics, mainly from the humanities and social sciences, stated in a declaration that academic freedom could not be divorced from the establishment of a free South Africa. The declaration also rejected "any form of victimisation" of the students who had participated in the protests.

The number of those who were prepared to condemn the disruption of O'Brien's lectures was disturbingly small. Ken Hughes, a remarkably versatile mathematics lecturer, argued in UCT's *Monday Paper* that it was quite possible to support the liberation movement and at the same time denounce an academic boycott as foolish.

Simkins wrote in an article in the *Cape Argus* that there was no justification for the disruption of a lecture where a view was expressed with which some members of the audience disagreed radically. While people had the right to pull the speaker's views apart in their criticism, they did not have the right to bar him from speaking. Freedom of speech was too precious a right for its violation to be condoned in the hope that a future state would reinstitute it.

Looking back on that time, Simkins recently wrote to me that his position on the O'Brien episode had put him firmly in a minority camp in the social sciences on the UCT campus. "I think that there was a great deal of romanticism plus the hope of escaping from the travail of the last apartheid years. Also people wanted to be on the right side of history, a phrase which I have always regarded with great suspicion."[99]

From the mid-1980s I started listening with considerable scepticism to the talk on campus about the ANC that would institute non-racialism after they had demolished apartheid.

## Questions about a border war

I made it clear that I did not conform to the fashionable leftist orthodoxy and also did not support the call for an end to the conscription system. During the 1980s the struggle was increasingly less about apartheid and more about a negotiated alternative. On its own, the permanent defence force was too small to provide the stable platform that would be required for a negotiated settlement. The spokespersons of the End Conscription Campaign on the campus were not conscientious objectors but political activists. I often wondered whether they would also have opposed conscription under an English-speaking government with a policy just slightly less blatant than that of apartheid.

At the same time, I endeavoured in my column in the English dailies to raise an independent voice on the issue of the defence of South Africa's borders. In particular, South African military involvement beyond our national borders was cause for great concern. Seeing that by the end of the 1970s there were more than 20 000 Cuban troops in Angola, the question arose whether our government's intervention in that country in 1975 to nip "communist involvement" in the bud had not had exactly the opposite effect.

The government never made it clear to the public why it had sent troops into a distant country and for how long we would continue to hear alarming reports of South African troops who had died in the "border war".

I still remember how upset Van Zyl Slabbert was about the undeclared war in a conversation with me. He had been an MP for just over a year when he visited the operational area in January 1976 as a member of a parliamentary group. On this tour, the group was informed that a South African battalion was in Angola, engaged in a war about which not a word had been uttered either in Parliament or the local press. His half-brother, Sean Taylor, was a member of the battalion. This was the first (but not the last) time he discovered that some of the government leaders were openly lying about the defence force's foreign interventions. It would become one of the reasons for his unexpected resignation from Parliament ten year later.

99   E-mail communication from Charles Simkins, 20 August 2014.

Early in 1981 the son of Ben Liebenberg, a valued colleague of mine at Unisa, died in Angola. I tried to convey my sympathies, but it was impossible to speak of such a death in terms of making "the supreme sacrifice" for the sake of the country's security.

From December 1983 to January 1984, during Operation Askari, 21 South African troops lost their lives in battles in Angola. The title of my column which appeared on 14 January was "Why did 21 South African troops die in Angola?" I quoted General Hein du Toit, former head of Military Intelligence, who said the government was running the risk of losing the support of the public if it did not inform them of the reason for the cross-border operations. It could not simply be assumed that the "*volkswil*" (public will) would remain blindly loyal.

I posed the question: "What is being achieved by fighting in Angola? It is no longer credible to maintain that Swapo can be defeated." I quoted Abraham Lincoln, who had said that "the difficult thing is not to thrash the enemy but to keep it thrashed". With Cuba and Russia involved in Angola, it was impossible "to keep Swapo thrashed".

The column concluded with the statement that everyone realised by now that Swapo would win a free election in South West Africa/Namibia, and that no country would recognise a settlement which excluded Swapo. There was only one question: What were we still doing in Angola?

# Chapter 8

# "All the voices of this land"

On my departure from the University of Stellenbosch I lost an important link with the Afrikaans community. The loss of this channel was exacerbated by the fact that both *Die Burger* after Piet Cillié's retirement and *Rapport* were no longer keen to publish my articles and those of other academics who were critical of the government. If you wanted to publish in Afrikaans, you had to start your own magazine and find your own readership.

In an interview published on 18 October 1985, the Stellenbosch student newspaper *Die Matie* wanted to know why I – now a lecturer at UCT – had launched an Afrikaans opinion magazine, *Die Suid-Afrikaan*. The Afrikaans press was dominated by the political centre or the *verligtes* and "no truly new ideas" were getting across, I explained, as well as "nothing of what the black community is saying or thinking".

I admitted that there was also a personal element. "The fact that I had moved to UCT was probably one of the main reasons why I felt the need to establish *Die Suid-Afrikaan*. I wanted to compensate in a sense for my departure. I doubt whether I would have done so if I had stayed at Stellenbosch."

André du Toit and I discussed the possibilities of such a venture. I founded a private company, Voorbrand Publikasies, of which I am still the director and sole shareholder. But I would never have embarked on the project without André as editorial partner, nor would it have succeeded without him.

In 1984, almost on the same day as the first session of the Tricameral Parliament, we launched *Die Suid-Afrikaan* as a quarterly magazine. We were soon joined by Welma Odendaal, Chris Louw and Riaan de Villiers as members of a team without hierarchy. Antjie Krog and Pierre de Vos joined our ranks in the 1990s. There was seldom harmony in the editorial team, but we were united by the belief that we were engaged in something special that would make its mark.

*Die Suid-Afrikaan* was an uncommon phenomenon in Afrikaner ranks: a political magazine that was independent of any political party but took a specific stand from the outset. The first editorial in the Spring issue of 1984 read: "The magazine has no party-political affiliations. But we do not intend to be a bland, neutral magazine. We choose sides for an open society, equal rights and a peaceful settlement in South Africa. While this will be the approach of our editorials, we also want to provide an open forum to all who are interested in promoting political and cultural dialogue across a wide spectrum."

We took the name *Suid-Afrikaan* from the nineteenth-century Cape journal *De Zuid-Afrikaan*, which had advocated an inclusive Afrikaner identity.

Publishing the magazine was an exhilarating experience. We believed in what we were doing and, in my opinion, we did it well. André du Toit edited the contributions incisively and with great devotion and wrote hard-hitting editorials, Chris Louw and Riaan de Villiers delivered excellent investigative journalism, and Welma Odendaal along with De Villiers ensured that the magazine was professionally designed and laid out. Santie Grosskopf and Rykie van Reenen made important contributions.

Distribution was a major problem. Fortunately, Ton Vosloo, the managing director of Nasionale Pers (Naspers), put the services of their distribution company NND at our disposal. This was despite the fact that *Die Suid-Afrikaan* competed with *Insig*, Naspers's own opinion magazine which made its appearance a year after ours. Vosloo never commented on the content of our magazine, even though Chris Louw levelled scathing criticism at *Die Burger*'s tendentious reporting on the Dakar conference at which a group of 61 "internal" South Africans and an ANC delegation had held talks.

Besides writing articles, I also had to secure funding. The income from subscriptions was woefully inadequate, and I persuaded big companies to sponsor the magazine through advertisements. Unless we had eight full-page adverts at R1 000 each (1984 monetary value) in every issue, the 48-page magazine, printed on fairly good paper, could not appear.

The trickiest problem was to obtain advertisements for the first issue. The magazine was an unknown factor in a loaded political atmosphere. My major breakthrough was the support of Elisabeth Bradley, the daughter of Albert Wessels of Toyota and the renowned Afrikaans poet Elisabeth Eybers. She had been at university with my wife Annette, and I had met "Oom Albert" on a tour to the United States in 1980.

Bradley persuaded her father to take a full-page advert in all four issues in the first year. Then Anton Rupert of Rembrandt and Ronnie Melck of Stellenbosch Farmers' Winery came in, followed by Naas Steenkamp (Gencor), a fellow member of the Synthesis discussion group, Fred Ferreira (Ford), Willem Pretorius (Metlife) and Tony Bloom (Premier Milling). The fact that Gavin

Relly, chairman of Anglo American Corporation, was also a member of Synthesis probably counted in our favour when we approached their Chairman's Fund for support. We could regularly place enough full-page adverts to ensure the magazine's appearance.

From the start, *Die Suid-Afrikaan* published a wide variety of excellent articles. Sometimes a contribution came from unexpected quarters. While we were compiling our very first issue, I received an article titled "Vryheid" (Freedom) by mail from a certain P Lourens.

He was the father of Jansie, a young woman who was in a relationship with Carl Niehaus, an ANC activist. The two young people were later sentenced to prison terms of four and fifteen years respectively for high treason. They were among the first of their generation of Afrikaners who served prison sentences on such a charge. Lourens recounted in a spare writing style how he had been informed by the police one day that his daughter was being detained in terms of security legislation, and that they could only visit her in ten days' time. The family was also harassed by anonymous phone calls. "Hell seeped quietly into our home."

The first issue also carried a thought-provoking article by André P Brink on the levels of correspondence between the dialectics of NP van Wyk Louw and that of George Orwell. Karel Schoeman called his own contribution a preliminary study for a book he was writing on Emily Hobhouse. JM Coetzee, in a review of Karel Schoeman's novel *'n Ander land*, referred to Schoeman's "superlative art" and the "magnificence of the last pages".

In his review of Nadine Gordimer's *The Essential Gesture: Writing, Politics and Places* in the same issue, Coetzee made an observation with which I concurred: "My sense is that Gordimer is not much read in the Afrikaans community, in part perhaps because she has never demonstrated much sympathy for the Afrikaner."

In a lighter vein, there was Rykie van Reenen's column "'n Woordjie van Waterlooweg" (A word from Waterloo Road). It included the joke about the Dutch Reformed dominee who refused flatly to conduct the funeral of a woman's dog until she happened to mention that she and her husband intended to donate R10 000 to whichever church laid the dog to rest. "My dear lady," the dominee exclaimed, "why didn't you tell me right from the start that it's a Dutch Reformed dog?"

Van Reenen also wrote about an Afrikaans translation of the *Communist Manifesto* that had appeared in 1937 in an independent paper. In a preface by Leon Trotsky, written specially for the edition, there was an appreciative reference to "*ons geesgenote op die Donker Vasteland*" (our kindred spirits on the Dark Continent).

The third issue featured interviews I had conducted with Louis le Grange, minister of law and order, and General Jannie Geldenhuys, head of the army. The fourth issue included an article on my conversations with Dr Nthato Motlana. In number five, Piet Cillié, who was chairman of Naspers at the time, took stock of apartheid. This issue also featured an in-depth conversation between André du Toit and Beyers Naudé about Naudé's eventful life.

In the sixth issue, the spotlight fell on a polemic in 1876 in the Pretoria newspaper *De Volksstem* about the treatment of black workers. A hundred years later, the same debate could have been conducted in virtually the same words. The former Springbok captain Morné du Plessis contributed a well-argued article titled "Die moeilikheid met ons rugby" (The trouble with our rugby).

After the third issue I could approach other companies with the backing of letters from writers, poets or public figures who had written approvingly about the magazine. Though the defence minister, General Magnus Malan, declined my request for an interview with the magazine, he introduced his letter of 11 April 1985 as follows:

> Let me start off by congratulating you on the quality of the magazine you publish and the exceptional perspective you maintain. I am appreciative of your efforts to establish objectivity in your magazine, and am by no means averse to talking to you in future for publication purposes.

Elisabeth Eybers wrote that the articles were extremely interesting, particularly the one by Richard van der Ross, then rector of the University of the Western Cape, "with its human and matter-of-fact tone" which must surely have moved whites "and put them to shame". Karel Schoeman, known for his acerbic criticism, sent a congratulatory letter after the third issue.[100]

Rykie van Reenen, one of the most outstanding journalists South Africa has ever produced, wrote to the chairman of the Anglo American Corporation's Chairman's Fund to solicit sponsorship for the magazine. Her letter (written in Afrikaans) read as follows:

> I wonder whether you as an English speaker can conceive of what this publication means to us as Afrikaners. Just at the time when we need it most, we have a magazine that puts us in touch in an impartial manner with what Jeremy Cronin has called 'all the voices of this land'.
>
> I consider it one of the truly important achievements of *Die Suid-*

100  Letter from Karel Schoeman, 9 June 1985.

*Afrikaan,* and more specifically of Hermann Giliomee, that he manages get people from such divergent backgrounds as, say, Louis le Grange and Ntatho Motlana to engage in conversation with *Die Suid-Afrikaan.* He achieves this by entering the conversation as interviewer from a different and more comprehensive perspective than that of the ordinary pressman; also, in my opinion, because he inspires confidence in his integrity and that of his magazine through his soberness . . .

Another thing: while the magazine is undoubtedly serious, it is not weighed down by its seriousness. It succeeds in frequently getting across more serious points in a lighter vein. It is capable of ridicule, but it is not mean.

Having said all of this, as Afrikaans speaker I have still not put the essence of my appreciation of the magazine into words. What it boils down to is that I rarely pick up any concealed malice towards the Afrikaner as such in its pages.

I suspect that liberal-minded Afrikaners too, and maybe they in particular, may not always grasp this, but it is this element which, I can assure you, lies at the root of much of the lack of openness to criticism that the Afrikaner *qua* Afrikaner has displayed in the past.

While *Die Suid-Afrikaan* does not gloss over the mistakes (to put it mildly) of an Afrikaner government, the magazine does not give the Afrikaner a sense that he is being picked on and singled out for criticism. The magazine exudes a much broader and more complex understanding of the country's problems, and challenges the Afrikaner to grapple with them together with all other South Africans.[101]

The countrywide unrest that prevailed from 1984 to 1986 increasingly dominated *Die Suid-Afrikaan*'s content. The eighth issue, dated Winter 1986, featured an interview I had conducted with General Malan. He had been surprisingly frank. In reality, the conflict was about winning the "hearts and minds" of the masses, he said. "The state must satisfy the expectations of the masses, who have huge needs. The radicals want to exploit this situation. I have on my desk Mao Zedong's Little Red Book – go read it; this is how the enemies of South Africa are driving their assault."

In response to my question whether the Algerian civil war was an example for us, he remarked that Algeria was a case where the government had lost the

101  Rykie van Reenen – Chairman of Anglo American Chairman's Fund, 21 July 1985.

fight. "Of course, it was not the military that lost the fight. You never lose this sort of fight militarily. You lose it diplomatically, politically, economically and on similar terrains. The military or security aspect is only a small component." The core of the entire conflict was to find a political solution. To him, a military dictatorship was not an option. "A military regime is never a solution, just a deferral of the problem."

Shortly before Malan's death 25 years later in 2012, I asked him for a postmortem on the NP's battle for control of the state. His reply was: "The battle of the 1980s to re-establish control and security we won decisively, but we lost the negotiations and thereby the political battle." When I asked whether the negotiations should not have been conducted sooner, he replied that the NP government could have negotiated earlier, but the ANC, with the Russians and Cubans still behind them, would then have made impossible demands. There would have been nothing that forced them to reach a settlement.

From the start I endeavoured to get the cooperation of Dr Neville Alexander, one of the leading black activists in the country and someone I held in high regard both as an individual and as a scholar. He had obtained a doctorate in German literature at the University of Tübingen in Germany. After his return to South Africa, he was convicted on a charge of conspiracy to commit sabotage in the early 1960s and sentenced to ten years' imprisonment. He served his sentence on Robben Island, where a good understanding developed between him and Nelson Mandela despite their political differences.

While Alexander had ample reason to be bitter about apartheid and his sentence, he had decided at an early stage of his imprisonment that bitterness would amount to the greatest defeat in life. Like Mandela, he left Robben Island a stronger person. Among the radical intelligentsia he was regarded as one of the most formidable critics of apartheid, capitalism and what he referred to as the Stalinism of the ANC in exile.

When I told him how a lack of money prevented us from expanding *Die Suid-Afrikaan*, Alexander wrote to Dr Beyers Naudé, who had access to foreign funds. At first he had been very sceptical of *Die Suid-Afrikaan* because it seemed to be directed only at a white Afrikaans readership, Alexander explained to Naudé. In time his assessment of the magazine became more positive, and he himself had contributed a review of JM Coetzee's novel *Foe*. Alexander added:

> *Die Suid-Afrikaan* has clearly begun to reach almost the entire South
> African intelligentsia. I know it is read widely and with great interest
> in the circles with which I am intimately associated. As such it is prob-
> ably unique since both blacks and English- and Afrikaans-speaking

whites read it. The lack of political and other sectarianisms is of the greatest importance to people in my circle because we believe that many other worthwhile efforts tend to be disfigured by a too rigid and dogmatic political stance.[102]

We published several articles that made a significant contribution to the political debate. Lawrence Schlemmer reported that the unrest of 1984 was supported much more widely in the black community than had been the case in 1976. It had become imperative that black leaders be included in the cabinet to help plan and implement further constitutional initiatives. The historian Albert Grundlingh, author of a striking work on the so-called handsuppers and joiners during the Anglo-Boer War, drew parallels between the divergent positions of the brothers Christiaan and Piet de Wet in that war, and those of the brothers Jan and Breyten Breytenbach in our own time.

One of our aims was to let coloured and black voices speak. We published essays in which black township children described their experiences in the "white city centre". Zwelakhe Sisulu, editor of *New Nation*, voiced the views of a new, undaunted generation of the black intelligentsia. Jakes Gerwel and Richard van der Ross, in articles from different perspectives, presented an exceptional angle on the coloured people's ambivalent position.

A few articles in particular were close to my heart. One was Samuel Huntington's "Whatever has gone wrong with reform?" (Winter 1986). Five years earlier, this renowned political scientist from Harvard had spelled out in a paper what PW Botha should do in order to reform the country successfully. His lecture had attracted great interest in the press as well as among some cabinet ministers.

Thanks to a sponsorship from the Mobil Foundation, I was able to invite Huntington to South Africa in the winter of 1986. He visited several campuses and presented a seminar on PW Botha's reforms at UCT. I asked him to adapt his presentation as an article for *Die Suid-Afrikaan*.

Huntington summarised the shortcomings of the government's reform strategy as follows: Too much had been promised and too little had been delivered; the reforms had been slow, laborious and full of contradictions; the government had tried to reform after its position had already weakened; the government had not succeeded in controlling the violence, and it had won over no important new black constituencies. The *Financial Mail* brazenly published this article, in my estimation one of the most important articles of the decade, without our permission.

---

102  Neville Alexander – Beyers Naudé, 31 August 1987.

Another article that was close to my heart was Piet Cillié's "Bestek van apartheid" (Taking stock of apartheid). He and I had agreed that he would respond to my document titled "Klagstaat teen apartheid" (Charge sheet against apartheid). In his response, Cillié posed the question: Has all of "grand apartheid" been in vain? His reply was: "What this experiment in social engineering achieved to the good is that the option of total racial and territorial separation has hopefully been closed off once and for all." This statement said nothing about the suffering and losses people endured under apartheid.

Cillié also opined that if a liberal government had ruled after 1948 instead of the NP government and were to have moved towards a surrender of white power, Afrikaners would have embarked on an intense struggle against such an "integrationist government". This struggle would have dominated politics completely. There was something in what he said. We simply do not know how South Africa would have fared economically and in terms of stability without apartheid. Argentina, which in the early 1930s had ranked among the top ten countries in the world, measured by GDP per capita, had slumped to the fiftieth position a few decades later – after uprisings, strikes, coups, regime changes and severe policy fluctuations.

The third article in my category of favourites was JM Coetzee's account of a rugby match between Western Province and Northern Transvaal at Newlands, which he had agreed to write in exchange for my ticket. Coetzee paid particular attention to the shortcomings of the match analyses that had appeared in the three Cape newspapers the following Monday. In his view, none of the rugby writers had succeeded in re-creating the drama of the match as he experienced it, or in shedding light on the parts where really good rugby had been played.

With professionalism just around the corner, Coetzee warned, rugby was at risk of losing its soul if the emphasis were to fall on the mere spectacle to entertain uninformed spectators rather than on the "internal" logic of the game. The spectacle of one-day cricket was undermining true cricket, namely test cricket. If rugby should go the same route, the rugby writers would be partly be blame.

I had fun with the column I wrote under the pseudonym "Die Man Wat Weet" (The man in the know). The first time I referred to PW Botha as the "Groot Krokodil" was in the February 1988 issue. I had come up with that nickname during an earlier conversation with Piet Cillié about a possible successor to Botha.

When I mentioned FW de Klerk, Cillié said he had also thought of him as a possibility. He then told me that he had once said to De Klerk: "FW, you know our people don't accept a man as leader unless they know he's a crocodile. Strijdom was a crocodile, Verwoerd was a crocodile, Vorster was a crocodile."

Whereupon I had interrupted Cillié: "Yes, and PW is the great crocodile." In my next column I wrote about the doings of "PW, the Groot Krokodil", of whom everyone in the NP caucus was terrified. The nickname started cropping up in parliamentary debates and soon became common currency. On my fiftieth birthday, my gift from Cora Coetzee was a sketch of me being chased by a crocodile. A portly crocodile in a dress cheered him on, yelling "*Hap hom, Pappie*" (Bite him, Daddy).

The article I most enjoyed writing, maybe because it was accompanied by a degree of risk, was the one in which I indirectly gave a platform to Joe Slovo, leader of the banned South African Communist Party (SACP). I met him in 1988 at an Idasa conference in Leverkusen, West Germany, which was attended by Russians, Afrikaner academics and ANC office-bearers. My interest lay in trying to ascertain what influence the Soviet Union and the SACP exerted on ANC policy. I requested permission from the state to quote him, but my request was declined.

My interview with Slovo took place on 22 October 1988. In the article, I wrote that Slovo had moved around comfortably among the conference delegates. "He looks like a successful small-town lawyer. One can easily mistake him for the president of the local golf club." Since I was prohibited from quoting him, I explained, the article contained my "observations" based on statements by people at the conference "whose thinking is close to that of Slovo's". In an interview with Nelson Mandela four years later, he told me he had been highly amused by my description of Slovo when he read the article in prison.

Slovo's pronouncements during the interview are still relevant today, given the standpoints Jacob Zuma and some other ANC leaders continue to express about the necessity of a national democratic revolution. According to my transcription, Slovo said that there had to be a mixed economy in the first stage. The ultimate policy was a socialist economy, a goal about which there was, according to him, no significant disagreement within the ANC.

Slovo envisaged a post-apartheid transitional period that would present huge challenges. They would have to endeavour to retain the whites with their skills, but, on the other hand, wealth had to be redistributed and blacks put in positions where they could learn on the job how to do the work. He added: "They are going to fuck things up, we know it."

A balance would have to be found between appointing inexperienced black people in senior positions and retaining white experience. With regard to the big commercial farms, it would be ridiculous to give "Joe Tshabalala" a patch of land and say: "Start farming". In order to build socialism, there had to be an initial period during which a free market and profit would be allowed. The interview left me with little doubt about Slovo's central position in the movement and the importance of the communist influence.

Long-term financial sustainability was *Die Suid-Afrikaan*'s chief problem. A shortage of money remained a concern until someone whispered a word in the ear of Marion von Dönhoff, editor of *Die Zeit*, a quality weekly paper in Hamburg. A generous donation by the paper lessened the burden of constant fundraising to some extent.

Up to 1990, when I withdrew voluntarily from *Die Suid-Afrikaan*, most of the money was still generated inside the country. I felt that we had to rely less on foreign sources of funding and more on domestic sources. Some members of the editorial team, however, were of the view that foreign funds could be used until the point when the struggle against apartheid was over.

In 1989 Ton Vosloo and I discussed the possibility of merging *Die Suid-Afrikaan* and *Insig* and creating one magazine in the Naspers stable. An independent board would guarantee its editorial independence and financial survival. Ton probably thought the name of such a new magazine should be "*Insig*, incorporating *Die Suid-Afrikaan*"; I was so forward as to think it could be "*Die Suid-Afrikaan*, incorporating *Insig*".

Denis Beckett, too, had earlier approached Vosloo when his independent magazine *Frontline* ran into financial trouble. Vosloo's offer was that Naspers would take a 50% stake. As Beckett put it, the deal would have meant "a new league" for *Frontline*. Unfortunately, the *Rand Daily Mail* wrote spitefully that Beckett "was selling out in slavish adherence to the National Party", which led to the collapse of the plan.[103]

I was the only one on *Die Suid-Afrikaan*'s editorial team who was enthusiastic about the merger with *Insig*. Though we were united in our rejection of apartheid, there was no consensus about what should come after apartheid. Most of my colleagues were in favour of individual-based majority rule, coupled with entrenched human rights.

My own preference was for a party that relied predominantly on minorities being made part of a new system built on power-sharing with a formation led by the ANC. As Schlemmer and I would contend in *From Apartheid to*

---

103  Denis Beckett, *Radical Middle: Confessions of an Accidental Revolutionary* (Cape Town: Tafelberg, 2010), p. 142.

*Nation-Building* (1989), it was imperative to build power-sharing into the new constitutional design in such as way that the majority party, which was bound to be the ANC, could not impose its will unilaterally.

None of my colleagues at *Die Suid-Afrikaan* were in favour of my and Vosloo's plan. Unlike Beckett, I had not established *Die Suid-Afrikaan* virtually single-handedly, and I did not wish to carry on on my own, either. I still regret the fact that the plan fell through. *Die Suid-Afrikaan* and *Frontline* both disappeared from the media scene. They left a huge void.

## After Rubicon

For almost four years after PW Botha's disastrous Rubicon speech on 15 August 1985, South Africa's internal politics were enveloped by a sense of political despondency. It was strange, as in this speech the NP government had admitted for the first time that black people whose "nations" had not become "independent" would in future have to be accommodated within a common system along with the white, coloured and Indian "minorities". In 1986 the government abolished the hated pass laws. Yet PW Botha's image as a reformer had been damaged beyond repair.

For all that, in respect of hard political power the state appeared to be unassailable. On 12 September 1987 the *Cape Times* published a damning speech by Mangosuthu Buthelezi. Twenty-five years after resorting to the armed struggle, he said, the ANC had gained little ground. All water and electricity supply systems were still functioning, and not a single factory had been forced to stop production on account of revolutionary activities. His conclusion was that the classic conditions under which an armed struggle gained the ascendancy – divisions in the security forces and civil service and large-scale popular support for a revolution – did not obtain in South Africa.

In 1987, under the heading "Once again, the government has rescued the ANC", I wrote that the West seemed to be getting tired of the ANC. I quoted the US secretary of state, George Shultz, who had remarked after a discussion with the ANC leader Oliver Tambo that there was no point in meeting again for as long as the ANC leadership's thinking about the struggle in South Africa remained so unrealistic. At a recent conference I had attended in England, journalists, diplomats and African politicians had spoken negatively about the ANC. African states were running out of patience with the ANC in exile, and were putting pressure on them to return to South Africa and wage their struggle inside the country.

I talked regularly to Lawrence Schlemmer, who was au fait with the latest opinion polls. According to the polls, the majority of black adults were keen to welcome the ANC, a movement with a 75-year-old history, back into the country to help liberate them. Remarkably, most of them felt closer to the NP than to the SACP. They preferred a government in which the minorities as well as the majority were represented in the cabinet, and were not in favour of sanctions, affirmative action or racial conflict. What they did want was for apartheid and all racial discrimination to be scrapped as soon as possible – they were fed up with being bossed around by whites.

There was, however, a serious political problem when it came to the black youth. In my *Cape Times* column of 1 August 1986, titled "Desocialisation of blacks big threat to state and business", I noted that the socialisation function of the education system for black youth was collapsing in urban areas.

In Soweto, only 7% of matriculants had passed with matric exemption (which gave access to university) compared to 16% in Bophuthatswana and 23% in Venda. Though black pupils in urban areas still attended school, there was very little learning taking place. The entire education system, constructed around the concepts of merit, standards, tests and examinations, was crumbling. The new slogan was "Pass one, pass all".

At the same time, anti-capitalism was gaining in popularity among the youth. Pamphlets on university campuses called on students to throw in their weight behind the black workers' struggle for improved working conditions. The South African state, despite all the "hard power" at its disposal, lacked the "soft power" capacity to restore the learning environment in black schools. Without this, it was hard to raise the extremely low levels of labour productivity. Sections of the business community started to believe that only the ANC would be capable of restoring the capitalist work ethic.

But the government, and specifically President PW Botha, had an equally big problem as the ANC leadership in exile. In August 1986 I wrote that Botha increasingly reminded me of the British general of whom it was said that his troops would follow him everywhere, but only out of curiosity about where he was leading them to. Every time the ANC found itself in a corner, the Botha government scored own goals that helped the ANC regain the moral high ground.

In February 1988 the government banned seventeen internally based black organisations that were organised under the umbrella of the United Democratic Front (UDF) . This action reinforced the impression that the government was incapable of tolerating radical opposition and that the ANC had grounds for claiming that it was the only true liberation movement. Not only did Botha refuse to talk to the ANC, he also did not get along with Mangosuthu Buthelezi, whose Inkatha organisation had a mass base.

The president was not even prepared to provide a declaration of intent for the negotiations with the internal black leaders that he envisaged. It seemed as if he would be quite happy with the indefinite continuation of the general state of emergency that had been proclaimed in 1986.

In these circumstances, I, like many others, was prepared to grab at any opportunity in an attempt to help break the impasse. The first was the general election of May 1987. Colin Eglin, Van Zyl Slabbert's successor as leader of the Progressive Federal Party (PFP), asked me to stand as the party's candidate in the Stellenbosch constituency.

I seriously considered acceding to his request until Esther Lategan announced that she would stand under the banner of Denis Worrall's Independent Movement. It made no sense to me to split the limited number of left-of-the-NP votes in Stellenbosch.

Subsequently, I was very glad about the way things turned out. For a writer on history and politics, independence from political parties was a vital asset, and I preferred to preserve mine.

## Slabbert's quest

Early in 1986 Van Zyl Slabbert, leader of the official opposition, walked out of Parliament after having labelled it an irrelevant institution in the face of the enormous crisis in which South Africa found itself. He immediately began searching for another role.

I regarded Slabbert's decision to write off Parliament as a positive step, while Stanley Uys, a very experienced analyst, called it "incomprehensible" in the *Financial Mail*. We debated the issue in an exchange of letters. I argued that Slabbert's dramatic step had been necessary to break the political impasse. He had received no significant support from the business sector. PW Botha, too, had shown little interest in the offer Slabbert had made to him in a private conversation to broker a political middle ground between the government and the ANC. It amounted to an attempt to get government backing for the idea of a convention in which the major white and black leaders would seek a compromise. Such an initiative would, as Slabbert put it during the conversation, "pull the ANC's teeth". By that he meant that the ANC would no longer be able to pass itself off as the only legitimate representative of the voteless.

Uys rejected Slabbert's plan. He firmly believed that the middle ground Slabbert was looking for was a chimera. In his view, it was incorrect to believe that the NP would never split and to argue, as Slabbert did, that Parliament had become irrelevant. Parliament would continue to be important because of the legitimacy it enjoyed in the eyes of whites. The place of white political leaders who advocated radical change was in Parliament, and their moment would come once the reformists in the NP started looking for new allies. Extra-parliamentary politics would doom white leaders to political impotence.

With hindsight, Uys was quite correct and I was wrong. By rejecting Parliament, Slabbert cut short his career in politics. Neither the ANC nor the NP would have any role for him. Like Jan Hofmeyr, he would become one of the great tragedies in liberal politics.

Had Slabbert remained in Parliament as PFP leader, things might have turned out very differently both for him and for the country. A reliable source in the NP government informed me that in 1990, just before the negotiations started in earnest, FW de Klerk had proposed in a conversation with Zach de Beer, leader of the PFP's successor the Democratic Party (DP), that their respective parties form a united front. De Beer subsequently came back to him and said he had been unable to obtain any support for the proposal in his caucus.

Tony Leon, who later became the DP leader, assured me that no such proposal was ever put to the DP caucus. In all likelihood Colin Eglin and Helen Suzman had rejected De Klerk's proposal at an early stage. I am almost certain that if Slabbert had still been leader of the liberal opposition in 1990, he would have jumped at De Klerk's proposal. Quite possibly he would have been one of the chief negotiators. But all of this is speculation. In 1987 the country was stuck in a political stalemate, and Slabbert was in search of a role in extra-parliamentary politics.

## The Dakar expedition

A few weeks after the general election of 1987, Slabbert asked me and my UCT colleague André du Toit to drop in at his cottage in Rondebosch. He wanted to gauge our views on his plan to fly a number of Afrikaner opinion-formers to an African state for the purpose of conducting a week-long debate with leading figures in the ANC in exile. "Just talking and feeling each other out, no issuing of declarations afterwards or any other obligations," he said. But that was not how things turned out. The ANC would fasten upon the Dakar conference to make maximum propaganda for its cause.

We encouraged Slabbert to proceed with the plan and suggested some names of Afrikaners who could make fruitful contributions to such a debate. The country was in the grip of ongoing violence. A peaceful outcome seemed unattainable. We felt sure that several opinion-formers would be willing to risk having their passports withdrawn as punishment for talks with ANC leaders.

After receiving a favourable reaction elsewhere in South Africa as well,

Slabbert went on a fundraising trip to the United States with Alex Boraine, who had joined him in resigning from Parliament and in founding the Institute for a Democratic Alternative for South Africa (Idasa). Slabbert recounted afterwards that in New York they had met a financier called George Soros, who was apparently loaded with money. Despite telling them that he feared South Africa was doomed and the conference futile, Soros had been willing to donate a substantial sum.

In the immediate aftermath of the conference, I tried to sum up in *Die Suid-Afrikaan* of September 1987 what I considered to have been the deciding factor for most of the Dakar travellers:

> We wanted to bring some measure of rationality into the propaganda war which has taken the place of serious political debate in South Africa. By sitting down with the ANC at the conference table, the internal delegation wanted to show that the country is not in the grip of a war that is being imposed from the outside. We wanted to say that the conflict is not between the forces of 'good' and 'evil': it is an internal conflict that is rooted in the country's history – a conflict that has to be resolved inside the country. Dakar is an effort to break through the propaganda war in which the government and the ANC demonise each other and each party holds the other solely responsible for the suffering and deaths of the past 34 months.

In early July 1987, a group of 61 South Africans flew to Dakar, Senegal, to meet a 17-strong ANC delegation headed by Thabo Mbeki. About half of the internal group were white Afrikaans speakers. The government probably knew about the planned expedition, but had decided to do nothing about it.

As the conference was held during the winter holidays, there was no need for me to request leave. In any case, I had reason to believe that the UCT executive would welcome participation in a conference of this nature. Theuns Eloff, then still a Reformed Church minister, was less fortunate and afterwards found himself in disfavour with the church authorities. Fred Mouton of *Die Burger* produced a good cartoon on the topic, with a church elder complaining to Eloff: "But dominee, I thought you'd said you're going to Senekal [a town in the Free State] for the week."

At Dakar Thabo Mbeki played a leading role among the group of ANC representatives who arrived in the city shortly after us. I was familiar with Mbeki's essay "The Historical Injustice", which had been published ten years earlier. It portrayed the history of black South Africans as 350 years of disaster for the black population as a result of Western colonisation – massacres, exploitation, enslavement and diseases, segregation, apartheid. Though blacks were the producers of the wealth, the white colonists and capitalists appropriated it for themselves. For Mbeki, the "Boers" were the opposite of all that was dynamic: they were feudalistic, primitive, stultified and reactionary.

At the conference the ANC leaders suggested that the Afrikaners could regain a moral identity for themselves in the country by renouncing their history. It reminded me of Lewis Gann's remark about ethnic minorities in eastern Europe for whom loss of power could easily mean the simultaneous loss of their history and culture (see p. 67).

My thoughts also went back to the NP leaders of the 1950s and 1960s. They had been inspired by their sense of injury about past defeats and humiliations and the belief that they now had a monopoly of political morality. Like the ANC leaders 20 to 30 years later, they believed their own righteousness would prevent them from abusing their power. Mbeki and his comrades wanted us to accept the ANC as a non-racial movement and as the only party that was fit to rule the country.[104]

The ANC gave the impression that they stood outside of history. Members of our group pointed out that a number of independent African states had made serious economic and administrative blunders over the past 20 to 25 years. Invariably the ANC delegation replied that they were too smart to repeat those mistakes.

Like the other "internal" South Africans, I struggled to grasp the theoretical context within which the ANC delegation spoke, which of course made it hard to engage them in a proper debate. The picture would only become clearer a year later, in the German city of Leverkusen. As I have mentioned, I was part of an Idasa group that held talks there with members of the ANC's communist faction under the leadership of Joe Slovo. Their ranks were supplemented by Russian officials and academics from Moscow.

At Leverkusen I soon clicked with the historian Irina Filatova, who was attached to a Moscow university. Her research area was the historical ties between Russia and South Africa, and in particular the relationship between the ANC and the Soviet Union. In the years prior to the Dakar conference, she had often met ANC leaders in Moscow at meetings held under the auspices of the Soviet Afro-Asian Solidarity Committee. She had been exposed to

---

104  For a debate that was conducted among myself, Breyten Breytenbach and Pallo Jordan directly after the conference, see *Die Suid-Afrikaan*, 13 February 1988, pp. 22-29.

communist doctrine from early on in her career, and was well placed to understand ANC thinking and interpret it to South Africans.

The ANC leaders she had met in Moscow, she told us, were deeply impressed by the communist model. The path they intended to follow in South Africa was the socialist policy of centralisation, nationalisation and central planning. While some leaders realised that this policy had gone badly awry in other African countries, most of them wished to take South Africa in the direction of a "National Democratic Revolution". In terms of this thinking, political liberation was only the first phase of the revolution; it had to lay the groundwork for the transition to the second phase, namely socialism. At the Dakar conference, Breyten Breytenbach was virtually the only participant who sounded a note of caution by pointing out what this road had led to in several other African countries.

In Filatova's view, the ANC leaders were also strongly influenced by the Soviet notion that imperialism and capitalism were the cause of all ethnic and nationalist conflicts. They firmly believed that phenomena such as racism, ethnic conflict or apartheid would no longer exist once capitalism had been eliminated in South Africa.

At Dakar speakers such as Pallo Jordan, at the time still falsely boasting a doctorate, declared with great assertiveness that the "real" divisions in South Africa did not run along ethnic or racial lines, but along class lines. It was a preposterous claim, given that a lack of ethnic and cultural unity had characterised Africa in the previous century and particularly in the post-independence period. Civil wars had erupted in a number of countries, with friction between different ethnic communities often a major factor in the conflict.

Jordan and his comrades Thabo Mbeki and Mac Maharaj, also present at Dakar, could get away with this interpretation because liberalism with its British foundation was also strongly inclined to hold that materialist notions (wealth, job opportunities, security and physical wellbeing) were always decisive. Against this, non-materialist notions (the survival of a particular history, language and cultural identity, and an insistence on not being dominated by other groups) were at bottom only misleading justifications for ethnic privilege and the retention of power.

It soon became clear to me that a future ANC government would not allow schools to teach a kind of history with which it disagreed. During the conference week Mbeki and I participated in a debate for an American television station on how the curricula for history as a school subject should be compiled in the "new" South Africa. I proposed that the professional organisation of South African historians appoint a panel on which the different approaches to historiography would be represented. The point of departure had to be that children should not slavishly accept one particular interpretation but instead see history as a debate about different interpretations.

"We have a better plan," Mbeki replied. "In a liberated South Africa, the political majority should appoint a committee to direct how the history of South Africa has to be rewritten." This committee would decide who the country's heroes were, both white and black. "There will be Afrikaner heroes too," Mbeki assured me, "people such as Bram Fischer and Beyers Naudé." Schlemmer observed after the conference that Mbeki and other ANC delegates confidently expected people to write off their history.[105]

Like Schlemmer, I had major doubts about the democratic credentials of the ANC. In general, however, the mood was euphoric, and some members of the South African delegation were bedazzled by the ANC. André P Brink's reaction could even be described as ecstatic. He would later write in his memoir 'n Vurk in die pad (A fork in the road) that at Dakar agreements had been sealed and lifelong friendships forged. "For many of us," he wrote, the encounter had "opened up new dimensions, new ways of thinking and seeing". But he added: "There were exceptions, too, such as the historian Hermann Giliomee, who assured me within the first few days: 'We can't trust these people', and a few others – even Breyten – who, according to their own lights, 'refused to be duped'." Brink enthused about the "scintillating intellectual" Mac Maharaj, the "ebullient" Steve Tshwete and the "endearing" Kader Asmal, whose "erudition" had captivated him.[106]

I gained a positive impression of Thabo Mbeki as a seasoned diplomat, but I was not bedazzled.

Like virtually all liberation movements, the ANC was not interested in freedom or equal opportunities for all, but in power and ideological domination inspired by the communist model.

My sense was that the ANC were not looking for partners to help build a successful South Africa, but for stooges to help carry out their radical plans. They embraced those who accepted their schemes and assurances at face value. Many years later, Chris Louw, a journalist who would create a furore in the year 2000 with his open letter Boetman is die bliksem in (Boetman is mad as hell), looked back ruefully on his Dakar experience:

---

105  Lawrence Schlemmer, "Politieke keuses en bebloede sitvlakke", Die Suid-Afrikaan, October 1988, p. 22.

106  André P Brink, 'n Vurk in die pad: 'n Memoir (Cape Town: Human & Rousseau, 2009), p. 404.

Only much later did I realize how naïve I was at Dakar. There was a kind of bravado among the younger Afrikaners, tired of the stereotyping of Afrikaners as rigid and racist. Shunned by the West, we considered it the highest priority to show that "we are not all like that". Most of us were more interested in demonstrating that difference, through our actions and words, and so to demolish stereotypes, than we were in confronting intellectually the arguments of the ANC delegation. We wanted to show we were even more African than the ANC; in that sense the meeting on our part was more about show and symbolism than substance. We were so very ashamed of our government, of PW Botha's boorish conduct, of the mishmash of NP policy, that we fell for the temptation to side with the ANC and its ideology and in that spirit dismissed any reference to minority or group rights as being code language for NP support. We wanted to create as much distance as possible between the NP and us.[107]

It was against this background that I caused a stir at the conference with my proposal of a bi-communal order that amounted to a system of mandatory power-sharing with the NP and the ANC as the major players, rather than a system dominated by the ANC on the basis of numbers. The NP would in all likelihood represent most of the white, coloured and Indian voters, and the ANC most of the black voters. Decisions would be taken on the basis of consensus, or what would later become known as "sufficient consensus".

This was anathema to the ANC participants. We simply had to believe that the movement had everybody's best interests at heart. It was not clear whether a future ANC government would tolerate the NP for long. At Dakar, Pallo Jordan spoke of a "liberatory intolerance" towards parties that had previously advocated race-based exclusion. The ANC delegates acted swiftly to isolate those who remained sceptical of their glib PR talk. Just after the conference, I was wryly amused to read in the Johannesburg *Sunday Times* that Jordan had referred to me as the "Boer in the woodpile".

But Jordan with his gravelly voice, who could switch with ease from English to Afrikaans, was also the one who told the best joke at the conference. This was after I had again raised the need for mandatory power-sharing between the major parties. I quoted Gérard Chaliand, author of the acclaimed *Revolution in the Third World* (1977), who had observed in an interview with *Die Suid-Afrikaan* that there was no record of an exiled liberation organisation

---

107   E-mail communication from Chris Louw, 29 May 2009.

(such as the ANC) turning itself into a non-violent legal movement competing with others for power.

Along with several others, I suggested that the ANC participate in new regional initiatives such as the KwaZulu-Natal indaba, which aimed to negotiate a democratic order for the region independently of the government, or other interim agreements that genuinely signalled a break with apartheid. It was during this discussion that Jordan told his joke.

A baboon, heeding the anguished cries of a python that lay pinned down under a rock, lifted the rock to set the reptile free. Immediately the python started to strangle the baboon. As they struggled, a fox came by and persuaded the two to accept his mediation. "The only way to solve the conflict," the fox said, "is for the python to assume his original position to see how it all started." The python obliged and the rock was replaced. "What do we do now?" the baboon said. "Let him be, you damn fool," the fox responded. "You know that he will swallow you."

In private conversations, ANC representatives confirmed the message conveyed by the joke: they revealed how deeply suspicious they were of being swallowed by the "python" of interim arrangements in which they were not assured of control. Yet the majority of the Dakar travellers were convinced that the lack of good faith was on the government's side rather than that of the ANC. Jannie Gagiano, my roommate in the hotel where the conference was held, told me later that some of the participants had remarked to him that they saw Dakar as the place where I "came out of the closet" and revealed my true colours as an "ultra-conservative Afrikaner nationalist".

Back in South Africa, a jeering AWB commando awaited us at the airport, but the police were evidently under strict orders to protect our safety. Jaap Durand, who was vice-rector of the University of the Western Cape at the time, wrote in his autobiography, *Protesstem* (2016), that Willie Esterhuyse told him he had pleaded with PW Botha not to throw Durand in jail. When Durand asked why, then, the NP-aligned academics had inveighed so negatively against him and the other Dakar travellers, Esterhuyse replied: "It was part of the package."

Durand recounted that he was deeply outraged by this.[108]

---

108  Jaap Durand, *Protesstem* (Wellington: Bybelkor, 2016), p. 201.

## Chapter 9

# "Witness to momentous times"[109]

From the early 1980s two urgent challenges dominated the political debate: a negotiated settlement and black urbanisation. The relation between the two had not been fully understood until the realisation sank in that a white government was incapable of dealing with rapid black urbanisation. Between 1946 and the 1970s the black population had doubled, and it would double again between 1970 and 1996. While the number of black people increased from 8 million to 31 million between 1946 and 1996, white numbers grew to just over 4 million.

Flip Smit and Jan Booysen's *Swart verstedeliking: Proses, patroon en strategie* (1981) and John Kane-Berman's *South Africa's Silent Revolution* (1990) changed the debate. These two studies highlighted how black people in search of work and housing were streaming to the urban areas, which used to be predominantly white. It was the "annihilation of distance" as a result of the progress of Western technology of which Arnold Toynbee had written 40 years earlier, which made it impossible for "the different fractions of mankind to retire into isolation from one another again". Much more than the ANC's armed struggle, the Achilles heel of white-minority domination was rapid black urbanisation and the growing power of the increasingly better-skilled black labour force.

Commuting between Stellenbosch and the UCT campus nearly every weekday from 1983 to 1998, I could witness the steady proliferation of squatter shacks next to the N2. Dr Jan Lombard, deputy director of the Reserve Bank, rightly observed that the migration of black people to the cities was the most important social development of our time.

By the mid-1980s there were for the first time in South Africa's history more people living in cities than in rural areas, and more black than white pupils

---

109 A translation of the title of the renowned Afrikaans journalist Schalk Pienaar's autobiography, *Getuie van groot tye*.

that passed matric. In my first-year class at UCT I saw the black and coloured component grow from about 15% in 1983 to more than 50% ten years later.

The failure of the homeland policy was visible to all, and a settlement that would replace apartheid had become imperative. There was, however, no consensus on how such as settlement should be reached and what system of democracy would be likely to work well in South Africa.

During the 1980s, in my UCT courses on the process of democratisation, I used to quote the views of three respected authorities and challenge my students to "pit their wits" against their arguments.

One of these experts was Elie Kedourie, author of an authoritative study on nationalism. Kedourie maintained that democracy only worked if there was a regular change of government, as was the case in Western Europe. But the application of the Western European model to deeply divided societies had repeatedly led to "the tyranny of the majority", he added.

Pierre van den Berghe, who had grown up in the Belgian Congo and became an influential sociologist in the United States, stated in his introduction to *The Liberal Dilemma in South Africa* (1979) that in plural societies such as South Africa, majority government could become a cloak for racial domination. With regard to black demands for an "ordinary" democracy, he wrote: "If your constituency has the good fortune to contain a demographic majority, racism can easily be disguised as democracy."

Then there was Donald Horowitz, a professor of law and political science at Duke University who had studied under Samuel Huntington at Harvard. He was generally recognised as one of the greatest authorities on ethnic conflict and constitution-making in deeply divided societies. In his seminal study *Ethnic Groups in Conflict* (1985), he noted that a well-functioning democracy was an exceptional phenomenon in a society with deep cleavages between different nationalities or racial groups.

Horowitz wrote in *A Democratic South Africa? Constitutional Engineering in a Divided Society* (1991): "If majority rule means black majority rule and white minority exclusion, something has gone wrong," and whites "will have no reason to choose an inclusive democracy for South Africa".

## Where do we fit in?

In 1979 Jeane Kirkpatrick, an American professor of political science who was a member of the Reagan administration's National Security Council and US ambassador to the United Nations in the 1980s, wrote: "No idea holds greater sway in the minds of educated Americans than that it is possible to democratize governments any time and anywhere under any circumstances." In 2007

*The Economist* affirmed this statement with the words: "Yes indeed." The same thought suggested itself to me virtually every time I had to hear from an American visitor how simple it was to institute a well-functioning democracy in South Africa.

From the late 1980s I was increasingly influenced by studies of societies that emphasised how politics and economics had to work in tandem to consolidate a democracy or, as a corollary, how poor political and economic decisions could cause a democracy to go under. This was illustrated particularly well by Huntington and the economist Joan Nelson in their book *No Easy Choice: Political Participation in Developing Countries* (1976). They distinguished between three different development paths: the technocratic model, the populist model and the liberal model.

The technocratic model is an apt description of the route South Africa followed from 1948 to 1990 under NP rule, if it had to be viewed by an uninvolved outsider. Shortly after 1948, the NP government curtailed voting and other rights. This was followed by high economic growth and considerable socio-economic development, but increasing socio-economic inequality between whites and blacks. Consequently there was less and less political stability from 1976, with a "participation explosion" from 1984 until the government had to transfer power in 1994.

The populist model, on the other hand, probably best describes what might have been South Africa's development path if a party such as the ANC had gained power in the early 1960s. It would have introduced a populist policy on the assumption that this would lead to more growth and greater socio-economic equality. The reality would in all likelihood have been quite different. The implementation of such a policy would have resulted in a flight of capital and skills, leading to less socio-economic development followed by less political stability and a "participation implosion" (i.e. a state of emergency that suspends democracy).

The third model, which Huntington and Nelson called the "benign liberal model", best describes the hypothetical course of events if a party such as the Progressive Federal Party were to have gained power. This is the model with which the majority of conventional liberals in South Africa work. It assumes that the country would have experienced strong economic growth, which would have led to greater socio-economic equality, which would in turn have promoted political stability. Racial and ethnic tensions would have dissolved, and greater prosperity and happiness would have ensued.

The big problem with this model is that in hardly any developing country has this trajectory ever manifested itself. Supporters of this model usually believe in the adage "all good things go together". It is predicated on the notion that a free labour market (where no one's advancement is determined by their race, colour or sex) and a free political system (universal adult franchise democracy) reinforce each other and work hand in hand to bring about high economic growth, political freedom and the easing of conflicts.

The work of Amy Chua, now a law professor at Yale, was in keeping with that of Huntington and Nelson. Her first teaching post had been at the Duke University Law School where Donald Horowitz was a professor. I got to know Horowitz in the late 1980s when he conducted research for his book *A Democratic South Africa?* He sent me Chua's unpublished papers, which eventually gave rise to her book *World on Fire: How Exporting Free Market Democracy Breeds Ethnic Hatred and Global Instability* (2002).

Chua used examples from Africa and Southeast Asia to show that the free-market system, which tends to give certain ethnic minorities an inside track, exacerbates ethnic and racial divisions in divided societies. But the wheel turns, and in time the previously subordinate majority comes into power. In Chua's view, democracy can then act as the vehicle for an ethnic backlash by the majority against "market-dominant" minorities with disproportionate economic power. The new government starts advantaging the majority and increasingly constrains the minorities through legislation. The civil service is packed with loyal supporters, industries are nationalised, and minorities' assets are confiscated and expropriated. Affirmative action intensifies for the sake of "transformation". Over the past 75 years this pattern of liberal democracy and liberal capitalism clashing, instead of reinforcing each other, had repeated itself in one country after the other, but the liberals had closed their eyes to it.

## A proposed framework for democracy

From the mid-1980s opinion polls indicated that the ANC's support was just above 60%, while that of the NP was just above 20%. If these support levels were to be reflected in the first free election, South Africa would have a dominant-party system in which the gap between the strongest and the second-strongest party would be among the highest in the world.

Hence the chance of a change of government during the first 20 to 25 years of a democracy was virtually zero. Research has shown that regular changes of the ruling party, rather than a good constitution, determine the health of a democracy.

Elsewhere, in democracies with a dominant party as electorally powerful as the ANC would be, the distinction between ruling party and state had dissolved over time. South Africa did have an abundance of vibrant civil society institutions such as trade unions, business organisations, cultural societies and religious organisations, but because of segregation and apartheid most of them were closely linked to a particular ethnic group.

In most deeply divided societies such as South Africa power-sharing was important, but such a system worked best where the election results impelled the parties to form coalitions. A leader such as Nelson Mandela declared explicitly in his prison conversations that he sought a balance between the interests of the majority and those of the minorities, but this idea was anathema to ANC leaders in exile who had been strongly influenced by the Soviet model. And on other occasions Mandela, too, had insisted on "ordinary majority government", by which he meant the "winner-takes-all" Westminster system.

After Dakar, Schlemmer and I decided to write more about the clash between what became known as majoritarianism (where the majority effectively has the say and the right to dismiss the views of minority parties) and power-sharing and pluralism (where minorities would participate in discussions in cabinet as well as Parliament, and where the thrust of politics would be to find the greatest possible degree of agreement). It was against the backdrop of this heated debate that we wrote our book *From Apartheid to Nation-Building*. The first part, which I wrote, dealt with the classic apartheid system and the reform phase of apartheid, which took shape in the 1970s and 1980s. The second part examined the possibility of an alternative to apartheid that would promote both stability and economic growth.

We noted in our introduction that there were various ways in which apartheid was misunderstood. Some radical analysts had argued up to the early 1970s that the material prosperity of the white community as a whole and the preservation of white supremacy went hand in hand. No one had anticipated that by the mid-1970s the NP government would embark on far-reaching reforms aimed at drastically reducing the racial disparities in pensions and salaries in the public sector.

By the early 1990s South Africa was spending more, as a percentage of GDP, on social assistance in the form of non-contributory schemes than many developed countries, and more on that than almost any country in the developing South. In 1993 interracial parity was achieved in old-age pensions.

Others argued that the Afrikaner "civil religion" – a very specific Calvinist belief system and worldview – permeated the Afrikaners' communal institutions and induced a sense of mission that made it impossible for them to abandon the system of white domination. But by the 1980s there were few signs left of a belief in Afrikaner group unity, except in some religious circles.

Then there was also the question whether a settlement would apply only to the era of apartheid, or whether it had to "redress" the consequences of the entire 330 years of white domination and white occupation of the land. We argued that whites would not easily vacate their power base if it meant ending up in a position where it would be impossible for them to determine policy in respect of issues that were important to them, for example property rights and their children's education. For that reason it was important that whites as a group should share in decision-making. Consequently, we proposed a system of entrenched power-sharing for at least two terms as a transitional arrangement.

Critics attacked this standpoint as "reheated apartheid" and an attempt to "cling to white privilege". But these commentators were seldom aware of the fact that several esteemed political scientists in Britain and the United States argued the exact opposite.

The constitutional expert Vernon Bogdanor, professor in politics and government at the University of Oxford, wrote in the respected American journal *Daedalus* that a form of power-sharing was a characteristic of all societies that had succeeded in overcoming their divisions and had prospered. He added that he was not aware of any divided society that had been able to achieve stability without power-sharing between groups or group-based parties.

But how should the groups be defined? PW Botha, and initially FW de Klerk as well, wanted to retain rigid classification by the state. It implied that the government could not yet bring itself to relinquish apartheid. Schlemmer and I contended that it was essential that the government abolish racial classification and guarantee free political participation. If that had to happen, we anticipated that the following formations would emerge:

- A majority, which favoured individual-based democracy and moderate redistribution.
- An alliance of minorities, which put the emphasis on economic growth and was committed to the protection of the political and cultural rights of minorities, along with the rights of businesspeople and property owners.
- Smaller parties to the right and the left of the above formations.

We suggested that the NP government, as the representative of an alliance of minorities, should approach the majority with the proposal that decisions be taken on the basis of consensus for a ten-year period.

Ten years later, the Good Friday Agreement would largely resolve the conflict in Northern Ireland through an electoral system that rewarded candidates who advocated reconciliation and a constitution that stipulated that, in the first session of the legislative body, all members had to designate themselves as Unionist, Nationalist or Other. Key decisions could only be taken with significant cross-community support.

The system Schlemmer and I proposed did not differ materially from this settlement. The common premise was that the majority party should not be able to impose its will unilaterally.

Robin Renwick, who was the British ambassador to South Africa between 1987 and 1991, told me that Dr Gerrit Viljoen, who would become minister of constitutional affairs in 1989, showed him a book in his office and encouraged him enthusiastically to read it. It was *From Apartheid to Nation-Building*. My impression, however, is that few other NP leaders had read the book.

As new president, FW de Klerk soon demonstrated that he was determined to find a way out of the political impasse. I was sceptical of him at first, as about half of the NP caucus had been in the election for an NP leader, but gradually started to believe that his mind was set on achieving a settlement.

## Elusive peace

Both the liberal opposition and the ANC defined the conflict in South Africa as a racial conflict – one in which the white community, driven by feelings of racial superiority, was bent on entrenching its position of dominance and privilege. I viewed it differently. It was a struggle between communities, each with its own history and value system, which did not seek to dominate other communities as such but desired a significant measure of "self-determination" in respect of education and other "own affairs".

I started reading more about Northern Ireland and Israel, two societies that shared a history of intractable communal conflict with South Africa. On the surface, these were conflicts between Protestants and Catholics and between Zionists and Muslims respectively, but in reality they were, as in South Africa, struggles between political communities, each with roots in the country and an obsession with land, which competed for power and status.

In all three of the conflicts there was a great fear about the possible loss of "homeland", culture and identity. In all three cases the conflict was not driven by the urge of the dominant group to dominate, but by the fear of domination and the concomitant loss of "self-determination".

Assimilation occurs on only a limited scale where communities are in competition with each other. In fact, the radical faction in the subjugated community yearns to get its hands on the ruling minority's power, land and jobs and thereby overcome the trauma of powerlessness.

All three conflicts were several centuries old but had fairly recently entered a new, more intense phase. In 1967 Israel occupied East Jerusalem, the West Bank and Gaza, and twenty years later the first intifada broke out; in Northern Ireland, British troops were first deployed in 1969. In South Africa, the Soweto uprising erupted in 1976 and in Ireland rioting in Belfast and Derry spread to other parts around the same time.

In 1987 I spent three months on the campus of the Hebrew University of Jerusalem as a fellow of the Harry S Truman Research Institute for the Advancement of Peace. What stood out for me was the adamant realism of the institute's researchers. The Israelis certainly had no intention of settling with the Palestinians if it held any risks for their security.

I asked an Israeli researcher at the Hebrew University with wide experience in various African countries what the Afrikaners should do if they lost power. "Forget about the state, the civil service, public universities and the big corporations that do business with the state," he replied. "There would soon be fewer and fewer opportunities for minorities in these sectors."

Flip Buys, executive chairperson of the trade union Solidarity, later told me that this advice had been spot-on. Between 1992 and 2007 well-qualified whites would indeed leave the employ of the state and big corporations on a large scale and opt for self-employment.

I visited Northern Ireland on two occasions and was able to interview several Irish political leaders with the help of the British diplomat Robin Renwick. With funding from Idasa and the Friedrich Naumann Foundation in Germany, I organised a conference on the conflicts in South Africa, Northern Ireland and Israel.

The conference was held in Bonn in September 1989. Seventeen scholars, each an authority on one of the three conflicts, delivered papers which were subsequently included as chapters in the book *The Elusive Search for Peace: South Africa, Israel and Northern Ireland* (Oxford University Press, 1990). I wrote the introduction and conclusion.

From the conference it was apparent that the differences among these conflicts were as significant as the similarities. Both the Jews in Israel and the Protestants (or "Ulstermen") in Northern Ireland were demographic majorities, while the white population in South Africa had shrunk from 15% in 1970 to a mere 10% in the 1990s. The Jews and the Protestants had powerful allies in the United States and Britain respectively.

In contrast, the whites in South Africa, particularly the Afrikaners, stood alone. Unlike in the case of the other two conflicts, there was no "patron" (the United States in the case of Israel and Britain in the case of Northern Ireland) that could intervene if a party violated the settlement. The whites in South Africa would get only one shot at negotiating an appropriate post-apartheid system. Should it fail, they would be on their own as a minority.

In all three conflicts the party in power regarded certain issues as non-negotiable. In the case of Northern Ireland it was the retention of the link with Britain, in Israel it was the insistence that the state should be Jewish, and in South Africa it was the whites' rejection of the possibility of a single mixed parliament with the majority in control. Only 7% of Afrikaners and 11% of English speakers supported this option in a 1988 poll.

There was, however, mounting support for power-sharing in South Africa. According to an opinion poll conducted in 1986 on the Witwatersrand, with its politicised communities, 75% of blacks and 60% of whites supported the idea of a joint government in which no group dominated.

Unlike the situation in Israel, where the electoral system had resulted in numerous small parties, the NP was sufficiently powerful to get a contentious settlement accepted among its supporters. Unlike Northern Ireland, where the budget was subsidised by Westminster, South Africa needed to boost its economic growth to provide jobs and food for all. Hence a political settlement could not be delayed for long. The key question was whether the NP leaders would have the ability to negotiate the right system for the country the first time.

## The wall comes down

In my contribution to the book *Can South Africa Survive? Five Minutes to Midnight* (1989), I predicted that the NP government would still be in power for quite some time. No significant support base in the broader white community was so alienated that it would defect to the other side, and the government was able to pay the salaries of all its civil servants and security personnel.

Between 2 February 1990, when De Klerk unbanned a number of organisations, and 22 September 1992, when the NP and the ANC signed the Record of Understanding, power slipped from the hands of the NP government. The health minister, Rina Venter, told me later that Kobie Coetsee, minister of justice, had said to her on the latter date: "Rina, today we've lost the country."

How could my forecast have been so wrong?

Like many other analysts, I had not anticipated the fall of the Berlin Wall and the collapse of the Soviet bloc. John Lewis Gaddis, professor in military and naval history at Yale University and a prominent scholar of Cold War history, has pointed out that not a single international relations expert foresaw the demise of the Soviet Union.[110]

Without the fall of the Berlin Wall, negotiations between the government

---

110  Jacqueline Stevens, "Political Scientists are Lousy Forecasters", *International Herald Tribune*, 23 June 2012.

and the ANC would probably not have taken place. The ANC in exile could no longer count on Soviet support. The South African government, too, was in a weaker position. With the disappearance of the threat of Russian intervention in southern Africa, it could no longer count on protection from the West.

Moreover, from early 1990 between ten and fifteen thousand ANC cadres streamed into South Africa from foreign countries. The majority of these returned exiles were unemployed and totally alienated from the political system. Many of them radicalised black politics in the townships.

The ANC's top leaders moved out of the political wilderness in Lusaka into the political centres of Johannesburg, Durban and Port Elizabeth. The normalisation of politics also meant that Nelson Mandela, the very embodiment of the black freedom struggle, would have to be released.

## Message from a prisoner

Towards the end of 1989 Izak de Villiers, then editor of *Rapport*, asked me to write a column for the paper. Ton Vosloo, managing director of Naspers, later told me he had suggested to De Villiers that he approach me. De Villiers made no secret of the fact that he was generally unimpressed with the readableness of professors' political commentary. To overcome his prejudice, I told him of the order Vladimir Lenin had issued in the early days of the Russian Revolution: "Shoot more professors and prostitutes."

My first column for *Rapport* appeared on 17 December 1989 under the heading "Day of the Vow 1989: Forgetting is not an option: We should remember together." I started by quoting Ernest Renan, the renowned French authority on nationalism: "Forgetting is a crucial factor in the creation of a nation."

I argued that, as far as the annual commemoration of the Battle of Blood River was concerned, forgetting was not an option, just as it could not be expected of Afrikaners in a new, democratic order to forget their communal identity.

The big task lay in trying to find a synthesis between different nationalisms. On the one side there was Afrikaner nationalism, a typical ethno-nationalism forged by bonds of descent, history and language. On the other side there was the ANC's African nationalism, which was a typical territorial idealism. It sought to build a new nation around the majority of the population. The ANC believed it was the only organisation that had the historical legitimacy to unite all the people in the country.

My standpoint was that nation-building and democracy could thrive only when communities respected each other and their respective historical legacies. History was not static, and other perspectives could be raised:

For both the Afrikaner and the Zulu, Blood River was a conflict over not being dominated by the other group. We understand the Voortrekkers' perspective, but do we grasp the political fears of the Zulu people of 1838? They were acutely aware of the fact that failure to act against the "interlopers" could result in their political order being totally undermined.

The Voortrekker leaders did not think of perpetual *baasskap* . . . They knew the survival of a tiny group amid the black majority was only possible if negotiated contracts were based on the principle of equality.

Hendrik Potgieter wrote as follows to [the Griqua leader] Adam Kok: "We are emigrants together with you and are regarded as such and regard ourselves as emigrants who together with you dwell in the savage strange land, and we desire to be regarded as neither more nor less than your fellow-emigrants, inhabitants of the country enjoying the same privileges with you."[111]

Only if Afrikaner leaders spell out clearly that Blood River is not the symbol of enduring white *baasskap* can it be commemorated as a historic battle, but then as one where heroism on both sides is honoured.

Shortly after the publication of the article, Trevor Manuel asked if he could come and see me at my home. At the time he was employed in Cape Town at the Mobil Foundation, of which I was a trustee. During his visit, Manuel explained that Nelson Mandela had instructed him to deliver a card to me. It was a conventional Christmas card with a printed message of good wishes for the festive season. On the blank side Mandela had written the following (in Afrikaans):

1335/88: Nelson Mandela 23.12.89

Dear Professor Giliomee

Your silence in the past few months on the national debate that is currently raging must have upset newspaper readers. No doubt it would have delighted them to ascertain from a recent article that you are still standing steadfastly in the front line.

Victor Verster Prison,

Private Bag x 6008

Southern Paarl 7624

---

111  *Griqua Records: The Philippolis Captaincy, 1825-1861*, compiled and edited by Karel Schoeman (Cape Town: Van Riebeeck Society, 1996), pp. 75-76.

Above: At the launch of *The Shaping of South African Society, 1652-1820* in Stellenbosch in 1979. From the left is Annette, my wife, Jan, my brother, Warnia, his wife, my parents, me and Hester Lambrechts, my sister.

Top left: My German grandfather, Hermann Buhr (1876-1966), whom I was named after.

Top right: As a student at Stellenbosch in the late 1950s, when furious debates took place regarding segregated universities and the question of South Africa becoming a republic.

Above: Carefree childhood days. On holiday in Melkbaai with from left at the back, my parents and an unknown aunt. Jan, Hester and me are in front.

Right: Me and Annette with our daughters, Adrienne (left) and Francine. Flippie and Jasper are with us.

Left: The Winter 1985 edition of the magazine *Die Suid-Afrikaan*. The lead article covered the discussions that I and others from Stellenbosch had with Dr Nthato Motlana of Soweto. Minister of Constitutional Development Chris Heunis keeps a slightly nervous eye on proceedings.

Bottom: Debate broke out in the letter pages of *Die Burger* when Stellenbosch academics took each other on about reform. Fred Mouton of *Die Burger* drew this cartoon, which was republished in *Frontline* magazine in November 1981 with an article by Helen Zille, called "The civil war that burst forth from The John". Left are Sampie Terreblanche, Julius Jeppe and Willie Esterhuyse as the *verligtes*; right are Johannes Degenaar, André du Toit and me. (*Fred Mouton/ Die Burger*)

Above: Nelson Mandela's message from prison, which Trevor Manuel personally delivered to me at my home.

Top: I first used the term "*die Groot Krokodil*" (the Big Crocodile) in my column under the pseudonym "*Die Man Wat Weet*" (The man in the know) in the June 1988 edition of *Die Suid-Afrikaan*. The term soon gained currency, and here Cora Coetzee puts a playful twist on it with a sketch that I got as a birthday present. (*Cora Coetzee*)

Above: Thabo Mbeki, Frederik van Zyl Slabbert and Breyten Breytenbach were key to the discussions at the first Dakar Conference in 1987. This photo appeared on the cover of *Die Suid-Afrikaan* after our return.

Top: A cartoon by Mynderd Vosloo that accompanied the article in *Rapport* (27 January 1997) in which I argued that the NP had suffered a knockout blow in the negotiations, an opinion that Dave Steward would later oppose vehemently. (*Rapport*)

Above: *New History of South Africa* was the first post–1994 illustrated general history of the country. Here I sign books in Johannesburg with co-editor Bernard Mbenga. (*BooksLIVE*)

Top: With Aaron Cupido at the launch of *Nog altyd hier gewees* (2007). The research for this book brought new insights into the price that certain communities had paid for apartheid.

Above: In Pretoria, in conversation with Pik Botha about the last leaders of the Afrikaners. This theatrical former cabinet minister has an astonishing memory and could throw light on numerous incidents from the inner circles of power. (*Gallo Images/Foto24/Alet Pretorius*)

Top: With Tony Leon, former leader of the Democratic Alliance, who spoke at the launch of *The Last Afrikaner Leaders*.

Above: At the 2016 award ceremony where I received the inaugural Jan H Marais prize for a contribution to the academic development of Afrikaans in any scientific field. The maquette is Coert Steynberg's first design for the statue that the University of Stellenbosch wanted to erect in honour of Marais's widow and brother-in-law rejected the design. The statue by Steynberg that currently stands on Marais Square was unveiled in 1950. (*Die Burger*)

Top: Lunch at Die Boord in Stellenbosch with dramatist Athol Fugard and author Dana Snyman, with whom I have shared many conversations about South African politics, our past and our future.

Apparently it was a reference to my column in *Rapport* that had appeared six days earlier.

By this time Mandela already knew that his release was imminent. It amazed me that, with so much on his mind, he had found the time to send me a card. I was of course only one of a great many people he drew closer to him in his inimitable way at that stage.

More than two years later, on 12 March 1992, I interviewed Mandela at his home in Soweto. He told me he had regularly read my contributions in the *Cape Times* and *Die Suid-Afrikaan*. With a twinkle in his eye he recalled my article in the latter on my conversation with Joe Slovo at the Leverkusen conference, where I had written that Slovo looked like the president of a small-town golf club.

I asked him about his decision to launch the armed struggle under the leadership of the ANC's military wing Umkhonto weSizwe on 16 December 1961, the same day as the commemoration of the Battle of Blood River. The date was not coincidental, he said. "The conflict is one between Afrikaner nationalism and an African nationalism based in South Africa. The conflict was so bitter because it took place in the same country. These two nationalisms now have to work together and solve the problems of the country."

This was also my own standpoint, which I had often advanced in academic and popular publications. For many academics, it was an unacceptable view. Radical academics only saw the conflict as a class struggle, while for liberal academics it was merely a struggle between the racism of apartheid and the non-racialism of the ANC.

## Support for De Klerk

After De Klerk delivered his watershed speech on 2 February 1990, I congratulated him py post on this giant step. Privately, however, I wondered whether the government had leaders in its ranks who would be able to conduct tough negotiations with the ANC. I had seen at the Dakar conference how the ANC claimed the moral high ground with ease and dismissed any notion of a balanced settlement.

Two months later I had my first interview with De Klerk. I was struck by the importance of moral considerations in his decision. With apartheid totally discredited, there was no ideology left with which he could attempt to justify white control.

I gained the impression that he deliberately put a clear distance between himself and his predecessor, as well as the security services, which had enjoyed great influence under PW Botha. It was significant that the defence minister, General Magnus Malan, was not part of the government's team that sat down for talks with an ANC delegation at the presidential residence Groote Schuur in early May 1990.

It seemed to me as if the critical decisions about the negotiations under De Klerk would be taken by a small circle of ministers in which expert advisers on security or negotiations would not be involved. It soon became known that De Klerk had sidelined both the State Security Council and the National Intelligence Service. I saw this as a cause for concern.

During the conversation with De Klerk I also realised suddenly that the specific circumstances of the Afrikaners excluded certain political possibilities. As long as South Africa was a white-controlled unitary state, it did not matter that the Afrikaners were dispersed throughout the country – a third lived in the western part, a third in what is today Gauteng, and a third were scattered across other parts. Under a democracy with universal franchise, however, the diffuseness of the Afrikaner community was a problem.

For me as a Bolander it was important that an attempt should be made to negotiate the establishment of a federal state with considerable powers in the western region of the country, where white and coloured people constitute the majority. Undoubtedly Afrikaans as an official language and medium of instruction would have a strong case here. But a strong base in the west could mean that white and coloured citizens elsewhere in the country would be put in a weaker position. Their question would be: "What will then become of us?"

In 1991 De Klerk surprised many by scrapping the Population Registration Act, which enforced racial classification. More than any other law, it had been the core of apartheid. I wrote to De Klerk:

> I would like to congratulate you on the great step you have taken in removing the apartheid albatross. From a historical perspective it is a step of the same order of magnitude as the abolition of slavery, which had regulated the entire social and political order, in 1834. Whereas the Afrikaner slaveowners in the Western Cape had regarded the abolition of that system with fear and resentment, you and the National Party have terminated the apartheid system yourselves and in an honourable manner. Huge problems lie ahead, but your leadership, and specifically the scrapping of apartheid, will assuredly unleash an unprecedented political creativity, particularly among Afrikaners.

## "Charming but naïve"

During the transition I wrote columns for *Rapport* and a number of English papers, except in the nine months between September 1992 and May 1993, when I was abroad. Since the country's politics were so extraordinarily riveting, it was easy to produce two and sometimes even three columns a month.

I could use the academic literature on the process of democratisation in the developing world as a frame of reference. In a column of 12 September 1991 I pointed out that South Africa lacked most of the requirements experts considered essential to a well-functioning democracy.

Half the population was functionally illiterate, and the inequality between the poorest half and the richest tenth was among the highest in the world. A strong middle class, which was generally regarded as a prerequisite for a democracy, was absent among black people. According to most calculations, less than 20% of the voters in a full-fledged democracy would be part of the middle class.

On 2 September 1993, in the *Cape Times*, I warned against the illusion that the ANC could be allowed to rule like a strong majority party in a developed country such as Britain or France, with the combating of corruption and abuse of power being left to the free press, pressure groups and trade unions. "This perspective is charming but naïve," I stated. "Only a strong countervailing political power in the form of an opposition party would prevent us from going down the road of Africa, where this too was lacking."

There was disagreement on whether South Africa should have a constitution based on individual rights or one that would protect the rights of communities in respect of education, language and culture. For most ANC leaders, federation had long been a dirty word. Serious conflicts loomed in respect of economic policy and contentious issues such as property rights. In September 1991 I wrote in a column about the necessity of an economic pact underwritten by all the parties.

The referendum of 17 March 1992, in which the De Klerk government sought a mandate for "the continuation of the reform process . . . which is aimed at a new constitution through negotiations", was of vital importance.

On 2 March 1992, two weeks before the referendum, I wrote that the referendum asked the voters to vote on a process rather than asking them to pass judgement on a draft constitution. Like other commentators, however, I failed to point out that there had never been any question of the electorate being asked to endorse a process rather than the proposed constitution itself.

De Klerk had first mooted the idea of a referendum on 30 March 1990, when he pledged that "after the completion of the negotiations the constitutional proposals will be tested in a constitutional manner among the electorate. And only with their support will a constitutional dispensation be introduced."

The second time the referendum issue was raised was in January 1992, when De Klerk said in Parliament that the government was "honour bound" to hold a referendum on any significant amendment to the existing constitution in each of the white, black, coloured and Indian communities. He envisaged referendums "in which every South African will be able to take part and whose result may be determined globally as well as by the parliamentary community".

In my estimation, the referendum, especially the referendum question, was perhaps the most important card De Klerk could play. Western leaders would understand if he took the line that he could not take his electorate into a new constitutional dispensation without their having had a chance to voice their opinion on the kind of constitution under which they would have to live in future.

The NP government's pre-referendum advertisements clearly conveyed the message that a yes vote was a vote against majority rule. Everyone knew that this was the form of government propagated by the ANC. Most of the yes votes in the referendum had not been cast with the intention of giving the De Klerk government a mandate to agree to majority rule.

In May 1992 the ANC decided to suspend its participation in the negotiations at the Convention for a Democratic South Africa (Codesa) and embarked on a programme of mass action to extract greater concessions from the government. I later asked Hernus Kriel, minister of law and order, whom I knew well from our student days, whether the stability of the state was ever seriously threatened. His answer was a categorical "no".

Nonetheless, the government dropped certain non-negotiable positions on a future constitution to lure the ANC back to the negotiating table. It sacrificed mandatory power-sharing and group rights for individual rights and majority government. Hereafter it would pin its hopes for the effective protection of minorities against discrimination on a progressive constitution and certain constitutional principles that would be interpreted by a constitutional court.

But this was a new, largely untested approach which by the mid-1980s had produced few encouraging results in the deeply divided societies of the developing world.

While I was on study leave in Washington in 1992 and 1993, I had ample opportunity to read about the negotiations and particularly the NP's promises to the electorate in respect of a referendum. On my return I observed in my *Rapport* column of 8 August that De Klerk had sounded a new note in a recent speech: "The new political dispensation should not frustrate the majority." I wrote: "At present the NP's entire constitutional approach rests on the personal guarantee President De Klerk has given not to deviate from his election promises. And is that good enough when the future of the Afrikaner people is at stake?"

I suggested that, as soon as possible after its completion, the draft constitution should be tested by way of a referendum in which all communities could take part. This was the process that would be followed five years later in Northern Ireland, when the voters were fully informed about the future constitution when they ratified the Good Friday Agreement in a referendum. A month later I repeated the plea for a referendum in *Rapport* under the heading "First test new constitution with a referendum". But the die had been cast.

The ANC largely got what it wanted in the negotiations, and its supporters were solidly behind it. While it had no reason to hold a referendum, there was likely to be strong opposition against a white referendum.

On 11 November 1993, with the negotiations completed, my *Cape Times* column appeared under the heading "ANC has played its role almost to perfection". The movement's leadership had steadfastly refused to be co-opted into the government and it had unified the black population, with the exception of the traditional Zulu people. The ANC had the world at its feet as a result of the iconic status Mandela had acquired.

The ANC had also attained its most important objective, namely that the final constitution would only be written after an election and that an electoral system was adopted which was ideal for the ANC leadership, in which communists were vastly overrepresented. Its biggest concession was on property rights, but there were enough loopholes in the clauses of the final constitution to widen the door for expropriation.

With his sharp writer's eye, JM Coetzee, who would receive the Nobel Prize for Literature in 2003, provided valuable commentary on my draft chapter on the transition to a new system for my book *The Afrikaners*. After the balance of power had tipped in the ANC's favour in mid-1992, he observed, the NP government spent much of its energy on avoiding the symbolism of defeat. There would be no guerrilla army parading through the streets in a victory march, no toppling of statues and no multi-party control of the security forces in the run-up to the election. The NP government also got its way when it came to its demand that the Tricameral Parliament had to pass the negotiated constitution as a law. This meant that there was constitutional continuity and not a revolutionary victory. Coetzee remarked: "The ANC was ready to indulge the NP in the matter of the symbolism and rituals of power, while it concentrated on the substance."

His commentary was again of great value when I worked on the second edition of *The Afrikaners,* which would appear in 2009. In response to my question about shortcomings in my account of the transition in the first edition, he replied:

> In the overall account you offer of the negotiations for a new constitution, the party that held political power at the time – the NP – got little of what it wanted and the party without power – the ANC – got what it wanted. There are two ways to explain this outcome. One is that the NP negotiators were incompetent. The other is that the strength of the NP and the weakness of the ANC were more apparent than real. You seem to incline toward the former explanation. What leads you to believe that, in the larger political context, the latter is not more valid?

This is still to me the best question about the nature of the settlement. I greatly underestimated the ANC's ability to recover so swiftly from its setbacks in Africa, when one country after the other kicked out the exiled organisation and even Zambia, its last refuge, was on the verge of doing the same.

Three dramatic events between early November 1989 and early February 1990 changed everything abruptly: the fall of the Berlin Wall, the unconditional release of Nelson Mandela, and the De Klerk government's unconditional invitation to all parties to negotiate.

Regarding the negotiations, I overestimated the NP's government will to insist on certain non-negotiable bottom lines, as it had promised in the referendum of 1992. It abandoned its ideology of group rights along with mandatory power-sharing and in its place accepted the sovereignty of the constitution instead of a sovereign parliament.

By September 1993 it was clear that there would be no power-sharing and neither entrenchment of minority or group rights nor guarantees for Afrikaans single-medium schools or universities. On 16 September 1993 Piet Marais, MP for Stellenbosch and the last NP minister for national education, wrote a letter to President De Klerk. A few years later Marais handed me a copy of the letter to use as I saw fit.

Marais was a competent minister and in charge of the important education portfolio, yet he was not a member of the NP's negotiating team or of the cabinet committee on the negotiations. In his letter he informed De Klerk that in informal talks he had had with ANC negotiators about a post-apartheid education system, he had gained the clear impression that they "displayed an intolerance to Afrikaans as a medium of instruction and to the demand that the Afrikaans universities could continue to imbue their mission with a cultural content". Marais attributed this to "a desire to do away with all institutions that in their view are stigmatised as racist or apartheid structures".

Marais also informed De Klerk that he felt uneasy about the question whether the undertakings the NP had given to its supporters in respect of education had been "sufficiently accommodated" in the documents the government had produced to date in the negotiating process. He added that "education was not the priority among our negotiators that it should be".

Marais proposed that the government compile a list of undertakings and bottom lines the NP had given to its voters. The negotiators should measure their actions against this list. He also recommended that before the NP finally accepted the constitution, it should be measured against the list.[112] Had Marais's proposal been accepted, the breakdown of trust between the NP and its voters that contributed to the party's rapid decline and inglorious demise might not have arisen later.

For the entire twentieth century white politics had centred on preventing what was destined to happen on 27 April 1994: black majority rule. Marion von Dönhoff, editor of the respected German weekly *Die Zeit*, once told me of a discussion in 1977 between the West German chancellor Helmut Schmidt and John Vorster on the possibility of black majority rule. Prior to the discussion Dönhoff had asked Schmidt to do his best to persuade Vorster to take the risk of granting the vote to all despite the chance that things might go wrong. Germany, Schmidt told Vorster, had survived two catastrophic world wars in the twentieth century, yet thirty years later West Germany was the richest country in Europe.

"You don't understand," Vorster replied. "For us Afrikaners there won't be a second chance if we lost power." In the same year Pik Botha said in an interview with the journalist Anna Starcke for her book *Survival: Taped Interviews with South Africa's Power Elite*: "For us a political system of one man one vote within one political system means our destruction."

Early in 1994 I wrote in *Rapport* on "The year in which everything changes". The big question was: "Why did the NP leadership, from a position of power, negotiate itself out of power in 1992-93?" Blaming five or six chief negotiators was a superficial view. Other, far weightier explanations had to be taken into account.

Firstly, population numbers were decisive. "In no other ethnic or racial conflict were the demographic scales tipped so inexorably against a ruling group," I wrote. Secondly, white parents had grown tired of sending their sons into the black townships to oppress people in their own country. Thirdly, the world

---

112   The letter is included in my document collection that is held in the Manuscripts Section of the University of Stellenbosch Library.

had developed a loathing for a pampered white group which was richer and far better educated than the rest of South Africa's people, yet did not feel equal to asserting itself without protection.

The major problem, I added, was that the NP leaders had not prepared their supporters properly for what lay ahead. "The NP's ineptness reminds one strongly of the white trade union leaders who had grown so accustomed to being coddled that they were defenceless when the Wiehahn reforms pulled the rug from under their feet."

## "Now we are all one"

On 27 April 1994 I drove through the Boland to Porterville, to observe the voting process in towns along the way and to cast my own vote in my home-town. I was accompanied by Simon Barber, a foreign journalist I had got to know well in Washington the year before, and by my daughter Adrienne and one of her classmates in the journalism course at Stellenbosch.

The long queues at every voting station, the patience of the people, and the democratic ritual of rich and poor standing in the same queue were striking symbols of the newly established democracy. I thought of 1 December 1838 when the Western Cape had experienced a similar symbolic moment – all of a sudden burghers, settlers, labourers and former slaves had found themselves equal before the law. Some masters had feared that the liberated slaves would get roaring drunk and rape white women. These fears proved to be just as unfounded as those of the doomsayers who had stockpiled supplies of tinned food before the election day of 1994.

At the voting station in Mbekweni, a township in Paarl, a black woman spon-taneously hugged Adrienne. On Barber's photo, which was published promi-nently in the *Cape Times* the following day, it seems as if she wants to say: "Now we are all one." All the spectators around them are clapping their hands.

Annette went to vote on a farm near Vlottenburg in the Stellenbosch dis-trict. On the way she gave a lift to a woman who was hitchhiking. She told Annette: "I voted yesterday already, for the white man. What's his name again? The bald one. He's looked so well after us all these years. People are now even getting more pension money."

At the voting station Annette bumped into a female friend who was a well-known ANC supporter. Back at home she described their encounter as follows: "We were happy to see each other, happy to see all the people around us, humble, simple people, all with a new sense of human dignity that was clearly visible in more than just facial expressions and attitude: neatly dressed, voters in a new South Africa, our country."

Just before the election I had written in the *Cape Times* that the new democratic South Africa required four tasks. Numerous other institutions, besides the political system, had to be democratised; societal stability had to be restored; the economy had to be put on a path of sustainable growth; and there had to be a sufficient measure of redistribution to improve the conditions of the disadvantaged communities.

The NP ministers and the white voters wrongly assumed that the ANC would soon discover they lacked the expertise and experience to govern the country on their own. I was mistaken when I wrote that the NP ministers in the cabinet, especially De Klerk and Derek Keys, the minister of finance, would have "great informal power" in the cabinet since investors would watch closely whether the ANC ministers heeded their advice. There was no question of resistance from the ranks of the security forces, as they were alienated from the NP leadership. With the ANC committed to a market-oriented economy, investors temporarily forgot their fears about nationalisation. For the ANC the transition in 1994 was easier than its leaders had ever dreamt it would be.

# Chapter 10

# End of the party

Shortly after the "liberation election" of 1994, the NP invited me to analyse the results at a special meeting of the party caucus under De Klerk's chairmanship. I observed a sense of relief among the participants, but also concern. The 20% of the total vote the party had won was considerably more than the 14% at which its support had stood a few months before the election, but far short of the 30% the leaders had expected on the eve of the election.

The party had six ministers in the cabinet and De Klerk was one of the two deputy presidents, but there was no certainty about whether they would really have an important say. The party's voters expected nevertheless that the NP would fulfil a vital "checks and balances" function in the government of national unity. Meanwhile, the ANC was ecstatic about the sudden victory after the long years in the wilderness. It was almost like the euphoria after the NP's election victory in 1948, which was summed up by the leader, Dr DF Malan, when he said: "Today South Africa belongs to us once more."

In my presentation, I pointed out that the NP had fared better than had been expected in the so-called "liberation election". It had attracted 66% of the coloured vote, 60% of the white vote and 50% of the Indian vote.

But the harsh truth was that NP had attracted less than 3% of the black vote – far lower than the 15% to 20% black support in 1990. In 1994 more than 90% of the black voters had voted for a party with a leadership profile that was unmistakably black. The same proportion of white voters had voted for a predominantly white party.

I emphasised the fact that the NP would have fared better if it had forced the ANC to make much greater compromises during the negotiations. The party should also have insisted on another electoral system than that of closed-list proportional representation. This system tends to create the semblance of inter-ethnic harmony in that the various parties put well-known personalities from communities other than their own on their respective lists. These people, however, do not represent those communities in the true sense of the word.

In his study *A Democratic South Africa?*, Donald Horowitz, an authority on deeply divided societies, recommended the so-called alternative vote electoral system, which is thought to promote reconciliation rather than polarisation.[113]

The electoral system that was adopted in the negotiations (a closed-list proportional representation system) in the first place served the immediate needs of both the ANC and the NP leadership. They wanted to exert strict control over their respective caucuses under a democratic system.

I highlighted the problems in the NP's election campaign for the black vote. The campaign had not focused on any specific groups within the community, but on the black community as whole. No strategies had been devised to get past the trade unions, "civics" and street committees, which were important gatekeepers in the black community.

Nor did the NP present an ideology which would have appealed to certain segments among the black electorate. The party should have focused more sharply on the black voters who had indicated that issues such as law and order, morality and economic growth were of importance to them. NP attacks on the ANC as a "reckless" and "dangerous" party had been counterproductive, as black voters saw this as a veiled way of expressing disdain for blacks in general.

The mistrust of the black voter was not likely to change until the party had attracted credible black leaders, I added. This would not happen until the NP had offices in the townships and was actively involved in addressing black people's problems. Moreover, the party had to guard against taking the white electorate for granted. The ideological differences between the NP and the DP had virtually disappeared. The party could not bank on the continued support of white business leaders. They were inclined to throw in their support behind the party that would help create a stable business environment.

I warned of the risks posed by the NP's participation in the government of national unity. It should maintain an independent public profile right from the start. Criticism of the ANC should not remain limited to NP propagandists or the party's backbenchers, and the party should not get sucked into the ANC's plans for a truth commission. De Klerk and the NP's provincial leaders should visit all corners of the country and develop a vision for the future together with black community leaders.

I also urged the party to prepare itself for moving to the opposition benches

---

113   In terms of this electoral system voters have more than one vote, which they can
      use to indicate their first, second and third choice of candidates in their constit-
      uencies. The theory is that this encourages voters to vote for centrist rather than
      radical candidates.

in the short to medium term. Samuel Huntington's advice to parties in negotiations was to obtain sufficient guarantees and assurances in respect of the
rights of the opposition.

## "Accept defeat"

For the first year or two after the transition the NP periodically patted itself
on the back. De Klerk and other leaders declared at public meetings that the
NP had abolished apartheid and thus was the co-liberator of the country.

This euphoria of self-congratulation could not last. The Afrikaners had lost
power, but were behaving like King Lear, who had renounced power but
naïvely expected everyone to continue treating him like a king.

On 6 August 1995 I wrote in *Rapport* that with an ANC that had "com-
manding power", the NP had two options. One was to develop such a strong
understanding with the ANC on key issues that it would invite the NP to
form a voluntary coalition in 1999. This would require great policy concessions and in effect put the NP in a position of dependency.

The other option was to prepare purposefully for an opposition role and
get as much powers, competencies and resources as possible for opposition
parties written into the final constitution. The NP leaders were divided on
this, however, with the result that in the negotiations for a final constitution
no resolute strategy with specific objectives was followed.

Nelson Mandela and other ANC leaders made it clear soon after the transition that they would not write mandatory power-sharing into the final constitution. In early May 1996 the final constitution was adopted – which provided
for ordinary majority government.

On 9 May 1996 De Klerk announced the NP's decision to withdraw from
the government of national unity. He explained that the ANC ignored the
emphasis he and other NP leaders had placed on the necessity of power-sharing
and joint decision-making for the most effective government. Hence the NP
had decided to meet the great need for a strong and confident opposition. This
opposition would be based on values rather than ethnic affiliation.

Over the following six months the NP maintained the illusion that it had
withdrawn voluntarily from the government of national unity in order to
build up a strong opposition party, even though it could have participated formally in such a government up to 1999. A realisation of what had really happened only sank in when De Klerk admitted frankly in January 1997, in a
speech in London, that the negotiations had not delivered a balanced political
settlement of the kind the NP had sought. What had actually occurred, he said,
was that whites had surrendered power and lost their "sovereignty". He continued:

The decision to surrender national sovereignty is certainly one of the most painful any leader can be asked to take. Most nations are prepared to risk war and catastrophe rather than to surrender this right. Yet this was the decision we had to take. We had to accept the necessity of giving up on the ideal on which we have been nurtured and the dream for which so many generations had struggled and for which so many of our people had died.

Ebbe Dommisse, editor of *Die Burger*, sent me a copy of the speech. I was able to use it immediately for a column in *Rapport* that appeared before any other paper had commented on it. I wrote:

In 1492 the Moors were defeated at Granada and 700 years of Moorish rule in Spain came to an end. The evening after the final battle the mother of the defeated general, Boabdil, found him in tears. She reportedly rebuked him with the words: "You do well, my son, to weep like a woman for what you failed to defend like a man."

A week or so ago the NP leader, Mr FW de Klerk, admitted for the first time that the Afrikaners had surrendered self-determination in the constitutional negotiations. Previously the NP still held up the fig leaf of power sharing; now there is little reason to gloss over the fact that the NP, as far as both power sharing and cultural self-determination are concerned, suffered a crushing defeat.

In the new Constitution that is now coming into effect, there is no effective guarantee for single-medium schools or mother-tongue education; there are no effective rights for Afrikaans as an official language; there is nothing that prevents the SABC from scaling down Afrikaans even more . . .

The dismal failure of the NP leadership in the area of minority rights and particularly rights in respect of language and schools can be attributed mainly to poor strategic planning and the absence of any non-negotiable principles, except for private ownership.

In carving out a niche for themselves in the new constitutional order, it is best for Afrikaners to start by openly admitting the great cultural defeat.

I compared the Afrikaners' position by 1997 with their position after their crushing defeat in the Anglo-Boer War. Then, too, there had been serious divisions in their ranks. By 1997 the Afrikaner middle class was split into two camps on account of conflicting definitions of Afrikaner identity and divergent opinions about the road ahead. I explained this as follows:

> The one camp comprises those who can be called pluralists. They have multiple identities – professional, class, cultural and religious – but put a special premium on their identity as Afrikaners and Afrikaans speakers. They are prepared to make their contribution to the survival of Afrikaans at all levels of society.
>
> The other camp, which I call the corporatists, views society as consisting of big corporations – organised labour, big business and the state. They also regard the historically Afrikaans universities such as Pretoria or Stellenbosch as semi-autonomous corporations that should be run with an eye to an impersonal market rather than a specific cultural community. For the sake of 'social harmony' they seek to consolidate the state-supported national culture and identity while simultaneously relegating the secondary cultures (including Afrikaans) to a lesser place.

I identified myself with the pluralists. Any deeply divided society ought to foster stability by giving people from different ethnic and cultural groups a sense of security and belonging. The demand that there should also be Afrikaans schools and universities that pursue academic excellence in their own way was a legitimate one.

It was a joke, I wrote, that the corporatists spitefully ran down the pluralists as "neo-apartheid warriors" and "rightists". It attested to ignorance on their part. They simply had no clue of the importance of cultural transfer at university level and the extent to which the ideology of corporatism was seen as oppressive and culturally sterile in Europe.

In response to De Klerk's speech in London, *Die Burger,* under the heading "Oorgawe" (Surrender), asked whether the leader of a party that had fared so poorly in the negotiations could continue in a leadership position.

During a short-lived political storm a spate of critical letters appeared in the Afrikaans press. One such letter read: "The NP had received a mandate from us to protect and secure our interests at all times. De Klerk did not get a mandate to lead, like a Judas goat, his unsuspecting people to the political abattoir." De Klerk pointed out that he had never promised a white minority veto, but he resigned from politics shortly afterwards.

More than sixteen years later, my role in this episode had unpleasant repercussions. On 9 December 2013, just after Nelson Mandela's death, Henry Jeffreys related in a column in *Die Burger* that in 1997 he had received a congratulatory telephone call from Mandela in response to his recent column in *Beeld*. In the 1997 column Jeffreys claimed I had written that De Klerk "sold out like a Judas in the negotiations and left whites in the lurch". He added: "If De Klerk was a Judas, was Mandela then a Pharisee who had provided the silver bribe money?" He had apparently confused the above-mentioned letter from a reader to *Rapport* in response to my article, with the article itself.

I wrote in a letter to *Die Burger*: "I would like to know what Jeffreys refers to when he attributes the standpoint that 'De Klerk sold out the Afrikaners like a Judas' to me. If he is unable to provide a source, he was guilty of gross misrepresentation in 1997 (and now as well)." Jeffreys still owes me a reply.

## Trouble with liberals

In the early 1990s I became a council member of the South African Institute of Race Relations (SAIRR), a research and policy think tank based in Johannesburg. The Institute was founded in 1929 and over time became the leading liberal organisation in the country. I considered it an honour when I was elected president for a two-year term in 1995. EG Malherbe, vice-chancellor of the University of Natal, and René de Villiers, editor of *The Star*, were other Afrikaners who had been elected to the presidency. As was customary, I became a vice-president on completion of my term, a position I would occupy until 2016.

Unintentionally, I caused a crisis shortly after becoming president. My hope had been that the Institute could be enlisted to promote the cultural and linguistic rights of communities in addition to their focus on the promotion of individual rights. In South Africa this would amount to the promotion of the rights of all minorities, including those of Afrikaans speakers. It would be a great boost for the struggle for multilingualism if the Institute fought for the right to receive mother-tongue education where practically possible. In so doing, the Institute would extend its sphere of influence beyond mainly white English speakers.

One of the miracles of the "New South Africa", I wrote in a column for *Rapport*, was that the Institute and the Afrikaner Broederbond (still the AB, but now renamed the Afrikanerbond) were now both fighting for liberal values. Both organisations had been founded in 1929 (in the case of the AB, it was reconstituted in that year after its establishment eleven years earlier). In time the AB and the Institute became the intellectual vanguards of Afrikaner nationalism and liberalism respectively.

In the almost seventy years of their existence there had never been an exchange of ideas between the councils of the two organisations, although they were well aware of each other and their head offices were only a few kilometres apart. In my column I proposed a meeting between the two councils where they could deliberate on ways of strengthening our young democracy and explore shared liberal values. I referred to the work of Charles Taylor, an influential Canadian writer on liberalism, who was a proponent of both Liberalism A (individual rights) and Liberalism B (group rights, such as linguistic rights, which in a deeply divided society are as important as individual rights). My proposal was that the liberals in South Africa stand up for Liberalism A as well as for Liberalism B.

The *Sunday Times* under the editorship of Ken Owen immediately slammed the proposal. Under the tendentious heading "Broeder plan shocks liberals", it reported that my suggestion had upset people with long-standing ties with the Institute. The paper quoted John Dugard, a law professor from Wits, who dismissed my notion as "absolute nonsense".

According to Dugard, there was no common ground between the Institute, which advocated individual rights, and the AB, which prioritised group interests. It was inconceivable to him that the AB could ever become a liberal organisation.

Sheena Duncan, a former leader of the Black Sash, expressed surprise that someone like me had been elected president. The politician Harry Schwarz warned of the danger of the Institute's image as the upholder of liberal values being besmirched by any association with an organisation which propagated values that were at odds with theirs.

The episode reminded me of the book *The Liberal Slideaway* by the veteran Institute supporter Jill Wentzel. Some liberals, she wrote, would rather condone abuses on the part of the liberation movement than support anything to do with the "Nats" or the previous government.

I suspect that some of the Institute's council members insisted on my resignation after the *Sunday Times* report. The Institute's CEO, John Kane-Berman, flew to Stellenbosch and the two of us agreed that he would issue a statement. It would spell out clearly that only the SAIRR council could decide on discussions with the AB's executive council. I had assumed that this was self-evident, but Kane-Berman judged correctly that the announcement would defuse the situation.

In a reply in a *Sunday Times*, I wrote that even government departments held talks with the AB on an issue such as fighting poverty in their own ranks. Why then the consternation about the proposal that the Institute and the AB should talk to each other? Was it because some South Africans still wanted to fight the old political battles? Is it perhaps true, I asked, that the intelligentsia, like the proverbial generals, are always fighting the last war?

My UCT colleague David Welsh came to my defence in an article in *Frontiers of Freedom*, a publication of the Institute. He noted that many other liberal thinkers apart from Taylor also advocated group rights. Under pressure from the ANC the country was adopting a constitution that amounted to majority domination. This was a system that would be just as detrimental to the ideal of a liberal democracy as apartheid had been.

Welsh advised the Institute to engage in conversation with all political tendencies rather than attempt to preserve its political purity. Kane-Berman later wrote to me that this episode did not redound to the credit of the SAIRR.

Something similar would happen four years later when the Democratic Party (DP) decided to enter into a coalition with the New National Party in the Western Cape in order to keep the ANC, which had won the most votes in the province, out of power.

In his autobiography, Tony Leon, leader of the DP and the later DA, tells of the reaction of Julian Ogilvie Thompson, chairman of the Anglo American Corporation and an important donor to his party: "Tony, you have gone to bed with people who have political AIDS and I have a good mind to switch off the taps." The role that the NP under De Klerk had played to bring about a settlement which suited the business sector down to the ground was completely forgotten.

## Founding myths

On 15 February 1996 I delivered my presidential address at the SAIRR on the major challenges for the new democratic order in South Africa.[114] While the establishment of our democracy with its impressive constitution was cause for celebration, I said, there were also grounds for concern. The ANC's majority was so overwhelming that our country might soon develop into a kind of dominant-party democracy, as in the case of Mexico, Taiwan, Malaysia and Zimbabwe. In a dominant-party state the rituals of democracy, such as elections and parliamentary debates, are observed, but democracy is hollowed out, notably as a result of a fusion between the ruling party and the state. This eventually becomes a cancer that leads to pervasive corruption.

I addressed a number of issues "awaiting new responses from liberals". The first was "the burden of our history", which could also be referred to as our

---

114  Hermann Giliomee, *Liberal and Populist Democracy in South Africa: Challenges, New Threats to Democracy* (SA Institute of Race Relations, 1996).

historical responsibility. It was an issue that had become particularly acute after the government established a Truth and Reconciliation Commission (TRC) in 1995. The TRC had to hear testimony on human rights abuses and, in cases where there had been full disclosure, grant amnesty to perpetrators.

I was opposed to the TRC from the outset because of the way in which it had been established. The ANC was only able to put the commission on the political agenda because the NP government had botched the chance of negotiating a general amnesty for all sides, and not because the security forces had suffered a defeat. Kobie Coetsee, the NP's minister of justice, dawdled over the issue of amnesty and De Klerk inexplicably failed to instruct him to finalise the matter while the NP government was still in the driver's seat.

The ANC succeeded in obtaining amnesty for 2 000 of its followers before the first session of the TRC. During the TRC process, however, the spotlight fell on the 280 members of the security forces under the NP government who had requested amnesty.

I pointed out the reprehensible manner in which ANC ministers sought to claim the moral high ground in the lead-up to the TRC. According to justice minister Dullah Omar, those who had fought against the ANC in the 1980s were like the German Nazis who had idolised Hitler or the French who had defended the Vichy regime during the Second World War. The ANC, on the other hand, had fought for democracy and freedom. I rejected this rhetoric as reckless propaganda.

The worst was the ANC's portrayal of the resolution in which the General Assembly of the United Nations (UN) declared apartheid a crime against humanity in 1973. The UN General Assembly also agreed to the drawing up of an International Convention on the Suppression and Punishment of the Crime of Apartheid. Omar and other ANC leaders regularly referred to this resolution and convention when they claimed that the "world community" had condemned apartheid as a crime against humanity.

The actual facts were rather different. The main sponsors of the draft resolution were the Soviet Union and Guinea, and the convention came into operation after twenty countries (including Hungary, Mongolia, Syria and Iraq), all members of the Soviet bloc, ratified it. The common goal of this bloc was to get a blow in against the West during the propaganda battle of the Cold War.

None of the above countries could be considered democracies in the normal sense of the word. Approximately seventy countries subsequently signed on, but all the major Western countries refused to ratify the convention. It was never adopted by the UN Security Council. The US ambassador stated in the General Assembly: "We cannot accept that apartheid can be made a crime against humanity. Crimes against humanity are so grave that they must be meticulously elaborated and strictly constructed under existing international law."

Nevertheless, the ANC propaganda claim that the "entire world community" had declared apartheid a crime against humanity was remarkably successful. It cropped up regularly in the TRC sessions.

Another theme I dealt with in my presidential address was that of "nation-building" and different approaches to this aim. The Jacobinical approach to building national unity, which enjoyed strong support among ANC leaders, was to have one national culture, one dominant language (English) and one interpretation of history in school curricula. I contrasted this with the pluralist approach, which regards a diversity of cultures, languages and historical interpretations as an asset and encourages real debate about history.

In my address I referred to the words of Nelson Mandela, who had said in early 1996 that any community which wished to retain its own schools, language and cultural background could do so, provided that coloured or black children who wanted to be taught in Afrikaans were not excluded. Some of the provincial education departments, however, were already planning to force Afrikaans schools and universities to teach in English as well.

Once the NP moved to the opposition benches, the ANC resumed its attacks on the party. The vice-president, Thabo Mbeki, said that reconciliation was impossible unless apartheid was acknowledged as a crime against humanity. What this amounted to, I wrote in a column in *Rapport* on 3 November 1996, was that your adversary would only forgive you if you apologised on his terms.

In the same year the book *Reconciliation through Truth: A Reckoning of Apartheid's Criminal Governance* (David Philip) appeared, co-authored by Kader Asmal, a cabinet minister. The theme was that the NP government had committed genocide as well as crimes against humanity. The allegation of genocide was perplexing, I stated in the *Cape Times* of 23 October 1996, given that the life expectancy of all population groups had risen steadily during the period of NP rule and infant mortality had declined. In the case of coloured infants, the decrease in the mortality rate was among the largest in the world.

With reference to ANC attempts to delegitimise the NP, I quoted Juan Linz, a distinguished authority on democratisation and regime transitions. Linz warned that efforts to paint the previous regime in the most negative light possible could be severely detrimental to the consolidation of a young democracy. In conclusion, I expressed my surprise that David Philip Publishers could have published such a book. This review damaged my relationship with my first English publisher irreparably.

John Kane-Berman asked me to sound out opinion-formers informally about a reply to the TRC's invitation to the Institute to testify before the commission. The Institute was wary of the TRC, especially when it became apparent that in terms of its composition (including the commissioners, the research staff and the historical context in which the overall conflict was framed) the scales were overwhelmingly tipped in the ANC's favour. I consulted influential people on the matter of the Institute's reply and also discussed it with a group of opinion-formers at a meeting in Johannesburg.

For me the most illuminating response was that of Van Zyl Slabbert, who refrained from adopting a public position on the TRC but was very sceptical of the commission in private. Characteristically, he dismissed the TRC's claim that public confession and penance would lead to reconciliation with a quip: "Tell that to any couple in a divorce case in which the one party is bent on running the other into the ground in court."

I recommended that the Institute did not testify. Kane-Berman declined the TRC's invitation, but offered to open the library of the Institute, which had arguably recorded human rights violations better than any other organisation, to TRC researchers.

Jacko Maree, the NP's parliamentary spokesperson on the TRC, later told me he had reported to De Klerk that Slabbert and I were of the view that the NP, in its own interest, should not participate in the TRC.

De Klerk had replied that it was too late to turn back. If the NP were to oppose the TRC bill, it would create the impression that the NP was afraid of having abuses under its rule investigated. According to De Klerk, the party had nothing to hide.[115] The TRC undoubtedly hastened the NP's demise.

## An awkward embrace

In the 1994 election the ANC received 63% of the votes compared to the NP's 20%. It was one of the widest gaps in the world between the victor and the second-largest party. From all indications, the results in the next three or four elections would be basically the same.

Nonetheless, in the first decade after 1994 there was a tendency among analysts to write as if South Africa was on the road to becoming a liberal democracy in the same mould as the modern industrialised democracies of the world.

I had reservations about this view from the outset. South Africa lacked three of the critical elements of a liberal democracy: a system where minorities are

---

115  Reply from Jacko Maree to a questionnaire compiled by Neil Southern, 4 December 2014.

regarded as loyal rather than potentially disloyal, where property rights are respected, and where the executive is held accountable and the lines between the state machinery and the ruling party are not blurred. In a liberal democracy the largest opposition party has a real chance of winning the next election, and the various parties mobilise voters on the basis of socio-economic priorities rather than race or ethnicity.

For me, all indications were that South Africa might see the emergence of a typical dominant-party regime in which the dominant party, which actually prefers an authoritarian system, is in an "awkward embrace" with democracy.

In 1995 I concluded an article in the American academic journal *Political Science Quarterly* as follows: "The evolution of a liberal democracy is most unlikely, and tensions between ethnic groups will be managed with great difficulty by a single dominant party."

From an early stage the ANC put demands for transformation on the basis of racial proportions of the population – rather than constitutional rights – at the centre and allowed no debate on the matter. Contracts, appointments and promotion at all levels of government soon depended to a large extent on party membership.

Even Nelson Mandela, at an ANC conference at Mafikeng in 1997, accused the "white" opposition parties of propagating a "reactionary, dangerous and opportunist position" and of being under the illusion that they had "a democratic obligation merely to discredit the ruling party, so that they may gain power after the next elections".[116]

In a particularly instructive 75-page study titled "Death of the Rainbow Nation", James Myburgh, one of my best students at UCT, wrote that within three years the ANC had replaced Mandela's vision of "an inspiringly united society" with a policy that incited racial conflict.[117] This was the basis of Tony Leon's decision to make "Fight Back" the theme of his party's campaign in the 1999 election.

I started exchanging views with Charles Simkins, who drew my attention to the book *Uncommon Democracies: The One-Party Dominant Regimes* (1990), edited by the American political scientist TJ Pempel. It was a study that focused on one-party dominance in advanced industrialised democracies such as Sweden, Italy and Japan. However, no comparative study had yet been done on similar regimes in developing countries.

---

116  Nelson Mandela, Political Report of the President of the ANC, Mafikeng, 16 December 1997.
117  Tony Leon, *On the Contrary* (Johannesburg and Cape Town: Jonathan Ball, 2008), p. 281.

Simkins and I decided to organise a conference that would examine dominant parties in semi-industrialised countries. The best-known examples were the Institutional Revolutionary Party (PRI) in Mexico, which at the time had been in power for more than 70 years, the Kuomintang (KMT), which had ruled Taiwan since 1949, the United Malays National Organisation (UMNO), which had dominated politics in Malaysia since independence in 1957, and the People's Action Party (PAP), which had determined Singapore's destiny since independence. There were also the dominant parties in Angola and Zimbabwe, which were of special importance to South Africa.

Dominant parties can be defined as those which:

- establish electoral dominance for an uninterrupted and prolonged period;
- enjoy dominance in the formation of successive governments;
- enjoy dominance in determining the public agenda;
- put the emphasis on the pursuit of a "historic project" that gives particular shape to the national political agenda. In the case of South Africa, the ANC's historic project soon shifted from affirmative action to transformation aimed at the achievement of demographic representivity on numerous levels of society, even sports teams and state-supported old-age homes.

At worst, a one-party-dominant regime undermines the essence of democracy. Distinctive features are a lack of accountability on the part of the executive, complete subordination of the judiciary to the executive, and pervasive corruption. Nevertheless, all of this takes place under the veneer of democracy.

The sociologist Pierre van den Berghe had noted years earlier that a study of democracy in Africa put one on one's guard against accepting the term "democracy" at face value. He pointed out that the liberal principle of majority rule represented "the great moral alibi of black nationalism" in Africa, which he explained as follows:

> If your constituency has the good fortune to contain a demographic majority, racism can easily be disguised as democracy. The ideological sleight of hand is, of course, that an ascriptive, racially-defined majority is a far cry from a majority made up of shifting coalitions of individuals on the basis of commonality of beliefs and interests.[118]

---

118  Pierre van den Berghe, "Introduction" in Van den Berghe (ed.), *The Liberal Dilemma in South Africa* (London: Croom Helm, 1979), p. 7.

At this time a settlement was reached in Northern Ireland on the basis that support from the majority party in both political communities was required to pass contentious legislation. It was highly probable that in deeply divided South Africa democracy might end up being not much more than a cloak for racial domination, since polls had indicated since the mid-1980s that the ANC would easily win more than 60% of electoral support.

## A private-sector based middle class?

In 1995 the government of Taiwan invited me for a two-week visit. Prior to 1994, South Africa had been one of the few countries that recognised Taiwan's sovereignty. The Taiwanese government was lobbying hard to persuade the Mandela government not to recognise only China, as Beijing's One China policy demanded. Their chances of success were slim, as many ANC leaders admired the Chinese form of communism.

At the conclusion of my visit I told my host, a deputy minister, that Taiwan's strongest selling point was its political system. It was undoubtedly democratic and had laid the foundation for the island's astounding economic growth. The dominant party, the Kuomintang (KMT), which originated in 1949 as a semi-autocratic party and became properly democratic over the next half-century, had played a key role.

The good example of his country's democratic system might help the ANC avoid the pitfalls of one-party dominance, I said. If that were to be the case, it might lead to rapprochement between Taipei and Pretoria.

On my way home I made contact with academics in Kuala Lumpur and Singapore who had grown up under one-party-dominant regimes. Some had spent years analysing the ways in which the dominant parties stayed in power.

I raised the necessary funds for a conference. Besides sponsorship from the Taiwanese government, I received support from the Chairman's Fund of Anglo American and De Beers, as well as from Standard Bank and Old Mutual. There were therefore business leaders who took the possibility of a one-party-dominant democracy seriously and thought more should be known about the nature of such regimes.

The conference took place in November 1996 at a centre in Waenhuiskrans. Authorities from various countries contributed papers under my editorship, which were later published as *The Awkward Embrace: One-Party Domination and Democracy* (1999).

I compared the systems in Taiwan, Mexico, Malaysia and South Africa and wrote the concluding chapter, while Charles Simkins analysed the relation between a country's level of broad-based socio-economic development and the quality of its democracy. The outlook for South Africa did not seem very promising. Simkins showed that the country was at a level where the prospects for movement in the direction of a liberal democracy with a competitive system were considerably poorer than in Mexico and Malaysia, where the dominant parties had been in power for 70 years and 40 years respectively. Taiwan's democratic prospects were a good deal brighter than those of the other three.

I gained important insights from the study. As TJ Pempel noted in his introduction to *The Awkward Embrace*, there were extensive differences between the various one-party-dominant democracies. Taiwan was able to move towards a mature democracy because its entrepreneurs had largely built up their small and medium enterprises without state patronage. It was in their interest to establish various opposition parties in order to keep the ruling party on its toes.

In my concluding chapter I pointed out that the relationship between democracy and an established middle class, which was generally assumed to exist, should be qualified. In ethnically divided societies there was good cause to question the theory that broad-based economic development goes hand in hand with the rise of a middle class committed to competitive politics. The crucial variable was whether or not the rise of the "indigenous" middle class was a product of state patronage. In Malaysia, where the Chinese community had long dominated the economy, the government tried in various ways to empower the "indigenous" Malay population through preferential treatment, but democracy declined more and more. Elsewhere I wrote: "As Malaysia shows, on which our empowerment policy is largely based, a state-sponsored middle class is more interested in the perpetuation and extension of patronage than in the checks and balances of a liberal democracy, particularly a virile opposition party ... Taiwan is the one place where the growth of small and medium businesses independent of state patronage promoted a viable democracy."[119]

Between 2005 and 2015 the question whether the efforts to increase black participation in the South African economy would be at the expense of democracy increasingly raised concern. In 2015 RW Johnson stated categorically in his book *How Long Will South Africa Survive? The Looming Crisis* that "South Africa can either have an ANC government or it can have a modern industrial economy. It cannot have both."

## Mbeki on the attack

At a conference organised by the trade union Solidarity in 2007, FW de Klerk and Pik Botha declared that the ANC was applying affirmative action and

---

119  Hermann Giliomee, *This Day*, 24 April 2004.

demographic representivity in an "unconstitutional and racist" manner. According to Botha, the NP would not have agreed to the interim constitution in 1993 if it had known what kind of labour legislation the ANC had up its sleeve.

De Klerk added: "The Constitution makes provision for demographic representivity being applied only in the civil service and judiciary. Now it is applied also to civil society, business and the field of culture . . . An unbalanced application of demographic representation has no basis in the Constitution."[120] Looking back in hindsight, Solidarity CEO Flip Buys observed in an e-mail to me on 12 February 2016: "Almost everything we're struggling with today reflects the NP negotiators' total lack of strategic thinking and the political trance they had fallen into as a result of the spirit of the times."

Roger Southall, a political scientist from the University of the Witwatersrand, referred to me in an article in 2005 as "the most prominent exponent of the 'party dominance' theory in South Africa".[121] According to him, the ANC's dominance and the accompanying lack of accountability were a major theme in the Democratic Alliance's election campaign in 2004.

As Southall points out, the ANC's response to critics who raised the notion of one-party dominance was penned in part by President Mbeki himself. For Mbeki the concept was inherently conservative, a cover for white interests and a manifestation of an inherent white distrust of black governance. The majority of South Africans wanted a unifying mode of politics such as that provided by the ANC-led government rather than "the racial divisiveness peddled by the DA".

In 2005 Mbeki responded to an academic paper I had prepared for a conference in Granada, Spain, in the same year, in which I pointed out the way in which the ANC enforced its project of transformation on the basis of representivity. Parliament and the Chapter Nine institutions offered little protection to minority groups. The main remaining shield of the minorities against an intolerant dominant party was the independence of the judiciary, and particularly that of the Constitutional Court.

But here too there was cause for concern, I said, when it came to the composition of this bench. While the chief justice, Arthur Chaskalson, denied having been a card-carrying member of the South African Communist Party, he had been closely associated with the party in the past. At the latest count,

---

120  Hermann Giliomee, *The Afrikaners: Biography of a People* (Cape Town: Tafelberg, 2009), pp. 706-07.
121  Roger Southall, "The 'Dominant Party Debate' in South Africa", *Africa Spectrum*, 40 (1), 2005, p. 61.

I went on, more than three-quarters of the Constitutional Court judges were either open or tacit ANC supporters. "This means that the difficult compromises made in the negotiations are now being interpreted by a bench perceived by the minorities to be biased in favour of the dominant party."[122]

James Myburgh published my paper on his blog *Everready News* and Mbeki responded to it a few days later in his 10 June 2005 issue of "Letter from the President", part of the online weekly newsletter "ANC Today". ZB du Toit reported in *Rapport* on this dressing-down under the heading "Mbeki hauls Giliomee over the coals". I had argued that government policy had reached a point where it was "an illusion that the Constitutional Court protects minorities," and that "transformation has replaced the constitution as the framework of government policy".

Mbeki weighed in with his customary royal "we": "We know of no instance where it [the Constitutional Court] has acted as 'an instrument of the overbearing dominant party'. Whatever the political sympathies of the individual members of the Constitutional Court, about which Professor Giliomee is obviously better informed than we are, I am certain that he would find it extremely difficult to prove that the Court has failed to protect such interests of 'the minorities' as might be provided for in our Constitution."

Commenting on the rebuke, I told *Rapport* that Joel Netshitenzhe, the ANC head of communications and a Mbeki confidant, had said the ANC was geared towards controlling all the levers of power, including the judiciary. By 2015 the ruling party designated at least three-quarters of the members of the Judicial Service Commission (JSC), the body which recommends judges to the executive for appointment.

The real bias was against candidates who are outstanding and fiercely independent. Top advocates such as Jeremy Gauntlett and Geoff Budlender who made themselves available for judicial appointments had scant hope of being accepted.

By 2016 there were, reportedly, increasingly fewer applications for vacant positions on the Constitutional Court bench, and vacancies had to be advertised more than once. Experts attributed this lack of interest to the nature of the questioning during the JSC's interviews and the perception that the chief justice and the president had too much say in the final choice.

---

122  Hermann Giliomee, "White-led Opposition Parties and White Minorities under South Africa's 'Liberal' Dominant Party System".

## The demise of the once-mighty NP

All the transitions from a dictatorship to a democracy during the second half of the twentieth century were characterised by the demise of a once-mighty party. In the election of 1999 more than half of the Afrikaner electorate voted for the DP. This was the main reason for the decline in support for the NP (now renamed the New National Party – NNP) among the electorate in general from 20% in 1994 to below 7%. The ANC united more than 69% of the voters behind it.

After the election the DP and the NNP formed the Democratic Alliance (DA) under the leadership of Tony Leon. I was pleased about this, as it offered the party of my and Annette's parents and grandparents a dignified end. As a Jewish South African, Leon showed a good understanding of the issues that troubled Afrikaners as a minority.

Unfortunately, a small NNP faction under the NNP leader, Marthinus van Schalkwyk, broke away and joined the ANC. The party fought the 2004 election in a coalition with the ANC, but was subsequently taken over by the ANC. The ANC exacted maximum symbolic tribute. The NNP members had to endorse the Freedom Charter and transfer the NNP's assets to the ANC on the party's dissolution. I described the NNP's demise as a "prostitute's funeral" in *Rapport*.

In the election of 2004 the NNP's overall support dropped from 6.9% in 1999 to 1.7%, while its support from Afrikaners declined to 8%. Nevertheless, the 11% support which the NNP attracted in the Western Cape enabled the ANC to come into power in that province and also in the city of Cape Town. The NNP was tossed the following crumbs from the ANC table: one ministership, two deputy ministerships, one ambassadorship and two consul-generalships. Only one person (Van Schalkwyk) would be high enough on the ANC list in the 2009 election to be elected to Parliament.

In 2007 Inus Aucamp and Johan Swanepoel, the last NNP leader in the Free State and the last chief secretary of the Free State NP respectively, asked me to write a foreword for their book on the Free State NP, *Einde van 'n groot party: 'n Vrystaatse perspektief op die (N)NP* (End of a great party: a Free State perspective on the (N)NP). The authors asked on the flyleaf how the NP, which had existed for almost a century and ruled the country for 55 years, had managed to "disintegrate" so disastrously and "become the laughing stock of the entire country". On the blurb I described the story as a combination of "a political farce and a Greek tragedy".

For my foreword I asked De Klerk and the Naspers chairman Ton Vosloo, a seasoned journalist and former editor of *Beeld*, why the NP had fared so poorly in the negotiations and gone downhill in the ten years after 1994.

Vosloo's reply pertained more to the period before 1990. He pointed out the "endless debates" in the NP on the colour question and the mounting international pressure. Conflicts between reformers and conservatives and the quarrels in Afrikaner ranks after the party split in 1982 had sapped the NP of its initiative.

> The NP had no vigour left in it by the time FW took over. This listless situation led to the poorly handled negotiations. Maybe PW would have driven a harder bargain, but he might never have achieved a deal . . .
>
> In the end the top dog had lost its vigour and there was no dynamism left to take the party by the scruff of its neck and drag it out of the morass . . . This malaise of ruling for too long and forming the laager within which the whites felt safe because it kept the blacks 'outside' our lives was a major contributing factor to the rapid implosion. In the end the house of cards proved not to have been built on rock. In the end the emperor turned out to be a streaker.[123]

De Klerk replied as follows:

> On the one hand the NP had to govern the country in the face of increasing violence on the part of the ANC, the IFP and elements within the security forces. It had to try and retain white support for the negotiating process in spite of the often perturbing statements and actions of the ANC and other groupings. And it had to attempt to negotiate the best possible constitutional settlement despite the fact that the party's power base had dwindled unavoidably in the lead-up to the negotiations.[124]

Vosloo's and De Klerk's replies reminded me of the illuminating comment by the political scientist Samuel Huntington, who had analysed transitions from autocratic to democratic systems in various countries in his influential work *Political Order in Changing Societies* (1968). On his first visit to South Africa in 1981, it seemed to Huntington as if white domination was still fairly stable. Yet he issued a warning: "Revolutionary violence does not have to be

---

123  E-mail communication from Ton Vosloo to the author, 12 April 2007.
124  E-mail communication from FW de Klerk to the author, 20 April 2007.

successful to be effective. It simply has to cause sufficient trouble to cause divisions among the dominant group over the ways to deal with it."[125] This was exactly what happened to the Afrikaners and their political arm, the National Party. As the historian Arnold Toynbee had predicted in 1959, it was not a military defeat but internal divisions, poor preparation and confusion that ended Afrikaner domination.

## Fissures about Fischer

In September 2004 the council of the University of Stellenbosch (US) decided to award an honorary doctorate to the late Abram "Bram" Fischer, an anti-apartheid hero and leading figure in the Communist Party. He had been convicted of conspiracy to overthrow the government by violent means and sentenced to life imprisonment in the mid-1960s.

In my book on the history of the Afrikaners, which had just appeared, I endeavoured to give an even-handed assessment of Fischer. I was nonetheless upset about the honorary degree. During my years at the US under NP rule the honorary degrees the university loved to dole out to government leaders had irritated me. But I had no objection to the US awarding honorary degrees after 1994 to people such as Nelson Mandela, Desmond Tutu, Beyers Naudé and Trevor Manuel. It was a good attempt to create a historical balance.

Fischer's honorary doctorate, however, was a different case. The degree would be awarded posthumously, which was only done in exceptional circumstances. He had no links with the US, and no other university, including his alma mater, the University of the Free State, had bestowed an honorary doctorate on him. The guidelines in respect of an honorary degree in the US statute specified that it had to reflect the aims and goals of the university. Obviously this included aims in favour of as well as against certain issues.

While Fischer's sacrifices in his struggle against apartheid were certainly praiseworthy, the following question immediately had to be posed: What were the aims Fischer strove for? The obituary which appeared in the *African Communist* after Fischer's death referred unequivocally to his "unswerving loyalty to the ideas of Marxist-Leninism and communism".

If the ANC were to have come to power in the 1960s, Fischer and his Communist Party SACP, which had such a strong presence in the ANC, would no doubt have tried to implement the radical plan for a National Democratic Revolution that the SACP had adopted as a policy document in 1962.

---

125 Samuel Huntington, "Reform and Stability in a Modernizing, Multi-Ethnic Society", *Politikon,* 8, 1981, p. 11.

Someone who was well placed to express an opinion was Alan Paton, leader of the Liberal Party, who had a warm affection for Fischer and even testified in his defence at his trial in 1966.

Paton had little doubt that communists with their hands on the levers of power at a time when the Cold War was at its most intense would spell great danger for South Africa. He disagreed with a fellow liberal who told him he would be the first to be killed if Fischer's party in alliance with the ANC seized power, but believed that if his friend Bram came to power, "an emissary would be sent to me with a one-way-ticket, and with a message 'Get out of here as fast as possible'."

The honorary doctorate reduced the US's aims to what could best be described as "being all things to all men". The decision was symptomatic of the ideological confusion about its own identity and values that the university has developed since the early 1990s. On the part of some members of the executive and senior academics there was a desire to break away totally from the past, and specifically from the university's history and the culture and language in which the institution had been built up.

At the annual meeting of the convocation I was one of the seconders of a motion proposed by a former SRC chairperson and former cabinet minister, Tertius Delport, which stated that the conferral of an honorary degree on Fischer was not compatible with the statutory criteria. It requested the council to review its decision. A compromise motion was adopted, in which it was declared that the correct procedures had been followed and that the university took note of unhappiness among its alumni about the decision. An amendment that Fischer be honoured for his struggle against injustice was voted down.

A member of the US council told me I should not waste my energy on the Fischer issue but rather save it for the big battle about Afrikaans as medium of instruction that lay ahead. I replied that the two matters were closely related.

## Chapter 11

# An uncommon biography

I embarked on my book on the history of the Afrikaners in 1992, a year or so after the publication of *The Mind of South Africa* by Allister Sparks. As a popular history, Sparks's book probably had a greater influence on international opinion-formers than any other work in the early 1990s. I was not impressed. In a comprehensive review in the magazine *SA International* in 1991, I argued that the book rehashed all the old stereotypes and myths about Afrikaner history. It seemed to be aimed at lending credibility to the ANC's struggle against the "historical injustice" to which black people had been subjected.

Sparks portrayed the Afrikaners' ancestors as the "most backward fragment" of Western civilisation in modern times. Even in the twentieth century the Afrikaners were still "locked in their seventeenth-century time capsule". According to him, the fact that the Afrikaners regarded themselves as a "Chosen People" until late in the twentieth century was the reason why Afrikaner nationalism became so extremist.

Sparks depicted Afrikaner nationalism as the historical stumbling block in the way of the modernisation of the political-economic system and liberty for all. In contrast, he waxed lyrical about the black people who, in his view, were infused with the *ubuntu* spirit of mutual respect.

I differed strongly with Sparks on the question whether Afrikaner nationalism represented the major stumbling block to a settlement. In reality, this nationalism had started crumbling from the late 1970s, a process which accelerated in the 1980s. Yet a settlement was not possible unless at least half of the Afrikaners were committed to it. Without the NP and without the elements of the Afrikaner nationalist movement – the press, the Broederbond, the Dutch Reformed Church and organised Afrikaans business – Afrikaner acceptance of a negotiated settlement would have been out of the question.

Most analysts ascribed the NP leaders' willingness to settle to the fact that the Afrikaners had increasingly become a middle class focused on consumerism and comfort. According to this view, sacrifices for the sake of the "Afrikaner cause" had become too costly. Hence the preparedness to settle was the inevitable consequence of the modernisation process.

I did not share this view. In my opinion, Afrikaners in leading positions increasingly rejected apartheid as a system that enforced injustice. They found themselves in a rapidly changing situation where the Afrikaner proportion of the population had declined from more than 11% in 1960 to 7% in 1996. The majority of Afrikaners were looking for an alternative that would give them a rightful place in South Africa. Such an alternative also necessitated a reassessment of history.

## The Afrikaners' story

When I started writing *The Afrikaners* in 1992, I knew that I faced a major challenge: Was it possible for me to write dispassionately and impartially about the Afrikaners? Every black and coloured person in South Africa carried the scars of white domination. "When are people morally obliged to remember?" Bernhard Schlink asked in *Der Vorleser (The Reader)*, the unforgettable German novel about the extermination of the Jews and the struggle to come to grips with the past. On a visit to South Africa, he answered his own question as follows: "When the victims insist on the right to have their identities, which have been shaped by the horror, acknowledged."[126] Books that prioritise the complexity of apartheid, especially when written by white South Africans, tend to create the impression that the author is blind to the feelings of those who have suffered severely under the system.

There was certainly a need for history books that acknowledge the suffering of victims and the callousness of the oppressors. One could even speak of a public demand for such works. C Vann Woodward, the great historian of the American South, wrote that after the end of segregation in the United States and the American defeat in Vietnam, there was a market for a particular product: "It was collective guilt that the buyers sought. Guilt inexpiable and probably ineradicable guilt over the long past, from the first settlers down to the present."[127]

After 1970 several historians in South Africa keenly sought to supply this market. Among the new generation of Afrikaners, too, some were almost desperate to show with how much revulsion they regarded the Afrikaners' history and recent political past. It seemed as if they wanted to make one point

---

126  *Die Burger*, 27 September 2003.
127  C Vann Woodward, *Thinking Back: The Perils of Writing History* (Baton Rouge: Louisiana State University Press, 1986), pp. 114-15.

clear at the outset: "We are not all like that." In extreme cases they appeared to harbour "a self-righteous self-hate" – a term the German writer Peter Schneider used with reference to his compatriots who protested loudly whenever anyone attempted to present a more nuanced picture of the Nazi era.[128]

Another option for a historian is not to prioritise guilt, but to write the history in such a detached fashion that no one might be able to guess in what community the writer had spent his formative years. I decided to write my book in neither of these two ways.

One of the most original modern historians and political commentators, Tony Judt, grew up in London as the son of Jewish parents. "History is a story, a story needs a narrator and a narrator needs to be standing somewhere," he wrote. "The view from nowhere does not work."[129] I decided I would attempt to write in such a way that my Afrikaans background would be a resource rather than a stumbling block, and that readers would be left in no doubt about the "corner" from which I told the story.

I did not want to write as a nationalist historian, but as a historian who did not hide his Afrikaans background. My hope was that my approach would be seen in a similar light to the German-born Hannah Arendt's identification with the Jewish community. She told Gershom Scholem, the fiercest critic of her book *Eichmann in Jerusalem: A Report on the Banality of Evil*: "I do not 'love' the Jews nor do I 'believe' in them. I merely belong to them as a matter of course, beyond dispute and argument."[130]

Though the two white communities in South Africa had much in common, certain things were distinctive to most politically aware Afrikaners. There was, for instance, the obsession among many Afrikaners about their small numbers and their anxieties about Afrikaner survival which culminated in their fatal embrace of apartheid. CW de Kiewiet, in my eyes the liberal historian with the greatest wisdom and insight, wrote in 1957 that "for the thoughtful man it is still important to understand how men [the Afrikaners] who are sincere in their Christian beliefs and staunch defenders of their own liberties can become identified with policies of discrimination and restriction".[131] I thought that someone who could explain apartheid with understanding would make an important contribution.

128  Laura Winters, "The Women Who Stood up to Hitler", *Financial Times Magazine* (London), 14 August 2004, p. 35.

129  Tony Judt, 'The Story of Everything', *New York Review of Books*, 21 September 2000, p. 66.

130  Gabriel Piterberg, "Hannah Arendt in Tel Aviv", *New Left Review*, 21, 2001, p. 145.

131  CW de Kiewiet, *Anatomy of South African Misery* (London, 1957), p. 45.

A book about survival and collective fears presupposes a degree of empathy. My challenge was to write with empathy and understanding but without condoning or explaining away the injustices perpetrated by the Afrikaners. In the book's introduction, written late in 2002, I would cite HDF Kitto, a scholar of slavery in ancient Greece: "To understand is not necessarily to pardon, but there is no harm in trying to understand."

This statement is not quite the safe position it seems. Neville Alexander, who spoke at the launch of *The Afrikaners* in April 2003, responded to Kitto by quoting Madame de Staël's *"tout comprendre rend très indulgent"*. The *Concise Oxford Dictionary of Quotations* translates this as: "To be totally understanding makes one very indulgent." One could also say: *"too* indulgent". Alexander's comment highlights the very fine but also very important line between apology and empathy.

The problem is especially acute when it comes to apartheid. There is certainly room for moral condemnation in the historiography of apartheid, but equally room for explanation. There is a particular tension between the two. A character in Schlink's *Der Vorleser* expresses it as follows: "When I tried to understand it, I had the feeling I was failing to condemn it as it must be condemned. When I condemned it as it must be condemned, there was no room for understanding . . . I could not resolve this. I wanted to pose myself both tasks – understanding and condemnation. But it was impossible to do both."

In post-1994 South Africa, historians were desperate to avoid anything that could be perceived as a vindication of apartheid. It was far easier to write about apartheid in pathological terms, to condemn it as a "cancer" or a "mental aberration", a flight into "nihilism", evil and economically disastrous, than to analyse it as the very complex system that it was. We live in a world in which "apology is easier than explaining", as Irish historian Roy Foster phrased it. He nevertheless urged historians to stick to their duty, which is to remind their public that "the continuums and the inheritances of history are matters of complex descent".[132]

An astute Brazilian anthropologist noted in a doctoral dissertation on apartheid that the policy was a strange creature for South Africans in the 1990s. Though they had all been born under it and had lived through it, "they seemed to regard it as some kind of strange nightmare or spell that was at last fortunately over. It could often be an object of their disgust and criticism, but seldom,

---

132  Roy Foster, "Fashion for apology can invite danger of amnesia", *Sunday Independent*, 25 July 1999.

if ever, an object of keen curiosity."[133] My decision was to approach apartheid as something that should be examined anew and described soberly.

The other question was whether I wanted to put the emphasis on a systematic analysis or on the narrative. I opted for a narrative history. Many professional historians lost their way in the 1960s and 1970s when historiography started to look more and more like a branch of sociology. As a result, their works were increasingly read only by fellow historians. I wanted to address my book to the general public.

Of great help in this regard was that Tafelberg Publishers took up the South African rights after Virginia University Press decided to publish the manuscript in the United States. Tafelberg specifically saw the general public as the target group and marketed the book accordingly. Christopher Hurst was the British publisher. The sales received a huge boost when *The Economist*, one of the most highly regarded magazines in the English-speaking world, published a long review. In the end, more than 30 000 copies were sold.

From the outset I decided to write the book as an "informed narrative".[134] I was blessed to have an American editor, Jeannette Hopkins, who drew a thick pencil line through my abstract generalisations and wrote in red in the margin: "Tell your story!"

Charles van Onselen made the apt comment that great works of history "should be akin to a fine novel, just as much as Emile Zola's most moving and best researched works can be read as fine history".[135] Karel Schoeman's novel *Verkenning*, which is set in the Batavian period, and his biography of Machtelt Smit, who lived in the same period, are almost two sides of the same coin – the novel is so much better for the historical research, and the history for its novelistic manner of telling.

Instead of sociological theories, I tried to employ the techniques of good story-tellers: the development of a narrative line, the fleshing out of characters, and the highlighting of irony, confusion and unintended consequences. I chose "the biography of a people" as the subtitle for my book to signal that I intended to tell the Afrikaners' story, but the term "biography" should be taken as a metaphor rather than a literal description.

---

133  Luiz Fernando Ferreira da Rosa Ribeiro, "Apartheid and *Democracia Racial*: South Africa and Brazil in contrast", doctoral dissertation, University of Utrecht, 1990, p. 33.

134  Lawrence Stone, "The Revival of Narrative: Reflections on a New Old History", *Past and Present,* 85, November 1979, pp. 3-24.

135  Text of his speech during the ceremony at which he was awarded the 1998 Alan Paton Prize.

I had the good fortune that two outstanding novelists, Karel Schoeman and JM Coetzee, read all the drafts of the chapters as I completed them. What struck me about their comments and criticism was how well they understood the task of constructing a story, their sharp eye for spotting irony, pathos, tragedy, self-deception and hypocrisy. Analysis can be woven into the narrative line, but the narrative line remains the framework around which the work is constructed.[136]

Neither Schoeman nor Coetzee would ever commit the cardinal sin of being ahistorical in their approach to history and modern politics. The British historian Herbert Butterfield has an apt metaphor for anachronisms and the ahistorical: "When we organise our general history with reference to the present we are producing what is really a giant optical illusion." It is quite wrong to abstract things from their historical context and judge them apart from their context. It is also wrong to see history as marching inexorably towards its fated outcome. In each generation there is what Butterfield calls "a clash of wills out of which there emerges something that probably no man ever willed".[137]

Historians should portray this clash. In 1992 FA van Jaarsveld, whose widely read textbook *From Van Riebeeck to Verwoerd* reaffirmed the apartheid ideology, admitted that he promoted apartheid because he thought it could succeed. He added that if he could rewrite his books, he would "present apartheid right from the beginning as an error, as a historical mistake".[138]

In my opinion, both approaches are flawed. Like novels, a good history should not look ahead, but should accept that the characters in the story in fact did not know the outcome of their actions. The Dutch historian Johan Huizinga advised historians to constantly put themselves "at a point in the past where the known factors will seem to permit different outcomes".[139]

Even without subscribing to the "great man theory" of history, it is easy to imagine different outcomes at critical junctures in Afrikaner history. Without President MT Steyn, there would have been no heroic *Bittereinder* resistance in the final phase of the Anglo-Boer War and no language rights entrenched

---

136  See my essay on Schoeman's commentary on my draft chapters in Willie Burger and Helize van Vuuren (eds), *Sluiswagters by die dam van stemme* (Pretoria: Protea Boekhuis, 2002), pp. 98–106.

137  Herbert Butterfield, *The Whig Interpretation of the Past* (New York: Norton, 1965), p. 28.

138  Remark by FA van Jaarsveld in an interview conducted in 1992. See Leonard Blussé et al., *Pilgrims to the Past* (Leiden: CNWS, 1996), p. 269.

139  Niall Ferguson, *Virtual History: Alternatives and Counter-factuals* (London: Picador, 1997), p.1.

at the National Convention; without Jan Smuts, no British agreement in 1902 to withhold the franchise from blacks until the defeated Boer republics had received self-rule; without Jannie Marais, no Afrikaans-language University of Stellenbosch and no Nasionale Pers (later Naspers); and without Hendrik Verwoerd, no coherent apartheid ideology that convinced the great majority of Afrikaners that there was indeed a proper plan for their survival and steeled their will to cling to power. Without an ideology such as apartheid, white control would have come to an end long before the fall of the Berlin Wall in 1989 – with unpredictable consequences.

As recently as the 1970s a different outcome from a black majority government in a unitary state was still possible. In 1977 Alan Paton urged the US secretary of state, Cyrus Vance, to press the South African government to establish a federal state in which the homelands were incorporated. He believed this would bring the country a significant step closer to an inclusive democracy.[140]

People read history books and novels to put themselves in the shoes of leaders who have to make decisions that test their moral character. The challenge for the novelist, and especially for the historian, is to capture the complex identities, the moral dilemmas and the momentous choices of the past.

## Apartheid and the Nazis?

I felt reasonably satisfied with some of the chapters of *The Afrikaners*, especially the ones that deal with slavery, the fear of social levelling, and the Cape Afrikaners. Yet from the start I knew there was a danger that the chapters on apartheid would overshadow everything else in the book.

I posed the following key questions about apartheid to myself: What did the comparative evidence from other countries suggest were the options for South Africa by the time the Second World War ended? To what extent did apartheid differ fundamentally from its precursor, the policy of racial segregation? And then there was the alleged Nazi influence on some of the architects of the idea of apartheid. In 2008 Richard Dowden, one of the most respected commentators on Africa, made the shocking claim that apartheid was "the last Nazi-inspired political system of the twentieth century".[141]

The view of apartheid as having been inspired by Nazi ideology dated from the years of the Second World War and was kept alive worldwide by the Communist Party of South Africa (later renamed the South African Commu-

140  Peter Alexander, *Alan Paton* (New York: Oxford University Press, 1994), p. 387.
141  Richard Dowden, *Africa: Altered States, Ordinary Miracles* (London: Public Affairs, 2008), p. 414.

nist Party). By the 1960s, however, it had disappeared from the country's political mainstream. Among academics, Heribert Adam, who had grown up in Germany, was one of the first to reject the Nazi analogy unequivocally.

But these views were not limited to foreigners. In 2013 the management of the University of Stellenbosch announced with barely concealed excitement at a press conference that a student had discovered a metal case of instruments used to measure human hair and eye types in the university museum. These physical anthropology measuring instruments had been left behind in the late 1930s by a German anthropologist with ties to the Nazi party who had been on study leave at the US.

The rector, Dr Russel Botman, stated that the discovery suggested that the work of US academics might have provided the foundations for apartheid, and the university would allocate funds for research in this regard. As was to be expected, however, the investigations failed to yield any results.

I wrote about the episode in *Rapport* under the heading "When will the nonsense end of comparing apartheid with Nazism?" No study of the literature would provide evidence that Nazi racial thinking lay behind the development of the apartheid ideology in the 1930s and 1940s.[142]

I cited Saul Dubow's *Scientific Racism in Modern South Africa* (1995). According to Dubow, the notion of essential racial differences as an explanation for social phenomena enjoyed wide adherence among English-speaking intellectuals and journalists during the earlier part of the twentieth century. He also pointed out that "scientific racism" had few adherents among the protagonists of apartheid during the 1930s and 1940s.

The Cape NP, which was influenced by Dr DF Malan, also had problems with the biblical foundations of apartheid, which had gained acceptance in the north of the country in particular.

So where did the concept of apartheid actually originate? Remarkably, in the jungle of books and articles written on apartheid no one had looked into this question. I corresponded with Richard Elphick, who had embarked on his major study that would be published in 2012 as *The Equality of Believers: Protestant Missionaries and the Racial Politics of South Africa*. In the course of his research Elphick came across a pamphlet from 1929 titled *Die NG Kerk van die OVS en die Naturellevraagstuk* (The Dutch Reformed Church of the Orange Free State and the native problem). It contained the speeches held in that year at a conference of the Free State Dutch Reformed Church (DRC) on mission work among blacks. The Reverend JC du Plessis of Bethlehem had used the

---

142  Hermann Giliomee, "Die wortels van apartheid", *Rapport*, 21 July 2013.

term "apartheid" in his speech.

I knew that in 1951 "Dawie", *Die Burger*'s political columnist, had inquired about the first recorded use of the term "apartheid'. In his next column he related that Rev. Du Plessis had referred him to his speech in this pamphlet: "In the fundamental idea of our missionary work, and not in racial prejudice, must one seek an explanation for the spirit of apartheid that has always characterised our [the DRC's] conduct and for which some censure us because of misunderstanding."[143]

By "apartheid" Du Plessis meant that "the heathen" should be christianised in a way that strengthened their "own character, nature and nationality" and that blacks had to be uplifted "on their own terrain, separate and apart". On the other hand he advocated an exclusively white DRC, "to ensure the survival of a handful of [Afrikaner] people cut off from their national ties in Europe".

In 1935 the Federal Council of the DRC declared themselves in favour of a mission and education policy based on each ethnic community's national culture, giving a prominent place to its history, language and customs. The DRC envisaged apartheid in its mission policy as a counter to the approach of English missionaries who, in the DRC's view, tried to gain converts by having them copy Western civilisation and religion. It would soon follow that the various "nations" had to govern themselves in their own towns and homelands.

Thus apartheid was in essence a product of Afrikaner nationalism as well as the DRC's approach to missionary work. DRC ministers and missionary strategists were the architects of the concept. A relative of Prof. TN Hanekom, later professor in church history at the Theological Seminary in Stellenbosch, told me that Hanekom used to say in private: "In the case of apartheid it was not what the NP had done to the DRC, but the DRC to the NP." *Die Burger* and NP politicians only started using the term "apartheid" in 1943.

Apartheid has become a metaphor for the cross of humiliation and contempt that black people across the world have had to carry in the past centuries. The eminent Kenyan political commentator Ali Mazrui rightly observed that "Africans are not necessarily the most brutalised of peoples, but they are almost certainly the most humiliated in modern history".[144]

Because apartheid had evil consequences, a question that arises is whether the NP leadership had malevolent intentions right from the start. It is significant that the two most prominent critics of apartheid in the Dutch Reformed

---

143  Louis Louw, *Dawie, 1946-1964* (Cape Town: Tafelberg, 1964), p. 49.
144  Ali A Mazrui, *The African Condition: A Political Diagnosis* (London: Heinemann, 1980).

Church at the time, Bennie Keet and Ben Marais, voted for the NP in 1948.
They were of the view that the policy of segregation had reached a dead end
and that apartheid, with its promise of greater upliftment of coloured and black
people, should be given a chance. It was considered possible for a morally
upright person to try to work within the Afrikaner structures for change. A
different voice was needed for this than the liberal one with its emphasis on
individual rights. Beyers Naudé, who would later found the Christian Institute,
explained that he and his colleagues in the DRC did not speak out against
apartheid in the 1950s because it would have alienated the Afrikaner people
completely from the church.[145]

There is currently a trend in the literature to describe apartheid purely in
moral terms and to dismiss any debate out of hand as an attempt to justify the
unjustifiable. Archbishop Emeritus Desmond Tutu, for instance, wrote in a
foreword to *South Africa: A Modern History* (by Rodney Davenport and Chris
Saunders, 2000): "Ultimately it is irrelevant whether racism or apartheid sometimes produced good results. Because the tree was bad the fruit was also bad."[146]

One might expect such a stance from an archbishop, but it also crops up in
academic journals. An Afrikaans philosopher wrote in a review of *The Afrikaners* that I adopted Kitto's statement in the introduction ("To understand is
not necessarily to pardon, but there is no harm in trying to understand") too
readily as a motto for the book. In his view, it was only partly true. When an
injustice had been committed, as in the case of apartheid, there was indeed
"harm in trying to understand".[147]

Lawrence Schlemmer wrote in response: "I have always thought that the
primary duty of an academic is to be fearless in trying to uncover the truth. I
can hardly believe that anyone could think that by refusing to try to understand
apartheid, racism or anything else, one can help the victims."[148]

In *The Afrikaners* I stated that I consider apartheid a "horrific" system of state
intervention in the lives of the subordinate population and briefly discussed
the psychological suffering and damage people experienced under the system.
In general, however, my emphasis fell on the material manifestations of the
policy. I cited generally accepted development indicators to show that the
well-being of black and coloured South Africans improved considerably from

145  *Die Suid-Afrikaan*, 5, 1985, pp. 21-23.
146  Desmond Tutu, "Foreword", Rodney Davenport and Christopher Saunders, *South
      Africa: A Modern History* (Johannesburg: Macmillan, 2000), p. xix.
147  Marius Vermaak, "Review of *The Afrikaners: Biography of a People*" in *African
      Sociological Review*, 7, 2, 2003, p. 165.
148  Lawrence Schlemmer, "Unintended absurdities", *This Day*, 9 April 2004.

1948 to 1994 as far as population growth rates, life expectancy, infant mortality and mass literacy were concerned. By 1994 the gap between whites and other communities was smaller than it had been in 1948 – though still substantial. But these indicators can never be used to justify apartheid.

Cold statistics and sober assessments are of little comfort to people who have suffered the viciousness of apartheid. Citing them exposes the historian to the charge of gross insensitivity to assaults on human dignity, the real horror of apartheid. Also to the charge of arrogance in trying to prove that black people did not really fare so badly under apartheid. Such a notion should be rejected in the strongest terms.

I thought that the journalist Jeremy Gordin's review of my book provided a good summary of my approach to the dilemma of an analysis of apartheid. "[Giliomee] has tried to find a path between, on the one hand, rationalising the sins of the Afrikaners and, on the other, simply denouncing the volk . . . his overall policy seems to be to let the facts do the talking and to keep comment to a minimum."[149]

An anonymous reviewer in *The Economist* came to more or less the same conclusion. The review stated that the book "soft pedals the remorseless cruelty of many of the South African government's acts", which I consider fair criticism. The same reviewer also gave an appraisal of the book that I find very gratifying: "Mr Giliomee struggles valiantly to offer a fair verdict on his own community. His ambivalence – instructive in the way it helps us consider how to avoid the alluring dark paths down which many nations have been lost – is not a weakness but the book's abiding strength, for it allows Mr Giliomee fully to explore the complexity of his subject."[150]

Robert Ross, an esteemed authority on early colonial South African history, said something similar in his review in the *Journal of Southern African Studies*:

> These ambivalences and uncertainties pervade the book. It might seem as if they would destroy it. However, the contrary is the case. Quite deep within Giliomee's apparently conventional narrative is a tension that drives it on. The book's strength comes from the emotional involvement of the author with his subject. This, of course, is history, not autobiography, and Giliomee ensures that it always remains so. However, it is precisely because Giliomee is able to let his emotions be

149 Jeremy Gordin, "Move our Marx, focus on women and religion", *The Star,* 19 June 2003.
150 "The ties that bound", *The Economist*, 19 July 2003, pp. 68-69.

subsumed in his academic analysis that this becomes a very fine book. Because that is, in the end, what it is.

When the reviews started coming in, Jeanette Hopkins, my editor, wrote to me. Twenty-five years earlier she had edited Eugene Genovese's *Roll, Jordan, Roll: The World the Slaves Made*, a work on the American South that rates among the books I most admire. She was at that stage in the process of editing *The Mind of the Master Class*, co-authored by Genovese and his wife, Elizabeth Fox-Genovese.

Hopkins wrote of what she called my inability to go as far as she would have liked "in acknowledging with greater candour and power the evils of apartheid". Her message read as follows:

> There is a danger that few historians are able wholly to avoid. Those who write of . . . issues that dominate the present and about which they care deeply and have so immersed themselves in studying the history, in both cases of oppressors [whites of the American South and Afrikaners] that they run the risk of some loss of detachment . . . For such historians it becomes a daunting task to achieve perfect objectivity and perspective, to understand and describe but not to yield to identification with the subjects of their study that in some degree affects the outcome in their books. It is a tribute to you, and to them [the Geneveses] that they have, most of the time, seldom let personal feelings determine what they write, and even more important, what they omit or fail to focus on. I would say of your book what Orlando Patterson wrote in a review of one of Genovese's books back in the 1970s, with which he took issue on some questions. He said that Genovese's intellectual integrity and vivid research was such that he provided the evidence on the basis of which others could arrive at wholly different conclusions.

This is a comment that I treasure. The same goes for the remark by JM Coetzee on the back cover: "A book to welcome . . . It contains an account of the origins and demise of apartheid that must rank as the most sober, objective and comprehensive we have." For the second edition the publisher could quote Athol Fugard's observation: "A stunning achievement". However, a number of reviewers, including Jonny Steinberg, viewed my interpretation of apartheid as an apology for apartheid.

## Afrikaner capitalism?

In South Africa and other deeply divided societies people tend not to vote as individuals, but as members of a community. From 1910 to 1970 the chief struggle was not between white and black, but the one in which the two white language communities competed for dominance and status.

Up to 1970 the more affluent English-speaking white community were in a much better economic position than the Afrikaners. It took the Afrikaners a long time to build big corporations that were comparable to those of the English and Jewish communities. Jan Hurter, managing director of Volkskas, remarked in 1968 that only four Afrikaner corporations had assets that exceeded R300 million – Volkskas, Trust Bank, Rembrandt and Sanlam.

Years later I asked Koos Bekker why the name of Nasionale Pers did not appear on that list. His reply was illuminating: "I doubt that the market value of Naspers's assets would have been close to R300 million in 1968. By 1984 the entire company's market capitalisation was only R24 million. (It was then still an unlisted but public company, with about 3 000 shareholders.)"[151]

The big question was: Why did the Afrikaners, despite an Afrikaner-based party being in power for most of the time up to the 1970s, lag so far behind economically? Just as I started working at full throttle on my book on the Afrikaners in 1996, Francis Fukuyama's comparative study *Trust: The Social Virtues and the Creation of Prosperity* appeared.

Fukuyama emphasises that social capital is as important as physical capital. A community is economically successful when it has a culture that puts a premium on persuading people to cooperate economically in their own best interests. Cultures that rate "social ties" highly and form associations are best positioned to build large-scale business enterprises that can compete, thrive and adapt when necessary.

Fukuyama considers "the failure of the Calvinist Afrikaners to develop a thriving capitalist system until the last quarter of the [twentieth] century" an anomaly that needs explanation. After all, the German sociologist Max Weber had made a convincing case for a strong correlation between Calvinism and capitalism.[152]

One reason is that up to the early twentieth century the majority of Afrikaners had been subsistence farmers in pioneering conditions. Apart from the church and the commando, they had little faith in institutions led by people

151  E-mail communication from Koos Bekker, 18 August 2008.
152  Francis Fukuyama, *Trust: The Social Virtues and the Creation of Prosperity* (New York: Free Press, 1995), pp. 44-45.

and groups beyond the family circle. Unfortunate experiences at the hands of itinerant traders and shopkeepers, the collapse of a number of district banks, and the English community's domination of mining, commerce and industry contributed to a strong distrust of the capitalist world among Afrikaners. Hendrik Verwoerd rightly pointed out at the First Economic *Volkskongres* in 1939 that the Afrikaners were over-organised when it came to religion and politics, but poorly organised economically.

A number of historians had focused their attention on the economic rise of the Afrikaners in the three decades after the conference. Some liberal and radical historians attributed it to state aid to Afrikaner business on the part of the NP government, while Afrikaner historians gave the credit to the Afrikaners who had pulled themselves up by their own bootstraps.

In the academic literature and in the English press, it was often alleged that the Afrikaners made their major economic breakthrough in the 1960s thanks to the goodwill of Harry Oppenheimer, who headed the Anglo American Corporation. He had supposedly allowed the sale of General Mining, an Anglo-controlled mining house, to the Sanlam subsidiary Federale Mynbou "at a fraction of its value".

The historian Grietjie Verhoef as well as Michael O'Dowd and Michael Spicer, two Anglo directors I interviewed, described this as a fabrication. Anglo not only sold its mining house at a market-related price but, in addition, Oppenheimer secured an important concession: Sanlam would not proceed with the development of its diamond interests and thereby threaten Anglo's diamond monopoly.

I did not analyse the Afrikaners' economic rise in depth in *The Afrikaners*, but tried to do this in an academic journal shortly after the publication of the book. It was a remark made by Dr Anton Rupert while I was still working on the book that had set me thinking. As I mentioned in an earlier chapter, I asked him whether he could think of any Afrikaans company that had been "empowered" by an English company. His reply was: "I cannot think of any, and I am very grateful for that."

This statement alerted me to the great value a business giant like Rupert attached to the fact that Afrikaner companies had to achieve success without state or English support. In the divided society of South Africa, there was only one route through which Afrikaners could gain recognition for their economic achievements from the English business elite. It was through establishing business enterprises that could attain success without state help.

The Afrikaners' advance in this regard was very slow; by 1954 their share in the manufacturing and construction sector was only 6%, and, in the case of the financial sector, only 10%. There was, however, also the parastatal sector, where Afrikaners predominated in management positions from the outset. This sector was an immensely important training school for emerging young business leaders.

A quite different form of advancement of an economically backward group is that driven largely by the state. Before it came to power, the African National Congress had studied the Malaysian model of empowerment where the state forced Chinese business companies to empower Malay-owned companies. The state also gave Malay companies preferential treatment when it came to contracts. The architect of this policy, known as the New Economic Policy, was Mahathir bin Mohamad, who later became prime minister.

In 2003, on retiring from politics after thirty years, Mahathir admitted that he had failed in his goal of making the Malays – a race that was supposed to win the respect of the Chinese community and others – as the "majority race" economically successful.

Mahathir found it regrettable that businesspeople in the Malay community were still dependent on the "crutches" of state contracts and state-imposed constraints on Chinese companies which they had got used to.

This is also the problem with many of the black companies in South Africa that have been empowered through state intervention. It seems as if the masses do not identify themselves with the achievements of black companies to the same extent that the Afrikaner community did with Afrikaner companies, which promoted a general sense of Afrikaner self-worth. The English business elite probably did the Afrikaners, and especially Afrikaner businesspeople, the biggest favour by compelling them to achieve success off their own bat in order to earn their respect.

## Unthinkable developments

In the five years after the appearance of *The Afrikaners,* the book sold well enough to justify a second edition. Any book is written in the shadow of the present. When I completed the last chapters of *The Afrikaners* in 2001, I never expected that the South African government would look on with tacit approval as Robert Mugabe's gangs plundered white farms in Zimbabwe.

It was still unthinkable that our government would enforce its policy of demographic representivity much further than what was provided for in the constitution, namely in the judiciary and the civil service. Corruption was not yet rampant, and I could not imagine that violent crime, service delivery failure, unemployment and xenophobia would reach such alarming proportions.

I had also not anticipated that the loss of power would catch the Afrikaners as unawares as it did. In 1994 the state, which used to serve as the hub of the wheel of the nationalist movement, fell away. The different organisations that make up the spokes were now separate and scattered, which made collective action practically impossible. The influence of the church declined and in the Democratic Alliance the leadership positions were dominated by English speakers. There was no institution capable of developing a collective response.

Worst of all, the Afrikaners had lost their ideology. This was not the idea that they should have exclusive power or that the country belonged to them, but rather the conviction that as a community they should have self-determination or participation in decision-making in respect of matters that affect them directly.

After 1994 the ANC soon instituted a form of majority domination coupled with "demographic representivity" that left little room for minorities. By 2005 there was already great concern about the question whether the minorities' language and cultural rights and assets were secure.

In a new chapter for the 2009 edition of *The Afrikaners* I put the emphasis on a dialogue that had taken place between Mbeki and former president De Klerk in 2005. It centred on Mbeki's assurance that the ANC did not want black domination to replace white domination.

In a speech De Klerk referred Mbeki to his statement in this regard, and then asked: "How will we be able to avoid black domination in a situation in which the black majority in effect now has a monopoly of power? What else is it if the black majority dictates the agenda for the white, Indian and coloured minorities, and negatively affects their core interests?" In his view the ANC policy of "representivity" meant the minorities "would become subject to the majority in every area of their lives – in their jobs, schools, universities and sports".

The Afrikaners and members of the other minorities increasingly have to learn to survive outside the state, as far as schools, universities and job opportunities are concerned. Everything depends on whether there is a sufficiently strong communal spirit to do so successfully. About three-quarters of the Afrikaners read only Afrikaans newspapers. In 2011 opinion polls indicated that Afrikaners felt a significantly greater need for political solidarity and cohesion than was the case among white English speakers. The biggest challenge is to rediscover their own particular identity and vitality, to organise, and to support innovative leadership.

*Chapter 12*

# Almost neighbours

As a young lecturer during the 1970s, I increasingly became aware that coloured people had all but been written out of the Afrikaners' history – whether as a community or as a class. Of the great many theses and dissertations completed at the US History Department in the preceding seventy years, only a handful dealt with coloured history. It was almost as if there was something that inhibited me, as well as other Afrikaner historians, from properly investigating the entwined historical roots of the two communities.[153]

Official commemorative volumes that celebrated the history of Stellenbosch, such as the one on the Victoria College in 1918 and the 1929 publication that marked the town's 250th anniversary, devote no more than a page or two to coloured residents. *Stellenbosch Three Centuries*, published in 1979 to commemorate the town's tercentenary, contains sixteen pages on the white schools and barely one on the coloured schools. The index lists ten references to Paul Roos, the renowned Springbok rugby captain and school principal, but there is no mention of the legendary PJ ("Oubaas") Coetzee who served as principal of the only coloured high school in the town, Lückhoff High School, for thirty years.

The emergence of an exclusive, race-conscious white group known as Afrikaners was not inevitable. The potential had always existed for an inclusive, non-racial Afrikaans-speaking community with class, rather than race, as the distinction. It is instructive that when Pieter Daniels, who was born in Stellenbosch, founded the first coloured political organisation in Kimberley in 1883, he called it the "Afrikander League (Coloured)". The term encapsulated the complexity well: in so many respects coloured Stelleboschers were nothing other than Afrikaners, but the colour consciousness of the white Afrikaners caused Daniels to qualify his Afrikaners as "coloureds".

---

153 A notable exception is EM Johnson's " 'n Krities-historiese waardebepaling van die ontstaan en opkoms van die Kleurlingonderwys in Stellenbosch se dorpsgebied tot 1963", MA thesis, UWC, 1986.

On the establishment of the Union of South Africa in 1910, the African Political Organisation (APO), a powerful coloured political body, briefly considered calling themselves the "Cape Afrikaners". This name did not gain acceptance among the coloured people of the Cape, especially because the APO leader, Dr Abdullah Abdurahman, was an ardent anglophile.

## Uncovering neglected history

After my retirement from UCT in 1998, I no longer had any links with an academic institution. It was on the initiative of Professor Albert Grundlingh, who had been appointed to the Jan Marais chair of history at Stellenbosch in 2001, that I renewed my ties with my old department at the US. I was appointed as extraordinary professor in history, with my own office and even on-campus parking. Albert and I largely saw eye to eye on historiography, and we became good friends.

In his previous position as lecturer at the University of South Africa, Albert had often exchanged views with historians at the University of the Witwatersrand, where investigations into the history of urban black communities, mainly based on oral history methodology, had become an important field of research. Works (produced by the Wits historians) on the communities of Pageview and Sophiatown in Johannesburg elicited favourable commentary.

In line with this tendency of uncovering neglected or suppressed histories, but without having consciously planned it on my side, I wrote a book on the history of coloured Stellenbosch, which was published in 2007. The idea of recording the neglected history of this community, with an emphasis on the central neighbourhood known as Die Vlakte, had arisen soon after 1994. It was advocated by coloured leaders such as the Reverend Simon Adams, while at the university acting rector Rolf Stumpf and Chris Brink, who became rector in 2002, supported it. Two mayors of the town, WF Ortell, a former resident of Die Vlakte, and Lauretta Maree, personally provided strong support.

Shortly after his arrival in Stellenbosch, Albert proposed that the envisaged history of coloured Stellenbosch be tackled as a departmental project. He obtained funding from the university and established a committee made up of several prominent coloured community leaders. Under the direction of the committee, the memories of a number of elderly Stelleboschers, selected mainly on the basis of their personal experience of life in Die Vlakte, were recorded on tape and video during individual and group interviews. Hilton Biscombe was chosen as the person who would compile the final text from the transcribed interviews. I was asked to contribute a historical introduction to contextualise the personal memories.[154]

---

154  Hilton Biscombe (compiler), *In ons bloed* (Stellenbosch: Sun Press, 2006).

There was a concern among some of the committee members that whites, and specifically the university, would "hijack" the coloured people's history. Six months after the work on the project started, one of them enquired at a committee meeting: "Who is going to edit Giliomee's historical introduction?"

When I replied that a language editor would edit my chapter as far as language and style were concerned, but that outsiders did not normally "edit" a particular historical interpretation, I saw at once that we were headed for a conflict. After the meeting I told Albert it would be better if I wrote my own book on the history of coloured Stelleboschers, with a special focus on Die Vlakte, which in 1965 had been home to about 3 000 coloured people. The result was *Nog altyd hier gewees: Die storie van 'n Stellenbosse gemeenskap* (Always been here: The story of a Stellenbosch community).

## "We were unknown"

My somewhat impulsive decision required a concerted effort on my part to understand the past from another angle. With *The Afrikaners*, the major challenge for me as an insider had been to maintain the necessary distance; now, as an outsider, it was to identify myself with a community which, unlike white South Africans, lacked power and, unlike black South Africans, could not rely on their numerical strength.

Even when it came to language and culture there was a particular problem in discussing the coloured community. In the years prior to the 1870s their ancestors had created Afrikaans as an everyday language together with the "Afrikaner" ancestors. Over time this fact of co-creation was generally recognised, but the Afrikaners would appropriate virtually all the credit for the development of Afrikaans as a literary and scientific language.

I sometimes wondered what my book on the Afrikaners would have looked like if I had written it after my book on Stellenbosch's coloured people. Aaron Cupido, who had spent his entire life of 98 years in the Stellenbosch district, told me in 2006: "The white people didn't know us. We knew them, because coloured people worked in their houses. The white people knew their servants, but we were unknown to them. They thought they could just push us around like on a map."

Like other whites, I never thought of what it meant to a coloured child to know that there were no equal opportunities with a white child. I had no inkling of what it must have felt like when your family home had to be vacated in terms of the Group Areas Act and you were forced to move to a place with inferior facilities and strangers as neighbours. I was oblivious of the grief and destruction that racial classification caused when a pair of lovers or members of the same family were classified in different "race groups". I have referred before to CW de Kiewiet's remark that "for the thoughtful man it is still important to understand how men [the Afrikaners] who are sincere in their Christian beliefs and staunch defenders of their own liberties can become identified with policies of discrimination and restriction". I realise now that I failed to come up with an answer to this question.

I decided to concentrate on a few critical moments: the emergence of separate white and coloured communities, the end of slavery, the competition for the "coloured vote" in the 1920s, the "Battle of Andringa Street", and the forced removals from Die Vlakte.

## Together apart

Like most other historians, I only realised after the publication of the genealogical researcher JA Heese's *Die herkoms van die Afrikaner* (1971) and that of his son HF Heese's *Groep sonder grense* (1984) how vague the boundaries were between white and coloured. The *stammoeder* or progenitress of numerous "white" families had been a former slave.

The pattern of descendants of Europeans mainly marrying each other only developed by about 1730. Children conceived by Europeans from extramarital liaisons were mostly absorbed in the ranks of the slaves and the free blacks, and after 1838 by the group now known as "coloureds". "Thus did the Boers keep their own race pure and [also] bring into existence a race of half-breeds,"[155] is the apt comment of JS Marais, the great historian of the Cape coloured people.

In 1950 General Jan Smuts, a son of the Swartland, was strongly opposed to the National Party government's plan to classify coloured South Africans as members of a separate group. In a House of Assembly debate on 8 March 1950 he pleaded: "Don't let us trifle with this thing. [We] are touching on things which go pretty deep in this land." He called it an attempt to "classify the unclassifiable".[156]

There was no rigid dividing line. Especially among the poorer classes white and coloured often married or lived together, and some of the children would be absorbed in the white community and others in the coloured community.

The coloured people considered with wry amusement the attempts of the apartheid propagandists to invent a completely separate identity. On one

---

155  Cited by Richard van der Ross, *Up from Slavery: Slaves at the Cape* (Cape Town: Ampersand, 2005), p. 133.
156  House of Assembly Debates, 8 March 1950.

occasion Piet Cillié, editor of *Die Burger* between 1954 and 1977, poked fun at the efforts to portray white and coloured Afrikaans speakers as two separate nations. He recounted the response of a coloured teacher to the suggestion from a white man that coloured people take pride in their "own identity":

> *Meneer*, you white people urge the brown people to be proud of their own history, be loyal to their own traditions and honour their ancestors. But let me tell you this: my history is your history, my traditions are your traditions, and I won't be surprised if some of your ancestors are also my ancestors.

I became convinced that it had been especially in Stellenbosch and on the surrounding farms that attempts to create a deep gulf between master and slave, white and coloured, were taken furthest. Cape Town was cosmopolitan, promiscuous and often colour-blind. Stellenbosch was remote, parochial, conservative and colour-conscious. Cape Town had a police force, known as the "Kaffirs", which could enforce order; Stellenbosch, on the other hand, had practically no police force, and hence the slaveowners themselves had to enforce the social order they had created.

How did they do this? Any answer needs to start with the most important fact: the Dutch Reformed Church in Stellenbosch at the time was a church of slaveowners. There were thousands of slaves in the town and in the district. Though the church never refused to baptise a slave, it soon became clear that it was reluctant to baptise too many and bring them into the congregation. This would antagonise the slaveowners. Slaves had to sit in separate pews. In 1825 the church council ordained that members who were not Europeans all had to sit together in the furthest pews in order to avoid "*aanstoot en onaangenaamheden*" (offence and unpleasantness).

In the early 1830s the slaveowners decided that their slave children could not attend the same school as others. It is not far-fetched to view Stellenbosch as the cradle of the institutions and practices that would later become known as apartheid.

Confronted with slaveowners who assiduously protected their status and interests, brown, black and "coloured" people in Stellenbosch seized every opportunity to make the most of their talents. For a long time Stellenbosch was the only place in the interior where there was a slave school.

Despite some resistance and disparagement, in the second half of the eighteenth century slaves started flocking to the various "*sending-gestigte*" (mission institutions): Meeuwe Jan Bakker's little school at 157 Dorp Street, Erasmus

Smit's school behind the Bletterman House in Plein Street, the Methodists' school situated on the site of the present-day town hall, and, last but not least, the school and church on the Braak that had been erected under the leadership of the Rhenish missionary Paul Daniël Lückhoff, who started his ministry in 1830. Of all the denominations, the *"Rynses"* with their emphasis on discipline, soberness and diligence exerted the biggest influence.

In the fifteen years before the end of slavery in 1838, the British government issued regulations aimed at ameliorating the lot of slaves. In 1831 the slave protector, an official appointed to watch over their treatment, was given the right to inspect slave quarters and farmers were compelled to hand in their punishment record books twice a year. It was only in Stellenbosch that the regulations caused a near-riot. *De Zuid-Afrikaan*, the mouthpiece of the colony's slaveowners, spoke openly of resistance and warned of "the rights of Dutch burghers and the length of farmers' rifles". The slave protector reported a deterioration in the relations between slaves and their masters.

We were never taught anything about this history at school or at university; nor about the way in which the Stellenbosch slaves reacted to their emancipation. As a resident of Stellenbosch I sometimes heard farmers referring to unseasonal rainfall in December as a *"slawereëntjie"* (a slave shower). I never imagined that the origin of the expression lay in the weather conditions that prevailed in the area at the time slavery came to an end.

The story of Emancipation Day in 1838 has been told in full by John Mason, an American student who was awarded a doctorate from Yale University in 1992 for his research on the emancipation of the slaves. Like 27 April 1994, when everyone in South Africa was suddenly free, 1 December 1838 was the day on which everyone at the Cape was free for the first time since the 1650s. (Though slavery had been abolished in British colonies in 1834, the slaves still had to serve a four-year apprenticeship until their final emancipation on 1 December 1838.)

Masters and slaves in the colony had widely divergent expectations of what that December would bring. The slaves had long prayed for this day, but they had no idea of what their fate would be under the new dispensation. The masters, on their part, feared the collapse of the social order.

Emancipation Day was a surprise to all. Instead of the heavens falling, they opened: heavy rainfall that persisted for three days caused rivers to burst their banks, while the mountaintops were covered in snow. The faithful speculated about the meaning of the heavenly message. For some former slaves, the rain was symbolic of the tears of slaves who had died in bondage before they could experience freedom. Some slaveowners decided that God had sent the rain to avert a disaster. A correspondent of *De Zuid-Afrikaan* in Tulbagh reported that the behaviour of the freed people was "quiet, proper and peaceful". The report continued:

> We look upon this weather as *providentially* happening . . . [it] occa-
> sioned the avoidance of idle assemblages, and its consequences; and
> also prevented . . . improper rejoicings and drunkenness, from which
> nothing but evil must have arisen.

In Stellenbosch the rain drizzled as former slaves streamed to the church of the Rhenish Missionary Society on the Braak. The church was filled to over-flowing at each of the three services that were held that day.

As early as the 1840s a traveller referred to the former slaves' neat houses in Stellenbosch. The observation probably pertained to the houses in Herte Street. By the 1850s houses started going up in the area east of the present-day Victoria Street and between the present-day Bird Street and Ryneveld Street. From the outset, this area was known as Die Vlakte. It forms the heart of the story of coloured Stellenbosch.

It is extremely difficult for historians of today to imagine the weal and woe of people who used to be slaves and suddenly found themselves free. How does one adapt to freedom overnight? How does someone start a new life as a free human being after a lifetime in which he or she was at the mercy of others, especially when he or she owns nothing, or very little, on emancipation? Slaves in Stellenbosch have left no documents behind which can assist us to understand their experiences. To gain an impression of the challenges with which the freed slaves of Stellenbosch were faced, I turned to the studies of historians in the United States, where literally hundreds of diaries have been preserved in which slaveowners in particular gave accounts of the fundamental way in which slavery had shaped both them and their slaves.

From this literature one can conclude that there were three major challenges. First, the slaves, as severely oppressed people whose assertiveness had been quashed, had to learn how to stop deferring to white people, the former slaveowners. Second, they had to learn not to put on the masks they had been obliged to wear while slaves, when their owners had the power to punish them virtually at will. "Masters" liked to see slaves clowning, joking and making fun of themselves. The great risk was that the mask might become permanent. Third, they had to learn not to hate and to make sure that their justified grievances did not consume their lives.[157]

---

157  See, in particular, Eugene D Genovese, *Roll, Jordan, Roll: The World the Slaves Made* (New York: André Deutsch, 1975) and Nathan Irvin Huggins, *Black Odyssey: The Afro-American Ordeal in Slavery* (New York: Pantheon Books, 1977).

A notable way in which freed slaves, including those of Stellenbosch, approached the challenge of a new life was to strive to enrich themselves spiritually. For many, religion and the church became the cornerstone of their life.[158] On some farms a paternalistic employment relationship continued with a degree of goodwill, but on many others the *dopstelsel* (tot system) perpetuated a form of continued enslavement.

Professor NJ Hofmeyr, a professor at the Theological Seminary in the second half of the nineteenth century, started a campaign against the use of all "*bedwelmende dranken*" (intoxicating beverages). His action led to "serious alienation" between him and the Stellenbosch church council, on which a number of wine farmers served.[159] Hofmeyr was even asked to stop preaching in the Moederkerk for a while for the sake of peace.

## A swing vote

The coloured vote was sought after in the constituencies of Stellenbosch and Paarl in parliamentary elections between 1915 and 1929. In both constituencies there were about a thousand coloured voters, who represented approximately a quarter of those registered. As swing voters, their votes could determine the outcome in either of these seats.

The late Aaron Cupido, the "walking historian" of Stellenbosch with his encyclopedic memory, told me about the lively meetings in the Temperance Hall behind the present-day town hall where candidates of the South African Party (SAP) and the National Party (NP) addressed coloured audiences. Though the meetings were stormy at times, no candidate was ever jeered from the stage.

Cupido related that coloured Stellenboschers thought Dr Abdullah Abdurahman and his APO were too radical and too pro-English. The majority saw their salvation in cooperation with white Afrikaners, with whom they had ties of blood, history and culture.[160] Shortly after the establishment of the Cape NP, a number of moderate coloured leaders held discussions with the leader, Dr DF Malan. He asked them to support the NP in elections, offering in exchange that every coloured man would get equality when the NP came to power.

The big sticking point was that from an early stage Dr Malan and other NP

158 James Backhouse, *A Narrative of a Visit to the Mauritius and South Africa* (London: Hamilton and Adams, 1844), p. 624.

159 Bun Booyens, "*De Gereformeerde Kerkbode* (1849-1923) as bron vir die Afrikaanse kultuurgeskiedenis", doctoral dissertation, US, 1993, pp. 576-84.

160 Interview with Aaron Cupido, 29 September 2005.

leaders had been attracted to separate voters' rolls for white and coloured and
to the idea of classifying coloureds as a group somewhere between whites and
blacks. In our conversations Cupido always emphasised that while the NP had
the potential to do very well among the coloured voters of Stellenbosch, there
was widespread mistrust among coloured people about separate voters' rolls and
little support for their own classification.

Coloured voters knew full well that their vote on a common voters' roll
offered the best guarantee that their interests and status would not be undermined. They were not interested in a separate list because they were not a
separate community. As Cupido put it to me: White and coloured had grown
up together and helped create what had been created. Why then vote separately?

In 1915 the SAP, with the formidable John X Merriman as its candidate,
won the Stellenbosch seat by 818 votes. In Paarl the SAP candidate obtained a
majority of 803. The NP candidate in Paarl was Bruckner de Villiers, the
philanthropist Jannie Marais's brother-in-law and private secretary. In 1911
De Villiers settled in Stellenbosch and played a major role in the establishment
of both Nasionale Pers and the University of Stellenbosch.

Cupido still had vivid memories of De Villiers. The coloured community
of Stellenbosch used to refer to him by the nickname "Oom Broekie", he recalled. In 1915 De Villiers promised to sign a declaration that he would resign
if he supported any measure detrimental to coloured interests. De Villiers
firmly believed the NP was capable of beating the SAP in rural areas in their
competition for the coloured Afrikaans vote.

According to Cupido, Oom Broekie used to send food baskets to influential
coloured families before elections. He bought up stands in Idas Valley, which
were still dirt cheap at the time, and dished them out judiciously just before
an election. In the Kylemore area his donation to a church-building fund was
the biggest. He assisted the Volkskerk van Afrika by donating land. He also
gave many cups and trophies to coloured societies.

After the 1915 election De Villiers, in close cooperation with Dr Malan,
the Cape NP leader and editor of *De Burger* (later *Die Burger*), devised plans to
woo the coloured vote. In 1919 he was instrumental in the founding of the
United Afrikaner League (UAL), a movement that pledged to support the NP
and its principle of "Afrika vir die Afrikaner" (Africa for the Afrikaner). It
published a newspaper, *The Clarion*, which was printed in the Nasionale Pers
building. *The Clarion* had ghost writers, who were in all probability NP politicians or *De Burger* journalists.

What strikes one about the newspaper when reading through it today is that it was quite evidently an opportunistic attempt to gain votes for the NP without accepting coloured people as part of the Afrikaner community. *The Clarion* committed itself to fighting for a "coloured nationalism" that strived to win "respect for our race, the education of our children, the rehabilitation of our people and our economic advancement". Its ghost writers depicted coloureds as a separate people or community who shared interests with the white Afrikaners.

Some of the contributors, however, proclaimed in their articles that coloured people "are Afrikaners, who speak Afrikaans and nothing else". JHH de Waal, author of one of the first Afrikaans novels and the NP MP for Piketberg, who favoured a racially inclusive Afrikaans-speaking community, maintained that British imperialists, "mining capitalists" and foreign "fortune-seekers" were the common enemy of white and coloured Afrikaans speakers. He saw the political struggle as one between these elements and the "permanent population", of which the coloured people were an indispensable part.

De Waal's objection to Dr Abdurahman's APO was that it supported the foreign "fortune-seekers" against the interests of the "permanent population". According to him, the APO wanted to set "the Coloured population against their fellow-Afrikaners, who speak the same language, have the same love for South Africa, have mostly the same history and interests and are hoodwinked by the same friends". He warned against the government's plans to bring in large numbers of British immigrants, who would take the bread out of the mouths of the "sorely tested sons of the soil", both white and coloured.[161]

In a series of editorials that appeared in *Die Burger* in 1923, Dr Malan spelled out clearly that there was no need for a policy of political or economic segregation between white and coloured. Only "the native" had to be segregated; for coloured people, "segregation is not possible, but it is also unnecessary". With "the degree of civilisation" they had attained, they posed no danger to whites. Both white and coloured had moved to the cities in their own interest, where they faced identical problems of poverty and a common threat from ultra-cheap black migrant labour. Malan added that through "proper guidance and sympathetic treatment", coloured people could become a "bulwark" for the defence of "white civilisation".[162]

The United Afrikaner League failed to deliver a significant increase in coloured votes for the NP in the 1921 election, and *The Clarion* promptly ceased publication.

Before the 1924 election General JBM Hertzog, the NP leader, addressed a

---

161  *The Clarion*, 3 May 1919.
162  The articles were published in a pamphlet titled *Die groot vlug* (The great flight).

large meeting in the Temperance Hall on 8 April. Hertzog shared the stage with Paul Sauer, the 26-year-old NP candidate, CM Neethling, the mayor, and Bruckner de Villiers. The vast majority of the audience was coloured, but there were also a number of whites.

Hertzog said that the black man was getting a vote in his own government in his own country. But the same could not be done in the case of the coloured people. They had adopted "white civilisation" and therefore belonged with whites politically and economically. Over time they could be "absorbed in the white community". This was greeted by shouts of "hear, hear" from the audience.

Socially, however, coloured people had to accept segregation. "Everyone is happy in his own circle. But we should treat each other with courtesy and respect." Coloured leaders should take pride in their "race" and serve the interests of their "own people". The meeting concluded with a unanimous motion of confidence in Hertzog.

## The 1924 election

For the coloured voters of Stellenbosch, the general election of 1924 was the first opportunity when they could weigh up the new SAP, which had recently swallowed the pro-British Unionist Party, against the NP. Calls had been mounting for protection against competition from cheap black migrant labour in the western Cape.

On 28 May the NP candidate, Paul Sauer, received a motion of confidence at a large meeting of coloured voters in the Temperance Hall. NP speakers emphasised that if the Pact alliance of the Labour Party and the NP came to power, they would protect "civilised labour". The policy created the expecta-tion among coloured workers that they would be protected equally with whites against black unskilled labour.

Nowhere were the results of the 1924 election awaited more eagerly than in the constituencies of Paarl and Stellenbosch. The NP and the Labour Party defeated the SAP countrywide by winning 81 seats (NP 63 and Labour 18) against the SAP's 52. But the NP failed to capture the Stellenbosch and Paarl seats. In Stellenbosch the SAP's majority was 470, and in Paarl 173.

The defeats in these two seats were a bitter pill for the NP leaders to swal-low. Years later Sauer told his biographers, Dirk and Johanna de Villiers, that the number of coloured voters on the Stellenbosch roll had increased by about 600 between 1923 and 1924. These voters had been registered by the SAP, and they had spelled the difference between victory and defeat.

It is common knowledge that Sauer was one of Dr Malan's closest confidants.

He had a major influence on the NP's new policy to put coloured voters on a separate roll, which was propagated from the early 1930s. Yet many years later he would tell his biographers how he hated "this dishonesty" on the part of the SAP in their competition with the NP, "this abuse" of coloured voters by registering them with the sole purpose of "voting out the Afrikaner nationalists".[163]

Early in 1924 Cape NP leaders founded the Afrikaanse Nasionale Bond (ANB) to replace the UAL. That Malan drew up the ANB constitution himself shows that the ANB was in fact the coloured wing of the NP. Malan's constitution distinguished among "three races", white, coloured and black, as "the constituents of the nation of South Africa". It also referred to coloured people as "coloured Afrikaners". Malan and several other NP leaders spoke at ANB congresses. They exhorted the audience to be proud of "their race" and not to intermarry with white or black people. In 1928 Dr Abdurahman estimated that the ANB had 10 000 members.

In the 1929 election the NP for the first time won power on its own. The party also captured the symbolically significant seats of Paarl and Stellenbosch. In Paarl the NP candidate, PP du Toit, obtained a majority of 65. In Stellenbosch Bruckner de Villiers turned the SAP majority of 470 in 1924 into an NP majority of 268. A group of coloured voters from Stellenbosch carried De Villiers shoulder-high into Parliament.

What was the reason for this swing in favour of the NP?

Just before the election day the ANB leadership had thanked the Pact government for what it had done for the coloured community. They referred to progress in the field of education, such as improved salaries for teachers, and better job opportunities, especially where the policy of civilised labour was interpreted in such a way that it benefited coloured workers as well. The government had bought the farm Kromme Rhee outside Stellenbosch to establish an industrial school for coloured children. Even *Die Volkstem*, a Pretoria-based SAP newspaper, acknowledged that the Pact government had done much for the coloured people.

For a moment it seemed possible that a non-racial Afrikaans community built around a common franchise could take root in the western Cape. But history took a different turn. In 1929 the New York stock exchange crashed, which in turn triggered the global Great Depression. In South Africa the crisis was exacerbated by the government's refusal to leave the gold standard. A severe economic recession and widespread unemployment among all communities followed. White politicians in South Africa agreed that the "rescue"

---

163  Dirk and Johanna de Villiers, *Paul Sauer* (Cape Town: Tafelberg, 1977), p. 31.

of poor whites was the main priority, and that to this end a "white" Parliament had become necessary.

Another problem was that the franchise provisions of the Union constitution of 1909 could no longer be accepted as far as the exclusion of women was concerned. Male objections to the enfranchisement of white women had crumbled in the course of the 1920s, but there were serious divisions over the extension of the vote to coloured women. Hertzog, who had always opposed the exclusion of coloured men from the voters' roll, was against the extension of the vote to coloured women. He believed, without much ground, that there was more and more mixing between black men and coloured women in the western Cape. Hence, in order to know who was genuinely "coloured", he first wanted to classify coloured people before extending the vote to coloured women. But the majority of coloured people were emphatically opposed to classification.

Early in 1934 Generals Smuts and Hertzog merged their respective parties to form the United Party (UP). For most of the coloured voters, the UP's strong support for a common voters' roll made it a more attractive prospect than the NP. (The NP had become the *Gesuiwerde* or Purified National Party, led by Dr DF Malan.) Nonetheless, in 1938 Bruckner de Villiers lost the Stellenbosch seat by only 30 votes to the UP's Henry Fagan, a strong candidate on account of his popularity among both the white language communities. With that, the last opportunity to create an inclusive Afrikaans community was doomed. De Villiers commented scathingly on the "bright young men" in Parliament whose "clever plans" had cost the party several Cape seats, while winning only one seat in the Transvaal.[164] But it was the "bright young men" such as Paul Sauer, PW Botha and Eben Dönges who now would set the tone in the NP.

## The Battle of Andringa Street

I first heard the story of the "Battle of Andringa Street" soon after enrolling at Stellenbosch as a first-year student in 1956. It was about a group of Stellenbosch students who in 1940, during the Second World War, had come to blows with coloured people in the town, assaulted coloured residents on a large scale and ransacked their houses. Strangely enough, in the accounts I heard the students' riotous behaviour was not condemned as a serious case of racial violence, but was seen as "student fun" that had got out of hand.

In my third year I read Jan Rabie's short story "Stellenbosch, my vallei",

---

164 Gert Pretorius, *Man van die daad: 'n Biografie van Bruckner de Villiers* (Cape Town: HAUM, 1959), pp. 116-7.

which is included in his collection *Een-en-twintig* (1956). In the story, Rabie as narrator, while mountaineering in the Swiss Alps in 1954, looks down on a valley far below and is suddenly reminded of another valley, the Eerste River valley, where he spent his student years.

He recalls a certain event which has lain hidden in his memory "without any shame" for fourteen years. Gradually a tone of dismay creeps into the narrative. Rabie's biographer, John Kannemeyer, puts it like this: "He is overcome by incredible anguish, forlornness and confusion. Is it anguish because years ago he participated in an act of inhumanity, a forlornness about an assault on the dignity of fellow human beings, which would haunt him all his life?"[165]

Rabie's student years at Stellenbosch, from 1937 to 1941, were turbulent times. The 1938 centenary celebrations of the Great Trek had sparked a surging Afrikaner nationalism which was radicalised in 1939 when Parliament decided on the basis of a slim majority of thirteen to declare war on Nazi Germany together with Britain. The vote had been split largely along ethnic divisions in the white community. The "great experiment" of the UP, which was formed in 1933-34 to unite the two white communities, now lay in tatters.

The premier Afrikaner man of letters, NP van Wyk Louw, typified the radicalisation which the declaration of war produced among the nationalist intelligentsia. He referred to it as a "great defeat" as, in his view, it emphasised South Africa's subservience to Britain. It was inconceivable to him that Afrikaners could fight for a country that had conquered the Boer republics, or could sing "God save the King", which had been imposed by force of arms. The nationalists' resistance to the war would later also find expression in aggression, with sporadic acts of sabotage and terror by the Ossewabrandwag in its most severe form.

Race relations quickly became polarised. According to *Die Burger,* the coloured people were becoming more "uppity" by the day, while a white UP canvasser asked a coloured audience: "How can people consider voting for a man like that [Bruckner de Villiers]? If you vote for his party, your voting rights will also be taken away . . . [and] within ten years all of you will be slaves again."

The year 1940 was a crisis year. It looked as if Germany under Hitler was well on its way to winning the war. Among many Afrikaners there was a rejection of parliamentary democracy because the system had landed the country in a war despite strong indications that the majority of voters were opposed to participation.

The UP government under Jan Smuts sought to nip any rebelliousness in

---

165  JC Kannemeyer, *Jan Rabie* (Cape Town: Tafelberg, 2004), p. 78.

the bud and, among other controversial war measures, ordered that all civilians hand in their firearms, and anything else that could be used as a weapon, at police stations. Dr Malan protested vehemently: "The Afrikaner is turned into an alien in his own land and is disarmed."[166]

In Cape Town the English-controlled city council proclaimed a compulsory pause for prayer at noon. On the firing of the noonday gun, everyone on the streets had to stop dead in their tracks for two minutes and pray silently for an Allied victory. Only after a bugle had sounded were they allowed to start walking again. There was a strong possibility that a soldier or policeman would rough up those who disregarded the order. This was the background against which the infamous Battle of Andringa Street took place on 27 and 28 July 1940.

When I started working on *Nog altyd hier gewees* in 2006, no historian had yet published anything on the "battle". Gustav Hendrich, my capable research assistant, combed through the newspapers of the period and the university archives.

Two students who had experienced the events at first hand had left written accounts. One was David van der Merwe, a former resident of Dagbreek, the university residence that was home to the majority of students who took part in the "battle". The other was the famed Schalk Pienaar, later editor of the Sunday paper *Die Beeld* and subsequently first editor of the Johannesburg daily *Beeld*. While Van der Merwe comes close to condoning the students' behaviour, Pienaar shows a measure of remorse. He wrote in his memoirs that while he could not defend his conduct, he had been "bitterly angry" at the time.

Here and there I was still able to find people from whom I could obtain oral testimony. They included the community leader Aaron Cupido and Willem Lubbe, a former mayor of the town.

In May and June 1940 the troops of Nazi Germany conquered the Netherlands, Belgium and France with surprising speed. A force of about 400 000 British and French troops fled across the English Channel to Britain. Towards the end of July Pienaar and a group of fellow students decided to defy the compulsory pause for prayer. As he put it: "We'll go to Cape Town and keep walking during the noonday pause. Any man who tries to beat us up will be given hell."[167]

When the noonday gun went off on 27 July 1940, two students walked down Adderley Street. As soon as the bugle announced that the two minutes of

---

166  SW Pienaar (ed.), *Glo in u volk: Dr. DF Malan as redenaar 1908-1954* (Cape Town: Tafelberg, 1964), p. 46.
167  Schalk Pienaar, *Getuie van groot tye* (Cape Town: Tafelberg, 1979), p. 24.

silence were up, a fierce fight erupted between the students and the many soldiers and sailors who were waiting to get their hands on them. Shouts of "Kill
the damn Dutchmen" and "Down with the bastard Nationalists" were heard
from among the spectators. Peace was only restored after half an hour.

It is hard to say who "won" this fight in Adderley Street. From Pienaar's
version it sounds as if neither the students nor the soldiers managed to get the
upper hand, but a considerable amount of blood flowed on both sides.

Everyone was eager to see how the events would be reported in the *Cape
Argus*, which was usually delivered in Stellenbosch between half past eight and
nine o'clock on Saturday evenings. The only place in town where the paper
was sold was Senitzsky's café in Andringa Street, opposite the present-day town
hall. White and coloured used to queue together to buy the paper at one of
two small windows in a door of the café.

Pienaar wrote: "Queue-jumping had long been a source of irritation." From
the context it is clear that he had coloured "queue-jumpers" in mind. He went
on: "Full of bravado and fervour about Adderley Street, it was decided over
the last beer that such behaviour would be dealt with properly that night."[168]

As could be expected, fights erupted on that Saturday evening among the
crowd of people queuing outside Senitzsky's café. The trigger was a white
student who had thrown a punch at a coloured man, an act for which he would
later be fined. Then chaos broke out.

White students whipped coloured children with switches they had torn
from trees. Coloured people attacked with stones and bricks they had found
on a building site. Property and vehicles were damaged on a large scale. Large
numbers of Dagbreek students went on the rampage and almost literally
invaded Die Vlakte. They burst into homes, smashed windows, radios and
tables, and damaged cars. Pienaar wrote: "Property belonging to coloured
people was damaged indiscriminately. It carried on until deep into the Sunday. Police reinforcements were called in from Paarl and Cape Town."

After peace was restored, the US tried to mend the badly damaged relations
between the residents of Die Vlakte and the white students. The SRC issued
a statement – a combination of excuses and qualified regret.

The university council paid out a total amount of £25 in damages (today
about R24 000, if inflation is taken into account). A further amount of five
shillings (today roughly R240) was paid to a messenger of the university who
had been assaulted by a student. It was a shameful story.

---

168  Pienaar, *Getuie van groot tye*, p. 27.

In 2006 Aaron Cupido told me that the older generation of coloured Stellenboschers still talked occasionally about the Andringa Street riot in the winter
of 1940. What they found especially hard to understand was why the students
had beaten coloured children in the queue ouside the café so viciously with
switches, and why they had damaged coloured families' homes in Andringa
Street.

The worst case, Cupido said, was the invasion of the home of Boetie Kannemeyer, a building contractor and one of the most respected people in the
community. His house stood on the corner of Merriman Avenue and Ryneveld
Street, which is today the site of the university's arts and social sciences building (previously the BJ Vorster building). On Sunday, 28 July 1940, while the
Kannemeyer family was having lunch, a mob of students ran into the house,
ripped the white tablecloth from the table and smashed the crockery.

With a twinkle in his eye Cupido recounted that in the 1980s he sometimes
made conversation with students standing in front of the BJ Vorster building.
"Do you see those parts of the cement path where the soil is lifting?" he
would ask. "It's Boetie Kannemeyer turning in his grave."

## Forced removal

In my first year in Stellenbosch in 1956, Die Vlakte was a neighbourhood
bounded by Victoria Street, Bird Street, Banhoek Road and Joubert Street, a
place that was home to some 3 000 coloured and 300 white people. It was
evidently a working-class neighbourhood, but there were also several attractive Cape Dutch houses in Ryneveld Street where prominent coloured families
lived. As a student, I never heard any calls for the coloured families to be removed from the area. It was a peaceful neighbourhood and, unlike in District
Six in Cape Town, crime was a rare occurrence.

During the 1960s the government increasingly indicated its intention to
force the people of Die Vlakte to move to the northern outskirts of Stellenbosch in terms of the Group Areas Act. An earlier plan had been even more
radical. In 1956 a local committee of the Group Areas Board considered relo-
cating all coloured Stellenboschers, including the residents of Idas Valley,
to a separate town between Jamestown and Vlottenburg, 8 km south of
Stellenbosch.

In his evidence before the committee, Cupido rejected the plan unequivocally and with dignity because, as he put it, it wrote the coloured people off as
Stellenboschers.

He said:

We have always been here in Stellenbosch. We were born here and grew up here and worked here, we helped establish what has been created here, and I don't see how it can be expected of us just to bid it all farewell. An Afrikaner remains an Afrikaner, he doesn't want to become a foreigner. The coloured people must remain part of Stellenbosch. We don't want to lose that identity, that we are no longer regarded as Stellenboschers.[169]

With these words Cupido ended the debate on the proposal. In a moving interview with Murray la Vita, published in *Die Burger* on 17 July 2007, he described what had happened that evening in 1956 after he testified before the Group Areas Board.

He had walked out of the venue together with some of the board members. "The chairman was Dr Van Rensburg. When we came to the corner, Van Rensburg walked up to me and patted me on the shoulder and said: 'Don't worry, Mr Cupido, I just want to give you the assurance: You will *not* lose Idas Valley.'

"Those were the sweetest words to me. And that is why we remained here, he whispered huskily."

But Die Vlakte still faced the threat of "the Group". In 1964 the government decided that Lückhoff High School, the heart of the coloured community, had to move from its position in Die Vlakte in central Stellenbosch to the established coloured neighbourhood of Idas Valley. Shortly afterwards Die Vlakte's residents were given notice that they, too, had to move to Idas Valley or to a new coloured area, Cloetesville, that was being laid out on the outskirts of the town. Besides the approximately 3 000 coloured residents, six schools, four churches, a cinema and ten business enterprises were also forced to relocate.

When La Vita interviewed Cupido in 2007, Cupido showed him the faded photo of the gabled house his father had built in the Cape Dutch style at 97 Ryneveld Street. Like nearly all the other houses in the neighbourhood, it was razed to the ground. Cupido told him:

They knocked down everything and I was bitterly unhappy. And I told them I can't understand how such a competent, such an educated town council can allow the demolition of such beautiful buildings. It would have been proof . . . we would have been able to say: my grandfather, my great-grandfather – they lived there and those were their houses.

169  Verslag van die ad hoc-komitee van die Groepsgebiederaad, 1956, pp. 83-4.

For the families of Die Vlakte the loss of the community they had built up caused tremendous heartache. The Rev. AP Hector, who had become minister of the Volkskerk van Afrika after graduating from the University of Cape Town, exclaimed: "A dark cloud hangs over the generations to come. A rich heritage, acquired through much sacrifice, dedication and the grace of God, is under threat. All we can do is trust in the Lord and pray earnestly to Him, who has led us through the years!"[170]

In spite of widespread opposition, *Die Burger* under Piet Cillié insisted that the people had to be moved as soon as possible. Three US academics who also served on the town council did their best to prevent the forced removals. They were Frans Smuts, professor in Latin, JC de Wet, professor in law, and Erika Theron, professor in social work. Their resistance delayed the removal of the community somewhat, but by 1969 it was a fait accompli. There were no longer any coloured Stellenboschers left in central Stellenbosch.

One wonders what might have happened if the removal could have been delayed for seven years. In 1976 riots erupted in Soweto and other areas, and for the first time coloured people participated in the protests in large numbers. The whites were suddenly urgently in search of allies.

Like most of the white residents of Stellenbosch, I did not pay serious attention to the forced removals. Annette and I lived in a flat in Crozier Street on the edge of Die Vlakte from 1967 to 1969, just when the evictions started. We were literally almost neighbours of some of the people who had to move. At many houses furniture stood outside on the stoep.

"Don't the people rather want to stay?" I asked an official who was supervising the moving of household goods. "No," he replied, "the people want to move." The rationalisation of the NP and the officials was that coloured people would now be able to own their own houses and business enterprises. Only 20% of the households in Die Vlakte owned the houses in which they lived, and perhaps it was true that at least some of the residents wished to move into a house of their own, although their opinion was never asked.

What was ignored was the residents' passionate love for Die Vlakte, a close-knit neighbourhood where they had family, friendship and social ties. A happy and orderly community was torn up by its roots and dumped elsewhere. They were now far from churches, schools, shops and other businesses they patronised. It was as if the evictions had ripped the heart out of coloured Stellenbosch.

---

170 Hermann Giliomee, *Nog altyd hier gewees: Die storie van 'n Stellenbosse gemeenskap* (Cape Town: Tafelberg, 2007), p. 207.

The removals of the late 1960s and early 1970s cut off the traditional communication channels between the white people and the people of Die Vlakte and led to a hardening of white-coloured relations. In the riots of 1976 coloured students and high school pupils took part in protests against apartheid for the first time.

A month or two after the unrest started, coloured youngsters in Idas Valley stoned my car as I drove through the area with an American visitor. I arrived at the campus with a bloody shirt as a result of a wound on my ear. Later I heard that here and there on the campus there had been spiteful delight at my misfortune.

Being the target of an enraged young man hurling a big stone at my car was an unsettling experience, and it left me perturbed. Shortly afterwards, in September 1976, I wrote a sombre article for *Die Burger* about the eruption of black violence in the ghettoes of the United States and South Africa. A repetition could only be prevented, I said, by eliminating the root causes of the violence.

In September 1976 rioting erupted in Stellenbosch's coloured areas as well, and the house of a white school principal was petrol-bombed twice in the same night. The local paper *Eikestadnuus* reported on 17 September 1976 that many people had realised that "civil defence is a reality". In several white neighbourhoods, including our own neighbourhood of Dalsig, residents formed patrols to protect properties.

I, too, patrolled our neighbourhood by car a few times in the middle of the night. But I increasingly had doubts about the project. It was absurd to believe that coloured people intended to attack the whites in Stellenbosch. On my arrival at home one morning at 3am, my revolver went off accidentally and the bullet narrowly missed me. I felt terribly ashamed about everything: the unfounded fears, the knee-jerk patrols, my near-fatal clumsiness.

Unlike in Cape Town, where seven coloured councillors were elected to the 45-member city council in 1963, Stellenbosch had never had any coloured town councillors. Coloured Stellenboschers found that while the municipality was always "prepared to listen", they had no leverage to force the town council to attend to their grievances.

During the 1970s I was secretary of the Stellenbosch Liaison Committee, which was aimed at eliminating the worst "sticking points" experienced by the coloured community. It did not manage to accomplish anything of significance. The NP government's plans for financially independent coloured municipalities was a dismal failure, in Stellenbosch as well.

In 2006, when I worked on *Nog altyd hier gewees*, the National Party had been in its grave for two years. There was a democratic system in the country and a coloured mayor in Stellenbosch. Yet there was no real social integration in the town. The legacy of slavery and apartheid will be part of our lives for a long time to come. But at least all the residents were now equal as voters.

I wondered how my book would be received by coloured Stellenboschers and those elsewhere in the country. After all, I was someone who had the privilege of attending the school and university of his choice and whose family had not been forcibly removed to places where they did not want to be.

The launch of *Nog altyd hier gewees* took place in 2007 in the Anglican Church on the Braak. A photo of me and Cupido looking at the book hangs in my study. He died in 2015 at the age of 98.

I was asked to say a few words at the memorial service in the Rhenish Church on the Braak. Nearly all the mourners were coloured, with just a few white faces here and there. Aaron Cupido was one of the great Stellenboschers, I said, and it was a tragedy that so few whites knew this.

Two members of the coloured intelligentsia gave positive assessments of the book. The historian Cornelius Thomas, currently head of the Cory Library in Grahamstown, wrote in 2008 in the journal *New Contree* that my book "debunks every myth fundamentalists, essentialists, political correctists held and may hold about the Coloured people". In his view, it "stands as an achievement to be emulated for many Coloured communities around the country".

The church leader and activist Allan Boesak remarked in his review in the *Vrye Afrikaan* of 14 April 2007 that among his circles in the Cape there had been "something of a mini debate" on the question: Can a white historian tell the story of coloured people? Boesak wrote:

> My answer is clear: "Yes, he can". And not because he has the "power" to do so, but because he has the ability and the knowledge and the sensitivity. Giliomee writes a history that cries out to be told and heard, and, whenever necessary, he lets himself be guided by the experience and standpoints of the people whose voices have never been heard.

For me, this study, and also a brief comparison I made with black disenfranchisement in the southern states of the United States during the 1890s, brought something important to light.[171] It is the nature of democratic competition that determines culture and ideology, and not the other way round. Extreme forms of racism in a society only take root after black or coloured people's right to vote has been taken away or is under serious threat. The Battle of Andringa Street in Stellenbosch in 1940 is a good example of this.

---

171  Hermann Giliomee, "The Non-Racial Franchise and Afrikaner and Coloured Identities, 1910-1994", *African Affairs*, 84, 375 (1995), pp. 199-226.

# Chapter 13

# New history

South Africa has a colourful past, with a multitude of records left by travellers, visual artists, photographers and writers who attempted to capture aspects of the country, its people and their unique history in word or image. Strangely enough, the first illustrated history books aimed at the general public only appeared as late as the 1980s. Hence I looked with interest at two works that were produced in quick succession during the last years of white rule.

In 1986 Human & Rousseau published *A New Illustrated History of South Africa* with Trewhella Cameron and Burridge Spies as editors. As they explain in the foreword, "the text includes many lively descriptions, enlightening biographical sketches, and dramatic or humorous accounts", while "the illustrations have been chosen to provide visual extensions of the narrative". The contributors, "a panel of professional historians", comprised fourteen white English speakers, five white Afrikaans speakers and one coloured Afrikaans speaker. With a few exceptions, it is a solid historical work presented from a broadly liberal perspective. The manuscript was completed before the final phase of the struggle for the South African state began.

Hot on its heels followed the *Reader's Digest Illustrated History of South Africa: The Real Story,* the first edition of which appeared in 1988 and the fourth in 1994. This hefty book, which ran to more than 500 pages, was a massive success in the market and sold over 130 000 copies.

As a historical work, the *Reader's Digest* history is an oddity. The names of only two historians appear on the inner title page – one described as a consultant and the other as an adviser. Also listed are the names of an "editor", twelve "writers" and five "researchers", none of whom are known as historians. The book seems to have been produced by obtaining approval from respected historians that the *Reader's Digest* "writers" could adapt their work in the style of the magazine. No one in particular appears to have taken responsibility for the interpretations of the past that are reflected in the text. The actual historians are absent – the voice is that of the ghost writers.

The subtitle – *The Real Story* – creates the impression that many of the facts about the South African past are revealed here for the first time, as if implying that before the 1980s South Africa was a country whose history no one had dared to write about. The anonymous editors proudly claim that "nearly every page broke new ground". It sounds as if previously there had not existed comprehensive accounts of South African history from the earliest times up to the 1990s, in both English and Afrikaans, and as if there had been no newspapers, magazines and pamphlets that persistently told the story of oppression and injustice, as well as of achievements and progress.

## The real Eve

Prior to 2006, the thought of collaborating on an illustrated history, not to mention acting as the editor of such a book, had never crossed my mind. But by the turn of the century there was a major impetus for a new illustrated history. This was not principally due to the birth of a non-racial democracy in 1994, but rather to the discovery that the whole of humankind descended from people who had once lived in Africa. Africa is literally and figuratively the cradle of humankind.

This was already known in some academic circles in the last decade of the twentieth century. It was the British geneticist Stephen Oppenheimer's television documentary of 2002, *The Real Eve*, followed by his book *Out of Africa's Eden: The Peopling of the World* (published in South Africa by Jonathan Ball in 2003), which transformed the way in which the general public viewed the origins of modern humans.

For the first time it became widely known that Africa was considered the cradle of humankind. According to the "African Eve" hypothesis, DNA types found today in our global human population can be traced back to a single common female ancestor who lived on this continent some 200 000 years ago. Not only did modern humans first emerge in Africa, but Africa was also the place where humans learnt to walk erect, to make tools, to decorate themselves, to decorate their dwellings, to organise themselves in groups, to sing, and to speak in syntactical language.

In the first years of this century, scholars inferred from shell beads excavated in the Blombos Cave near Still Bay that the people who inhabited the cave about 75 000 years ago had a fully syntactical (in other words, modern) language. It must be added, however, that the linguist Rudolf Botha has argued by means of the "windows approach" that this inference cannot be proved.[172]

---

172 Rudolf Botha, *Language Evolution: The Windows Approach* (Cambridge: Cambridge University Press, 2016).

Oppenheimer's work also supported the "out of Africa" theory, which argues that today's global population originated from a single wave of migration of a few hundred modern humans from Africa. From the Horn of Africa, a relatively small number of these early people are thought to have crossed the Red Sea some 70 000 years ago. They first settled in Yemen and India, and gradually became dispersed across Europe and the Americas.

After the Neanderthals became extinct, these anatomically modern humans which had migrated from Africa were the only modern human species left. Hence white people, too, have a special bond with Africa, in the sense that their early ancestors came from this continent.

Along with this fresh perspective on the origins of modern humans, scientists showed how outdated the prevailing views on skin colour and "race" were. Skin colour is actually one of the least significant and most unstable characteristics of humans. Depending on the amount of radiation received from the sun in the environment in which a community settled, people could change from white to black and vice versa within a period of about 13 000 years.

Gabriël Botma, formerly a journalist at Media24 and now a lecturer in journalism at the University of Stellenbosch, recounts how Koos Bekker, then managing director of Media24's parent company, Naspers, publicised the new insights into the evolution of modern humans in Africa and the peopling of the world by migrants from Africa.

Bekker's plea was that people should stop thinking that the continent had played an inferior role in global history. "Africa is no sideshow in the epic story of mankind."[173] At the same time, black people needed to realise Africa was a special place that belonged not only to them and on which not only they could pass judgement.

The themes Bekker raised under the banner of the "So where do we come from" project were disseminated by Naspers through the print media and television talk shows on M–Net and kykNET in which scientists, journalists and celebrities took part.[174]

## We are all "*inkommers*"

According to the history I learnt at school and university, South Africa was empty and unpopulated by the 1650s, except for relatively small numbers of

---

173  Koos Bekker, "Africa is no sideshow", *City Press*, 30 April 2006.
174  Gabriël Botma, "'Koos sê so': 'n Kritiese diskoersanalise van die metakapitaal van 'n invloedryke Suid-Afrikaanse mediamagnaat", *Tydskrif vir Geesteswetenskappe*, 56, 1 (2016), pp. 153 –68.

"Bushmen" and "Hottentots" who were scattered across a wide area. During the 1960s archaeologists and historians debunked this interpretation as a result of advances in knowledge. In Afrikaans there is the word *inkommers* – those who have moved in or are later arrivals. In terms of the new view, all people in South Africa were *inkommers,* except for the San. The earlier rigid distinction between Bushmen people, now called San, and Hottentots, now called Khoikhoi, became obsolete, and historians and anthropologists coined the term "Khoisan".

By the beginning of the modern era, San or Bushmen in what is today Botswana acquired domesticated cattle and sheep from Bantu-speaking agriculturists. They abandoned their hunter-gatherer mode of existence and adopted a pastoral economy. They called themselves Khoikhoi. If a community lost their livestock through a disaster of some or other kind, Khoikhoi herders frequently reverted to a hunter-gatherer economy. Hence the term Khoisan refers to a society in which boundaries between lifestyles were fluid.

Some 2 000 years ago the Khoisan crossed the Limpopo River and migrated into the western and southern parts of what is today South Africa. At about the same time, the first Iron Age Bantu-speaking peoples settled south of the Limpopo and then moved rapidly into the eastern half of the country. They were settled in what is now KwaZulu-Natal by AD 400 and in the present-day Eastern Cape by AD 600. A thousand years later the last *inkommmers* arrived, when ninety Europeans disembarked at the Cape of Good Hope in 1652 to establish a refreshment station.

## A request

In 2006 Erika Oosthuysen from Tafelberg Publishers, with whom I had enjoyed working on *The Afrikaners*, approached me with a request. Would I consider compiling a new illustrated history of South Africa? The idea was that the book should cover the entire history of the region that is today known as South Africa. It had to provide an outline of the most recent discoveries regarding the earliest modern humans in Africa and the migration to other continents. Thereafter recognised scholars would recount and analyse the history of South Africa from the earliest times to the first years of the twenty-first century, with the latest available research woven into a readable narrative history. I saw the task as one of putting South Africa's history together in such a way that it would acknowledge all the wrongs and blunders, while also stressing our people's ability to survive, adapt and make progress.

I was given free rein to choose a co-editor and the panel of contributors. The payment per word for contributors was considerably more generous than the usual rates offered to historians and archaeologists.

The deadline was inexorable: the manuscript, together with the numerous illustrations that accompanied the text, had to be submitted within a year. In practice, it meant that contributors were chosen on the basis of their contribution to substantive research which they had either already published or were about to publish.

In the end, besides me and my co-editor, Professor Bernard Mbenga from the History Department of North-West University's Mafikeng campus, 28 academics collaborated on the project. Mbenga and I worked well together as editors. A Zambian by birth who later became a naturalised South African, he regarded other South Africans' claims and utterances with a healthy scepticism. We also complemented each other well as far as our specialist research areas were concerned. Mbenga had written a doctoral dissertation as well as academic articles on black societies and chiefly authorities in the northwestern Transvaal during the second half of the nineteenth century. I had focused mainly on the Cape eastern frontier and the history of the Afrikaners.

In March 2007, almost exactly a year after embarking on the project, we delivered the manuscript to Tafelberg. All the contributors had met the deadline, and everyone's work was of a high quality. I insisted that the writer of each chapter or subsection be identified by name. Photos of all the contributors were included at the back of the book.

With tact and discretion, Erika, the responsible editor at Tafelberg, helped keep together the various components of the project. As there was considerable overlapping, there was always the risk that an important event might fall through the cracks. I discovered at a late stage that two major events had been omitted: Blood River and Rivonia. Fortunately the mistake could be rectified, otherwise the book would have been a disaster. It is said of Napoleon that before appointing a general, he would first ask whether the man's record showed that he was lucky. When Erika and I finally handed the manuscript to the printers, we decided that we had definitely had luck on our side.

*New History of South Africa*, published in both English and Afrikaans, was printed on good paper and beautifully laid out, with a striking cover design by Abdul Amien that featured the Keiskamma Tapestry, an embroidered artwork depicting the history of South Africa. Of all the books I have been involved in as author or editor, *Nuwe geskiedenis/New History* is the one that gives me most pleasure when I see it on someone's bookshelf or on a coffee table. Its Afrikaans and English editions both sold more than 20 000 copies.

## An exceptional history

The period between 1652 and 1910 can be regarded broadly as the colonial era, with Britain dominating politics, the economy and culture in the course of the nineteenth century. By the time of unification in 1910, South Africa, when viewed comparatively, had emerged as an exceptional country. Virtually unique in the history of Western colonisation, it contained within it signifi-cant numbers of the indigenous population who had survived. The reason was that the different communities beyond the first mountain ranges – with the exception of the San – had all been largely dependent on stock farming. The first European stock farmers learnt from the Khoikhoi how to survive in the interior. On the eastern frontier attempts at territorial separation were imped-ed because so many farmers insisted on retaining the services of their Xhosa herdsmen. Cornelius Thomas was correct in his review of *New History* in which he observed: "The editors break with tradition and state up front that we were 'migrants all'. The sub-text here is that no one can claim 'the land belongs to us'."[175]

The view that South Africa was a shared country did not suddenly fall away after the National Party assumed power in 1948. In 1953 Prime Minis-ter DF Malan said in his New Year's message: "Living as we do in a multiracial society, we must recognise each other's right of existence unreservedly. South Africa is our common heritage and belongs to all of us."[176] Two years later the African National Congress would commit itself to the Freedom Charter, which declares that "South Africa belongs to all who live in it, black and white".

One of the shortcomings of *New History* is that the interdependence of the different communities was not given enough attention and insufficient em-phasis was put on the conflicting conceptions of landownership and land rights. In the critical frontier expansion phase of the Cape Colony, roughly between 1700 and 1820, the loan farm system applied to the burghers. The holder of a loan farm did not have proprietary rights, but could renew his lease on an annual basis. The boundaries of farms were vague, which frequently gave rise to conflict.

The severe isolation experienced by most farmers in the interior and the lack of a decisive military capability encouraged them to take in outsiders as tenants, who were sharecroppers or kept livestock or helped with defence. Initially it was white men who were *bywoners* (tenant farmers) and who went on commando. Later, coloured and black people increasingly fulfilled these functions.

The notion of landownership on the basis of conquest was not unknown to the burghers, nor was the idea that the group that first settled on a piece of

---

175  Cornelius Thomas, "New History of South Africa", *New Contree*, 56 (2008), pp. 145-46.
176  *Die Burger*, 3 January 1953.

land had a right to occupy it. As late as the second decade of the nineteenth century the British system of property rights was introduced in the interior, beyond the first mountain ranges, by which a demarcated piece of land was granted exclusively to a particular person. It was only with the passing of the Natives Land Act in 1913 that shared farming between white and black was finally prohibited.

After power passed to a black majority government in 1994, landownership again became a burning issue, with the government proposing that farms be divided between a farmer and his workers on a 50/50 basis.

## A distinct type of colony

It was not only the survival of a substantial part of the indigenous population that distinguished South Africa from other colonies. Other colonies also had rich mineral resources, but as the economic historian Charles Feinstein points out, nothing could match the vast mineral riches of the Witwatersrand. The discovery of gold in 1886, together with the discovery of diamonds fifteen years earlier, transformed South Africa.[177] It was low-grade gold ore that could only be mined profitably by cheap labour. Before long, migrant labour on the mines was introduced in the factories as well. The system disrupted black family life severely.

There was another factor, too, that made South Africa unique. The debate about policies regarding local populations and the political morality of these policies was more vehement in South Africa than in almost any other colony. As Richard Elphick shows in his contribution to *New History,* southern Africa was one of the first regions in the world to be flooded by Protestant missionaries. Protestantism took root on a large scale among black and coloured people at an earlier stage – and across a bigger area of the interior – than in most other places in Africa or elsewhere. In no other country did Protestant missionaries play such a major role in both politics and education, initially mainly as defenders but later as critics of the prevailing political order.

Initially the Union of South Africa struggled to find its feet. By 1930, when the country entered a deep recession, observers had no reason to anticipate a bright future for South Africa. Around this time the historian CW de Kiewiet remarked that South Africa was a country of low-grade land, low-grade ore and low-grade people. By the last term he meant poorly educated people, which was true for all population groups. Apart from a small, overwhelmingly

---

177  Charles H Feinstein, *An Economic History of South Africa: Conquest, Discrimination and Development* (Cambridge: Cambridge University Press, 2005), pp. 1–2.

English-speaking upper stratum, few whites were really wealthy. Coloured and black people were poor or destitute. By the 1930s the capacity of the "native" reserves to feed their inhabitants was starting to collapse. The slums in South African cities were considered to be among the worst in the world.

There were major defects in the economic structure. In 1931 Jan Hofmeyr, who would soon become minister of finance, wrote that it was an illusion that South Africa was a rich country with vast mineral resources and boundless agricultural possibilities. The gold mines, the only reliable source of foreign exchange, were a wasting asset, the manufacturing sector was sluggish, and agriculture "no easy oyster for man's opening". The country was in a race against time to provide food and work for a rapidly growing population. Hofmeyr warned that the future of "white civilisation" was at risk if the country failed to develop speedily a modern manufacturing sector.

SP Viljoen, a leading economist, observed in 1983: "It is seldom appreciated today how poor a mining and agricultural country South Africa was [up to the 1930s]." By 1925 South Africa had a gross domestic product (GDP) of only R537 million (at 1982 values), to which agriculture contributed 21%, mining 16.2% and secondary industry a mere 7.8%. Viljoen continued: "Since industry tends invariably to act as the growth sector in a newly developing country, South Africa's economic structure was then as undeveloped as those of most African countries [in the early 1980s]."[178]

In the 1930s the state intervened to resolve the so-called poor white question and employed large numbers of poor whites. In some state schemes they received sufficient training to secure a job in the private sector. The state also put pressure on the private sector, excluding the mining sector, to employ "healthy quotas" of "civilised labour".

By 1933 no one would have predicted South Africa's astounding growth over the next forty to fifty years. In 1949 the elderly Jan Smuts observed: "The whole world is moving into a Colour phase of history, with results none can foresee and South Africa should dread most. Still, the worst, like the best, never happens [in South Africa]."

The worst did not happen. By the 1970s the government started withdrawing its protection from white workers and also embarked on a process of closing the racial gap in salaries and pensions. On the social and economic terrains, the foundations were laid for the establishment of a democracy. Strong and resourceful black and multiracial trade unions arose, the independent press

---

178 SP Viljoen, "The Industrial Achievement of South Africa", *South African Journal of Economics,* 51, 1 (1983), p. 31.

challenged the government, coloured and black pupil numbers in secondary and tertiary education increased dramatically after the early 1970s, and home-ownership expanded. The racial gaps in wages, salaries and pensions narrowed. Black workers streamed to the town and cities and liberated themselves from the pass laws.

The feared bloodbath did not occur when the black mass movement and the state joined battle in the contest for control of the state in the 1980s and early 1990s. Between 1984 and 1994, just over 20 000 people died in the conflict in South Africa. In terms of political deaths as a proportion of the population, it is, along with Northern Ireland, among the lowest of all the major ethnic or racial conflicts since 1945.

In 2003, just before we started working on *New History*, the South African economy was the 20th largest in the world measured by purchasing power, 17th in terms of market capitalisation, and 27th with regard to the services sector output.

In the book, we never really delved properly into the question why South Africa, despite all its shortcomings, grew so dramatically. Why did the country not remain, as it had been in the first decades of the twentieth century, a mining camp dependent largely on imports for manufactured goods, with struggling farmers and a poor white question that dominated politics?

There were three factors in particular on which we put far too little emphasis.

First, in the twentieth century South Africa had a professional civil service that was to a large extent independent of the ruling party. It was instituted by Alfred Milner, that bête noire of the Afrikaner nationalists, after the end of the Anglo-Boer War. His perspective was: "All good government is good administration, all the rest is rot."

Michael O'Dowd, an economist, political analyst and later chairman of the board of the Anglo American Corporation and De Beers, concurs with the view that from early on South Africa had a better civil service than any country could expect at that stage of its development. For whites, there was effective local government, proper tax collection and a clean civil service. Apart from a few isolated cases, corruption on the higher levels was rare. There was no insistence that the top levels of the civil service had to reflect the proportions of the white population. It was only in the early 1960s, more than fifty years after unification, that the higher ranks reflected the fact that Afrikaners represented about 55% of the white population.

Second, the successive governments had a plan. The country had to be developed, but not only so that whites could enjoy a better life. Both liberals

and segregationists argued that higher spending on white education was justified in order to establish a "healthy core group". There was, however, an important condition: the superior education white children received ultimately had
to be to the advantage of the other groups as well.

Third, no obligation was imposed on the English-speaking business community to "empower" the Afrikaners or any other group. The Afrikaners were
content with acquiring managerial expertise in running large corporations
through the parastatal sector. Iscor and Eskom were soon followed by other
state bodies such as the Industrial Development Corporation, which contributed
greatly to the rise of a local manufacturing sector. There was never any serious
demand for nationalisation, although the English corporations and companies
dominated the private sector completely.

In 1937 Hendrik Verwoerd became the only opinion-maker who proposed
Afrikaner quotas in the professions and the retail sector to ensure a "proper
share" for the Afrikaners. No political leader in the National Party supported
him. In the early 1950s a meeting of the Executive Council of the Afrikaner
Broederbond was asked to consider the idea of quotas for Afrikaner compa-
nies in the various sectors of the economy. Anton Rupert of Rembrandt and
Andreas Wassenaar of Sanlam persuaded them to drop the idea, insisting that
"Afrikaner enterprises have to learn to compete".

After the publication of *New History,* I occasionally had conversations with
black intellectuals about the question whether the book had any message for
black people striving to command respect in the economic sphere by establishing successful companies.

I remember one particular occasion very well. It was when I told Professor
Njabulo Ndebele, vice-chancellor of the University of Cape Town from 2000
to 2008 and an esteemed novelist, that the economic position of Afrikaners
and that of black people had been very similar in the early twentieth century.
Large numbers of both communities were forced to urbanise, both groups were
regarded with contempt by trade union leaders of British descent, and the government harshly suppressed strikes by both white and black workers. Up to the
1930s there were virtually no Afrikaner-owned businesses in Johannesburg
or other big cities.

"Yes", Ndebele replied, "that is so. But remember: the Afrikaners had
the land."

## Chapter 14

# Surrender without defeat?

My book on the Afrikaners covered such a wide field that there was no room to describe the last leaders' strengths and weaknesses, their special bond with the Afrikaners, or their respective solutions to the mounting political crisis. When I was working on the 2003 HF Verwoerd memorial lecture, however, a seed was planted for a book that would appear ten years later: *The Last Afrikaner Leaders: A Supreme Test of Power* (Tafelberg, 2012).

Forming a balanced judgement of Verwoerd presented a severe challenge. After the change of power in 1994, it was almost as if it was incumbent on white academics not to pronounce themselves on Verwoerd without excoriating his policy in advance.

Strangely, Verwoerd had acquired a unifying function: virtually all opinion formers in South Africa regarded him as the architect of most of South Africa's problems. The position Verwoerd occupies in public debate reminds me of a remark by a character in Julian Barnes's novel *The Sense of an Ending*, which won the 2011 Man Booker Prize: "We want to blame an individual so that everyone else is exculpated. Or we blame an historical process as a way of exonerating individuals." As far as NP rule is concerned, Verwoerd is the individual and apartheid the process that is singled out for blame.

I had no intention of singling out Verwoerd as the major scapegoat, although I accepted that he had had a greater impact on the last 35 years of white rule than anyone else. I told his son-in-law Professor Carel Boshoff, who had been living in Orania for twelve years by then, that delivering a Verwoerd memorial lecture at Orania would be an interesting challenge for me. The biggest challenge was that of assessing Verwoerd within the context of his own time and not in the light of how apartheid took shape in the twenty years after his death.

The first Verwoerd memorial lecture was delivered in 1975 by the minister of finance Dr Nico Diederichs; the second by the prime minister, John Vorster, and the third by MC Botha, minister of Bantu administration and development. Between 1977 and 2004, when the National Party in its final guise was dissolved, no NP leader was invited.

## The man with a plan

In my Verwoerd lecture in Orania I said that most of Verwoerd's critics view him as an ideologue incapable of changing course from the apartheid route he had taken. By that they usually mean he would have clung rigidly to the homelands as the best solution to black numerical domination.

I disagreed with this view. On several occasions Verwoerd had radically changed course and done the unexpected. Also noteworthy is the impression of David de Villiers, a respected senior advocate who led South Africa's legal team in the World Court case on South West Africa, who worked closely with Verwoerd for several years. In a book compiled by Verwoerd's eldest son, Wilhelm, De Villiers wrote that Verwoerd "listened intensely and as a result he would often change, adapt or ditch an opinion, an intention or a plan he had mooted".[179]

I find it very hard to believe that Verwoerd would have persisted with the homeland policy as a final blueprint after it became clear in 1969 that by the year 2000 there would be between 10 and 15 million more black South Africans than the number expected in the early 1950s, when the homeland policy had been planned on the basis of Professor Jan Sadie's population projections. As far as urban blacks were concerned, Verwoerd believed that black urbanisation could be curbed through tough influx measures, but by 2000 there would be 15 million blacks in urban areas compared with the 2 to 3 million the planners had had in mind.

In my speech in Orania I also pointed out a liberal myth that had long prevented debate about Verwoerd, which could be summarised as follows: "After a period of relatively good and easy race relations before 1948, South Africa, after a change of government, was suddenly plunged into nearly four decades of increasing racial tension and racial hatred."[180]

Liberal thinkers of the 1930s and 1940s, I said, would have found this myth of relatively benign race relations before 1948 astonishing. The philosopher Alfred Hoernlé, arguably the most respected liberal thinker of the early twentieth century in South Africa, remarked in 1936 that a visitor from Mars would immediately be struck by the pervasiveness of racial exclusion and discrimination in the country. Such a visitor, he wrote, could come to only one conclusion: "[There] was a dominant urge towards segregation, which has moulded the structure of South African society and made it what it now is."

---

179  David de Villiers, "Die wêreldhofsaak in Den Haag", WJ Verwoerd (compiler): *HF Verwoerd: Só onthou ons hom* (Pretoria: Protea, 2001), p. 139.
180  Piet Cillié, "Wat is (was) apartheid?", *Die Suid-Afrikaan*, 5 (1985), p. 17.

On the idea that the state should take control of the education of black children, Hoernlé observed that while a large section of whites would not object to "Native education" as such, it would be "political suicide in most constituencies" for a candidate to advocate that "Whites should be taxed in order that Natives may be educated".[181]

After the 1948 election the National Party classified people in racial groups, banned sexual intercourse between white and coloured (the ban on black–white sexual relations had been instituted as far back as 1927), and introduced Group Areas. In my opinion, these laws and especially the way in which they were implemented are among the most callous deeds committed by Afrikaners.

But I questioned why Verwoerd was primarily held liable for all of this. It was the Cape Nationalists under Dr DF Malan who had laid the foundations of apartheid with the 1947 report of the Sauer Commission and the legislation that was passed between 1948 and 1954. And it was *Die Burger* of Phil Weber and Piet Cillié that endorsed this legislation, although the newspaper knew full well that these laws would cause great suffering among the coloured population in particular.

Because coloured people, who represented neither a threat to white power nor a different culture, were also forcibly removed and disenfranchised under this legislation, international opinion rightly concluded that apartheid was driven by racial obsessions rather than cultural differences.

## "Someone who would want to remain a Bantu"

Along with the homelands, Bantu education is Verwoerd's most notorious legacy.

In 2012 President Jacob Zuma remarked: "What is happening today is what Verwoerd did, where the black majority were historically not given education. We are dealing with a system that had put black people back for centuries."[182]

In my Orania lecture, I said that among the urban black elite of the time there was a strong suspicion that Verwoerd envisaged inferior education for black children. They saw the educational policy as subservient to the political policy, which aimed to channel all black representation and advancement through the homelands. This impression was reinforced by successive ministers of black education, such as WA Maree, who said in 1959 as minister of

---

181  RF Alfred Hoernlé, *Race and Reason* (Johannesburg: University of the Witwatersrand Press, 1945), pp. 96–7.
182  *The Citizen*, 23 July 2012.

Bantu education that the aim of black education was "to keep the Bantu child a Bantu child, someone who would want to remain a Bantu".

Although the black urban elite strongly opposed the policy, they did not attract much support for boycotts from the majority of black parents, especially the less literate. A study by Jonathan Hyslop, *The Classroom Struggle: Policy and Resistance in South Africa 1940-1990,* published in 1999, describes an almost complete absence of protest on the part of parents between 1954 and 1976. According to him, most parents accepted the system because there was such a desperate need for education and no alternatives available. The expansion of mass education was also welcomed because parents felt schools kept pupils "safe from accidents and juvenile delinquency" while they were at work.

After my lecture I became embroiled in several polemics about Bantu education. They were generally unpleasant. The assumption was that any attempt at a balanced evaluation of Verwoerd's policy could only be inspired by covert racism.

The critics tended to start off by quoting what Verwoerd had said in 1954: "The Bantu must be guided to serve his own community in all respects. There is no place for him in the European community above the level of certain forms of labour." He had qualified this comment by adding: "Within his own community, however, all doors are open."[183] This sentence was often omitted in later discussions.

What was also ignored was that the policy of the United Party government prior to 1948 had not been substantially different. It reserved skilled and even semi-skilled posts in the "white areas" for whites.

The critics invariably mentioned that the racial gap in per capita spending on each black and each white pupil widened from 7:1 in 1953 to 18:1 in 1969, mostly ignoring that the main reason for this had been the dramatic increase in the number of black pupils, from 800 000 in 1950 to 2.75 million in 1970.

I only established recently from retired officials of the department of Bantu education that after a few years Verwoerd abandoned as unrealistic the stated policy of linking spending on black education in part to the revenue from black taxpayers. To avoid putting the spotlight on the growth in expenditure on black education, the NP government concealed capital expenditure, including spending on school buildings in particular, in the budget of the department of public works. It is estimated that capital expenditure would have represented roughly 15% to 20% of the spending on black education if all expenses had been brought into the budget of the department of Bantu education.

---

183  AN Pelzer, *Verwoerd Speaks,* p. 83.

Prior to 1989, no one had analysed the real expenditure. A table in this regard, based on research done by Lawrence Schlemmer and Monica Bot, was published for the first time in that year in a book I co-authored with Schlemmer. It showed that the total spending on black education grew by 50% in real terms from 1962 to 1967, and by 87% from 1967 to 1972.[184]

In September 2012 I became involved in a polemic on Bantu education with Matthew Prew, a researcher at the Centre for Education Policy Development, on the *Politicsweb* blog. I pointed out some of the above points and quoted from the work of Kathleen Heugh, an acknowledged authority on language use in education. She wrote in the academic journal *International Journal of Educational Development* (1999):

> Between 1955 and 1975, there was a steady improvement in the achievement in literacy and numeracy . . . Eight years of MTE (Mother Tongue Education) resourced with terminological development, text-book production, competent teacher education and competent teaching of English, resulted in a school-leaving pass rate of 83,7% for African students in 1976. This is the highest pass rate to date.

In 2013 Heugh concluded in the *Annual Review of Applied Linguistics* that the education policy of the NP government consisted of two phases: the first phase (1955 to 1976) worked to the educational advantage of black pupils; the second phase, from 1976 on, to their disadvantage, with mother-tongue education being limited to three or four years.

I have often wondered why the radical opposition in South Africa singles out Verwoerd as the ultimate political scapegoat. During his term of office, considerably fewer black people died in detention or during riots than under the other NP leaders in the twenty years after his death. He was always impeccably correct in his behaviour towards leaders of other groups, both white and black. Under his watch, the economy grew faster and the unemployment rate was lower than during any other period.

Verwoerd, however, has become the symbol of implacable, uncompromising white power. I believe it has to do with the fact that he was the first leader to break away from the idea of a common South African nation, to which even Dr DF Malan had subscribed. For Verwoerd, only white people constituted the South African nation.

---

184  Hermann Giliomee and Lawrence Schlemmer, *From Apartheid to Nation-building* (Cape Town: Oxford University Press, 1989), p. 106.

Three months after the Republic was proclaimed on 31 May 1961, Verwoerd declared: "When I talk about the nation, I talk about the white people of South Africa." It meant, the coloured leader Dr Richard van der Ross responded, that "in future no non-white South African need regard 'Die Stem' as his national anthem or the South African national flag as his flag".

In 1965 Verwoerd stated that just as Ceylon (now Sri Lanka) was the country of the Sinhalese despite the presence of the Tamils, South Africa was a white state despite the presence of other groups.[185] Verwoerd became the embodiment of the policy of excluding black and coloured people from nationhood.

## John Vorster: The man who kept waiting

John Vorster was the most enigmatic of all the leaders I spoke to. As I mentioned earlier, I interviewed him three months before his death on 10 September 1983. My impressions of this interview were published in Denis Beckett's magazine *Frontline* in the same year.

The man I interviewed was tired and crushed, but mentally still very alert. He harboured a burning resentment against his cabinet colleagues who had forced him out of politics, first as prime minister and then as president. It was the same cabinet he used to dominate and the same ministers he had protected after major blunders such as that of Jimmy Kruger, minister of justice, when he remarked that Steve Biko's death left him cold. His sense of collegial loyalty had prevented him from expelling Kruger from the cabinet, as he should have done.

Vorster's colleagues, however, abandoned him when it became known that he had been involved in the department of information's illegal machinations and had allowed the responsible minister to mislead Parliament. Twenty-five years later, in 2008, when I worked on my chapter on Vorster for *The Last Afrikaner Leaders*, I looked at the *Frontline* article with new eyes. In the 1980s prominent authorities on African history, such as the historians Roland Oliver, author of *The African Experience* (1991), and Terence Ranger, introduced the idea that the modern entity "tribe" had been unknown to African people in the pre-colonial period.

"Tribe" was in fact a colonial-era invention on the part of the white rulers. As a relatively small ruling group, white people in Africa needed to divide the black population in colonies so as to be able to govern them. In South Africa, the notion of "tribe" was used to set aside limited territories as "Native reserves". Since 1910 the basic idea had been to exclude as many black people as possible

---

185 *House of Assembly Debates,* 1965, columns 403–410.

as citizens and eligible voters. By linking the independence of homelands to de-nationalisation, this was exactly what Vorster sought to do when he negotiated with homeland leaders about independence.

Vorster described to me the final negotiations between himself and Lucas Mangope of Bophuthatswana as follows:

> Mangope and I agreed about everything as far as independence was concerned. Then Mangope came up with the idea that he wanted to take only those people who were within Bophuthatswana territory. I then said to him the policy of my party is not to make territories independent but to make nations independent. I said to him that if he expected to take only some Tswanas and expected me to take the rest and give them South African citizenship, then I was not prepared to come to an independence agreement with him. On the eve of independence Mangope again came with a proposal: he was prepared to take all the Tswanas but they should be allowed a choice whether they wanted to accept his citizenship. I then said to him I was not prepared to give blacks South African citizenship.

Vorster was prepared to wait until all black people had accepted the government's offer of "independence" for their respective "nations" and thereby relinquished their South African citizenship before he would tackle any constitutional settlement. He waited in vain. During his twelve years in office, the government did not move a step closer to a solution. Eli Louw, who entered Parliament in 1977 and ten years later would become minister of manpower, replied as follows when his wife asked in 1977 what his main impression of his first parliamentary session had been: "Two things: the enormous power and influence of John Vorster and the fact that he does nothing with it. It looks as if things have come to a standstill, have become stuck. There is no dynamic movement."[186]

## PW Botha: The dog that didn't bark

The Rubicon speech that President PW Botha delivered to the congress of the Natal NP in Durban on 15 August 1985 was supposed to be the highlight of his career. If everything had gone according to plan, the whole world would have accepted that South Africa had finally renounced apartheid and that the release of political prisoners and negotiations towards a political settlement

---

186  Interview with Eli Louw, 30 December 2010.

would soon become a reality. Instead, things went awry so spectacularly that PW Botha's credibility as a reformer lay in shreds.

In this case I discovered only too well to what extent expectations can determine the assessment of a landmark speech. I had spent the ten days prior to the Durban NP congress in idyllic seclusion in an Italian villa on Lake Como, where as a guest one could dream about one's next book. Only the Italian media were available, and I was unaware of the excitement that was building in South Africa about the speech.

I flew home during the night of 15 August and bought a newspaper on my arrival. "There has been progress," I thought. After all, Botha had announced that blacks whose homelands had not accepted independence would be treated as South African citizens with the right to representation at all levels of government.

I was amazed at the glum faces I saw all around me. Evidently much bolder announcements had been expected. The only explanation I could get was the allegation that Pik Botha, minister of foreign affairs, had raised unrealistic expectations of radical reforms on the part of the German, British and United States governments, including the release of Mandela and the start of negotiations with the ANC. PW Botha had blown a gasket. He had torn up the draft speech that had been prepared for him and in its place delivered a belligerent speech of his own.

In the end, from my interviews and inquiries I could piece together an answer that was reminiscent of the Sherlock Holmes story of "the dog that didn't bark". PW Botha's leadership style, I discovered, was as follows: If ministers approached him with a proposal for a controversial reform initiative, he would immediately express his disapproval if he did not like it. No minister would then dare to put the matter before cabinet. If Botha gave the proposal the nod, however, he would encourage the minister to submit it to cabinet and quite possibly throw his weight behind it.

The cabinet, supplemented by other members of the NP leadership, met at the Ou Sterrewag (Old Observatory) in Pretoria on 2 August 1985 to discuss constitutional reform. President Botha had undertaken to announce decisions made there at the congress of the Natal NP on 15 August. Chris Heunis, minister of constitutional affairs and development, presented his proposal for an expanded cabinet in which initially homeland leaders and later also other black leaders with proven support would serve. Other ministers discussed how representatives of black people who had not lost their South African citizenship could be given a say in decision-making at all levels of government. Pik Botha came with the most radical proposal: within a reasonable time the ANC should be unbanned, Nelson Mandela and the other ANC leaders freed, and negoti-ations take place. No minutes were kept, and no one really knew what was decided.

The proposals were far-reaching, but an extraordinary thing had happened, as I established from the interviews: PW Botha kept quiet during the meeting. The dog of the Sherlock Holmes story failed to bark. I subsequently talked to four or five of the most prominent role-players, and each person commented on PW Botha's unusual silence. No one could provide an explanation.

Pik Botha drew his own conclusions, assuming that Botha's silence meant approval of the major reforms that were proposed. He immediately flew to Europe to inform representatives of the major Western countries of the im-minent bold reforms. He left himself a loophole by saying that the president obviously still had to approve the proposals. The South African media started speculating wildly about the speech, with newspaper posters trumpeting the news that power-sharing with blacks could be imminent. PW Botha became intensely irritated and summoned the NP's provincial leaders. He threw the draft speech compiled by Heunis's department, with inputs from foreign affairs, on the table, and humiliated those present by forcing them to listen for nearly 45 minutes to his "own speech". This was the speech that would un-leash so much anger and disappointment.

My question was: Why didn't the dog bark at the meeting on 2 August? What had caused PW Botha to keep quiet? My speculation led to my com-mitting the worst error in my career as historian.

Early in 1989 PW Botha suffered a stroke, but resumed his duties after a month or two. In the opinion of Professor JC (Kay) de Villiers, the neuro-surgeon I interviewed, the stroke had been a serious one. I asked several doc-tors what their advice to such a patient would be. They were unanimous in their view that the patient had to rest and avoid becoming emotionally upset.

Meanwhile, there was a rumour going around that Botha had already suf-fered his first stroke four or five years earlier. One day a neurologist I knew showed me a letter from early March 1985 (in other words, before the Rubi-con speech), in which Botha thanked him for what he had done for him as his patient. I assumed incorrectly that the neurologist had treated Botha for a stroke which was hushed up, but Botha's condition had been of a different nature. The neurologist later explained to me that in 1985 the problem had been a nervous facial twitch. Laypersons tend to confuse such a symptom of nervous strain with that of a stroke.

I inserted a correction in the second edition of *The Last Afrikaner Leaders*. Unfortunately I was unable to do anything about the erroneous passage in the American edition.

I never managed to get an interview with PW Botha. As a matter of fact, even my requests for interviews went unanswered. Several people who had worked closely with Botha expressed positive views about him. They include Dr Niël Barnard, head of the National Intelligence Service, General Magnus Malan and Professor Erika Theron, who told me that of all the ministers she worked with, he had come to meetings the best prepared. Barnard recounted how well Botha had kept his hand on the government as an effective administrator.

Nelson Mandela told me in an interview that one of his greatest regrets was that he did not get the opportunity to negotiate a new constitution with PW Botha. One can only speculate about how that would have turned out. I asked Barnard, who sometimes talked to both men on the same day during Mandela's last years in prison, what would have happened if the negotiations had been left up to the two leaders. In Barnard's view, Botha would have said: "Let's govern together for ten years and see how it goes." He added that he believed Mandela would have given serious consideration to such a proposal.

Irina Filatova, who came to know most of the ANC leaders well in Moscow, wrote to me on 27 October 2013 that the ANC would not have accepted power-sharing under any circumstances. Even if they accepted the principle formally, they would have subverted it from the outset. The only realistic possibility was minority rights, and while the ANC would have subverted those too, it would have given Afrikaans a better chance than it has today. She added: "De Klerk certainly did not know who he was negotiating with; ANC leaders certainly believed that once they got to power they would replace whatever has been negotiated."

## Slabbert: The man who was not there

My choice of Van Zyl Slabbert as the fifth leader for *The Last Afrikaner Leaders* raised eyebrows. In all likelihood he had never enjoyed the support of more than 10% to 20% of Afrikaners. My argument was that he had been an Afrikaner who played a major role in a leadership position. Between 1974 and 1986 in Parliament he had relentlessly spelled out the risks of clinging to apartheid better than anyone else. A new generation of Afrikaners respected him as one of the first Afrikaner intellectuals to renounce apartheid unequivocally. The NP government would not have relinquished apartheid if it had not been totally discredited in the ranks of the Afrikaner intelligentsia as well.

Why was Slabbert never appointed to a top position in politics? People tend to attribute it to the fickleness of Thabo Mbeki. After 1994 Slabbert moved closer to the ANC and adopted positions on many issues that did not differ much from those of Mbeki.

Before the 1999 election I once spent a night at his home in Johannesburg. Late that evening he asked me bluntly: "I've noticed a slight stiffness towards me among my old friends. What is your problem?" I replied: "The major problem in our democracy is the lack of opposition, and now you, too, want to jump into bed with the ANC."

Slabbert's real opposition was the ANC leaders who officially or covertly supported the South African Communist Party. It was unclear whether Slabbert saw any meaningful role for the Democratic Party (DP) under the leadership of Tony Leon. Before the 1999 election, Leon, in the presence of RW Johnson, briefly considered the idea of Slabbert standing as DP candidate for the office of premier of the Western Cape.

Slabbert emphasised that in the event of a hung Parliament, he would insist that the DP in the Western Cape form a coalition with the ANC, not the NP. Leon was shocked, as he had little chance of selling such a proposition to his voters, who expected more resolute opposition to the ANC. Slabbert's demand was incompatible with the DP election call to "fight back". Contrary to Slabbert's expectations, Mbeki did not offer him a senior position in the ANC government after becoming president in 1999. Slabbert died in 2010 a tragic figure.

From 2007 to 2014 the Democratic Alliance (DA) under Helen Zille made steady progress. The party consolidated its power in the Western Cape, and in 2014 Zille said the party was well positioned to capture Gauteng as well. The burning question was: How could the DA attract enough black voters to secure the victory? Should it become more like the constructive section of the ANC, or should it present a clear-cut alternative to the ANC?

The speculation was that Helen Zille was overhasty and was in fact jumping the gun.

My book on the last Afrikaner leaders with a chapter devoted to Slabbert had been out for a while when Wilmot James invited me to address the DA's parliamentary caucus. James, an old friend and colleague from my UCT days, had become an MP in 2009 and was elected unopposed as the party's national chairperson the following year. James asked me to talk about Van Zyl Slabbert. I inferred from this that the DA was confronted with the same choice Slabbert had faced: Should it become more like the ANC, or should it offer stronger and more consistent opposition?

Slabbert's major shortcoming, I told the caucus, had been his lack of patience. Charisma and intelligence, which Slabbert possessed in abundance, were important qualities, but even more important for a leader and a party was "digging in for the long haul and keeping in touch with the concerns and wishes of its constituency". While Slabbert's brilliant mind was indisputable, he underestimated the importance of building the party slowly but surely through patient persuasion and keeping closely in touch with its earliest followers. It was also better for the DA to project the party as a viable coalition of classes and communities, each with their own histories and expectations, rather than as a vehicle for the "true (liberal) faith".

I was especially critical of the DA's claim that it could implement black economic empowerment (BEE) better than the ANC. During Slabbert's best years as parliamentarian he used to adhere to a key principle: "Never bat on your opponent's pitch."

At no stage did Slabbert argue that his party, the Progressive Federal Party (PFP), could placate the whites better than the NP. He rejected race-based policies unambiguously and never tried to "improve" apartheid. The DA's major challenge, I said, was to offer an alternative to a race-based society. I also contended that the ANC was terminally ill. The mounting debt burden and the combination of misguided policies and an external crisis would lead to a tectonic shift in politics, as had been the case in 1932-33.

Helen Zille had been unable to attend the caucus meeting I addressed, but we subsequently exchanged views on the speech via e-mail. Her explanation for Slabbert's conduct is considerably more convincing than the emphasis I had put on his lack of political patience. I quote Zille's message of 19 July 2016 in full:

1   Slabbert fundamentally misunderstood the ANC as an organisation.
2   It was a patronage organisation, yes, but it was also a fundamentally ideologically divided one.
3   Mbeki was vying in the succession stakes with Chris Hani and Cyril Ramaphosa.
4   There was no way that Mbeki could take any risks whatsoever with his power base by favouring a person who was seen to come from outside the ranks of the ANC, where positions are the equivalent of a gold watch for long service and loyalty to a particular faction.
5   Mbeki was in the difficult position, in what was then a predominantly Marxist organisation, of having to steer a path that would defend the market economy.
6   This put him at a distinct disadvantage vis-à-vis Hani and Ramaphosa (with his trade union credentials).
7   Race always had to be Thabo Mbeki's weapon against the materialist analysis – to mobilise a constituency for himself.

8  Van Zyl brought absolutely no constituency of any significance with
him at all – so he added no value to Thabo's support base, and could
only detract from it.

9  Van Zyl's fundamental misunderstanding was that the ANC would
value skill and ability and competence. They don't. It is all contesting factions, and who can use patronage more effectively to lever
power. That is what liberals often fail to understand.

I would add to this that none of the three major parties had room for Slabbert. The PFP would never trust Slabbert again, and to the ANC he was too
independent in his thinking. The NP under De Klerk knew that Slabbert
loathed the party and its policy. When negotiations started in 1990, Van Zyl
Slabbert was, in the words of ex-editor Ken Owen, "the man who was not
there".

## FW de Klerk and the negotiations

In January 2014 a polemic arose between me and Dave Steward, chief of staff
in the office of President FW de Klerk and currently attached to the FW de
Klerk Foundation, about what had really happened in the negotiations. It was
sparked by an article I wrote on Nelson Mandela's retirement at the invitation
of the Dutch journal *Maandblad Zuid-Afrika*, which was published on the
journal's website in January 2014.

Among other things, I wrote: "The big question about the change of government is not how the ANC overthrew the government, but why the De
Klerk government let power slip from its hands. De Klerk made little use of
the advice of his military generals and even that of his National Intelligence
Service."

Steward responded to my article as follows:

It is remarkable that one of South Africa's most famous historians – who has
studied the transitional process and written extensively on it – evidently has
so little understanding of what really happened in the early 1990s; the options
available to President De Klerk; and the correct role of the security forces.

To start with, it is not true that the ANC "overthrew" the NP government
(as Giliomee himself concedes at the beginning of the article). There was
constitutional continuity at all times during the transitional process. Our first
democratic election took place on 27 April 1994 in terms of the interim constitution that had been passed by the old South African Parliament in Decem-

ber 1993. In 1996 the newly elected Parliament – sitting as a Constitutional Assembly – adopted the final constitution, within the framework of 34 immutable constitutional principles. The constitutions of 1993 and 1996 fully provided for the establishment of a non-racial constitutional democracy, subject to the rule of law, and protected the reasonable rights of all South Africans and all our communities.

On 10 May 1994, when President Nelson Mandela was inaugurated, FW de Klerk did not transfer power to the ANC: he transferred power to a new and sovereign constitution. The ANC definitely did not "overthrow" the NP government, just as President Obama did not "overthrow" the Republican administration in 2008.

Does Giliomee really believe it would have been possible or advisable for President De Klerk to retain power in his hands? The whole point of the negotiating process was to get rid of the aberration of white minority domination and create a new dispensation – a dispensation in which power, as in the case of all normal democracies, would vest in the hands of all citizens within the framework of a strong constitution.

De Klerk would have been foolish if he had failed to utilise the conjuncture of opportunities that arose by the end of 1989 to embark on negotiations. These included, inter alia, the collapse of international communism, the restoration of order inside South Africa, and the successful implementation of the UN's independence plan for Namibia. De Klerk realised that the balance of forces would never again be as favourable for the negotiation of a balanced constitution. But he also realised negotiations would inevitably mean that power would and should no longer remain exclusively in the hands of the white minority.

And what does Giliomee think the role of the "military generals" and the NIS [National Intelligence Service] should have been at this stage? De Klerk made it clear to them that their role was to continue defending the state and maintaining public order – tasks that they generally performed under difficult circumstances with success and commitment. Solutions to the country's constitutional problems and the negotiations, however, were rightly the responsibility of the representatives of all of South Africa's major political parties – and not of military and intelligence advisers.

De Klerk agrees with Giliomee that it would have been better if the negotiating parties could have agreed on the inclusion of some or other form of power sharing at the executive level in the final constitution. De Klerk and the National Party did all in their power to achieve such an agreement, but they were unsuccessful – mainly because the other minority parties refused to support power sharing.

Be that as it may, the new constitutional dispensation has functioned reasonably well since 1994. Despite all the current challenges, South Africa is a functioning constitutional democracy with a strong bill of rights; the country has experienced twenty years of economic growth (except in 2009), and it is once again a respected member of the international community. This would not have happened if De Klerk had not decided to "let power slip from his hands" – and from the hands of the white minority.

On 9 March 2014 I wrote in response to Steward's letter:

At pivotal moments in history leaders are compelled to take decisions under great pressure. Historians sometimes tend to abuse their hindsight knowledge to pass unfair judgements on political leaders who had to take momentous decisions at such moments. I do not wish to be guilty of that.

I reply to Steward's criticism because the manner in which white domination was ended between 1990 and 1996 still fascinates both experts and the general public. Seldom if ever in history did a regime surrender power while its security forces, civil servants and primary support groups were largely united behind it and the economy, though under pressure, was not on its knees.

In my article in *Maandblad Zuid-Afrika* I summarised in only three lines a story I told in more than 150 pages in *The Last Afrikaner Leaders: A Supreme Test of Power*. The book was published recently [2012] by the University of Virginia Press in the United States and Europe.

Steward writes in response to my article that it is remarkable that I have "so little understanding of what really happened in the early 1990s; the options available to President De Klerk; and the correct role of the security forces".

Not everyone shares this view. Tony Leon, who participated in the negotiations and later became leader of the Democratic Alliance, refers to my book as "utterly mesmerising" on the front cover, and Professor David Welsh, who had assisted the DP as an expert adviser, describes it as "an excellent book that breaks new ground". But perhaps Steward believes they, too, have a limited understanding of the negotiations and the transition.

When I started working on the book in 2009, I corresponded with the novelist and Nobel laureate JM Coetzee about the challenge for a historian who seeks to understand the transfer of power in 1994 correctly. In his reply Coetzee referred to the final chapters of my earlier book *The Afrikaners: Biography of a People* (University of Virginia Press, 2003), and continued:

> In the overall account you offered of the negotiations the party that held
> political power – the NP – got little of what it wanted and the party
> without power – the ANC – got what it wanted. There are two ways
> to explain the outcome. One is that the NP negotiators were incom-
> petent. The other is that the strength of the NP and the weakness of
> the ANC were more apparent than real. You seem to incline toward the
> former explanation. What leads you to believe that, in the larger con-
> text, the latter is not more valid?[187]

This is indeed the key question. The NP had all the "hard power", and by
hard power is meant coercive or punitive measures such as detention without
trial when there were reasonable grounds to suspect that certain leaders of a
previously banned movement had been involved in murders or assaults. These
were measures that were used in the second half of the 1980s in particular. By
contrast, De Klerk as president mainly used "soft power" (persuasion).[188]

Under De Klerk's predecessor, President PW Botha, there was a willingness
to use hard power within limits and detain people on a large scale. De Klerk
was not prepared to do the same. The only manner in which hard power could
impose a more balanced settlement would be not to go further than compulsory power sharing, to hope that the ANC would split and to isolate the
radical wing.

What makes the conflict difficult to analyse is its asymmetrical nature.
The government had the security forces behind it; the ANC had broad legitimacy, internationally as well as among a large section of the South African
population. Shooting down opposition was not an option for the De Klerk
government. It would only have exacerbated its legitimacy crisis and might
have led to what the business leader Anton Rupert warned President Botha
against in January 1986: Nuremberg-style trials of the NP leaders.

Steward writes that I fail to understand the options that were available to
De Klerk. I am convinced, however, that moderate political leaders here and
overseas would have had sympathy for De Klerk if he had indicated from the
start that he would not be able to transfer power without the approval of the

---

187   E-mail communication, JM Coetzee to author, 14 December 2009.
188   When certain police officers were prosecuted as a consequence of the Goldstone
      Commission, General Johan van der Merwe, head of the police, insisted that
      ANC leaders be arrested on the grounds of prima facie evidence that they had
      helped to plan murders. When De Klerk mentioned the intention to charge ANC
      leaders to Mandela, he threatened to pull out of the negotiations.

people who had voted for him – and that meant the white voters. The more pragmatic ANC leaders, too, realised it would be virtually impossible for the movement to govern the country if the white voters, who were also the biggest taxpayers, were alienated. De Klerk, and not Nelson Mandela, held the key to white acceptance of an ANC government and a peaceful transfer of power.

In the case of the conflict in Northern Ireland, the British government realised full well that it was imperative for the transition to a new system to be regarded as legitimate by all the parties. In terms of the Good Friday Agreement of 1998, the voters had to be fully informed about the negotiated constitution before voting on it in a referendum. The fact that there was a referendum waiting at the end of the process kept the negotiators focused on achieving a settlement that would enjoy broad acceptance.

In South Africa the last white election was held in 1989, which was also the first election under De Klerk's leadership. The NP won, but for the first time in thirty years its support among the electorate dropped to below 50%. The election was won on the basis of the party's constitutional proposals, which were fairly conservative. They made provision for "races" having self-determination over groups' own affairs and for power sharing for general affairs.

On 31 March 1990, six weeks after the De Klerk government lifted the ban on the ANC and a number of other extra-parliamentary organisations, De Klerk already held out the prospect of negotiations for a new constitution and pledged that "the constitutional proposals will be tested in a constitutional manner among the electorate. And only with their support will a constitutional dispensation be introduced."

In September 1991, before the start of the negotiations in the Codesa forum, the NP's federal congress adopted a new set of constitutional guidelines: multi-party representation in the cabinet, which would take decisions by consensus, and a presidency consisting of the leaders of the three biggest parties and a rotating chairmanship. For the local level it proposed two electoral rolls, one in which the names of all residents appeared, and one containing the names of owners, lessees and ratepayers.

In January 1992 De Klerk said in Parliament that any substantive changes to the NP proposals would require a referendum "in which every South African will be able to take part and whose result may be determined globally as well as by the parliamentary community".[189]

Nine months later, with the NP having increasingly moved away from its own policy in the negotiations, Colin Eglin of the Democratic Party said De

---

189 Giliomee, *The Afrikaners*, p. 633.

Klerk was being "very naughty" in claiming he kept to undertakings he had given. He pointed out that in his referendum campaign, De Klerk had said he was not asking for a blank cheque; he was asking for a "Yes" vote for the 1991 policy adopted by the NP's federal congress.[190]

The NP's explicit policy was power sharing. The major promise made personally by De Klerk and by the NP as a party in the referendum campaign of February and March 1992 was that the NP would only settle for power sharing and that it rejected majority rule in the form in which it functioned in Britain and the United States. The banner headline of a full-page advertisement the NP placed in the Afrikaans papers a day before the referendum read: "*As jy bang is vir meerderheidsregering, stem 'Ja'*" (If you are afraid of majority rule, vote "Yes").[191]

The question posed in the referendum was: "Do you support the continuation of the reform process that the state president started on 2 February 1990 and which is aimed at a new constitution through negotiations?" Lawrence Schlemmer, probably the most astute and best-informed political analyst in the country, noted that a "yes" vote was no mandate for majority rule. There would never have been a "yes" vote with a two-thirds majority if there had been a prospect of the ANC getting into a position where it could rule on its own.

The harsh truth is that the De Klerk government did not have a mandate for the interim constitution that was passed by Parliament in 1994. Today one can only speculate about what the ANC leadership would have done if they had known from the outset that the NP would only agree to a constitution for which it had received a mandate from its voters.

In the press debate about the future political system, De Klerk's insistence on power sharing was sometimes dismissed as a desire to cling to the "perks of office". The reality is that a deeply divided society such as South Africa can probably only be governed successfully through power sharing. In 1997 Vernon Bogdanor, professor of government at Oxford University, wrote in the influential journal *Daedalus*: "Some kind of power-sharing has been a feature of all societies that have successfully overcome their internal divisions."[192]

It was the programme of rolling mass action the ANC embarked on in June 1992, which lasted for more than three months, that caused the government to capitulate. In the so-called Record of Understanding of 26 Septem-

---

190  O'Malley Archives, Interview with Colin Eglin, 3 August 1992.
191  See the second-last photo in the photo section of Hermann Giliomee, *The Last Afrikaner Leaders: A Supreme Test of Power* (Cape Town: Tafelberg, 2012).
192  Vernon Bogdanor, "Forms of Autonomy and the Protection of Minorities", *Daedalus*, 126, 2 (1997), p. 66.

ber 1992, signed by the government and the ANC, the ANC gained the upper hand. It was on this day that Justice Minister Kobie Coetsee, usually a strong De Klerk ally, told Health Minister Rina Venter: "Today we have lost the country."[193] In the course of the next fifteen months the ANC would sweep all the government's proposals for power sharing off the table.

Hernus Kriel, minister of police, believed it was a mistake on the part of the De Klerk government not to have stuck it out in the winter months of 1992 when the ANC started its programme of rolling mass action. He rejected any suggestion that the government was losing its grip. In his view, the ANC, too, should have been forced to make a major concession to get the negotiations back on track. "We let the power slip from our hands," was his assessment.[194]

In his stimulating work *Summits: Six Meetings that Shaped the Twentieth Century,* David Reynolds analysed some of the major summits between world leaders. He concluded that such summits were only successful when both parties possessed a credible deterrent. In this regard General Johan van der Merwe, who headed the Security Police in the 1980s and was appointed commissioner of the South African Police in January 1990, commented as follows:

> Ultimately, the De Klerk government had no fall-back mechanism. At all times I had the impression that the National Party, from the moment it embarked on the negotiations, found itself in a crush pen. There was no going back. According to all indications, they would not have won another election in terms of the Constitution that applied at the time. I personally attended several discussions in cases where a crisis had arisen during the negotiations and certain of the principles that were initially labelled non-negotiable had been rejected by the ANC. I recall that on one occasion Pik Botha exclaimed angrily and snidely that the ANC was not interested in power sharing, they wanted all the power. Each time FW de Klerk asked the one question: "Do we break on this point?" And then the harsh reality registered with everyone again and each time they ended up conceding to the demands of the ANC.
>
> My personal impression is that particularly FW de Klerk and his advisers were to a large extent misled by Mandela's initially accommodating and benevolent attitude. Because we had had the opportunity over many years to conduct an intensive study of Mandela as a person, I warned repeatedly that he was a dangerous political opponent. FW

193  Interview with Rina Venter by author, 10 November 2011.
194  Interview with Hernus Kriel by author, 8 September 2010.

de Klerk himself later admitted to me that he had greatly misjudged Mandela. As a result of all these factors, FW de Klerk and the NP lacked the boldness to take a stand during the negotiations and, when a deadlock occurred, to act according to the courage of their convictions.[195]

De Klerk could not rely on support from the international community in this regard. Anthea Jeffery, author of *People's War: New Light on the Struggle for South Africa*, rightly observes:

> The international community let De Klerk down: for example, after Codesa 1 when he demanded the disbanding of Umkhonto and Mandela refused. If the West had backed him, it would have strengthened his position in insisting on this reasonable demand. The West must also have understood the ANC's role in violence, yet it never went public in condemning this.[196]

But the NP's biggest problem lay in the cabinet itself. Hernus Kriel described it as follows:

> We had no plan, no strategy, no bottom line where we would refuse to yield any further. We had no clarity on the goal at which we wanted to arrive. On numerous occasions in cabinet FW [de Klerk] would thump the table when Roelf [Meyer, the government's chief negotiator] reported that the ANC had rejected yet another aspect of our negotiating position and come with their own demand. FW would say: "That we cannot concede, that we cannot accept, here we draw the line." Then Roelf goes back and Cyril [Ramaphosa, the ANC's chief negotiator] takes a stand, and three weeks later the same issues come up again and then we accept the ANC's demand without offering any further resistance.
>
> During the entire final year of the negotiations three or four of us kept insisting that the amnesty question should be finalised before we continued with the negotiations. Then Kobie Coetsee would say: "Don't worry, colleagues, I have everything under control. Soon I'll have everything settled." And then FW would just let him be and we followed suit.[197]

195  E-mail communication, Johan van der Merwe – Author, 31 January 2010.
196  Anthea Jeffery – Author, 4 January 2010.
197  Interview with Hernus Kriel by author, 8 September 2010.

Steward writes: "The constitutions of 1993 and 1996 fully provided for the establishment of a non-racial constitutional democracy, subject to the rule of law, and protected the reasonable rights of all South Africans and all our communities." He also criticises my statement that the De Klerk government allowed power to slip from its hands, and that one reason for this was that De Klerk had made limited use of the advice of his military generals and intelligence service. He continues: "De Klerk made it clear to them that their role was to continue defending the state and maintaining public order . . . Solutions to the country's constitutional problems and the negotiations, however, were rightly the responsibility of the representatives of all of South Africa's major political parties – and not of military and intelligence advisers."

Of course the elected leaders are the ones who ultimately have to take the final decisions. But leaders of modern states that are engaged in a struggle against sophisticated resistance movements rely to an important extent on the expert advice of their strategic advisers. This happens on a regular basis. Israel is a good example.

It is doubtful that South Africa would have regained control of the security situation in the 1980s without the deliberations that took place within the State Security Council (SSC) and the strategies that emanated from it. There was little reason to assume in 1990 that stability and normal politics in the townships would become the order of the day simply because the NP government had announced that constitutional negotiations would take place. Yet De Klerk sidelined the SSC.

As Jeffery shows in *People's War*, from 1990 onwards the ANC took control of many townships with considerable violence.[198] The destabilising activities of a section of the security forces could also have been better kept in check through a body such as the SSC.

By expert advice from the side of the military and national intelligence service I mean their strategic insights and the knowledge they had acquired over the years, especially in discussions with contacts in countries such as Britain, Israel, etc. What the NP government also lacked was profile analyses of the ANC leaders and expert advice on negotiating strategies and tactics. In the mining companies there were people such as Naas Steenkamp and Johan Liebenberg, who in wage negotiations during the 1980s had acquired extensive experience of the former trade union leader Cyril Ramaphosa, who headed the ANC team in the constitutional negotiations. As negotiators, De

---

198  Anthea Jeffery, *People's War: New Light on the Struggle for South Africa* (Johannesburg: Jonathan Ball, 2009).

Klerk chose politicians who had little experience, particularly of the formidable negotiators of the ANC.

This brings me to the last and perhaps the most important point. The NP was left with no choice but to trust that the ANC would implement the constitution in the spirit in which it had been negotiated and adopted. The two parties had totally different conceptions of the meaning of a constitution: for the NP, it was a binding contract that could only be changed with the consent of both parties; for most ANC leaders, it was merely a half-way station on the road to a national democratic revolution in which ANC control of key positions and state control of the economy would be pursued.

In January 1997 De Klerk acknowledged in a speech in London that the negotiations did not bring about the balanced political settlement of the kind that the NP had sought. The white population had surrendered power and lost their "sovereignty".

It is unrealistic to believe, as Steward evidently does, that the constitution and the Constitutional Court could settle these disputes satisfactorily. Neither the ANC nor the NP had a tradition of allowing a court to resolve burning political disputes. A new doctrine emerged in the Western world in the 1970s: that minority rights in the developing world could be protected adequately through entrenched individual rights, independent courts and a vibrant civil society. By the early 1990s disillusion had set in.[199] A general trend was that on burning issues opposition parties tried to circumvent the legislature by turning to the courts and the ruling party countered this by manipulating judicial appointments.

This has been happening in South Africa in recent years. The bench of the Constitutional Court and those of several other courts have increasingly come under fire from the government's side.

There is a widespread feeling in the legal profession that the Judicial Service Commission, with a big ANC-aligned majority, tends to follow the party line in appointments to the bench.

Steward replied to my article as follows:

As Hermann Giliomee observes, "the manner in which white domination was ended between 1990 and 1996 still fascinates both experts and the general public". Because this debate is so important and because the issues involved

---

199 Samuel Moyn, *The Last Utopia: Human Rights in History* (Cambridge: Harvard University Press, 2010).

are so widely misunderstood, I feel that I must reply to Giliomee's very long comment on my rejection of his earlier thesis that the De Klerk government should not have allowed power to slip from its hands.

Giliomee takes exception to my criticism of this remarkable view.

He cites the praise expressed by Tony Leon and David Welsh for his book *The Last Afrikaner Leaders* as somehow refuting my views. However, I was not commenting on his widely applauded book, but on his opinion that De Klerk should not have allowed power to slip from his hands. I would be very surprised if either Leon or Welsh agree that De Klerk could have, or should have, retained some kind of veto power in the hands of the white minority under the guise of power sharing – particularly in view of the fact that Leon refused to support power sharing during the negotiations.

I am responding to Giliomee with some trepidation. He is, after all, our leading historian and has delved – more deeply perhaps than anyone else – into the forces, factors and individuals involved in the transformation of our society.

What then are my own qualifications? For twenty years I was a South African diplomat – who experienced on a daily basis the closing net of international isolation. As Ambassador to the United Nations (1981-82) I reached three conclusions: firstly, regarding the deep involvement of the Soviet Union in the ANC and in the international anti-apartheid campaign; secondly, that we could not rely on the West for help; and thirdly that we could expect no recognition for reforms – even for the significant reforms that PW Botha initiated between 1978 and 1986.

The global demand was for "one-man, one-vote" and – in effect – the transfer of power to a majority (i.e. ANC) government. Anyone who imagines that the West would have supported anything less is deluded. The most we could have hoped for – even from Reagan and Thatcher – was support for a strong non-racial constitution and the rule of law – along the lines of the constitution that we ultimately negotiated.

Similarly, Giliomee is mistaken when he says that "moderate leaders here and overseas would have had sympathy for De Klerk if he had from the start indicated that he would not be able to transfer power without the approval of the people who had voted for him – and that means the white voters". There is no way that any significant country would have accepted that the white electorate had a veto over future constitutional developments – any more than they were concerned about the views of the white Rhodesian electorate.

In 1986 I was appointed Head of the new South African Communication Service (SACS). I was a member of the expanded State Security Council and regularly visited our regional offices during the height of the state of emergency.

I witnessed at first hand the impossibility and unacceptability of maintaining minority rule over an increasingly restive and angry black population. I supported the state of emergency's goals to restore order; to restore services and to create an environment for negotiations.

I watched the contortions through which the PW Botha government went in its reform-minded efforts to find a constitutional solution that would not end in the loss of white power. However, its principal manifestation, the Tricameral Parliament, never enjoyed the support of a majority of Indians and Coloureds – and still retained final power in white hands. I watched the President's Council wrestling with proposals for the accommodation of black political rights – through the establishment of a "fourth chamber" – or mini-states in the black urban areas. None of these proposals would have stood the slightest chance of being acceptable to black South Africans or to the international community.

The Rubicon that PW Botha would not cross was the extremely painful acceptance that there could be no solution that did not include negotiations with the genuine representatives of all South Africa's people – and that would not inevitably lead to the loss of exclusive white sovereignty. Giliomee is shocked that FW de Klerk should have admitted as much in a speech in London in 1997. But how does Giliomee imagine that whites could realistically have retained sovereignty (i.e. own government and armed forces) in a country where they comprise a diminishing 10% minority – and in which there is no region in which they come close to constituting a majority?

Anyone who imagined that negotiations would not culminate in an ANC government was also deluded. Since 1986 SACS had been briefing the cabinet on regular opinion surveys that it had commissioned which showed ANC support of about 63%; NP support of about 20% and IFP support of 10%.

The best prospect for white South Africans was the negotiation of a strong and justiciable constitution and some form of power sharing.

This is what De Klerk promised.

From 1989 onwards I worked closely with the President – first as his communication adviser and then from October 1992 as the Director-General in his Office. In these capacities I shared the sometimes frightening roller-coaster ride of negotiations.

In any negotiations, the determining factor is perceptions of the relative power of the negotiating parties. In our situation, power was inevitably going to shift away from us as we approached a final agreement. The key to success was accordingly to launch the process when the balance of forces was most strongly in our favour.

Such an opportunity arose at the beginning of 1990 – when suddenly all the traffic lights turned green: De Klerk had been elected leader by a caucus that supported fundamental change; Cuban forces had been withdrawn from Angola; the Namibian independence plan had been successfully implemented; and – after the success of the state of emergency – all sides had finally agreed that there could be neither a revolutionary victory nor a solution imposed by the security forces.

Most importantly, the fall of the Berlin Wall in November 1989 and the collapse of international communism changed the global strategic and economic paradigm and significantly reduced the threat posed by the South African Communist Party.

De Klerk moved quickly to take advantage of the window of opportunity that history had suddenly flung open. He seized the initiative by removing at one stroke all the remaining obstacles to negotiations. He did so to the alarm of many of his security advisers – to whose advice Giliomee attaches such importance. In his speech of 2 February 1990 and again before the referendum in March 1992, De Klerk promised that he would negotiate a strong justiciable constitution and power sharing.

As General Van der Merwe points out, there was no going back once negotiations had begun. De Klerk has often commented that it was like a canoeist paddling out of a stagnant swamp. Before he reaches the river that flows to the sea, he must go through frightening rapids. Once the canoeist enters the rapids he is no longer fully in control: he can try to avoid the rocks and the whirlpools and he can try to right the canoe if it capsizes. Unleashing the forces of history inevitably involves risks. However, the risks of doing nothing are much greater.

Giliomee questions De Klerk's failure to use "hard force", as PW Botha had done from time to time. He suggests that "the only manner in which hard force could impose a more balanced settlement, would be not to go further than compulsory power sharing and to isolate the radical wing of the ANC, which was led by exiles".

Does Giliomee really think that De Klerk could have used "hard force"[200] to impose a power sharing solution against the will of the vast majority of South Africans? And how exactly could 'hard force' have been used to "iso-

---

200  Steward responded in English to my article, which was written in Afrikaans. He translated my Afrikaans term "*harde mag*" as "hard force", whereas the translation "hard power" is used for the English version of my article in this chapter (in the context of the distinction between hard and soft power as highlighted by the political scientist Joseph Nye).

late" the exile-led radical wing – which included the ANC's main leadership? Would this have involved banning, arresting or exiling them? Does he imagine for a moment that Mandela and the rest of the ANC leadership would have gone along with this?

Any such action would almost certainly have resulted in the collapse of the negotiations and a national and international crisis of catastrophic proportions. It would have immediately isolated South Africa in the international community and generated enormous internal and external support for the ANC. Sooner or later the government would have been forced to resume negotiations – but only after the balance of forces had shifted decisively against it. That is the kind of fatal mistake that Ian Smith made in Rhodesia.

Giliomee claims that the government lost control of the situation during the ANC's rolling mass action between June and September 1992 and that De Klerk did not consult his military and police advisers 'at this critical hour'. This is simply not true. I was there. He was in daily – sometimes hourly – communication with his security advisers – and certainly did not back down under ANC pressure.

Of course he wanted the ANC to stop its rolling mass action and worked day and night to bring them back to the negotiations. But he did not unleash his security forces against ANC protesters to 're-establish order' as some of his security advisers wanted. Instead, he kept his cool. In September 1992 – after the Bisho crisis – the ANC moderates regained control and agreed to resume talks on the basis of the Record of Understanding which was signed on 26 September.

Like many other observers, Giliomee completely misreads the significance of the Record of Understanding and cites it as the moment when the ANC gained the upper hand. He refers to Hernus Kriel's remark that "in his opinion, the ANC should have been forced to make a large concession to get the negotiations under way again".

In fact, the Record of Understanding included massive concessions by the ANC. From its position at the end of June – when it had turned its back on negotiations; when it had rejected the Codesa agreements; and when it had openly embarked on a non-negotiated seizure of power – it completely reversed itself. *It returned to the negotiations and signed off on all the main agreements that had been reached at Codesa.* These included the critically important concessions that

- the final constitution would be drawn up within the framework of constitutional principles that would have to be agreed to by the minority parties;
- during the interim period there would be constitutional continuity;

- there would be a transitional government of national unity;
- the interim constitution would provide for regional governments; and
- there would be justiciable fundamental rights and freedoms.

By any objective measure it was the ANC – and not the government – that had backed down. The concessions that the government made were largely symbolic and related to the banning of traditional weapons and the fencing of hostels. The exception was the ANC's demand for the blanket release of all its members still in prison, regardless of the crimes that they had committed. De Klerk found this most offensive and was prepared to break on it – but was dissuaded from doing so by his security advisers.

After the transition De Klerk continued to work for the inclusion of some form of power sharing in the final constitution – as he had repeatedly promised to do. However, he did not succeed – primarily because the IFP and the DP refused to support him. De Klerk felt so strongly about the ANC's refusal to accept some form of power sharing that it was the principal reason for his decision to withdraw from the government of national unity in 1996.

However, he did not support the idea of a minority veto – either in the GNU or in some subsequent power-sharing dispensation. He believed that a racial veto would at the first impasse inevitably precipitate a constitutional crisis that would have jeopardised the whole constitutional settlement. He favoured instead the establishment of a Council of State that would include minority parties and that would sit alongside the cabinet and consider all issues of common interest – but without a veto power.

Parties seldom succeed in achieving all their initial negotiation goals. The NP did not – and neither did the ANC. Initially, the ANC wanted nationalisation and a centralised state with no provinces or regions. It was not enthusiastic about constitutional curbs on executive and legislative power. These misgivings were eloquently expressed by Ngoako Ramatlhodi, one of the ANC's principal ideologists, in an article in September 2011.

He claimed that the balance of forces at the time of the constitutional negotiations had forced the ANC to make fatal concessions. During the negotiations the 'regime' had given up elements of political power to the black majority but had migrated substantial power away from the legislature and the executive and had vested it in the judiciary, Chapter 9 institutions and civil society. As a result, "the black majority enjoys empty political power while forces against change reign supreme in the economy, judiciary, public opinion and civil society".

So, Ramatlhodi certainly does not agree with Giliomee and JM Coetzee that "the party that held political power – the NP – got little of what it wanted and the party without power – the ANC – got what it wanted . . ."

Ramatlhodi conceded that the new constitution effectively limited the power of the majority to do as it pleased. He also attested to the effectiveness of the judicial system by complaining that white economic interests consistently and successfully challenged government policy in the courts. He clearly attaches more significance to the constitution than Giliomee who criticises De Klerk for putting too much faith in its provisions and in the independence of our courts.

However, De Klerk did not put all his eggs in one basket – as Giliomee claims. On 20 May, 1994, he told an audience in London that although South Africa had taken a leap of faith, it had done so with "constitutional parachutes and judicial safety devices". Other safety mechanisms included

- "strong and well-established organs of society, including professional and civil organisations; an independent and outspoken media; and a large and dynamic private sector;"
- the international community – which he believed would help to ensure that all sides would honour constitutional agreements; and
- "the symbiotic relationship which exists between all our communities." Government would not be able to harm the reasonable interests of whites without destroying national unity and jeopardising the interests of all South Africans.

Giliomee's contention that the "NP's biggest problem lay in the cabinet" is simply untrue. I know – because I was the Secretary of the Cabinet. Despite the enormously difficult decisions that it had to take, and despite deep misgivings and concern about the future, the cabinet and the NP caucus retained their unity and support for De Klerk throughout the whole tumultuous period.

Of course, there were anguished discussions about the concessions that affected the NP's bottom line – as there no doubt were within the ANC at the same time. That is what happens in tough negotiations. Hardly anyone was happy – but nobody resigned. De Klerk succeeded in retaining the support of his white constituency throughout the process. As is evident from the result of the 1994 election, he also attracted the support of a majority of coloured and Indian South Africans as well as an estimated 600 000 black South Africans.

Perhaps Giliomee's main criticisms of De Klerk are that he had no mandate to negotiate a majoritarian outcome – and that he did not submit the final constitutional proposals to the white electorate in a second referendum. De Klerk believed that his 69% victory in the 1992 referendum gave him a sufficiently strong mandate to reach agreement on the interim constitution. The interim constitution did not include power sharing beyond the idea of a Government of National Unity for the first five years. However, it also did not prevent the NP from continuing to work for power sharing in the final constitution.

However, by December 1993 there was no possibility of exiting the rapids of change and of trying to paddle upstream. A referendum at that stage would have been unacceptable to all the other parties and to the international community. De Klerk would probably have won – but with a smaller majority than he achieved in 1992. However, had he lost, he would have had to resign as president and call a new all-white election in the teeth of universal international condemnation and mounting domestic insurrection. Not surprisingly, there were few demands from his supporters for a second referendum and no dissension from their representatives in parliament when they adopted the interim constitution.

De Klerk's decision was vindicated on 27 April 1994 when an overwhelming majority of the white electorate voted for the National Party. Surely, they would not have done so had they not broadly approved of the constitution that the NP had negotiated.

Nevertheless, there were, of course, failures in the NP's negotiating approach:

- It could have made use of stronger negotiators.
- More could have been done to nail down an agreement on amnesty before April 1994 – although the interim constitution unambiguously states that "…amnesty shall be granted in respect of acts, omissions and offences associated with political objectives and committed in the course of the conflicts of the past".
- the NP should have reached a firm agreement on the nature and scope of the truth and reconciliation process that the ANC launched in 1996.

Giliomee also correctly points to the fact that the ANC did not negotiate in good faith and is committed to the implementation of its unconstitutional National Democratic Revolution. As a result, important facets of our constitutional settlement are under pressure. We know this only too well. The FW de Klerk Foundation has played a leading role in warning the public of these dangers and in defending the constitution.

The real challenge is to mobilise civil society, the media, business and public opinion to uphold the constitution and the values and rights that it enshrines. Nobody ever said that managing our new society was going to be easy – but upholding the constitution is a lot easier – and a lot more likely to enjoy domestic and international support – than defending the idea of a white minority veto.

None of this detracts from the central reality that – with the exception of power sharing (which it did not exclude) – the interim constitution effectively delivered virtually all of the promises that De Klerk made on 2 February 1990.

De Klerk stands out as one of the very few leaders in history who have successfully managed the radical transformation of a society. Unlike his friend Mikhail Gorbachev, he did not lose control of his revolution.

Since 1994 South Africa has made significant progress. Ironically, the principal beneficiaries have often been whites. We have enjoyed twenty years of relative peace and economic growth. We are once again a respected member of the international community. Our economy is three times as large as it was in 1994. Tens of millions of South Africans have been able to proceed with their lives in relative peace, prosperity and freedom – and without the degradation of institutionalised racial discrimination and without the calumny of being international outcasts.

During this period Prof Giliomee has written wonderful histories, surrounded by the tranquillity and unparalleled beauty of Stellenbosch. He has been able to meet with his friends in the dappled sunlight of the town's delightful sidewalk restaurants and, no doubt, discuss over a glass of cabernet sauvignon the grievous mistakes that he thinks De Klerk made in handling the transition to our new society. This has always been the role of those who write history. Those who make history – and who have had to wrestle with enormous social, economic and political questions – often have other perceptions of the past.

I can, however, assure Prof Giliomee, from my own experience of the history of that period, that there would have been no tranquillity, no prosperity, no international acceptance, and no prospects for the future had De Klerk decided to use 'hard force' to impose a constitutional system on South Africa in which 10% of the people, on the basis of their race, retained an effective veto over the decisions of a democratically elected government.

And De Klerk? At the age of almost 78 he continues his work to defend the constitutional order that he helped to negotiate more than 20 years ago.

This ends Stuart's letter. On 9 March 2014 I concluded the correspondence as follows:

I have trouble understanding Dave Steward's basic argument. He writes that no informed expert – and he mentions Tony Leon, who participated in the negotiations as a representative of the Democratic Party – would agree that De Klerk could have, or should have, retained some kind of veto power in the hands of the white minority under the guise of power sharing. He adds: "Particularly in view of the fact that Leon refused to support power sharing during the negotiations."

But why would Leon agree? At no stage did he and his party, as the NP did on the eve of the 1992 referendum, place a full-page advertisement that trumpeted: "If you are afraid of majority government, vote 'Yes'". He never promised, as De Klerk had done, that if the settlement deviated substantially from the NP's proposals another white referendum would be held.

What the ANC managed to negotiate was a system that did not differ materially from ordinary majority rule. In the final hours of negotiations for a transitional constitution in November 1993 the ANC rejected De Klerk's proposals that would have tempered majority rule. The final agreement read that the cabinet should function in the spirit of seeking consensus, but that when this failed, the majority would take the decision.

Contrary to what the ANC likes to suggest, power sharing is not unnatural or old-fashioned. Vernon Bogdanor, a constitutional expert from Oxford University, writes: "Some kind of power-sharing has been a feature of governments in all societies that have successfully overcome their internal divisions . . . The essence of power-sharing is the departure from majority rule that enables all major groups to play their role in government; majority rule is bound to lead to alienation and instability . . ."[201]

During the past decade we have been witnessing increasing signs of "alienation and instability" in South Africa. Commentators were unbelievably short-sighted during the negotiations when they dismissed President FW de Klerk's demand for power sharing as an attempt to cling to the privileges of NP rule.

What options were available to the De Klerk government after it announced in early February 1990 that it had decided to negotiate a democratic constitution? If the NP government had been on its knees, a settlement that reduced the NP to a lame-duck minority party would have been understandable. But there is no indication that that had been the case.

Addressing the Cape Town Press Club on 30 March 1990, De Klerk declared that the government was not acting from a position of weakness. "We did not

---

201 "Forms of Autonomy and the Protection of Minorities", *Daedelus*, Spring 1997, p. 66.

wait until the balance of forces had shifted against us before we decided on the course of peaceful settlement through negotiations." Two years later Chester Crocker, who had been the US assistant secretary of state in the 1980s, wrote that while the NP government would not be able to regain its legitimacy, "the resistance [movements] had no hope of forcing the government to capitulate".[202]

In the early 1990s Donald Horowitz, one of the world's leading authorities on constitution making in deeply divided societies, published a book titled *A Democratic South Africa?* in which he outlined the big challenge for South Africa: How should it prevent majority domination and minority exclusion? "If majority rule means black majority rule and white minority exclusion, something has gone wrong. It need not and should not mean that; and . . . if it does mean that, Whites will have no reason to choose an inclusive democracy for South Africa."[203]

Twenty years later Horowitz, who at the time had just completed a book on the constitutional negotiations in Indonesia, was highly critical of the NP's performance in the negotiations. In an e-mail message to me about *The Last Afrikaner Leaders* he wrote:

> De Klerk's failings were astounding. Did he think he was going to negotiate the purchase of a used car? Not to know the goals, the endgame, and not to have a list of what was and was not acceptable – this was a prescription for failure. On your account, he did not even have a conception of what he really wanted. These were negotiating failures much worse than in Northern Ireland, Bosnia, etc., and far worse than Indonesia.[204]

Steward incorrectly assumes that I propose some kind of veto power for the white minority under the guise of power sharing. But there are many other possibilities that could have been pursued: for example, electoral systems that are aimed at rewarding moderation and multiracial support (something that Horowitz advocates); federation (to which the NP never gave serious consideration) and weighted majorities. The settlement in Northern Ireland provided that crucial decisions could only be taken if they enjoyed sufficient support from both communities. No one condemns this settlement as unacceptable.

---

202  *High Noon in Southern Africa*, p. 496.
203  *A Democratic South Africa?* p. 94.
204  University of Stellenbosch Library Manuscript Section, Donald Horowitz to author, 24 July 2016.

In September 1991 an NP federal congress accepted far-reaching proposals for power sharing. It even included a proposal for a Second House in which parties that won a specified minimum number of votes in a regional election would all be given an equal number of seats.

Steward argues that "there is no way that any significant country would have accepted that the white electorate had a veto over future constitutional developments – any more than they were concerned about the views of the white Rhodesian electorate".

But surely South Africa was not the same as Rhodesia. Governments capitulate when their security forces have lost the battle or become demoralised, or when a more powerful neighbour puts the screws on them (as John Vorster did in the case of Ian Smith's Rhodesia). In South Africa's case the security forces were loyal and on standby to the end.

Of course the major countries of the world were eager to have a settlement in South Africa, but I doubt whether there was among all countries that mattered the unanimous will to put the screws on the De Klerk government until it had settled on the ANC's terms. My hunch is that the outcome surprised them as much as it did the De Klerk government's own legal advisers. One of them, Jan Heunis, wrote of his "shock" when he was told that the NP negotiators had agreed to majority rule. It was not the agreement itself that shocked him, but the fact that the NP had made an agreement for which it had no mandate from its voters.[205]

There is consensus among commentators that the turning point in the negotiations was the Record of Understanding signed between the NP government and the ANC on 26 September 1992. In the preceding three months the ANC had withdrawn from negotiations and launched a campaign of rolling mass action, accompanied by violence and disruptions. At times it seemed as if the ANC intended to bring the government to a fall through these actions.

There was no indication that the government was tottering. Police Minister Hernus Kriel told the journalist Padraig O'Malley at the time that the government "was not affected by the ANC mass action at all. We will not be forced through mass action to hand over the government to the ANC." He felt that the Record of Understanding was a huge blunder, and that as Kobie Coetsee, minister of justice, had told Rina Venter, minister of health: "We have lost the country."

Steward writes that it was in fact the ANC that had to make massive concessions. I am not aware of a single respected commentator who supports such

205  Heunis, *Binnekring*, p. 150.

an interpretation. The general view is that the ANC gained the upper hand for the first time and the NP would henceforth play second fiddle.

I argued in my book that there were actually two occasions on which De Klerk radically changed his position. The first was in December 1991, when he changed course and accepted an elected constitution-drafting body. This was an idea De Klerk had publicly rejected and on which the ANC had insisted.

De Klerk probably took this step because he believed that the NP, in co-operation with Inkatha, would be able to negotiate strong protection for minorities and a form of power sharing in an interim constitution. The expectation was that the ANC would struggle to get the prescribed increased majority to change a constitution that had been negotiated by a great number of parties.

The second big concession was in the Record of Understanding. With this bilateral pact the ANC succeeded in rupturing the informal alliance between the government and Inkatha. The ANC's demand that certain hostels with large numbers of Inkatha followers be fenced was largely aimed at this, and the ANC's move was highly successful. Thereafter the NP was isolated at the negotiating table. In my book I cite Mangosuthu Buthelezi who told me recently that Kriel had been quite correct when he said after the signing of the Record of Understanding that this spelled the end of the NP-Inkatha alliance.

The other gain for the ANC was that the NP government acceded to its unreasonable demand that ANC prisoners receive amnesty even if they did not meet the requirements of the internationally accepted Norgaard principles for amnesty for political crimes.

Another setback for De Klerk was that he failed to persuade Mandela that the ANC should stop using mass action as an instrument of political pressure to extract concessions at the negotiating table.

Up to May 1992 the plan had been that Codesa 2 would write an interim constitution. An elected constitutional assembly would then have been able to amend this constitution with a prescribed increased majority. Certain increased majorities would also apply when amendments were made.

After the Record of Understanding this mode of constitution making was off. The ANC would now have a clean slate when the delegates gathered to write an interim constitution. All it had to do was to obtain the specified increased majority and ensure that it stayed within vague agreed-upon constitutional principles.

To informed observers, it was clear that Nelson Mandela personally, and the ANC as movement, had gained the upper hand. The only "gain" for the NP was that the ANC returned to the negotiating table. But as Joe Slovo rightly observed to Patti Waldmeir of the *Financial Times*: "They caved in on everything."[206]

Besides, the ANC did not intend to pay much notice to the interim constitution that was finalised in November 1993. A year after the transition Thabo Mbeki, the deputy president, told an ANC conference that the negotiations for an interim constitution were "contrived elements of a transition" necessary to end white domination. At no time did the ANC consider them as "elements of permanence".[207]

By the time the final constitution was negotiated in 1995–96, the NP no longer had any power. In response to a recent statement by De Klerk that the ANC had not consulted the NP about its radical plans for transformation, Cyril Ramaphosa, the ANC's chief negotiator, said: "De Klerk seems to forget that the constitution was drawn up by the Constitutional Assembly, a democratically elected body that represented the collective will of the South African people."[208]

Steward does not reply to my most important point of criticism: that De Klerk did not have a mandate from his voters for the constitution that was negotiated. De Klerk's promise to voters was that he would prevent majority rule, and majority rule is what South Africa got. Not much came of the checks and balances of which De Klerk spoke so often.

Admittedly, there is a measure of protection in the fact that in South Africa the constitution, rather than Parliament, is sovereign. The Constitutional Court has the power to declare laws unconstitutional. But this crucial issue, too, was poorly negotiated. Nowadays the Judicial Service Commission (JSC), which recommends judges for appointment, time and again votes three to one against any judge who does not meet the approval of the ANC leadership. The JSC is completely dominated by people appointed by the legislative and executive branches, where the ANC has the majority.

The constitution has made it possible that private enterprises are not burdened by excessive taxes and government dictates. In particular companies that also have interests outside of South Africa are flourishing. But it seems as if the ANC is increasingly moving in a more populist direction. The decision to reopen land claims, without any money being available to pay out all the claims, may lead to a form of nationalisation of land and subversion of private

---

206  Waldmeir, *Anatomy of a Miracle*, p. 216.
207  SAPA PR Wire Service, Speech of Thabo Mbeki at ANC National Constitutional Conference, 31 March to 2 April 1995.
208  *Politicsweb*, 24 February 2014.

ownership. The Institute of Race Relations has recently sounded a strong warning in this regard.

Lastly, there is the issue of medium of instruction and language rights. By forcing Afrikaans schools and universities to introduce an English stream (in order to grant "access"), the government has dramatically weakened the position of Afrikaans.

The historian Arnold Toynbee detected a certain pattern in the rise and fall of civilisations. Minorities, and the Afrikaners in particular, are faced with formidable challenges. Nonetheless, it can be argued that the available social capital offers possibilities for a creative response. It will not be easy, but our history abounds in examples of communities which, in spite of huge obstacles, seized the existing opportunities and also consolidated their cultural goods.

With this article, the correspondence came to an end.

## In retrospect

Looking back on the period of white domination and specifically the years 1948 to 1994, one is struck by the great extent to which successive governments gave priority to tactical manoeuvres over any strategic planning. The crucial factor, the shrinking demographic base of the white population, was seldom taken properly into account.

The development of a formidable defence force between 1966 and 1990 would in the longer term make little difference to the South African government's ability to control the growing community of urban blacks. Only in the 1960s did the homelands offer the semblance of a solution. Derek Keys, the NP's last minister of finance, told me in 2010: "It was a failed system. The homeland elites raked off the system. There was a huge salary bill, but very little service delivery or tax returns. The national government got very little from these centres of administration."

As Arnold Toynbee warned in his 1959 article, "History's Warning to Africa", there comes a time when minority rulers have to accept a new status. Minorities who are descendants of colonists from the Netherlands and Britain find it particularly hard to take the critically important political decisions in good time and are then forced to accept majority rule.

In South Africa the race problem was further complicated by the fact that the white minority consisted of two communities. They battled each other for political domination while they jointly subjugated the communities that were not white. In 1960 Nelson Mandela proposed in a letter to Hendrik Verwoerd that black people elect sixty representatives to Parliament as a transitional measure. It is virtually certain that most of the sixty would have voted with the United Party, which represented the predominantly English-speaking community.

Ironically, it was Verwoerd who, shortly after he became minister of native affairs, made a proposal that had much more potential than the homelands or giving black people limited representation in Parliament. In 1950 he proposed to members of the Natives Representative Council (NRC) that "the greatest possible measure of self-government" be given to urban blacks. Black people needed to be educated to be sufficiently competent in many spheres so that they could do all the work in these townships.[209]

I wrote in *The Last Afrikaner Leaders* that this was a fateful turning point. A new field for black politics could have opened up if this offer had been accepted — particularly if it set in motion a political process that entailed talks between government and the urban black leadership on the election of urban black councils, the formula for the allocation of revenue, the staffing of the local councils' bureaucracy, property ownership and opportunities for black business. It would have opened up a whole new area for the development of black managerial and administrative capacity, something that the country would sorely lack when whites handed over power in 1994.

The members of the NRC did not take up the offer because the urban black elite demanded representation at all levels of government in common with whites. Of course, they did not know at the time that the NP would still rule for forty years and that "self-government" in the respective "homelands" was the alternative Verwoerd and his successors would impose. It is interesting to speculate about what might have happened had they accepted Verwoerd's offer — as in the case of the leaders of the independent trade unions who accepted the Wiehahn recommendations for a new labour relations system in 1979 despite their serious objections to certain aspects of it. Over the next seven years the government increasingly lost control of the system.

---

209  AN Pelzer (ed.), *Verwoerd Speaks*, pp. 28-30.

# Chapter 15

# To know who you are

In 1998 I resigned from the University of Cape Town (UCT) with the aim of completing my book on the Afrikaners over the next three or four years. Resignation was an easy choice. My classes on problems related to democratisation in South Africa and in other developing countries no longer offered the same challenge as in the 1980s and early 1990s, when the possibility of a peaceful transition in the country had been a burning issue.

I resigned at the age of sixty, cleared out my office in the Leslie Building below the slopes of Table Mountain and moved to my workplace in our home in the Stellenbosch suburb of Dalsig, where we had lived for the past thirty years. Our daughters, Francine and Adrienne, had both embarked on their careers. I was ready to devote all my time to writing, and had no appetite for Stellenbosch battles.

I sometimes joked that Stellenbosch was a good town to live in as long as one was not attached to the university. It is a peculiar place with a blend of megalomania and parochialism. Several professors think the town exists for the benefit of the university and the university for the benefit of the professors, rather than that of the students. Some professors have started to believe they are entitled to perform their teaching task in a manner that suits them, rather than their students, and that the university has no responsibility towards that which past generations have built up or what future generations may want. This applies particularly to Afrikaans as medium of instruction.

The University of Stellenbosch (US) was quick to embrace the ANC policy of transformation without asking whether a class-based form of redressing inequalities would not be preferable to the race-based model. Nor did the US reflect creatively on the way in which the university, with Afrikaans as language medium, could contribute independently towards building a liberal democracy characterised by cultural pluralism. A question that was never posed was how the US should position itself against the ANC with its zeal to introduce English as the lingua franca and foist "struggle" history on everyone. The result was a language battle in which the university's credibility became the biggest casualty.

The Afrikaans communities have reverted to what they were in the last decades of the nineteenth century before Afrikaner nationalism developed. The people in the south are once again loyal subjects, this time not of the queen and her empire, but of the Anglo-American economic and cultural empire. The northern Afrikaners, with the Solidarity movement at the forefront, have again become citizens like the republicans of yore, who intercede for a particular community.

## Afrikaans and the ANC

In 1987 already I had butted heads with the ANC delegation at the Dakar conference. The ANC participants at the talks even rejected a bill of rights as superfluous. According to them, the Freedom Charter offered enough guarantees for minorities. They simply refused to concede that speakers of a minority language had to be able to rely on enforceable language rights. Pallo Jordan stated that the future of Afrikaans was assured because it was the language of many black people.[210] This was far from a reassurance.

Alex Boraine, co-organiser of the conference, later expressed his displeasure about the emphasis a few of the Dakar travellers had put on language rights. In his *A Life in Transition* (2008) he wrote: "Hermann Giliomee, Lawrie Schlemmer and others kept raising the issue of the future of the Afrikaans language. Pallo Jordan put these people in their place when he replied in fluent Afrikaans that they should not worry only about Afrikaans but about Xhosa and Zulu as well." Boraine noted with irritation that we had not been reassured by the ANC about the position of Afrikaans in a future democratic system.

I found it alarming that there were so few among the roughly thirty Afrikaans-speaking Dakar travellers who were prepared to stand up for language rights in the new order. They were afraid that it would come across as a covert form of racism.

These Dakar travellers were the precursors of the language defectors on the university campuses after 1994. The storm clouds had started gathering for Afrikaans.

---

210  ANC document, "Paris-Dakar meetings", pp. 26-27.

## An uncertain future

On the eve of the 1994 election the philosopher Johan Degenaar and I drove to Onrus to visit the writer Jan Rabie and his wife, Marjorie Wallace. Jan had become known for his words *"Sonder Afrikaans is ek niks"* (Without Afrikaans I am nothing). I, too, felt that Afrikaans had made me the person I was. It involved an identification with an increasingly non-racial Afrikaans community, with all its virtues and vices, and the conviction that I expressed myself, in both writing and conversation, more eloquently and creatively in Afrikaans than in English.

Over lunch I asked Jan: "What will now become of Afrikaans?" He replied with a wry smile: *"Allesverloren"* (a lost cause).

By 1994 Jan's view was marked by a sombreness about the future of Afrikaans. The wave of globalism, with English as the primary medium, had engulfed South Africa. Like other liberation organisations the ANC government elevated English, the colonial language, and portrayed it as the key to success. The language clauses in the constitution could offer little effective protection against a government that was intent on circumventing them.

In 1990 Jan Rabie spoke in one of his last speeches of his dream that "nationwide, Afrikaans, and not skin colour, would be the umbilical cord of a big Afrikaans country". Jan's dream was not realised. The coloured elite in Cape Town and in bigger towns were anglicising at a rapid rate while the predominantly Afrikaans-speaking bottom third of the coloured community was still trapped in the same culture of poverty that the Theron report had described in 1976.

Among the estimated population between 18 and 24 years, university enrolments were as follows in 1994: whites 28.3%, Asians 23.3%, blacks 4.7% and coloureds 3.5%. One of the biggest challenges that faced the Afrikaans community was to prepare increased numbers of coloured pupils for university education. But the council and management of the US did not talk about this with a sense of urgency.

Most of the big companies with Afrikaans roots dropped Afrikaans without any compunction and embraced English. Affluent Afrikaners increasingly became what Niek Grové, registrar of the University of Pretoria, calls "a personalised society". People migrated inwards and now lived for themselves. Ties with friends, clubs, the community and institutions such as their alma maters have all become looser.

## Afrikaans at a crossroads

In 1999 Lawrence Schlemmer and I compiled a report on the US's language profile at the request of the then rector, Professor Andreas van Wyk. He wanted to send it to the then minister of education, Professor Kader Asmal, who had scant sympathy with the desire to retain Afrikaans at school and university level.

In our report, I wrote the following about the US's language policy at that stage:

> The present ambiguities tempt lecturers to adopt the language policy that suits their or their department's needs even if such action conflicts with the university's language policy. If the language policy is not firmly regulated there is a real possibility of serious conflicts erupting over the issue between staff and the university administration and between student groups. It is imperative that an unambiguous language policy towards tertiary education be formulated that will eliminate uncertainties.

Van Wyk did not hesitate to deal firmly with departments that defied the policy openly. One was the Anthropology Department, which had become known as a serial language-policy offender over the years.

Schlemmer and I followed up our report with chapters in a book that also raised other aspects of the problem. It was published in 2001 under the title *Kruispad: Die toekoms van Afrikaans as openbare taal* (Crossroads: the future of Afrikaans as public language). Other contributors were Neville Alexander, a language activist, Bertie du Plessis, a market researcher, and Max Loubser, a law professor.

The book was a stocktaking of Afrikaans. At the level of *use* or *consumption*, I wrote, Afrikaans appeared to be thriving. Newspapers, magazines, books, music, arts festivals, a national radio station and a television channel attested to a vibrant culture.

But I warned that the blossoming of Afrikaans could be misleading – almost like a sunset where the colours are intense just after the sun has gone down. This was certainly true when one looked beyond *production* and *use* at *reproduction*. Without Afrikaans instruction in schools and universities where a new generation of users of Afrikaans had to be cultivated, the production and use of Afrikaans as language of literature and science would decline progressively. Since 1990 the number of single-medium Afrikaans schools had decreased dramatically and the technical and teacher training colleges that used Afrikaans as medium of instruction had disappeared.

Schlemmer made the following statement in *Kruispad*: "The single greatest danger for Afrikaans is, however, that if Afrikaans as university language should diminish or disappear, it would mean the downfall of Afrikaans as language of science, as academic language, as language of intellectual discourse, and eventually also as literary language." He added: "Many languages have survived at grassroots level . . . There is little doubt that Afrikaans will survive in sport stadiums, bars, cafés, lounges and bedrooms. But who will take it seriously if it does not excel at the intellectual and professional level? As with other indigenous African languages, Afrikaans would in such a case be decapitated."

We pointed out that Afrikaans was confronted with serious challenges. Though in South Africa Afrikaans was still the most important literary language, measured by the number of books published locally, internationally English had increasingly become the language in which scientific articles and books were published. In our final chapter we stated categorically: "At university level Afrikaans is seriously endangered."

We advanced several reasons for this conclusion. Besides the pressure at postgraduate level, there was the wave of English-speaking students who had fled to the campuses of the historically Afrikaans universities. There was a strong suspicion that in many cases these students were seeking to escape from transformation at the established English universities. Between 1995 and 2015 students with English as home language or language of preference on the Stellenbosch campus would increase from 3 039 (20% of the total) to 13 316 (44%). During this time the numbers of Afrikaans speakers varied between 11 000 and 13 000.

The table below shows the growth in the number of English speakers, of whom at least 90% were white:

## Language profile of students

|      | Afrikaans     | Engels       | Totaal  |
| ---- | ------------- | ------------ | ------- |
| 1995 | 10 985 (74%)  | 3 039 (20%)  | 14 946  |
| 2005 | 11 338 (50%)  | 7 364 (33%)  | 22 569  |
| 2015 | 12 754 (42%)  | 13 316 (44%) | 30 150  |

Experience at Afrikaans-medium universities that had anglicised showed that there was a tipping point: once the English-speaking component on an Afrikaans campus constituted more than a quarter of the student body, these students increasingly demanded English-medium instruction. Stellenbosch passed this tipping point early in the new century.

The policy at all South African universities that lecturers receive no extra compensation for lectures they repeat in the other language accelerated the shift towards English. It is a global tendency that, as the American commentator Thomas Friedman puts it: "Faculty follows its own interests." Many academics saw parallel-medium instruction as an extra burden to which they had to devote time that could be used for research. Their attitude was: "If Afrikaans as language medium is lost in the process, we can't be blamed for that. Our task is mainly to publish."

There was an additional problem, even bigger than the other two daunting problems: Afrikaners had lost their communal spirit. Up to 1990 there had been among this group in particular a sense of solidarity with a community that included rights as well as obligations. Parents considered it their right to demand mother-tongue schools and universities if this was justified by local demographics. They saw it as their obligation to support Afrikaans educational institutions and businesses.

In the propaganda war waged by the ANC in the last fifteen years of NP rule, Afrikaans was a soft target. The narrative was propagated that the development of Afrikaans into a language of literature and science had been the result of special advantaging by the state – a notion that was utterly unfounded. The 1909 constitution of the Union of South Africa recognised both Dutch (later Afrikaans) and English as official languages with equal status. Effective bilingualism was the primary symbol of reconciliation between the two white communities.

Without the recognition of two official languages and a system of both Afrikaans and English schools and universities, South Africa would in all probability not have experienced the political stability and material prosperity of the greater part of the twentieth century. And without the establishment of a sophisticated economy and efficient state, there would have been no question of an inclusive democracy in the 1990s.

## "Transforming academics"

In the final chapter of our book Schlemmer and I highlighted a new phenomenon that had emerged on the Afrikaans campuses from the early 1990s. This was the rise of what we called "transforming academics" – those who believed they had "a more compelling and important calling than becoming concerned about Afrikaans and other smaller languages". For them, excellence, competitiveness and international scientific interaction and recognition carried much more weight. This was how they wanted to acquire academic status. While there were other academics who still wanted a proper place for Afrikaans on their campuses, they were too scared to say anything that might sound racist.

In this chapter we also identified strongly with the liberal philosopher Charles Taylor, whose interesting article "The Dynamics of Democratic Exclusion" was published in the *Journal of Democracy* in 1998. Taylor argues convincingly that the masses who make up "the people" in modern democracies find it hard to achieve consensus on crucial questions. Instead of the opinion of elected representatives carrying weight, a symbolic community of opinion formers push themselves to the fore and attempt to dominate public debate, even though they have no proven support on the ground.

Lawrence Schlemmer depicted opinion-formers of this kind as "a club of people with the correct attitudes". These include non-racism and the empowerment of the previously disadvantaged. They see themselves as a vanguard that have to transform institutions so that they conform to their values. They attach little value to the transmission of cultures other than the British-American world culture. To them, English is free of ideological and ethnic contamination.

They are suspicious of those who question the hegemony of English on a campus and try to marginalise them with a tactic Taylor refers to as "democratic exclusion". He warns that debates that focus on the victimhood of people and social groups that were previously excluded soon become sterile as it is assumed no common ground can be found with other groups. It is much better that people from different communities learn from each other and about their respective cultures through reciprocal recognition and exchange.

In the language debate at Stellenbosch, the "democratic excluders" soon denounced those who pointed out the risks of the increasing use of English as "rightists" and "*taalbulle*" (language bulls) who hankered after apartheid. The "people with the correct attitudes" consider it beneath them to debate an issue such as language by way of arguments. It is sufficient to discredit opponents by branding them as "undemocratic" and "hidebound".

## An emerging "taalstryder"

At UCT I made no pronouncements on matters to do with language, except on one occasion. In 1991 the executive proposed the scrapping of a provision dating back to 1919, which allowed students to take their examinations in both Dutch (or Afrikaans) and English. In the senate, my colleague in the Political Studies Department Professor David Welsh and I proposed that no decision be taken before the conclusion of the constitutional negotiations. As expected, we received virtually no support, but we were convinced that the executive's proposal was premature.

By the late 1990s I realised that unless Afrikaans speakers were mobilised, there would be little left of their formal language rights. The Pan South African

Language Board (Pansalb) existed as a watchdog of sorts, but most national and provincial government departments simply took no notice when a body of any kind brought contraventions of the language legislation to their attention.

The voice of Afrikaans organisations had gone quiet. In 1996 the chairman of Sanlam, Marinus Daling, recounted that President Nelson Mandela had asked him in a discussion on Afrikaans speakers' interests: "How can I take the Afrikaans speakers seriously when they cannot even organise themselves properly?"[211]

On a visit to Flanders and the Netherlands shortly after the transition in 1994 I heard about the Vlaamse Oorlegplatform or VOP (Flemish Consultation Platform), a forum in which most of the Flemish organisations were represented. They used the VOP as a platform where representatives of the respective organisations could reach consensus on matters before directing a collective request to the government or municipalities.

I started propagating the idea of an Afrikaanse Oorlegplatform (AOP) to act as a pressure group for language rights. Ton Vosloo of Naspers responded to this idea. He was almost the only business leader who expressed himself unequivocally and frequently on the diminishing role of Afrikaans in many facets of public life and the need for an organised response. He reacted positively after I had asked at a 1996 congress of the Afrikaanse Taal- en Kultuur-vereniging (the Afrikaans Language and Culture Association) that a flexible Afrikaanse Oorlegplatform be established where Afrikaans speakers of all colours would feel at home.

Our idea was that such a body would raise a powerful voice with regard to the marginalisation of Afrikaans and ill-considered forms of affirmative action. Breyten Breytenbach also made a plea for a coordinating body – "a standing-together, a clearing house address that can be approached for information, advice and assistance". Together with Vosloo and Breytenbach I planned a meeting for Saturday, 30 November 1996, at which the idea of an umbrella organisation would be discussed. It was attended by about 200 people from the business and professional spheres along with artists, writers and journalists. There was no unanimity about the way forward. The poet and radio personality Antjie Krog said she did not wish to stand under an umbrella of colours that were "anti-government, anti-ANC, anti-Truth and Reconciliation Commission, anti-English, anti-nation-building" including the "never-ending moaners about the SABC". Breytenbach responded with a question:

---

211 JC Steyn, "Nuwe aktiwiteite rondom Afrikaans: Die totstandkoming van 'n 'Afrikaanse Oorlegplatform'", *Rapport*, 17 November 1996.

"Antjie, what do you want us to do? March to Greenmarket Square with a noose around our necks and ask: 'Please just hang us?'"

A committee was set up to reflect on the question whether we should proceed with the establishment of an AOP. We decided to have an opinion poll conducted to gauge the feelings of Afrikaans speakers. More than 70% of white as well as coloured Afrikaans speakers indicated that an independent organisation for the protection of language interests was "extremely important". A total of 80% of the white respondents (compared to 32% of the coloureds) indicated that they were very unhappy about the manner in which their language and cultural values were treated under the new government. Close to 60% of the white Afrikaans speakers expected that their language would "weaken or die out".

On 28 July 1998 I was one of 14 people who attended the founding meeting of the Afrikaanse Oorlegplatform in Johannesburg at the invitation of Vosloo. Vosloo asked the meeting to come up with "an inspiring vision" that could lead the Afrikaans community to "balanced self-confidence". Jakes Gerwel asked: How do we as Afrikaans speakers deal with our past if we want to become a community?

Neville Alexander pointed out that, unlike Afrikaans speakers, the indigenous language groups did not believe in mother-tongue education. If the AOP intended to help foster mother-tongue instruction in other South African languages, he would welcome the platform. I warned that we needed to be careful in how we used concepts such as community and minority rights. In the literature in English there was a tendency to use the term "minority rights" in respect of groups that had been historically stigmatised. The experience of the white and the coloured Afrikaans communities differed strongly in this regard. Alexander asked that a secretariat be set up that could focus on issues such as mother-tongue education. Other proposals included talks with other minorities about the problems and the challenges they were experiencing, and the development of expertise regarding constitutional rights and social responsibilities.

Vosloo closed the meeting with the words: "We have found something of an overarching and common nature in the discussions that we should work on and refine within the framework of the constitution."[212]

The AOP played a catalyst role in a First Language Summit that took place at Oude Libertas in Stellenbosch on 22 July 2000. Most of the Afrikaans

---

212 Afrikaanse Oorlegplatform, "Dinkwinkel", 21-22 August 1998, US Library Manuscript Section.

language and culture organisations were present, as well as officials from Pansalb and the department of arts, culture, science and technology, who attended as observers.

With the help of Slabbert and Neville Alexander I drafted a memorandum that was submitted to the summit and subsequently sent to President Thabo Mbeki. The memorandum pointed out the strong pressure from government circles to elevate English as the lingua franca. This was in direct conflict with the wishes of the majority of South Africans, who preferred to be served by the government in their home languages.

The people who came to the Oude Libertas meeting expected us to demand immediate action from the government, but we would soon discover that government officials were in no hurry to attend to our representations. A request received an acknowledgement of receipt, followed by deafening silence. I referred to it as polite contempt.

Shortly after becoming president, Mbeki announced his intention to institute a "language mechanism" in the presidency to review all changes in language policy. Deputy President Jacob Zuma would be in charge of this.

When I heard that the department of justice was proposing to do away with Afrikaans as a language of record in the courts, I phoned the ANC head office and explained what we wanted to discuss with Zuma. I was informed that he would see us from 9:00 to 10:00 on Monday morning 10 January 2001 in his office at Shell House (later Luthuli House) in Johannesburg. I had to fly from George and Ton from Swakopmund for this appointment, while Van Zyl had to travel by car from Swaziland.

At the appointed time Zuma walked into his office and seated himself behind his desk with a broad smile. "Well, gentlemen," he said, "what brings you here to see me? I am just the baggage carrier of the ANC." He made no notes during our meeting and had no one in his office who could keep minutes. After 15 minutes I asked whether I could keep minutes of the meeting to send to everyone afterwards.

When the hour was up, we said our goodbyes. A week later I sent my "minutes" to the deputy president's office. There was no acknowledgement of receipt. When I told the story of our visit to Jakes Gerwel, who had been director-general in the office of President Nelson Mandela, he just shook his head and remarked: "That's Jacob Zuma for you." Mbeki's "language mechanism" was stillborn.

Ton Vosloo and I realised that it was almost impossible for the AOP to function well as a pressure group. The expectations from the Afrikaans side about such a pressure group were too high, and the government was unwilling to act constructively. Another problem was that Afrikaans organisations and institutions such as schools and universities often competed with each other for funds or pupils or students. In the event of conflicts of interest they would not easily submit to mediation. A few years later the Afrikaanse Taalraad (Afrikaans Language Council) came into being, which started focusing on the need for collective action in the field of language.

## The fatal T option

At the end of 2001 Professor Van Wyk retired as rector of the US and was succeeded by Professor Chris Brink, a mathematician who was then attached to an Australian university. Brink won the election in the council by a vote or two. What proved to be decisive was his response to the question: "How do you see the future of Afrikaans?" His reply was: "Relax, it is not a problem; it is a situation that needs to be managed. Afrikaans will not be in danger at Stellenbosch if it is managed correctly."

It is puzzling that Brink, who put such a premium on the management of the language problem, showed so little interest in an analysis of the problem. At a conference overseas he saw an analogy between Afrikaans and particularly Finnish among the smaller languages in Scandinavia. In Finland Swedish was historically the dominant language and is still one of the official languages. Finnish acquired official status by the end of the nineteenth century and is able to maintain itself today thanks to government help and the support of Finns in other countries.

Hence there was no analogy between Afrikaans and Finnish. Afrikaans could only rely on its speakers in South Africa, and after 1994 it suddenly had to get by without a state that was willing to enforce the language clauses.

At the end of 2002 the US council and management adopted a language policy and language plan. The core principle was: Afrikaans-medium instruction was the "default" or "automatic" option. Provision was also made for parallel-medium instruction (separate language streams).

Then there was also the Tweetalige Opsie (the bilingual option, known as the T option), which would only apply to the first year of study. Here the lecturer alternated between Afrikaans and English, with the rule being that he or she would speak in Afrikaans for at least 50% of the time. The assumption was that this exposure to Afrikaans would enable students to study in Afrikaans from their second year.

Unlike dual medium, which is based on the assumption that learners are fluent in both languages, the T option was an untested method. Van Zyl Slabbert referred to it from the outset as "a pedagogic absurdity".

There was a Unit for Afrikaans on the campus that offered courses to help students become proficient in Afrikaans. But students received no credits for these courses. Nor were they advised to report to the centre to improve their language proficiency before embarking on their studies In classes the content was usually repeated in English, and lecturers were obliged to provide bilingual class notes. Collena Blanckenberg, former head of the Unit for Afrikaans, wrote to me: "There was no intrinsic motivation for the non-Afrikaans student to acquire Afrikaans."[213]

The "democratic excluders" that Taylor spoke of soon referred to Afrikaans as the language of exclusion. In reality, the blame lay with the university for attempting to solve the language problem by means of a flawed vehicle such as the T option. The US did not require students to pass language proficiency tests. Nor did the university create any mechanism to make it possible for students to complain without fear of victimisation if lecturers contravened the language policy by increasingly teaching in English under the T option.

The language committee played a central role in the process of moving from a university that taught predominantly in Afrikaans to one that taught predominantly in English. It was a subcommittee of the council, but up to 2008, when I was appointed a council member, all the members were either lecturers or officials, and normally one student. And for those who were keen on anglicising the US, packing the language committee was as easy as pie.

## The gate is opened wider

In the second term of 2005 a small number of council members took certain steps that would lead to Afrikaans at the US being radically scaled down over the next ten years to a point where the phasing out of the language seemed inevitable.

The process was driven by the executive committee of the council (ECC), on which the following key figures served: Dr Edwin Hertzog, the council chairperson, Dr Gerhard van Niekerk, the deputy chairperson, and the rector, Dr Chris Brink. Along with the ECC, the language committee chaired by Professor Anton van Niekerk also played a key role. One of them later recounted the story to me as follows: "Early in 2005 a few of us posed the question: 'Should the gate for English as medium of instruction be opened slightly, or widely?' Our decision was to open it widely."

The ECC's first step was to persuade the faculty of arts and social sciences

---

213  Hermann Giliomee and Lawrence Schlemmer, *'n Vaste plek vir Afrikaans: Taaluitdagings op kampus* (Stellenbosch: Sun Press, 2006), p. 256.

to use the T option in all the undergraduate years. Other faculties could then also decide to follow this course. Thus the original motivation, namely that it would help students to gain proficiency in Afrikaans during their first year, was dropped, but no alternative motivation was presented.

According to the minutes of the language committee, the members resolved at a meeting towards the end of April 2005 that "the language policy and plan of the University of Stellenbosch [should] not be drastically changed at this stage". Professor Anton van Niekerk informed the committee, however, that the ECC had requested that the language policy be revised in the near future and that the wording had to emphasise "flexibility".

The language committee went along with the ECC's wishes. The minutes of 19 May 2005 read: "In line with the recommendations of the Language Plan it appears that the flexibility of the T option is being implemented to such an extent that it is being positioned as a default option in the language specifications for the different modules."

The language policy does not provide for such "positioning", and by definition there cannot be more than one default option. It is noteworthy how little regard was paid to the wishes of students or academics. In an opinion poll that the management commissioned among academics and students in 2004, they were not asked what language medium they preferred and whether they desired greater flexibility in the language policy.

In June 2005 the faculty of arts and social sciences formally proposed to the university council that every lecturer in the faculty be obliged to use the T option in all modules in all three years of undergraduate study. The document that explained the language policy and plan, however, did not make provision for such a choice.

It is sometimes said that business leaders on the US council pushed the university in the direction of English, but this needs to be qualified. Van Niekerk and Hertzog were both executive directors of big companies, but Koos Bekker and Jannie Mouton, who also served on the US council, were strong advocates of a predominantly Afrikaans university.

After the language struggle ignited in September 2005, Hertzog tried to explain his standpoint in *Die Burger* of 5 October 2005. The main reason he advanced for the view that the US should not be a predominantly Afrikaans university was the risk of isolation and academic mediocrity.

In a book I co-wrote with Schlemmer, *'n Vaste plek vir Afrikaans: Taaluitdagings op kampus* (A fixed place for Afrikaans: language challenges on campus), I showed what a strange argument this was. In the preceding ten years the US's researchers, who were nearly all Afrikaans speaking, had improved their research outputs considerably. In 2003 the US was second only to UCT as far as the number of scholars with a rating from the National Research Foundation was concerned.

Hertzog also warned that the US could lose 30% of its students in arts and social sciences and also in various other faculties if it taught only in Afrikaans. The question was why Hertzog was so worried about shrinking numbers. It was generally accepted that in terms of the government subsidy, the optimal number of students was 15 000. By 2005 there were already more than 22 000 students registered at the US. More money could be generated from research outputs through better appointments and more incentives for academics to publish.

The insistence on flexibility, therefore, did not come from students or lecturers, but from a few members of the ECC. The issue was never discussed in principle in the council or senate. The term "flexible" or "flexibility" does not appear in the document that sets out the language policy and plan.

In June 2005 the decision to prioritise "flexibility" was reflected in the formal proposal of the faculty of arts and social sciences to the council about the language medium in which it wanted to present its modules in 2006.

At the council meeting of July 2005 the chairperson did not draw the members' attention to the proposal of arts and social sciences, and the council approved the agenda in its entirety. When I later asked a council member to support a campaign against the council's decision, her reply was: "I can't, I don't know what I voted for."

When a polemic about the decision erupted shortly afterwards in *Die Burger*, the US management feigned surprise: "But it is recorded in the council documents," was the reaction. Yet everyone had been caught off guard. In November 2005 the council even held an informal meeting to reflect on the way in which the decision had been taken and the damage it had done to the US's image.

In 2006 a curious book by Chris Brink, *No Lesser Place: The Taaldebat at Stellenbosch*, was published. Brink offers no convincing argument to prove that a predominantly Afrikaans university at Stellenbosch is unsustainable. Nor does the book try to persuade the Afrikaans community about the merits of the language-medium policy. Brink rather seems intent on signalling to the government that those at the helm at the US are "people with the correct attitudes" and that they are being thwarted by reactionaries who cling to the old order.

Brink dismisses a predominantly Afrikaans-medium university as "a volkstaat of the mind". He draws the lines between oppressors and liberators, and neo-apartheid and inclusion.[214] The term "culture" or the notion of cultural transmission as a fundamentally important function of a university receives no mention.

When one looks back on the development of the US's language policy from 2002, certain things stand out. For one, there was the disgraceful neglect to send experts to Europe to learn how to manage a multilingual campus. When I explained the US's language policy to François Grin, one of the expert advisers of the European Union, he remarked: "I have never heard of a university where each faculty unit does as it pleases."[215] This was exactly what Stellenbosch did.

In 2006 I sent an e-mail to Jean Laponce, a renowned expert on language displacement, about the T option, which would in 2006 be used for the first time in all three undergraduate years in the faculty of arts and social sciences. "A total of 853 students enrolled for the first year and in the case of 253 tests showed that the student's proficiency in Afrikaans was so poor that he or she was advised to follow the course in the Unit for Afrikaans. Only 24 did so."

Laponce replied that this system was "absurd". "The system is to the eventual advantage of English, Afrikaans being retained as a mere decoration."[216]

When Collena Blanckenberg of the Unit for Afrikaans once spelled out the deficiencies of the T option in a conversation with Brink, he said: "I don't have the power to force the deans." This was after the T option had already been introduced. No dean who had chosen the T option would return voluntarily to Afrikaans medium. At the same time the deans of three important faculties (law, economic and management sciences, and engineering) decided not to switch to the T option and to remain primarily Afrikaans medium.

A question that soon arose was how long it would take before English-speaking students in these faculties started insisting on also being taught via the T option or the medium of English. I had little doubt that the T option in arts and social sciences was the Trojan horse for the introduction of English. What surprised me was the brazenness of the people who decided on their own to anglicise the US.

214  See the reviews of Chris Brink's book by Lawrence Schlemmer and Philip John in 'n Vaste plek vir Afrikaans, pp. 201-16, 227-29.
215  E-mail communication from F Grin to author, US Library Manuscript Section; F Grin, "Language Planning and Economics", Current Issues in Language Planning, 4,1 (2003), p. 166.
216  My correspondence with Laponce has been published in 'n Vaste plek vir Afrikaans (Stellenbosch: Sun Press, 2006), pp. 253-56.

But the US was not an exception. In 2006 Lawrence Schlemmer and I showed in *'n Vaste plek vir Afrikaans* that on nearly all the historically Afrikaans campuses untransparent and sometimes dishonest ways had been used to scale down Afrikaans before it disappeared as language medium.

The process was spelled out strikingly to me by a lecturer from the Nelson Mandela Metropolitan University in Port Elizabeth, which used to have a full parallel-medium offering but eventually anglicised completely: "As far as staff are aware the transition to English medium alone never took place. It is a creeping illness that no one wants to admit to – very much like leprosy or Alzheimer's disease."

## In the ring

In September 2005 I saw a short report in *Die Burger* in which the poet Lina Spies from the Afrikaans Department expressed her dismay about the fact that her faculty had made the T option compulsory in all three years of under-graduate study. I made enquiries and discovered that everyone was as surprised about this move as I was. If one could talk of a "language coup", this was exactly what had happened here.

I sat down and wrote a letter of protest to *Die Burger*. To my great joy, Brey-ten Breytenbach and Van Zyl Slabbert agreed to add their names as signato-ries. It was published on 22 September 2005. The letter strongly criticised the decision to use Afrikaans and English on a 50-50 basis in the same class in all courses in arts and social sciences from 2006. We pointed out that Afrikaans had soon vanished at other institutions in the country where dual-medium teaching was used. We asked: "When will the US realise how dangerous the T option is?"

From several subsequent letters from readers it was clear that there was huge public opposition to plans to anglicise the university. Of the 165 letters on this topic published in *Die Burger* and *Rapport* in the last months of 2005, 80% were in favour of Afrikaans being retained as the primary medium at the US. A group of 134 literary writers in Afrikaans declared that the US had not advanced any convincing arguments that dual-medium instruction worked at tertiary level, while convincing evidence existed that it was fatal to the smaller language.

A contribution that attracted special attention was an article by Koos Bekker, who at that point was CEO of Naspers and a US council member who had been elected by the convocation. He posed three questions: What kind of community do we want to build in the Western Cape? What is the everyday language in Stellenbosch? Who can Afrikaans rely on? If the US becomes anglicised, he wrote, "it chooses in my view the road of cowardice. It turns our backs on our roots in Africa and our brown brothers and sisters."[217]

On 10 November 2005 more than a thousand people turned up at the annual convocation meeting that was held in the Paul Roos Centre. Here I proposed a motion that was seconded by, inter alia, Richard van der Ross, Ton Vosloo, Lauretta Maree, Van Zyl Slabbert, Gys Steyn, Jan Lochner and Amanda Lochner. The motion expressed grave concern about the perception that the US was moving away from its commitment to Afrikaans as medium of instruction. It also asked that transformation at the US should take place decisively through the medium of Afrikaans.

During the debate, Chris Brink contended that isolation was a far greater risk than a slippery slope in the direction of English. He also made other controversial statements, such as that academics had the right to choose what they wanted to teach and in which language. The interests of parents and students were apparently irrelevant. My motion was adopted with an overwhelming majority.

On 25 November 2005 the board of the arts and social sciences faculty reconfirmed the proposed language specifications it had adopted earlier in the year. Evidently to pacify people, it was added that the introduction of the T option up to third-year level should only be regarded as experimental and that it would be reconsidered after three years.

It would later turn out that the faculty had forgotten about its promise until some council members drew attention to it in 2008. There were no clearly formulated hypotheses, control groups or monitoring that might be expected in the case of an experiment. There was no literature study. No outside experts were invited to investigate the pedagogic effectiveness of the T option.[218] The "experiment" was a complete flop.

At its last meeting of 2005 the council approved the recommendations from senate. Professor Anton van Niekerk, chair of the language committee and a council member, told *Die Burger*: "The council would have been very unwise to overturn the senate's recommendation, which was based on academic grounds."

I asked Professor Van Niekerk in an e-mail what the academic grounds were on which the statement was based. His reply was that some of his colleagues from linguistics maintained that the significance of mother-tongue instruction was being exaggerated. According to them, a movement in language-teaching theory that had recently gained much ground claimed that, as a result of

---

217  *Die Burger*, 26 October 2005.
218  Marié Heese, Letter to the *Mail & Guardian*, 9-15 October 2009.

globalisation and the right of all people to communicate correctly in the wider world, it has become increasingly important to educate people bilingually. Van Niekerk sent me a list of six sources that in his view substantiated this claim.

A study of these sources, however, yielded a surprising result: the books did not deal with tertiary education at all, but with school education and specifically the first stage of second-language acquisition. None of them offered any scientific substantiation for any benefits of the use of dual-medium instruction (or the T option) at university level. Moreover, in the sources the emphasis fell on stigmatised ethnic groups in Europe such as the *Gastarbeiter* or the children of recent immigrants who struggled to acquire a new language. The books contributed literally nothing to an understanding of the US's "language-medium problem".

Kathleen Heugh, an acknowledged authority on language use in education, contends in various articles in academic journals that not a shred of credible scientific evidence to date supports the weak reasons that are provided for the lack of provision of proper mother-tongue instruction up to tertiary level. Against this, there is robust research that underscores the significance of mother-tongue instruction.[219]

## Election as council member

In February 2006 an election was held in which I, along with Christo Viljoen, a former vice-rector, and Lina Spies, a prominent poet, was appointed as representatives of the US convocation of alumni on the university council. The three of us each received roughly 7 000 votes and defeated two incumbent members who had also stood for election, Christo Wiese and Ruda Landman, by far. In the same election donors of the university elected Jacko Maree as member instead of the deputy chair of the council, Gerhard van Niekerk.

I could not have asked for better comrades in arms: Viljoen understood the inner workings of the university management better than anyone else; Maree, with the acumen of an experienced lawyer, racked up facts for the cause we were fighting for; and Spies spoke with poetic inspiration about the place of Afrikaans in her life and her career. And then there was Pieter Kapp, president of the convocation, who kept a detailed record of the battle in all its facets.

---

219  See the following articles by Kathleen Heugh: "Multilingual education policy in South Africa constrained by theoretical and historical disconnections", *Annual Review of Applied Linguistics,* 33 (2013), pp. 215-37, and "Languages, development and reconstructing education in South Africa", *International Journal of Educational Development,* 19 (1999), pp. 301-13.

At my first council meeting I requested permission to attend the T-option classes in the arts faculty together with one or two other former lecturers on the council in order to assess its pedagogic value at first hand. The request was refused because this would supposedly have damaged the relationship of trust between lecturers and students.

We would, however, also have been satisfied with an alternative – that a panel of experts attend the classes with the aim of compiling a report for the council on the pedagogic advantages and disadvantages of the T option. At that stage there was no other university which, to our knowledge, used this language-medium option. The council would certainly have benefited from such a report.

I am fairly sure that the advocates of the T option in the council did not really want to know what was happening in the classes, and they decidedly did not want to allow independent observers. It became increasingly clear that for some in the council and management the T option was merely a means to the end of arriving at a predominantly English university.

## The Vlottenburg report

Relations in the council grew increasingly fractious on account of the mismanagement of the language policy. The major problem was that the council was not informed of the true state of affairs regarding the language-medium options. Even the questions we asked as council members about the language proficiency of lecturers went unanswered. The particulars were supposedly not in the management database.

Initially the arts faculty and management argued that the T option would attract black students, but between 2004 and 2008 their numbers as a proportion of undergraduate students declined from 3% to 2%. By 2009 there were fewer black students registered in the arts faculty than there had been in 2005. To this can be added that Lawrence Schlemmer found in a survey that black students preferred parallel medium to the T option.

The language committee did not keep the council abreast of the strong expansion of the T option. The A option (Afrikaans medium), which was supposed to be the "automatic" choice and the first in the "hierarchy" of options, became the minority option. The T option, which was supposed to serve merely as a transitional mechanism, became the majority option.

I only found out about this when a sympathetic official leaked a revealing table to me. Between 2004 and 2009 the A option had dropped from 70% to 38% while the T option had risen from 24% to 45%. Parallel medium, which was a much more legitimate choice than the T option, had stagnated at between

6% and 8%, but this was of course because few lecturers were enthusiastic about it.

Certain faculties, such as economic and management sciences, law (until 2009), engineering and education, still used Afrikaans medium as the primary or sole choice, but other faculties increasingly used the open gate of "flexibility" to introduce the T option.

The language committee, which as a subcommittee of the council had to implement policy, had in fact become the decision-making body. The whole policy was to manufacture "facts" that would make the shift to an English-medium university inevitable.

A need arose on the part of management for a new language policy whereby they could "legalise" the status quo retrospectively. To this end Brink appointed a language task team that consisted mainly of academics and officials who saw eye to eye with him.

However, Russel Botman, the vice-rector, convinced Brink that the ongoing conflict between the convocation executive and the university management was detrimental to the university. He recommended that I be asked to draft a policy on behalf of the convocation, which would then be submitted to the council together with management's report.

I accepted the offer, but made it a condition that a comprehensive opinion survey be conducted to determine student attitudes towards the language-medium policy. I requested that Lawrence Schlemmer, who had done various surveys on language preferences, be asked to lead the investigation, and that it be supervised academically by Dr Neville Alexander, director of the Project for the Study of Alternative Education in South Africa (Praesa) at UCT.

I had great respect for Alexander's personal integrity and academic insights. He had strong views on the language-medium issue. He had recognised the value of mother-tongue tuition at an early stage and realised what damage could be done if people without adequate proficiency in English had to use it as medium of instruction at high school or university.

Alexander had a good understanding of the real nature of the language-medium issue. The nature of this problem would also become apparent a few years later from research done at UCT on black schools where mother-tongue tuition was only offered to grade 4. By the time such learners reached grade 12, they were on average five years behind their fellow learners who had received mother-tongue tuition up to matric. This explains in part why the failure rate among black students in particular at universities is so alarmingly high.

Theodorus du Plessis, head of the Unit for Language Facilitation and

Empowerment at the University of the Free State, rightly observes: "The obsession with doing away with Afrikaans medium at university level deflects attention from this much greater national crisis – the crisis in black education."[220]

Afrikaans-speaking children in Afrikaans schools, on the other hand, achieve better results. In 2015 they had a pass rate of 93% compared to the national average of 70.7%. Nationally, Afrikaans-speaking matriculants form the majority of learners who achieve more than 80% in maths and physics.

The group I got together to help formulate a language policy on behalf of the convocation gathered at a restaurant on the farm Vredenheim near Vlottenburg station outside Stellenbosch. They included Professor Jakes Gerwel, a former rector of the University of the Western Cape (UWC), Professor Jaap Durand, former vice-rector of UWC, Dr Van Zyl Slabbert, who would become chancellor of the US a few years later, Professors Arnold Schoonwinkel and Johan de Villiers, deans of engineering and economic and management sciences respectively, Lawrence Schlemmer, Dr Neville Alexander and a lecturer from arts and social sciences who prefers to remain anonymous. After debating the topic extensively, we unanimously adopted the report Durand had formulated. It became known as the Vlottenburg report.

The Vlottenburg report set out its premises as follows:

- A sensible language policy can only be formulated against the background of the diversity of South African society. In the light of the striving towards a non-racial society, it is important that this diversity is not seen as race based but as a variety of interest groups as provided for in Section 18 of the Constitution.
- As far as language interests are concerned, all Afrikaans-speaking South Africans are in respect of language rights an interest group, not an ethnic group.
- A university is eminently an institution where the higher functions of Afrikaans, or of any of our other languages, can be developed and promoted in order to prevent that it becomes reduced to a private vernacular.

220 Theo du Plessis, "Ongelykhede in taal en onderwys – perspektiewe op moedertaalonderrig in Suid-Afrika", text of address delivered on 23 February 2016, published online on Litnet, University Seminar, 2016.

The report argued that the availability of at least one university where teaching in Afrikaans took place at undergraduate level followed as a matter of course from the above. Only in that way could Afrikaans speakers be taught most effectively. The lack of an Afrikaans-medium university would inevitably lead to a loss of the higher functions of Afrikaans. While the university would obviously also use English, its primary language of meetings, communication and tuition should be Afrikaans.

At my request, council member Jacko Maree wrote a research report on the manner in which the language policy had been implemented in the preceding five years. As Pieter Kapp observes in his study of the language debate, the Maree report is exceptionally thorough and illuminating.[221] He conducted interviews with senior members of management and perused about seventy memoranda of people who had commented on the language policy and its implementation. Maree indicated that the T option did not enjoy strong support on the campus, that management had not investigated the demand for Afrikaans-medium tuition properly, and that management had failed to inform the council adequately about many aspects of the implementation of the policy.[222]

In 2007 Lawrence Schlemmer conducted an extensive opinion survey on student attitudes regarding the undergraduate language policy. He submitted his report in 2008 and it was also published on the university's website.

Among Afrikaans students, the A option was the most popular: more than 80% of the Afrikaans-speaking students wanted Afrikaans "primarily and consistently" or would go along with it. If one added to this the fact that 60% of the English-speaking students indicated that they were proficient in Afrikaans, there seemed to be no real reason why classes could not be presented predominantly through the medium of Afrikaans.

The report made a number of significant points: More than a third of the students regarded the T option as irritating and frustrating because switching between languages broke their concentration. It was particularly students who expected to do badly who complained about the T option.

In June 2006 Brink announced out of the blue that he was leaving the US to accept the position of vice-chancellor at the University of Newcastle in the United Kingdom. Just after I heard the news, I had an appointment with him

---

221  Pieter Kapp, *Maties en Afrikaans, 1911-2011: 'n Besondere verhouding* (Pretoria: Protea Boekhuis, 2013), pp. 146-49.

222  See his comprehensive report "Die verengelsing van die Universiteit van Stellenbosch" in *Verantwoording* (Stellenbosch: US Convocation, 2007), pp. 30-73.

about another matter. When I asked him about the reason for his unexpected departure, he said he had come to the US with the expectation that he would have to wage a conventional war on the language-medium issue. "But," he continued, "it turned into a guerrilla war, and one can't win a guerrilla war."

Towards the end of 2006, on the eve of Brink's departure, the council again held one of its extraordinary meetings in the hope that a language-medium "miracle" might happen. The question was asked whether we were ready to choose between the proposal of management and that of the Vlottenburg group. The voting resulted in a tie, and no decision was taken. As a compromise, the council now started looking at the possibility of a minimum offering of Afrikaans-medium classes alongside an English offering.

Christo Viljoen, who proposed the motion, made it clear that it could only work if all the faculties had a minimum offering of 65%. But once again faculties that wanted to continue with the T option were strong enough to refuse their participation.

## A false peace

Up to the end of 2006 the language battle at the US had been so closely linked to the person of Professor Chris Brink that there was strong hope that his resignation would usher in a new era. It seemed as if his successor, Professor Russel Botman, was well suited to play a conciliatory role. But the problem was that the crisis had not been resolved, and that Professor Botman inherited a language practice that was practically insoluble without firm leadership.

In the 2008 election of council members from the ranks of the alumni and donors, the voters again unequivocally expressed their preference for candidates that advocated the A option and rejected the T option. Notably, Jannie Mouton and Marié Heese represented important views and approaches. Mouton as business leader strongly insisted that the US should serve its Afrikaans-speaking niche market and that the wave of Anglicisation should be rolled back. Heese, a former Unisa lecturer with vast experience in language research, emphasised the pedagogic value of Afrikaans tuition for Afrikaans speakers and the academic flaws of the T option.

Like those who had been elected in 2006 as pro-Afrikaans-medium candidates by the convocation, the new council members soon became frustrated with the council's modus operandi. Under successive chairpersons procedures left much to be desired. Evidently some council members were more equal than others, and management's word on the issue of language policy counted much more than that of other members. Few efforts were made to insist that council decisions or recommendations on language be implemented.

In an attempt to heal the rift between council members elected by the convocation and the members of the language committee, Paul Cluver, who replaced Hertzog as chairperson in 2008, arranged that I obtain a seat on the language committee. I soon discovered that there was no support for my standpoints. Their attitude was that the language policy was something which only members of management and lecturers in the committee were allowed to decide. It became clear to me that the committee paid scant attention to the language policy of 2002, as revised in 2008.

In terms of the policy, the A option was the "automatic" choice. Valid reasons were required to replace it with another option. It seemed to me that the committee allowed the A option to be edged out further for virtually any reason, and that alternative options such as parallel medium were hardly considered. Suggestions or recommendations from the council were ignored.

In a memorandum that Jacko Maree made available to council members on 20 May 2009, he made the following finding: "The US is undoubtedly anglicising head over heels. If existing trends continue, by 2016 the majority of undergraduate students will be English speaking." In 2016 it would prove that his prediction had been spot-on.

On 30 July 2009 I wrote in a memorandum to the language committee:

> The council decided in 2008 to recommend parallel medium (alongside Afrikaans single medium and interpretation). What happened then? There was a big jump towards the T option and a further decline of the A option, maybe precisely to avoid parallel medium. What is the status of the council's recommendations after protracted debates? A mere mumbling in the wind?[223]

## Law changes its tune

In June 2009 the language committee approved the application of the law faculty to switch its entire undergraduate offering from the A option to the T option. The law faculty came with this request in spite of the arts faculty's failure to attract black students by means of the T option and black students' insistence on parallel medium.

The law faculty's switch to the T option had primarily to do with the 40%

---

223  US Library Manuscript Section. Insake die meerderheidskommunikasie uit die Taalkomitee aan die Raad oor Raadslid H. Giliomee: 'n Persoonlike reaksie, undated.

growth in the numbers of white English speakers between 2005 and 2009. It can be assumed that certain lecturers and some students pressed for the increased use of English in lectures.

As could be predicted, the law faculty used the terminology of what Charles Taylor calls democratic exclusion. As motivation for its step the faculty argued that the A option did not meet the needs of the significant number of current students who preferred tuition in English. The faculty contended that students who wanted to learn in English were being exposed to unequal treatment, and that this might be in conflict with the Constitution and legislation regarding access at university level – "the more so because the language policy of the department of education in fact does not make provision for exclusively Afrikaans universities".[224]

It was strange that the faculty had not already expressed its concern in 2001, when the relevant legislation was passed. In the 2009 election campaign, three of the opposition parties, the Democratic Alliance, Inkatha and the Freedom Front, pronounced themselves unambiguously in favour of the US as a predominantly Afrikaans university.

At this stage a council member asked Advocate Jan Heunis SC to write a legal opinion on this issue. This opinion, which was presented to the US management, pointed out that the ministry of education had declared its willingness in writing to enter into discussions with the historically Afrikaans universities about language-medium issues, including Afrikaans medium as the primary, but not the exclusive, choice.

Advocate Heunis came to the conclusion that there was no reason to assume that the US's language policy of 2002, as amended in 2008, which regards Afrikaans as the default language and allows English to be used 'in particular circumstances', was in conflict with either the Constitution or government policy.

I was still a member of the language committee when the law faculty's request to switch to the T option was tabled. I opposed the proposal, but was outvoted by far. I then requested that it be recorded in the language committee's minutes that the law faculty's request to switch to the T option was an act of "language betrayal", especially in light of the massive work done by predecessors such as JC de Wet towards the establishment of Afrikaans as a legal language. The majority of the committee members signed a memorandum in which they requested the council to replace me as representative as, in their view, I had a disruptive effect on the committee's activities.

Soon afterwards Jannie Mouton and Marié Heese resigned as council mem-

---

224  US Fakulteit Regsgeleerdheid, Taalplan, 2009, pp. 4–5.

bers because they felt, in Mouton's words, that the US was "too white and too English".[225] Heese expressed her distrust of the management's implementation of policy. She pointed out that the management and the council had allowed the university's language policy to be determined by its lecturers' preference, with the university thereby being governed from the bottom up.[226]

Whereas Afrikaans medium had still been the automatic option in 2002, from mid-2009 the management and certain lecturers typified this option more and more openly as a stumbling block. In contrast to an earlier tendency of being defensive or evasive, proponents of the increased use of English became progressively more confident.

On 10 October 2009 Professor Magda Fourie, vice-rector: teaching, described the A option negatively: "This option excludes non-Afrikaans speakers and those who did not study Afrikaans at school."[227] Fourie omitted to mention, however, that there were 23 universities, three of them in the Western Cape, which were at that stage already primarily English medium or English single-medium. All things considered, Stellenbosch was the only university in the country, given its geographic location and historical background, that was in a position to remain primarily Afrikaans medium.

Sandra Liebenberg, professor in human rights law, wrote in her criticism of an article of mine,"A deadly war of languages" (*Mail and Guardian,* 2-8 October 2009), that the law faculty's decision should be seen as an attempt to increase the diversity of the students and lecturers at the US. She made no mention of the fact that three other universities in the region taught exclusively in English.

She stated that the Constitution required the state to take measures to promote the indigenous languages that were previously discriminated against, and continued: "No single language *particularly not a historically privileged language such as Afrikaans* [my emphasis] can claim that it has an exclusive right to be used at a higher educational institution funded by the state."[228]

She seemed to be unaware of the constitutional settlement of 1909 in which the two white communities committed themselves to reconciliation on the basis of the recognition, also in practice, of the equality of the two official languages. The statement that Afrikaans was "privileged" between 1910 and 1994 is false. Professor Jan Sadie, who had consulted numerous government publications on the economy and demographics written predominantly in English, told me that if any language had been privileged, it was English.

---

225  *Rapport*, "Jannie Mouton sê hoekom hy loop by US", 17 October 2009.
226  *Die Burger*, 19 July 2009, article in *By*.
227  *Die Burger*, 10 October 2009, article in *By*.
228  *Mail & Guardian*, 9-15 October 2009.

Liebenberg is probably also blissfully unaware of what Nelson Mandela said at Stellenbosch in 1996 when he was awarded an honorary doctorate by the US: "[W]ithin a system comprising more than twenty universities, surely it must be possible to reach an accommodation to the effect that there will be at least one university whose main tasks will include that of seeing to the sustained development of Afrikaans as an academic medium. How that institution is to accommodate languages other than Afrikaans is one of the details that can be settled through a process of negotiation."[229] In 2001 Dr Jakes Gerwel was commissioned by a committee of the department of education to head an investigation that resulted in the recommendation that the government give a special mandate to two universities to promote Afrikaans "systematically" and "consciously" as a language of instruction and research. They had to report annually to Parliament on how they had fulfilled these functions.

As Gerwel put it: "Without two such academic pillars Afrikaans would not be able to survive in the long run." It is remarkable that Liebenberg as a professor specialising in human rights is so indifferent to the rights of Afrikaans speakers. It is probably only at Stellenbosch in its new guise that one can expect such an anomaly.

At the annual general meeting of the convocation on 11 December 2009 the president, Pieter Kapp, said that the executive committee of the convocation and the six council members elected by the convocation had consistently maintained that Stellenbosch should remain a primarily Afrikaans university that promotes multilingualism. What had happened in reality was that the Afrikaans offering at undergraduate and postgraduate level had declined to about 40%. "Stellenbosch has therefore opted for a minimal position for Afrikaans and a maximal position for English."

Some of the lecturers who felt somewhat guilty about the transition of the US to a primarily English-medium university contended that the students merely reacted to the demands of the local and international market, and that Afrikaans students also insisted on English medium. I argued in letters to *Die Burger* that this claim had to be called into question, especially in light of the finding of the Schlemmer report of 2008 that more than 80% of the Afrikaans students preferred tuition primarily in Afrikaans. According to all indications, Afrikaans students' proficiency in English was much better than it had been in 1994.

The strangest contribution came from Anton van Niekerk, who was chair-

229  Address by President Nelson Mandela, 25 October 1996, http://www.sun.ac.za/
    english/Documents/Madiba/Madibaspeech1996.pdf

person of the language committee for a considerable time. He contributed a chapter to a book titled *Woordeloos tot verhaal: Trauma en narratief in Nederlands en Afrikaans* (2012) in which Dutch and Afrikaans writers reflect on accounts of social trauma in both fiction and non-fiction. One of the most striking chapters deals with how the Dutch looked on passively during the Second World War as Jews were rounded up to be sent to concentration camps.

Van Niekerk's contribution is about the language battle at Stellenbosch. He starts off by saying that the language debate was triggered by the "emotional" letter Van Slabbert, Breyten Breytenbach and I wrote in September 2012. He labels us and the other opponents of the T option as people who are experiencing "the trauma of a threatening loss of identity".

Van Niekerk concedes that in three successive elections of council members by the convocation of alumni, proponents of Afrikaans as primary language medium "overwhelmingly" defeated proponents of the increased use of English. But not too much should be read into this, according to him, because fewer convocation members voted in the 2010 convocation election "than there were mourners at Eugène Terre'Blanche's funeral".

I can speak for myself, but to suggest that the participation of people such as Van Zyl Slabbert, Breyten Breytenbach, Jacko Maree, Christo Viljoen and Lina Spies in the language battle was motivated by a traumatic identity crisis is one of the most far-fetched interpretations I have ever come across.

## English triumphant

In 2014 the US council decided to give Afrikaans and English equal status, but in 2015 a new rector, after pressure from black students, made English the sole medium of instruction and official communication. In a lawsuit the management admitted that it had violated its own language policy on a large scale.

In 2016 the university management tabled a draft language policy as part of a formal process of policy review. It allowed (but did not prescribe) parallel medium to a limited extent, and in all other courses English was elevated to the dominant language. In spite of the disastrous consequences of devolving decision-making on language medium to faculties, departments and even lecturers, which had spelled ruin to Afrikaans between 2002 and 2012, the management again allowed precisely the same.

The overriding impression one gets from the draft language policy is that management was desperately searching for a way in which to make the de facto dominance of English, which was the result of poor management, the de jure position. They could count on an inbuilt majority in the council – in the previous years the council had been loaded with members of management, representatives of academics and people nominated by the government. For all practical purposes, the management had an inbuilt majority to anglicise the university regardless of the will of several generations that had studied there and regardless of the pedagogic needs of the Afrikaans-speaking community. Several experts were of the opinion that this was in conflict with the King code on corporate governance.

Jan Heunis, president of the convocation, asked me, Christo Viljoen and Flip Smit, a former rector of the University of Pretoria, to formulate a proposal which he submitted on behalf of the convocation as part of the process of policy review the university had embarked on.

The proposed policy of the rector's management team not only ignores regional demographics but also one of the most important functions of the modern university, namely cultural transmission. JM Coetzee, novelist and Nobel laureate, puts it as follows:

> My sympathies are all on your side. The crucial fact, for me, is that the official Taalbeleid document does not once use the word "kultuur". The university management seems to conceive of language as an instrumental communication system without any culture-bearing role.[230]

Moreover, there is not a single reference to the value of mother-tongue instruction, which also applies to tuition at university level. Dr Marié Heese, an authority on the methodology of university tuition, remarked:

> During my time at Unisa I conducted such research myself, with the aim of determining how best we could assist struggling students. We used questionnaires as part of our research, as well as a number of focus groups. One of the main findings was that students who struggle often overestimate their own abilities by far. They do not realise what a core variable language is, and how badly a wrong language choice can trip them up. They are caught completely off guard when their results are unexpectedly poor. They then blame the lecturers. The best way to support these students is not to offer extra "help", which they in any case experience as insulting. It is to make the language of learning as accessible as possible, therefore, inter alia, mother-tongue options for as many students as possible.

---

230 Communication to H Giliomee, 16 April 2016.

As in her term as council member, Marié Heese figured as a voice of reason in a sanatorium of lost souls. Flip Smit, Christo Viljoen and I made the following proposal in our memorandum for the convocation executive, which accommodates the demands of both people wishing to study in Afrikaans and those who prefer English medium:

- That the university council reconfirms its 2014 policy that accords equal status to Afrikaans and English and gives full expression to it;
- that the US every year when it takes in first years allocate 50% of the available places to students wishing to study in the Afrikaans stream and 50% to those wishing to study in the English stream; and
- that during their undergraduate studies students remain in the language stream that they have chosen at the outset. Thereby the Afrikaans stream will remain constant. It is likely that the university will attract many talented Afrikaans-speaking students. Only in this way can Afrikaans be assured of a fixed, sustainable and full-status place at the US.

The Federation of Governing Bodies of South African Schools (Fedsas) warned in a memorandum to the US management about the grave consequences for Afrikaans instruction at schools if there was no longer a full-fledged Afrikaans-medium offering available at any university. There was a real need for the training and development of Afrikaans teachers to supply the needs of Afrikaans-medium schools, most of which were in the Western Cape.

The Gelyke Kanse-inisiatief (Equal Chances initiative), which was started by Breyten Breytenbach and Ebbe Dommisse, former editor of *Die Burger*, enlisted support for the idea that English and Afrikaans be treated on a 50-50 basis at the US by means of an internet website, in tandem with our proposals and those of Fedsas.

Some of the public figures, opinion formers and creative writers who have given their support to the idea of a 50-50 offering in Afrikaans and English include:

- Fritz Brand, recently retired Appeal Court judge
- Breyten Breytenbach, poet
- JM Coetzee, Nobel laureate
- Paul Colditz, CEO of Fedsas, which represents 1 974 school governing bodies countrywide
- Ebbe Dommisse, former editor of *Die Burger*

- Theo du Plessis, head of the Unit for Language Facilitation and Empowerment at the University of the Free State
- Marié Heese, educationist and researcher of the methodology of bilingual education
- RW Johnson, author of *How Long Will South Africa Survive?* (1977 and 2015)
- Rhoda Kadalie, activist and recipient of an honorary doctorate from the US
- Tony Leon, columnist, former politician and ambassador
- Lord Renwick of Clifton, former British ambassador to South Africa
- Danie van Wyk, Goeie Hoop initiative
- David Welsh, author of *The Rise and Fall of Apartheid* (2009)

The council rejected the 50-50 proposal for Afrikaans and English and adopted a language policy that makes English medium so dominant that in the view of authorities it would in the short term lead to the phasing out of Afrikaans as language of instruction and meetings at Stellenbosch.

## "Knowing who you are"

A few weeks after the US decided not to accord Afrikaans equal status, I became the first recipient of the Jan H Marais prize for my contribution to the academic development of Afrikaans. Scientific research in Afrikaans across the entire spectrum of disciplines was taken into consideration. The following principles carried the most weight: (1) originality, (2) critical insight, (3) purposefulness, (4) impartiality and (5) accessible presentation.

The sponsors were the University of Stellenbosch, Naspers and the Het Jan Marais Nationale Fonds. In all three cases, Jannie Marais had made an indispensable financial contribution towards the establishment of the institution.

In my speech after the award ceremony I said that South African universities of today have a duty not to become trapped in what the philosopher Hennie Rossouw called the "parochial narrow-mindedness and group-centred exclusivity" of the apartheid years. But there was also a great danger at the opposite end of the spectrum: the complete negation of the obligation to talk about cultural transmission and to conduct constructive debates on our history.

When I talked of cultural reflection, I said, I had the following in mind:

- On what aspects of our history do we agree or differ?
- What are the core societal values in our history on which we can agree, and where do we differ?
- What kind of future are we striving for?

In the history writing of prominent historians there are no prescriptions for action with regard to cultural transmission, but their works do offer a perspective on vital questions. Leszek Kolakowski, the great Polish authority on Marxism who was later forced to move to Oxford, said: "We learn history not in order to know how to behave or how to succeed, but to know who we are."

I concluded by thanking the selection committee for their decision to award the first Jan H Marais prize to a historian. History has been my life, I said, and few countries have a more challenging history than South Africa.

*Chapter 16*

# Proud *and* ashamed

*The most effective way to destroy a people is to destroy and obliterate their own understanding of their history.*

George Orwell

*The writer should always be ready to change at the drop of a hat. He speaks up for the victims, and the victims change.*

Graham Greene

During a stay in Israel in 1987 I made the acquaintance of Meron Benvenisti, former deputy mayor of Jerusalem and administrator of East Jerusalem. With his sharp intellect and charismatic personality, he immediately reminded me of Van Zyl Slabbert, who had walked out of the white-controlled Parliament in protest shortly before.

Benvenisti, a medievalist with a doctorate in conflict management, had been a newspaper editor before entering politics in 1972. A mere six years later he abandoned politics because, as he explained to me, "one cannot govern a city as if a third of its population does not exist".

In his small office in the centre of Jerusalem he documented and monitored the growing number of Jewish settlements on the West Bank. He predicted that they would lead Israel to perdition.

We talked about the differences and similarities between the Afrikaners and the Israeli Jews. The latter were not biological racists, as they included all Jewish people irrespective of colour; the Afrikaners, on the other hand, excluded people who spoke the same language and had largely the same history as themselves purely on the ground of colour. But there was also a similarity: like the Afrikaners, the Israelis had a "Herrenvolk" democracy that accorded self-determination only to the master race and treated the subordinate groups as serfs or strangers within the city gates.

After he had read *The Afrikaners: Biography of a People*, Benvenisti wrote to me: "What touches me is your profound identification, pride and worry about your tribe and the struggle to reconcile deep attachment with a sense of guilt. Maybe I read in your words my own feelings, for I feel the same about my tribe: pride and shame. There is a Jewish saying: 'Israel, even if he has sinned, Israel he is.' One can never escape the contradictions and one shouldn't. From this perspective we are similar and I have learnt a lot from you."

There is much in the Afrikaner history of the past hundred years of which I am proud, and also much of which I am ashamed. When it comes to the positive, I think particularly of the upliftment of the "poor whites", to which my mother had contributed more than her share in Porterville, and of people like my father who, like so many Afrikaner teachers countrywide, had inspired his pupils to make use of study opportunities to progress in life while always ploughing something back into his community.

There were also the humble beginnings in the late 1930s of the "Ekonomiese Volksbeweging" (economic people's movement), which worked to increase Afrikaners' share of the economy by encouraging entrepreneurship. One of the chief organisers, Dr Eben Dönges, stated explicitly that Afrikaners had no right to expect others to help them find economic salvation. All that they asked of the English business world was that it maintain a "benign neutrality" while the Afrikaners were finding their economic feet.

And then there was the astounding rise of Afrikaans as a language of literature and science. As Susan Roets, a language practitioner, describes it: "There never was generous funding for the implementation of bilingualism and the development of technical terminology. It was more a case of Afrikaans blossoming because some Afrikaners worked with great and sometimes life-long devotion (with no glory and at the lowest remuneration conceivable) to create and develop scientific, technical and academic terminology – at tertiary institutions, in the media, and as writers and poets – everywhere, because the former kitchen language was so incredibly close to their hearts."[231]

The Afrikaner nationalist movement experienced its heyday from the mid-1930s to the advent of a republic in 1961. It generated an unprecedented enthusiasm and idealism and shaped me for life, as an individual, an academic and a historian. Apartheid piggybacked on the nationalist movement and progressively polluted it.

When I consider feeling ashamed at the conduct of one's "tribe", to use Benvenisti's term, well-known events such as the Sharpeville massacre and the death of Steve Biko immediately come to mind. But there are also largely unknown incidents, such as the "Battle of Andringa Street" in 1940 in Stellenbosch, where a mob of white students attacked the homes of the coloured community and terrorised the residents in an orgy of hate and violence, which fill me with shame.

231  Commentary by Susan Roets, language practitioner, 10 December 2004.

One thinks of the many coloured and Indian businesses that were destroyed by the Group Areas Act once the central business districts in cities and towns were reserved for whites. One out of four coloured people and one out of six Indian South Africans were forced to move to their "own group area"; only one out of 666 whites ever had to do the same.

For me as a Bolander, the NP government's homeland policy initially was not much more than an abstract intellectual construct. It was only after my 1979 visit to Dr Nthato Motlana in his Soweto home that I fully grasped the absurdity of a policy that sought not only to disenfranchise but also to denationalise even the most respected black South Africans. My visit to resettlement camps in the Ciskei showed starkly how a policy reduced cast-out people to a permanent state of helplessness. I returned with the firm resolve to make the abolition of the pass laws and influx control a central theme in my writing. Unless that happened, South Africa would never normalise.

Although I had been a long-time resident of Stellenbosch, it was only with the writing of *Nog altyd hier gewees* that I became aware of the trauma suffered by a community of 3 000 people on my doorstep, uprooted from their established neighbourhood in central Stellenbosch and dumped at the outskirts of the town.

As apartheid was systematically being imposed across South Africa, the poet Dirk Opperman wrote: "The Afrikaner had built his own world and had made himself strong," and in the process had alienated his fellow South Africans. People in a heterogeneous society had to be able to attract others to survive, he said. Apartheid had had the opposite effect. Afrikaners had developed "a strong power to repel".[232] Piet Cillié, editor of *Die Burger*, warned that apartheid had made South Africa the "polecat of the world".

Historians, including several Afrikaans-speaking historians, played a major role in discrediting apartheid as an ideology. By the 1960s it was already fairly well known that long before 1652 Khoisan and Bantu-speaking people had inhabited large parts of the region that would later become South Africa. In my work with Richard Elphick, I pointed out that Afrikaner ancestors neither held dogmatic views on racial purity nor had a Calvinist sense of being a chosen people. It was, instead, the statutory groups instituted in the period of Dutch East India Company rule – Company officials, burghers and slaves – that distinguished between people and determined their relations. In the 1850s, Afrikaner politicians insisted on low franchise qualifications in the Cape Colony so that white, coloured and black could all have representation.

232  DJ Opperman, "Uitdyende heelal?" *Die Burger,* 25 May 1960.

Systems such as Zionism, socialism and apartheid, which seek to transform an entire society in accordance with its particular radical ideology, feel obliged to justify their views on historical grounds. Hence historians loyal to the party and the ideology are vitally important to the party bosses.

But historians that are worth their salt prefer to be faithful to their discipline. The great historian Eric Hobsbawm, who was both a Marxist and a member of the British Communist Party, recounts the rebellion that erupted when Moscow asked him and his fellow members of the party's group of historians to condone the revelation of Stalin's crimes and Khrushchev's succession. They refused because, as Hobsbawm remarks: "Why should we simply approve Khrushchev? We do not know, we can only endorse policy, but historians go by evidence."[233] Along with their counterparts who wrote in English, Afrikaner historians increasingly related a different, more complex story of Afrikaner history. And much of this writing did not offer a rose-tinted picture.

In Israel Meron Benvenisti had to witness how his Zionism degenerated into the occupation of the West Bank and injustices perpetrated against the Palestinians. He writes: "Our Zionist liberal-socialist philosophy did not escape the fate of other great liberating ideologies. Its failure to adapt to changing realities enabled dark forces to usurp its revered symbols . . . and turn enlightened, moral and progressive ideas into reactionary beliefs and immoral deeds."[234]

Shortly after the Soweto uprising in 1976, I wrote in *Die Burger* that we were running the risk that ideological blueprints and politics that put a premium on race "will in the long run destroy everything that is worth preserving in this divided country of ours".[235]

What I attempted to do as historian, commentator and Afrikaner was to explain the origins and development of racial conflict in South Africa and to recommend reforms without becoming sucked into party politics. The challenge was to stay objective and to strive for humanity, fairness and justice – to try to take a broader view and to judge soberly. There were many others who tried to do the same.

The profound change in Afrikaners' understanding of themselves and their society, brought about mostly by critical writers and journalists writing in Afrikaans, has been almost universally overlooked in the literature on the

---

233  Eric Hobsbawm, *Interesting Times: A Twentieth-Century Life* (London: Abacus, 2002), p. 207.
234  Meron Benvenisti, *Conflicts and Contradictions* (New York: Villard Books, 1986), p. 78.
235  *Die Burger*, 26 August 1976.

transition in South Africa in the 1990s. It was this change in self-conception and outlook on life among its voters that made it possible for the NP to implement radical reforms, which ultimately led to the constitutional settlement.

In the 1970s it was an Afrikaner businessman, Wim de Villiers, who took the lead in the reform of South Africa's industrial relations system; it was also the Afrikaner members of the Wiehahn Commission who played the decisive role in the redesign of labour legislation.

In 1986 it was Anton Rupert, doyen of Afrikaner businessmen, who told President PW Botha that apartheid threatened the survival of white South Africans. He wrote: "[Apartheid] is crucifying us; it is destroying our language; it is relegating a once heroic nation to the position of the lepers of the world. Remove the curse of a crime against humanity from the backs of our children and their children." He concluded with a sombre warning: "Should you fail in this God-given task, then one day we shall surely end up with a Nuremberg."

But this reassessment of old assumptions was not limited to the elite only. In a comprehensive study of changes in white opinion between the years 1970 and 1994, the respected analyst and pollster Lawrence Schlemmer came to a significant conclusion: More so than white English speakers, the Afrikaners increasingly identified with their religion rather than with class interests or ethnic identity. Living an ethical life had supplanted serving the Afrikaner community as the prime value.[236] Without this mental shift, it would not have been possible for FW de Klerk to carry through his sweeping reforms. In the referendum of 1992 at least half of all Afrikaners voted yes: they approved of the abolition of apartheid.

After De Klerk lifted the ban on a number of extra-parliamentary movements in February 1990, I wrote to him about a leftist Israeli academic who had told me a month earlier in Tel Aviv: "I have prayed for years that the Jews should not become like the Afrikaners. Now my prayer is the opposite." I concluded my letter with the words: "You have given the Afrikaners back their self-respect which apartheid damaged so badly. For the first time in many years one can hold one's head high again."

---

236  L Schlemmer, "Factors in the Persistence or Decline of Ethnic Group Mobilisation: A Conceptual Review and Case Study of Cultural Group Responses among Afrikaners in Post-Apartheid South Africa", doctoral dissertation, University of Cape Town, 1999.

# Acknowledgements

I would like to thank the following people: Firstly, my wife, Annette, who in our time as life partners has proven to me the adage that two are better than one. The second is Erika Oosthuysen, my editor at Tafelberg since 2002. She has managed me with insight, patience, and charm – even as I indulged my tendency to endless rewriting. I was fortunate to have Dolf Els, an experienced and expert professional, as copy-editor of the original Afrikaans manuscript. Linde Dietrich, who rendered the Afrikaans text into English, was more than a translator; she made a valued contribution to the manuscript itself. Albert Grundlingh, friend and head of the history department at Stellenbosch University, gave solid feedback throughout. It is always stimulating to talk history with him. Johannes du Bruyn provided invaluable feedback as well as research material. Anton Naudé, my research assistant, found wonderfully relevant material that I had completely forgotten about. Lindie Koorts and Danelle van Zyl-Hermann, members of an exciting new generation of historians, read certain chapters and gave useful comment.

In chapter 14, an exchange of letters between me and Dave Steward, Chief of Staff in President FW de Klerk's office, is published for the first time. It originally appeared on the blog *Maandblad Zuid-Afrika*. I have added a few sentences to make the distinction between hard and soft power clear. I wish to thank Dave Steward for his permission to publish the letters here.

Lastly, I would like to thank JM Coetzee, for valuable feedback on each concept chapter. *The Good Story: Exchanges on Truth, Fiction and Psychotherapy* (2015), which he co-authored with the psychotherapist Arabella Kurtz, made me very aware of the temptation to tell a better story about your own life than the one that actually happened.

# Books by Hermann Giliomee

1974 *Die Kaap tydens die eerste Britse bewind*

1979 *The Rise and Crisis of Afrikaner Power / Afrikanermag: Opkoms en toekoms* (co-author Heribert Adam)

1982 *The Parting of the Ways: South African Politics, 1976–1982*

1982 *The Shaping of South African Society, 1652–1820 / 'n Samelewing in wording: Suid-Afrika, 1652–1820* (co-editor Richard Elphick)

1983 *Afrikaner Political Thought: vol. 1: 1780–1850 – Documents and Analyses* (co-author André du Toit)

1985 *Up Against the Fences: Poverty, Passes and Privilege in South Africa* (co-editor Lawrence Schlemmer)

1989 *From Apartheid to Nation-building* (co-author Lawrence Schlemmer)

1989 *Negotiating South Africa's future* (co-editor Lawrence Schlemmer)

1990 *The Elusive Search for Peace: South Africa, Israel and Northern Ireland* (co-editor Jannie Gagiano)

1994 *The Bold Experiment: South Africa's New Democracy* (co-editors Lawrence Schlemmer and Surita Hauptfleisch)

1999 *The Awkward Embrace: One-Party Domination and Democracy in Industrialising Countries* (co-editor Charles Simkins [e-book])

2001 *Kruispad: Die toekoms van Afrikaans as openbare taal* (co-editor Lawrence Schlemmer)

2003 *The Afrikaners: Biography of a people / Die Afrikaners: 'n Biografie*

2006 *'n Vaste plek vir Afrikaans: Taaluitdagings op kampus* (co-author Lawrence Schlemmer)

2007 *New History of South Africa / Nuwe geskiedenis van Suid-Afrika* (co-editor Bernard Mbenga)

2007 *Nog altyd hier gewees: Die storie van 'n Stellenbosse gemeenskap*

2012 *The Last Afrikaner Leaders: A Crucial Test of Power / Die laaste Afrikanerleiers: 'n Opperste toets van mag*

2015 *Buhr van die Bokveld: 'n Bloemlesing uit die werk van Johann Buhr* (compiler)

# Index

# Reconsiderations in Southern African History

Milton Shain, *The Roots of Antisemitism in South Africa*

Timothy Keegan, *Colonial South Africa and the Origins of the Racial Order*

Ineke van Kessel, *"Beyond Our Wildest Dreams":*
*The United Democratic Front and the Transformation of South Africa*

Benedict Carton, *Blood from Your Children:*
*The Colonial Origins of Generational Conflict in South Africa*

Diana Wylie, *Starving on a Full Stomach:*
*Hunger and the Triumph of Cultural Racism in Modern South Africa*

Jeff Guy, *The View across the River:*
*Harriette Colenso and the Zulu Struggle against Imperialism*

John Edwin Mason, *Social Death and Resurrection:*
*Slavery and Emancipation in South Africa*

Hermann Giliomee, *The Afrikaners: Biography of a People*

Tim Couzens, *Murder at Morija:*
*Faith, Mystery, and Tragedy on an African Mission*

Diana Wylie, *Art and Revolution:*
*The Life and Death of Thami Mnyele, South African Artist*

David Welsh, *The Rise and Fall of Apartheid*

John Edwin Mason, *One Love, Ghoema Beat:*
*Inside the Cape Town Carnival*

Eric Allina, *Slavery by Any Other Name:*
*African Life under Company Rule in Colonial Mozambique*

Richard Elphick, *The Equality of Believers:*
*Protestant Missionaries and the Racial Politics of South Africa*

Hermann Giliomee, *The Last Afrikaner Leaders: A Supreme Test of Power*

Meghan Healy-Clancy, *A World of Their Own:*
*A History of South African Women's Education*

Ruramisai Charumbira, *Imagining a Nation:*
*History and Memory in Making Zimbabwe*

Jeffrey Butler, edited by Richard Elphick and Jeannette Hopkins,
*Cradock: How Segregation and Apartheid Came to a South African Town*

Hermann Giliomee, *Historian: An Autobiography*